Data Science for Fundraising

Data Science for Fundraising
Build Data-Driven Solutions Using R

Ashutosh R. Nandeshwar, PhD
Rodger Devine, MS
2018

Copyright © 2018 by Data Insight Partners LLC

All rights reserved. No portion of this book may be reproduced in any form without permission from the publisher, except as permitted by U.S. copyright law. For permissions contact:

rodger.devine@gmail.com

Visit authors' websites:
http://www.nandeshwar.info
http://www.rodgerdevine.blog/

Published by Data Insight Partners LLC, Los Angeles, California.

978-0-692-05784-1

All rights reserved.

First edition: February 2018

The greatest data-driven value for a non-profit comes of better targeting your fundraising campaigns. Done correctly, this can multiply their sheer ROI. "Data Science for Fundraising" delivers solid, comprehensive coverage of today's state of the art data science techniques – not only for targeting your fundraising, but also optimizing it in various other ways. Brought to you by two seasoned veterans, this book will guide you with detailed, hands-on instructions. I greatly recommend it!

— Eric Siegel, Ph.D., founder of Predictive Analytics World and author of "Predictive Analytics: The Power to Predict Who Will Click, Buy, Lie, or Die"

Data Science for Fundraising is packed full of recipes for building a fundraising analytics team from scratch. Its content covers the full spectrum of the field: from the high-level details of building a case, hiring, strategy, and return on investment, to the day-to-day details of data analysis, visualizations, and predictive modeling. I suspect this book will remain within easy reach of many fundraising professionals even as their teams evolve and grow in sophistication. And because the examples are based entirely in R (a free, open-source software package for data analysis) the material is accessible regardless of budget. Whether you are a large team or a one-person shop; whether you are new to fundraising, new to analytics, or new to both, you are likely to find a lot of ideas here. Even seasoned veterans are likely to learn some tips and tricks— I certainly came away with a few of my own!

— Brett Lantz, author of "Machine Learning with R"

With their new book, Data Science for Fundraising, Ashutosh and Rodger have done a wonderful and humorous job in addressing the challenges, pitfalls and joys of creating a data analytics program. Their thoughtful and generous sharing of ideas (and code!) that users can put to use immediately is incredibly helpful, but the time spent on the importance of developing the "people skills" required to create an effective program is what I found most valuable. Having lived through this process with Ashutosh many years ago, I appreciated that they address topics like the messiness and persistence needed to be successful, the need to know your audience and gain their trust, the need for experimentation and continuous improvement, and – most importantly – the necessity of "creating actionable" business intelligence that is adopted by the organization vs. the lure of answering lots of "interesting" questions. A great addition to any fundraiser's or data analyst's library.   **— Karen T. Isble, Associate Vice Chancellor, University of California, Irvine**

While there is a surfeit of books addressing general data science, there are very few that have a sharp focus on solving a specific set of domain problems. This book is one of them. That does not mean a general practitioner cannot benefit from this. The objective, organization and content of the book make it an invaluable addition to any serious data scientist's library.
— Bala Deshpande, Ph.D. Senior Managing Consultant, Watson and AI Solutions Center of Competence, and author of "Predictive Analytics and Data Mining"

Over the past twenty years, fundraising has become one of the most competitive industries on the planet. Future fundraising success for organizations of all shapes and sizes will depend almost entirely on the ability to effectively and seamlessly integrate strategy, technology, and human capital. This book takes an "over the horizon" view of data science and highlights

the growing role the field of analytics is playing to drive innovation while optimizing results. Ashutosh and Rodger have done a masterful job of packaging a broad spectrum of tools, philosophy, and best practices that every fundraising shop can benefit from.
— **Dondi Cupp, Associate Vice President, University of Michigan**

Leavened with anecdotes and touches of humour, this book cuts through the abundance and confusion of technical materials available, delivering a package that manages to be both highly readable and comprehensive. A book that is as much about people as it is about data, "Data Science for Fundraising" takes the reader from beginner to advanced, always keeping in mind that the end goal is not the analytics but the actions it suggests or supports. This is must-have for every fundraising team that is data-driven, or aspires to be. **— Kevin MacDonell, author of "Score!" and Acting Executive Director, Dalhousie University**

Ashutosh and Rodger provide astonishing insight on how to transform prospect attribute and behavior theory into strategies that will better inform your fundraising and constituent engagement. Whether you're a data scientist, analyst or a development professional that's driven by information, Data Science for Fundraising is a definitive and comprehensive study that will inspire you to turn data into action. This is really a fantastic work. **— Ben Tompkins, Senior Associate Vice President and Chief Operating Officer, Emory University**

Ashutosh and Rodger are two individuals leading with thought and action on the vanguard of the data science revolution in the Advancement profession. This book represents a "how to guide" for analysts at all levels to transform static data into dynamic insights. Advancement leaders must get familiar with this aspect Advancement Services as we continue to approach the business of philanthropy with more sophistication in an ever changing world.

— Aaron Westfall, Director of Development, University of Cambridge

Data Science for Fundraising provides both technical and non-technical people an effective path to learning how to turn their organization's data into actionable insights. The use-cases are clear and one's fundraisers will understand. This book is an important addition to the data science for good library.

— David M. Lawson, author of Big Good: Philanthropy in the Age of Big Data & Cognitive Computing

Over the years I've had the benefit of working both as a research consultant and a fundraising practitioner, and have rarely come across a book that addresses so directly some of the major data and analytics challenges that advancement shops face. What I find especially impressive about the book is that it's clear it was written by fundraising professionals for fundraising professionals. The diverse range of use case demonstrations along with step-by-step instructions for performing analyses renders the book akin to a 'cookbook' with detailed, time-saving data recipes. I highly recommend it to those working in advancement roles that involve data, analytics, and strategy development.

— A.J. Nagaraj, Senior Consultant (Former), EAB

Whether operations, fundraiser or aspiring advancement team member, this is a great book filled with pertinent, easily explained do-it-yourself information.

— Janiece Richard, Assistant Director of Annual Giving, USC Shoah Foundation

Contents

List of Tables		xi
List of Figures		xiii
Foreword		xix
Preface		**xxiii**
	Why read this book	xxiii
	Structure of the book	xxv
	Not Technical?	xxvi
	Other reading	xxvi
	Software information and conventions	xxviii
	Acknowledgments	xxx
1	**Introduction**	**1**
	1.1 Quick Introduction to Analytics	2
	1.2 When Do You Need a Data Science Team?	2
	1.3 Analytics Maturity Model	3
	1.4 What Will Data Science Do For You	5
	1.5 How to Build a Case for an Analytics Team	8
	1.6 Differentiate Actionable from "Interesting"	10
	1.7 Mindset	10

ii CONTENTS

1.7.1	Curiosity	11
1.7.2	Balanced Skepticism	11
1.7.3	Persistence	12
1.7.4	Hunger to Learn and Improve	12
1.7.5	Motivation	13
1.7.6	Portfolio Approach	13
1.7.7	Selling	13
1.8	Technical Expertise	14
1.9	Areas of Importance	14
1.9.1	Data Mining / Machine Learning / Statistics	14
1.10	Where to Find Them	17
	Sample Job Description	19
	Summary	19
	Job Responsibilities	19
	Qualifications	20

2 Analytics Adoption   **21**

2.1	Journey from Operations to Strategic Partner	22
2.2	Translating Problems into Opportunities	26
2.3	Create a Road map	27
2.4	Identify Your Champions	28
2.5	Defining Business Purpose	30
2.6	Analytics Maturity	30
2.6.1	Descriptive Analytics	31
2.6.2	Predictive Analytics	31
2.6.3	Prescriptive Analytics	31
2.6.4	Data Pyramid	32
2.6.5	Pathways to Wisdom	32
2.6.6	Wisdom is Competitive Advantage	33
2.7	Adoption Barriers	34
2.7.1	Know Your Audience	35
2.7.2	Adoption is Change	37
2.7.3	Competency and Motivation	37
2.7.4	Building Trust	38
2.7.5	Quick Wins	38

CONTENTS   iii

	2.7.6	Build Your Brand	39
	2.7.7	Purpose	39
	2.8	People, Talent, and Culture	40
	2.9	Change Management	41
	2.10	Managing Hype, Priorities, and Expectations	42
	2.11	Critical Mass	43
	2.12	Diffusion of Innovation	44
	2.13	Continuous Improvement	45
	2.14	Wrapping Up	46
3	**Success in Analytics**		**47**
	3.1	Products	48
	3.2	People	54
	3.3	Passion	60
	3.4	Storytelling	61
4	**Data Science Applications for Fundraising**		**63**
	4.1	What is Data Science?	63
	4.2	How to Use Data Science for Fundraising?	64
	4.3	Problems in Fundraising	64
	4.3.1	Finding Prospective Donors	64
	4.4	Maximizing Resources	65
	4.5	Are they Really Problems?	65
	4.6	How to Use Data Science to Solve These Problems?	66
	4.6.1	Outward Looking	67
	4.6.2	Inward Looking	68
5	**Getting Started with R**		**69**
	5.1	Why R?	69
	5.2	Download R (Required)	70
	5.3	Install RStudio (Optional)	70
	5.4	Install Packages	71
	5.5	Learning R	73
	5.6	R Console	74
	5.7	Built-in Functions	77

iv CONTENTS

	5.8	Variables	79
	5.9	Conditional Logic	80
	5.10	Data Types	82
	5.11	Vectors	82
	5.12	Sequences	83
	5.13	Matrices	84
	5.14	Lists	84
	5.15	Factors	85
	5.16	Data Frame	86
	5.17	Data Types	87
	5.18	Additional Support	88
6	**Loading Data**		**89**
	6.1	Read CSV Files	90
	6.2	Read Delimited CSV and TSV Files	91
	6.3	List Session Variables	91
	6.4	List Data Frame Variable Names	91
	6.5	Inspect Data Object	92
	6.6	Read Excel files	93
	6.7	Read from a Database	94
7	**Cleaning Data**		**97**
	7.1	Remove Extra Spaces	99
	7.2	Change Data Types	100
	7.3	Replace Values with NA	100
	7.4	Change Order of Values	101
	7.5	Clean ZIP Codes	101
	7.6	Manipulate Dates	103
	7.7	Remove Non-Numeric Characters	104
	7.8	Convert from Character to Numeric Data Type	105
	7.9	Export Cleaned Data File	106
8	**Manipulating Data**		**107**
	8.1	Chaining Operations	112
	8.2	Selecting Columns	114

CONTENTS   v

8.3	Filtering Rows		120
8.4	Creating Columns		121
8.5	Creating Aggregate Data Frames		124
8.6	Creating Joins		125
8.7	Transforming Data		130
8.7.1	Transforming from Wide to Long Layout		131
8.7.2	Transforming Data from Long to Wide Layout		133

9 Exploratory Data Analysis   **137**

9.1	Heads or Tails		138
9.2	Glimpse		139
9.3	Slice and Dice		139
9.4	Indexing Notation		140
9.5	Deselect Rows and Columns		140
9.6	Select Columns by Name		141
9.7	Summary		141
9.8	Average Gift Size		142
9.9	Measures of Spread		143
9.10	Two-Way Contingency Table		144
9.11	Group By		145
9.12	Histograms and Bar plots		146
9.13	Boxplots with Outliers		149
9.14	Correlation Matrix		153
9.15	Missing Values (NA)		155
9.16	Correlation Matrix Revisited		156
9.17	Scatter Plot Matrix		157
9.18	Summary		162

10 Data Visualization   **165**

10.1	Creating Better Charts		165
10.2	Understanding Perception		166
10.3	Process		171
10.3.1	Chart Junk		173
10.3.2	Critical Thinking		174
10.4	Improving Effectiveness of Visuals		176

vi CONTENTS

10.4.1	Design Principles	176
10.4.2	Clarity	177
10.4.3	Format	178
10.4.4	Color	179
10.4.5	Distractions	180
10.4.6	Accessibility	180
10.4.7	Incorrect Encoding	181
10.4.8	Aspect Ratio and Axis Values	182
10.4.9	Context	185
10.5	Choosing the Right Chart Types	185
10.5.1	Tables	185
10.5.2	Simple Bar Charts	186
10.5.3	Line Charts	186
10.5.4	Pie Charts	187
10.5.5	Stacked Bar Charts	189
10.5.6	Scatter Plots	190
10.5.7	Maps	192
10.6	Creating Data Visualizations with `ggplot`	193
10.6.1	`geom`	193
10.6.2	Aesthetics (`aes`) Mapping	194
10.6.3	Using `scales` Functions	196
10.6.4	Use `theme` to Control the Look and Feel	198
10.7	Creating Bar Charts	202
10.8	Creating Dot Charts	212
10.9	Creating Line Charts	219
10.10	Creating Scatter/Text Plots	223
10.10.1	Text Plots	228
10.10.2	Creating Bubble Plots	234
10.11	Creating Slopegraphs	239
10.12	Creating Heat Maps	243
10.13	Creating Panels/Facets	245
10.14	Geographic Mapping	247
10.14.1	Points on a map	247
10.14.2	Filled a.k.a. Choropleth Maps	261
10.15	Creating Dashboards	266

10.16	Creating Animated Charts	272
10.16.1	Gathering, Cleaning-Up, and Summarizing Data	272
10.16.2	Get the Store Openings Data	273
10.16.3	Creating Maps	275
10.16.4	Creating the Walmart Growth Movie	278
10.17	Summary	280

11 RFM Modeling — 281

11.1	Calculate RFM Values	281
11.2	Create Quintiles	286
11.3	Plot Ranks	289
11.4	Use Cases	297

12 Machine Learning Recipes — 301

12.1	Feature Selection	302
12.2	Supervised Learning	303
12.2.1	Classification	304
12.2.2	Instance-Based Learning	304
12.2.3	Probabilistic Machine Learning	313
12.2.4	Decision Trees	320
12.2.5	Rule-Based Classification	344
12.2.6	Regression	362
12.3	Unsupervised Learning	376
12.3.1	K-Means	377
12.3.2	Association Rule Mining	382
12.4	Model Diagnostics	391
12.5	Summary	393

13 Predicting Gift Size — 395

13.1	Simple Forecasting	396
13.2	Quantile Regression	399
13.3	Gradient Tree	403
13.4	Neural Networks	408
13.5	Method Evaluation	409

14 Text Mining — 417

viii CONTENTS

14.1   Bio Generation 418
14.2   Endowment Benchmarking 421
14.3   Geo-Coded Prospect Identification 424
14.4   Social Media Analytics 430
14.5   Text Classification 434
14.6   Sentiment Analysis 441
14.7   Summary 445

15 Social Network Analysis   447

15.1   Key Concepts 449
15.2   Data Structure 452
15.3   Creating Your First Network 455
15.4   Creating a Game of Thrones™ Network 460
15.5   Adding Interactivity 474

16 Finding Prospects   477

16.1   Prospect Segments 478
16.2   RFM 480
16.3   Giving Velocity 480
16.4   Social Network Analysis 481
16.5   Gift Capacity and Inclination 481
16.6   Engagement Scores 482
16.7   Annual Giving 483
16.8   Planned Giving 488
16.9   Summary 492

17 New Trends   493

17.1   USC's Action Center 493
       Donor News 494
       Prospect Recommendations 494
       Gift Alerts 494
       Proposal and Portfolio Cleanup 496
17.2   Opportunity or Proposal Generation 496
17.3   Bio Generation 499
17.4   Web Giving 500

17.5	Trackers + Ads	500
17.6	Event Suggestor	501
17.7	Donor Platforms	502
17.8	Crawling + MTurks	503
17.9	Auto-Generated Emails	504
17.10	Interactive Data Analysis	505

Bibliography 509

Index 519

x CONTENTS

List of Tables

1.1	Making a case for an analytics team	9
3.1	Analytics road map	52
4.1	Inward-looking fundraising problems and data science applications	68
10.1	Same statistical properties datasets but different shapes (Matejka et al. 2017)	170
11.1	Sample gift transaction table	283
11.2	Median giving by recency bins	289
11.3	Median giving by frequency bins	290
12.1	'TensorFlow' evaluation using test data	361
12.2	'TensorFlow' evaluation using full data	361
15.1	Edges-only data	453
15.2	Edge and vertex data	453
16.1	Annual giving mailing segments example	487
16.2	Test results from a mailing	491

xii LIST OF TABLES

List of Figures

1.1	IBM's analytics maturity model	4
1.2	Lift obtained using predictive analytics over regular practice	7
2.1	BM25 document ranking	22
2.2	Rodger's social network map circa 2011	23
2.3	Heat map calendar to help the hungry	24
2.4	Backroom software engineer	24
2.5	Business process map	25
2.6	Enterprise systems	25
2.7	Hanging out in the server room	26
3.1	Mean and variance of kicks: Kicker A	53
3.2	Mean and variance of kicks: Kicker B	53
3.3	Bigger decision tree with 78% accuracy	56
3.4	Smaller decision tree with 77% accuracy	56
3.5	Quality, acceptance, and effectiveness (Jerry Allyne, INFORMS presentation)	59
4.1	Data science applied to the donor journey	67
5.1	Command prompt	74

xiv LIST OF FIGURES

5.2	Interactive output	76
5.3	RStudio command prompt	76
5.4	RStudio interactive output	77
8.1	Wide layout	131
8.2	Long layout	131
10.1	Bar and line graphs testing (Zacks and Tversky 1999)	167
10.2	Bar and line graphs testing (Chua, Yates, and Shah 2006)	168
10.3	Anscombe's quartet: four different data sets with similar statistical distributions	170
10.4	Anscombe's quartet: four different data sets with similar statistical properties	171
10.5	Same statistical properties datasets but different shapes (Matejka et al. 2017)	172
10.6	Redesigned chart on state spending	174
10.7	Idea-generation framework	175
10.8	Encoding of circle sizes by radius and area	182
10.9	Apple performance with an aspect ratio of 5	183
10.10	Apple performance with an aspect ratio of 1	183
10.11	Apple performance with an aspect ratio of 0.4	183
10.12	Apple performance with the Y axis starting at 0	183
10.13	Apple performance with the Y axis starting at 10	184
10.14	Meeting = pie chart	188
10.15	Scatter plot of age and length (Ashton et al. 2014)	191
10.16	Aesthetics mapping using 'ggplot'	195
10.17	Aesthetics mapping using 'geom'	196
10.18	Y-axis limits changed	198
10.19	Y-axis gridlines changed	199
10.20	Y axis transformed with a square root	200
10.21	Y-axis label removed	201
10.22	Axis labels modified	202
10.23	Bar graph of number of prospects by wealth ratings	203

10.24	Horizontal bar graph of number of prospects by wealth ratings	204
10.25	Horizontal bar graph of number of prospects by wealth ratings with commas	205
10.26	Horizontal bar graph of number of prospects by ordered wealth ratings	206
10.27	Horizontal bar graph of number of prospects with unknown values removed	207
10.28	Horizontal bar graph of number of prospects. Cleaning up	209
10.29	Horizontal bar graph of number of prospects with added titles	210
10.30	Horizontal bar graph of number of prospects with vertical gridlines	211
10.31	Horizontal bar graph of number of prospects with axis labels reformatted	212
10.32	Wealth rating count. A dot chart example using 'ggplot'	214
10.33	Wealth rating count. A dot chart example using 'dotchart'	215
10.34	Wealth rating count. A dot chart example using 'ggplot'	217
10.35	Wealth rating count. A dot chart example using the 'dotchart' function	218
10.36	Comparing stock values with a line chart	221
10.37	Comparing stock values with a line chart. Legends on the line.	222
10.38	A scatter plot of age and total giving	224
10.39	A scatter plot of age and total giving with currency format	225
10.40	Scatter plot of age and total giving	226
10.41	A scatter plot of age and total giving with transparency	227
10.42	Fictional name plot	229
10.43	Fictional name plot with colors	231

xvi LIST OF FIGURES

10.44	Alumni size and participation rates (FY15)	233
10.45	Gapminder bubble plot	235
10.46	Gapminder bubble plot with increased size	236
10.47	Gapminder bubble plot with colors	237
10.48	Gapminder bubble plot with better colors	238
10.49	Gapminder bubble plot with changed scale	238
10.50	Gapminder bubble plot with labels	239
10.51	Changes in alumni participation seen using a slope-graph	242
10.52	Contact activity heat map	244
10.53	Contact activity heat map with labels	245
10.54	A faceted box plot	246
10.55	Number of prospects by ZIP code on the US map	252
10.56	Number of prospects by ZIP code on the U.S. map, colored by density	254
10.57	Bay Area map	255
10.58	Various maps of Los Angeles	256
10.59	Prospects in the Bay Area	257
10.60	Prospects mapped on a street	261
10.61	State filled map	264
10.62	County filled map	265
10.63	A quick and dirty mockup of a dashboard	267
10.64	Dashboard using gridextra	271
10.65	Walmart locations	279
11.1	Density distribution	287
11.2	RFM scores and counts	291
11.3	RFM scores and giving	292
11.4	Recency rank, frequency rank, and giving	293
11.5	Box plot of giving	294
11.6	Recency and frequency rank along with giving . .	296
11.7	Recency and frequency rank along with giving . .	297
12.1	A neural network representation	348
12.2	Donor neural network using neuralnet	351

12.3	K-means donor cluster analysis		381
13.1	Actual versus prediction of current FY giving using simple average		398
13.2	Actual versus prediction of current FY giving using quantile regression		402
13.3	Actual versus prediction of current FY giving using TDBoost		407
13.4	Actual versus prediction of current FY giving using neural networks		410
13.5	RMSE of many models		414
13.6	Violin plot to compare models using the 'mlr' package		415
13.7	Box plot to compare models using the 'mlr' package		415
14.1	Forbes bio example		422
14.2	Twitter wordcloud: MachineLearning DeepLearning AI		433
15.1	Different layouts for networks		452
15.2	Customized vertex options		454
15.3	Fruchterman-Reingold layout		462
15.4	Circle layout		463
15.5	Kamada-Kawai layout		464
15.6	Large graph layout		465
15.7	Multi-dimensional scaling layout		466
15.8	Auto layout		467
15.9	Star-shaped layout		468
15.10	Sphere layout		469
15.11	Game of Thrones™ interactive network		476
16.1	Prospect quadrant		479
16.2	Gift capacity versus giving likelihood		482
16.3	Gift capacity versus engagement		484
17.1	USC's action center		495

xviii   LIST OF FIGURES

17.2	Auto proposal generation	. . . .	497
17.3	Event suggestor	. . . .	502
17.4	Event seating suggestor	. . . .	503
17.5	Crawling + MTurks	. . . .	504
17.6	A Shiny app for fundraiser performance scoring (using fake data)	. . . .	506

FOREWORD

2013 was a magical year. You remember it, right? We shared some great memories.

Together, we enjoyed:

- Destiny's Child reunion at the Super Bowl.
- U.S. Customs taking custody of a monkey from Justin Bieber as he tried to take it to the Grammys.
- The Federal Government shutting itself down.
- The all-new Cool Ranch® Doritos Locos® were introduced and the absolutely delicious new … Ramen Burger!

And to personalize this a bit, I'll add one of my personal favorite memories from 2013:

Meeting Ashutosh Nandeshwar.

Here's how it all went down:

My email box gets pinged one day by this guy at the University of Michigan who tells me that he thinks he'd be a great speaker at a conference that I was helping put on. He's very kind in his note and asks if I'd be willing to have a phone call to chat about what he'd like to present about. I say sure and we set up a call.

xx FOREWORD

Before the date of our call, I start to do a little homework on Ashu and become intrigued. I hear about his background and some of the great work that he's done at Michigan and think that we could really be in for a treat with him as a speaker.

So we end up having our phone call, and he's absolutely delightful to talk to. He's sharp, articulate and more than anything: desires to help people by sharing what he knows.

I tell him we'd love to have him as a speaker. I could sense his excitement and it's game on.

Next thing you know, conference time is here and I'm at the event having a coffee and then it happens. This guy walks up, best dressed in the room (by far) puts his hand out and says:

'Chris, it's Ashu!'

One day later, we're scrambling with conference facility staff to find more chairs for his room (of course it was overflowing) and I quickly realize: this guy is a legend in the making.

People couldn't get enough of him at the event in 2013.

Not surprisingly, they can't get enough of him now.

This book you're about to enjoy will serve as a series of keys to help you unlock your potential in the dynamic field of information and data technology. Ashutosh and co-pilot, Rodger Devine, take you on a journey that will have you arrive at technical excellence.

Their simple to grasp introduction to concepts, in-depth examples and ability to express why it matters: give you the perfect companion on your path to becoming an industry expert.

As you become an industry expert, consider the example laid before you in this book. Give back. Mentor, just like Ashutosh and Rodger have done.

For as their example shows: far better it is to give, than to receive.

But for now, it's time to receive … some of the best content you'll ever read on the subject of data, analytics and beyond.

Go, get after it!

Chris Sorensen
Creator of the DRIVE/ conference (now owned by CASE)

xxii FOREWORD

PREFACE

Why read this book

There are many books that cover various topics in fundraising. There are many books that explore the R programming language, data analytics, and machine learning. However, there are few books that explore how to use R to build data-driven solutions for fundraising problems. This was one of the key motivations for writing this book.

At the time of writing this, a quick web search of "fundraising analytics" produces 1,850,000 results (in 0.46 seconds), which clearly suggests there is appetite, curiosity, and demand for useful material regarding this subject. Fundraising analytics articles, products, and webinars tend to focus on technical tools and approaches such as data visualization and predictive modeling across many fundraising areas, including, to name a few, prospect identification, donor segmentation, pipeline management, direct response marketing, and fundraising forecasts.

As lifelong learners, we strongly encourage you to search, study, and explore as much as you can about the art of fundraising and

xxiv   PREFACE

the science of data, visualization, and machine learning because the future of fundraising, like many other industries, will continue to be shaped and strongly influenced by advancements in technology. And why do institutions and firms (for-profit and non-profit) invest in technology? To gain competitive advantage. To gain efficiency. To increase results.

Contact reports are no longer dictated or hand-typed on a typewriter. In fact, some customer relationship management (CRM) software and donor databases allow you to enter contact reports via voice entry on your mobile device using speech-to-text technology. Speech-to-text and natural language processing software is far from perfect, but it's still a useful step forward to a technology-driven future. And what's the point of all these bells and whistles? In the case of contact reports, one could argue that minimizing the effort required to enter contact reports saves time and energy (scarce resources), which fundraisers could apply towards other important areas, such as fundraising strategy, donor outreach, qualification, cultivation, and solicitation.

Why read this book?

Because you're curious. Because you've already read many articles about the potential of analytics to improve your fundraising programs, but you want a clear path and practical methods on how to analyze and distill the actionable insights in your data. Also, because you're ready. As Rodger's beloved piano teacher, Katherine, says, "I can teach you something in 10 minutes that took me 10 years to figure out." Many of you reading this book may have heard or been interested in data science, analytics, and machine learning for years, but never had an opportunity to dive in. After reading the book and executing the code, you will understand and learn about 80 to 90% of the knowledge of applied data science, specifically as applied to fundraising. You're lucky because it took more than 10 years to acquire that knowledge.

This book will help get you going on your data science journey. So, no more waiting, rainy days, or "maybe someday" stalling. This is the future, and the time is now.

The value proposition of this book is simple: There are countless resources on data science and its applications, but this one book will take you from a beginner to an advanced level of understanding. From there, you must continue to sharpen your skills to attain mastery.

Structure of the book

This book is organized into 17 chapters, with chapters 1 through 4 beginning with an introduction to analytics, analytics adoption, and fundraising application examples. Chapters 5 through 9 introduce the R programming language and provide a series of recipes to help familiarize you with basic tasks such as loading, cleaning, manipulating and exploring data for patterns.

Chapter 10, Data Visualization, explores a broad set of data visualization methods and best practices that you can incorporate into your own solutions. Chapter 11 explores Recency, Frequency, Monetary (RFM) modeling, which is a descriptive analytics technique drawn from direct marketing and is commonly used in fundraising. Chapter 12 covers machine learning concepts (including both supervised and unsupervised learning methods) and provides R recipes (coding scripts) that you can explore with an example donor file to demystify the application of machine learning techniques to donor data.

Chapters 13 explores predicting next gift size, including simple forecasting and some of the challenges with this task. Chapter 14 focuses on text mining, which is a form of data analytics focused on gleaning patterns from text-based data. Chapter 14 also introduces you

xxvi PREFACE

to some powerful R packages you can use to generate reports, acquire web-based data, and enhance your analysis by blending data sources and generating comparative insights.

Chapter 15 explores social network analysis, which uses graph theory to visualize and analyze information as networks of connections or relationships. Chapters 16 explores the concept of finding prospects, including some popular use cases that are frequently discussed, researched, and debated. Chapter 17 concludes with a survey of new trends and applications that highlight future fundraising applications and beyond.

Not Technical?

This book does not assume any previous programming knowledge, experience, or background. A familiarity with basic statistical concepts is helpful, but not required as additional reading and resources are introduced and suggested in each chapter.

If you are a manager or leader and not interested in directly learning data science, we encourage you to get a copy of this book for your data-driven staff or curious colleagues who would benefit from learning the best-in-class machine learning methods to build solutions and add value to your organization.

Other reading

This book will not satisfy all readers because of omissions, intentional or not. Let's go over the intentional omissions. We don't cover all the issues you will face when you're just getting started with R. We don't discuss any big data tools or techniques. We don't explain the machine learning algorithms. If we did so, this book would've never been completed. We want to help you get to the 80 to 90% of knowledge level in a short time. We highly recommend these books to fill any gaps as well as to sharpen your skills.

- *R Cookbook* by Paul Teetor, 2011: http://a.co/bMrC9ot. This book covers many of the basics of R using recipes. An easy to follow book and a must read.
- *R for Data Science* by Hadley Wickham et al., 2017: http://a.co/4luF7t. Learn from a master. Not only is this book well written, but it also teaches you efficient ways to complete complicated tasks.
- *Machine Learning with R* by Brett Lantz, 2015: http://a.co/6pRrjGb. Rodger and I have both been fortunate to know and work with Brett. He's written elegantly and explained complicated algorithms in this book.
- *Data Mining: Practical Machine Learning Tools and Techniques* by Ian H. Witten et al., 2011: http://a.co/ifmkIvh. This book will help you easily understand many machine learning techniques and concepts. Its simple language and explanations will speed up your understanding.
- *Code Complete* by Steve McConnell, 2004: http://a.co/9f27xQc. If you want to write code that you can understand even after many years, you must read this book. Steve provides hundreds of recommendations on writing good code.
- *Making Things Happen* by Scott Berkun, 2008: http://a.co/5hWXU18. Analysis is wasted if it's unused. In this book, Scott explains how to manage projects to make things happen. Every analyst should read this book.
- *Information Dashboard Design (1st edition)* by Stephen Few, 2006: http://a.co/bVGINJ5. If you are just getting started in data visualization, you should read this book. You will never see charts the same way again.
- *Confessions of a Public Speaker* by Scott Berkun, 2011: http://a.co/5Ym5nqV. Another Berkun book, and an-

other gem. Ashutosh got his start in public speaking after reading this book, but more importantly, ¥ he learned the skills he needed to explain his analysis.

- *Presentation Zen* by Garr Reynolds, 2011: http://a.co/e9OduPx. After all your hard work, don't let your presentation fail you. Read this book to create beautiful slides and effectively present your points.

Software information and conventions

All the code in each chapter needs to be run in order as examples tend to build on previous examples.

We encourage you to explore the book's content according to your interest and need, but advise against jumping into the middle of a chapter and expecting your code results to match without running the code introduced earlier in the chapter.

Please note the following information and coding conventions used within this book:

This is a note.

Any text displayed within this text box is intended to be an important note, concept, or takeaway.

This is a quote.

Any text displayed within this text box is intended to be an important quoted reference.

This is an exercise.

Any text displayed within this text box is designed to be a challenge or exercise to help you learn how to customize the solution or recipe to explore your own questions.

If you're reading an electronic copy of this book, you may have difficulty copying and pasting the code directly. All the code and data used in each chapter are available as standalone files. You can download them from http://www.nandeshwar.info/ds4fundraisingcode.

Every time you see the `library` command along with a library name, such as `library(tidyverse)`, we assume that the package is installed on your computer. If not, use the `install.packages(<package_name>)` command to install the library. Note that we are using the words "library" and "package" interchangeably.

You will notice that the code chunks are in a grey box and R code is highlighted, and the output is shown in orange. The output in the book always begins with `#>` characters. Since `#` denotes the beginning of comments in R, you can safely copy the output on your console. (The output in your console will show up without the `#>` characters.)

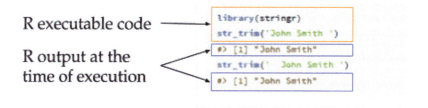

Although all the code will run on the base R application/console, we highly recommend you to use RStudio as an editor (integrated development environment (IDE)). RStudio makes coding faster and comes with many wonderful functionalities, which you will uncover as you follow the recipes in this book.

xxx   PREFACE

The R ecosystem is continuously evolving, and although we made sure that all the code in this book runs on multiple computers, it is likely that some library will be out of date or may cause errors. Feel free to reach out to us so that we can help you and update the code in the book. The last compilation of this book used this configuration:

```
#> R nickname: Kite-Eating Tree
#> R version 3.4.3 (2017-11-30)
#> On platform: x86_64-apple-darwin15.6.0 (64-bit)
#> Running: macOS Sierra 10.12.6
```

 If you can't reproduce the output using the code from the book, try setting the seed to 777 with this command: set.seed(777).

Acknowledgments

Ashutosh Nandeshwar

I'm thankful to many people for various reasons. There are some who have helped me every time I've stumbled. Then there are those who helped me before I could stumble. There are some who showed me the light. There are a few who paved the way for me. Some helped me without knowing. Let me list a few names, but this list isn't exhaustive, and I apologize for my omissions.

Dr. B. R. Ambedkar for creating opportunities for all the marginalized communities of India. I would be far from writing this if it were not for him.

Mom and Dad for believing in me, especially when I failed, and setting the path for my future. Unfortunately, my father passed away before he could see this book. Thank you for everything, *Baba*. I miss you.

Mr. Prabhu, my math tutor in high school, for building the belief that I could do math (my brother will tell you how hopeless I was). Dr. Rakesh Chandran for helping me out through the tough years of graduate school. Dr. Tim Menzies for teaching not only machine learning, but also the value of simplicity. Mike Sperko for giving me a chance to do data analysis for a living. Karen Isble for taking a chance on me and letting me apply analytics to fundraising.

All my terrific colleagues at USC. Tracey Vranich for seeing the value of data science for fundraising and letting me run free with my ideas. Doug Byers for helping me in immeasurable ways. Al Checcio for his vision and belief in data-driven fundraising.

Chris Sorenson for helping me spread my ideas and for writing the fantastic foreword.

My wonderful wife, Utpalvarna, for taking care of *everything* while I focused on this book on weekends and evenings. Asanga and Dinnaga, my amazing children, for teaching me so many things, including the value of spending time with your loved ones. They understood when I could not attend their soccer and Taekwondo practice.

Many thanks to everyone who provided feedback on the book: Andrew Schultz, Michie Spradling, and Dibyendu Mondal. Thanks also to our editors: Madhusudan Uchil and Kathy Osborn.

Lastly, huge thanks to the R community. It would have been impossible to do anything without the work of every package builder and every Stackoverflow [r] answerer. A few R developers deserve special mention: Hadley Wickham, author of "R for Data Science" and `ggplot`, `dplyr`, `devtools`, and others. Yihui Xie, author of the `bookdown` and `knitr` packages (we wrote this book using `bookdown`). Because of RStudio and all the people behind this great product, literate programming and interactive analysis has never been this easy. Thanks #rstats!

And, of course, my co-author Rodger! :)

xxxii PREFACE

Rodger Devine

This book would not have been possible without the support and encouragement of many friends, family, and mentors over the years, including:

Lada Adamic, Prabhanshu Agrawal, Kaleena Bajo, Reginald Becton, Kerri Bennett, Donald Boettner, Russell Brown, Bob Burdenski, John and Susan Butler, Carly Capitula, Cathleen Conway-Perrin, Kevin Corbett, Gin Corden, Dondi Cupp, "Lo" de Janvry, Hui Cha "Kim" Devine, Lindsay Devine, Rodger A. Devine, Terri Devine, Ryan Donnelly, Susan Engel, Nathan Fay, Nicole Ferguson, Josh Fields, Tyson FitzGerald, Patrick Franklin, Christina Frendo, Knekoh Frugé, Jennifer Dunn Greenspan, Renee Haraburda, Kelli Harrington, Yuping He, Christina Hendershaw, Salijo Hendershaw, Chere Hooks, Dianna Gladstone, Mike Glier, Risa Gotlib, Lorri Grubaugh, Nathan Gulick, Karen Isble, Josh Jacobson, Kim "Bella" Jacobson, Sonya Vanhoof Jimenez, Caitlin Johnson, Bob Jones, Kevin and Liz Jones, Sam Jones, Justin Joque, Frieda Kahn, Nick Kennedy, Jim King, Jennifer Kranz, Margaret Krebsbach, Dan Kugler, Andrew Kulpa, Brett Lantz, Karen Latora, Deborah Lennington, Jessie Lipkowitz, Shalonda Martin, Kim "McData" McDade, Qiaozhu Mei, Jaime Miranda, Xiomara Moncada, Chandra Montgomery, Andrew Mortensen, Tadd and Nayiri Mullinix, Ashutosh Nandeshwar, Leah Nickel, Kathy Osborn, Todd Osborn, Linda Pavich, Michael Pawlus, Jayne Perilstein, Andrea Perry, Joseph "Cacaww" Person, Matthew Pickus, Fabian Primera, Cynthia Radecki, Christopher Rael, Janiece Richard, Matthew Rizner, Jane Roach, Rose Romani, Jesse Ruf, Shahan Sanossian, Steve Sarrica, Eddie Sartin, James Sinclair, Jeff Sims, Alison Sommers-Sayre, Chris Sorensen, Katherine Teves, Henry Tyler, Jarrod Van Kirk, Tyler Varing, Tracey Vranich, Andrea Waldron, Tom Wamsley, Kathy Welch, Aaron Westfall, Hanah Wilkins, William Winston, Paul Worster, Jeff Wright, Julie Wright, Jing Zhou, R Community, Stack Overflow, WLAP Group, U-M Information and Technology Services, U-M MIDAS, U-M Ross School of Business Development and Alumni Relations, U-M

School of Information, USC Dornsife Advancement, USC University-sity Advancement, APRA, CASE, @DRIVE, Innovation Enterprise, MOTM, and all of my other friends, colleagues and teachers who have been a positive influence. Thank you for your support and encouragement. Onward and upward!

Many thanks to everyone who provided feedback on the book and, of course, special thanks to our editors, Kathy Osborn and Madhusu-dan Uchil. Lastly, thank you to Lada Adamic for making me learn R, Qiaozhu Mei for teaching me to develop intuition and apply my knowledge to real-world problems, Katherine Teves for inspiring passion and discipline, Eddie Sartin for his vision and leadership, and Todd Osborn for always keeping in real. I am forever grateful.

If you like this book, consider sharing it with your network by running `source("http://arn.la/shareds4fr")` in your R console.

Ashutosh R. Nandeshwar
Rodger Devine
February 2018

xxxiv PREFACE

1

INTRODUCTION

Data science is everywhere. Most likely you have heard that data science can do wonders for you, that you will boost your appeal responses, that you will find new major donors, and that you will be a rock star. Although there is some truth in these statements, do not conclude that you need an analytics team. Performing quality analysis is a hard task, but most organizations fail in its execution. Most people are reluctant to change, and selling analytics to such people is difficult (Mankins & Sherer 2014). Even if you're interested in learning only the *hows* of data science, you still must understand the *whys*.

Let's look at the *whys* from three different perspectives.

1. Need for analytics
2. Adoption of analytics
3. Success in analytics

2 INTRODUCTION

1.1 Quick Introduction to Analytics

This field has many names: statistical analysis, quantitative analysis, data mining, machine learning, data analytics, business intelligence, and data science. While some names have fallen out of favor, some are trending.

Regardless of the size of ythe data, the common goal in all these fields is to learn something from your data. It requires grit and skill, however, to learn something useful and actionable. In recent years, the data has grown so rapidly that it has become unmanageable. Plus, management leaders and data professionals have realized the derived value of such data (Amatriain & Basilico 2011).

The growth of available data and the increased need of insights from such data has given birth to specialized tools to manage and store data as well as to learn from it. We will not talk about these specialized tools, such as Hadoop, Hive, Mahout, and other tools that sound like names of animals or diseases, in this book. You can extend the principles and methods discussed here to learn and use such "big data" tools.

1.2 When Do You Need a Data Science Team?

As a believer in discovering insights from data, I am biased: I believe that data-driven decisions will make you and your organization more effective (Brynjolfsson et al. 2011). The question is not whether you should use data or analytics, but which insights you would find most applicable.

After seeing countless news articles on big data, you may find it easy to believe that you need scores of data scientists or that you need in-

ANALYTICS MATURITY MODEL 3

fographics. For simple aggregation of data or calculation of descriptive statistics, you just need an introduction to statistics class.

To do (what I consider) data science, you need advanced knowledge of analytical concepts and, more importantly, you need heightened judgment to reject questions that yield "interesting" yet non-actionable results. These skills come with practice and at a cost.

1.3 Analytics Maturity Model

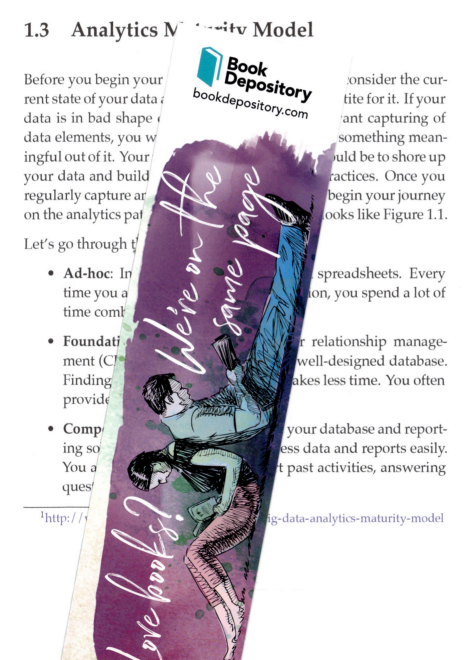

Before you begin your [journey], consider the current state of your data and [your appe]tite for it. If your data is in bad shape or [you don't w]ant capturing of data elements, you w[ill struggle to get] something meaningful out of it. Your [first step sho]uld be to shore up your data and build [strong data p]ractices. Once you regularly capture a[nd store data, you can] begin your journey on the analytics pat[h. This path l]ooks like Figure 1.1.

Let's go through the [stages:]

- **Ad-hoc**: In [this stage, you use] spreadsheets. Every time you a[sk a questi]on, you spend a lot of time comb[ining data.]

- **Foundati[onal**: You have a custome]r relationship management (C[RM system or a] well-designed database. Finding [data t]akes less time. You often provide [reports.]

- **Comp[etent**: You integrate] your database and reporting so[ftware. You can acc]ess data and reports easily. You a[re looking a]t past activities, answering ques[tions.]

---
[1]http://[...]ig-data-analytics-maturity-model

4 INTRODUCTION

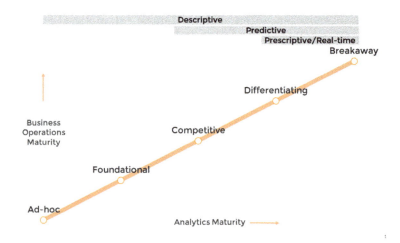

Figure 1.1: IBM's analytics maturity model

- **Differentiating**: You generate forward-looking information. The decision makers rely on this type of information to plan for the future. You answer questions like "What will happen?" and "Why did X happen?"

- **Breakaway**: You help automate decision making and/or generate real-time information. The decision makers have the latest information readily available along with recommendations for subsequent steps. You answer questions like "What should we do?"

As proposed in the IBM model, your goal should always be to advance the status from the basics of getting and storing the right data and building the best data practices to measuring objectives and goals.

Although you should always attempt to increase data usage in your decision making, you need to assess whether you need an analytics team.

If you work for a smaller organization (say an organization with fewer than 1,000 prospects) then, yes, you can improve your solicitation success rates or increase your retention rates using analytics. The costs of doing so, however, using a full-time analyst could be higher than any efficiency you gain.

For example, let's say the cost of an appeal is $5 per piece and you send this appeal to 1,000 people. That appeal will cost you $5,000. But instead, you develop a model that predicts people who are likely to respond. Based on that model, you choose to send the appeal to 600 people. Your cost of sending the mail now is $5 X 600 = $3,000, a total savings of $2,000.

Not bad.

But if these savings came at a cost of a $55,000 employee or a $15,000 model purchased from a vendor, you did not even break even on the money you spent on modeling.

The true value of an analytics person is less in what models he or she can develop, but more in his or her critical thinking. Any analyst should be able to solve a given problem, but good analysts will ask the questions nobody has asked before and provide new solutions to previously undiscovered problems. And that ability is worth acquiring.

1.4   What Will Data Science Do For You

After reading the first section, you may wonder, "But what about *Moneyball*?" or "What about all the news of how 'big data' is going to save the world?". If you cut through the hype and find some problems in your organization worth solving, yes, analytics can indeed add a lot of value. Let's look at an example of how analytics can add value.

Lift is a common way to measure this value. *Lift* measures the improvement achieved by a predictive model over the standard, baseline approach.

Let's say your annual appeal has a response rate of 8%, but then you send your appeal to only a selected population using a predictive model. From this selected population, 16% of the people respond, thus, giving you a $16/8 = 2$ lift.

Another way to look at it is by creating a *cumulative gains chart*, as shown in Figure 1.2. This chart shows the response rates using traditional methods of selecting whom to contact and the response rates using predictive models. Most likely, you will see improvements over your baseline methods.

For example, in this chart you see that if you contact 20% of the population using your baseline method, you will get a response of 20%. With a predictive model, if you contact 20% of the population, you will get a response of 50%. You gain efficiency by contacting people likely to respond as predicted by the models.

If applied thoughtfully, insights generated using analytics can help your organization do all of these better:

- Find more prospects
- Build a stronger prospect base
- Retain more donors
- Increase giving
- Manage the right prospects
- Recommend giving options to your donors
- Find volunteers
- Recruit gift officers

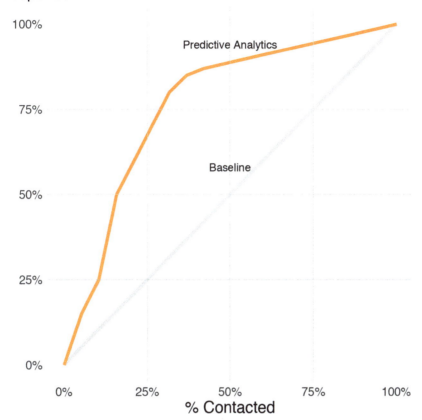

Figure 1.2: Lift obtained using predictive analytics over regular practice

- Invite people to events
- "Up-sell" online giving
- Create stewardship articles
- Staff the right geographic regions
- Assess campaign readiness
- Scale prospect research

8 INTRODUCTION

- Measure performance

1.5 How to Build a Case for an Analytics Team

The best way to build a case for an analytics team is to report on the return on investment (ROI) on analytics as applied to your organization's existing problems.

Are there any problems that worry you about the future of your organization? Problems such as how to retain donors, how to find new donors, how to increase giving, how to increase participation rates, how to focus your gift officers' efforts, how to provide timely information on your prospects to your staff, or how to know that you have enough prospects to reach a campaign goal?

The following is a simple way to document these problems.

Create a table with five columns as shown in Table 1.1. In the first column, list all the problems that worry you about the future of your organization[2]. In the second column, record your thoughts about solving those problems.

Take a break.

Go over the list again and add any other information that you can think of. In the third column, make notes of any problems that you think can be solved by data-driven decision making. In the fourth column, make notes of any outcomes such as improved processes, saved time, or increased giving. In the last column, enter estimated savings or earnings.

---

[2]Don't note the lack of your promotion as a worry – numbers will always be against you!

HOW TO BUILD A CASE FOR AN ANALYTICS TEAM 9

Table 1.1: Making a case for an analytics team

Problem	Solution	Data use	Outcomes	Cost
Acquire more prospects	Purchase lists	yes, we can purchase lists based on profiles of our existing donors	1,000 more prospects in the database	$5,000
Increase retention	Learn interests of donors	yes, we can build a dataset of donor interests	improved response and retention rates	$10,000
Shortage of donors	Find new markets	yes, using geographic modeling, we can find new regions	new opportunities	$500,000

Once you complete the list, you may find that an outcome of fixing a single problem could be worth thousands, if not millions of dollars to you. If that is the case, congratulations! You just built a strong case for your analytics team.

Summarize all the outcomes, provide the estimated dollar amounts in savings or new income, and present the findings to your management team. When leaders see significant risks or opportunities, they are more likely to invest and support the idea.

> When leaders see significant risks or opportunities, they are more likely to invest and support the idea.

If your organization is unwilling to invest in a new team or you just don't have resources to do so (though you have a solid case), just start doing. Doing is far more powerful than saying. Lead with an example. Tackle a reasonable problem and generate an analytical

10   INTRODUCTION

solution to it. Show the results and projected outcomes to a potential consumer of your information. Be very picky about choosing your first consumer. This consumer should be your champion and should be able to communicate the power of analytics to other people, including your leadership.

1.6   Differentiate Actionable from "Interesting"

It is very easy to think that you can apply analytics to every problem—true, you can—but the bigger challenge is separating "interesting" from "actionable." For example, social network analysis is quite cool and you may apply it to your data to find network graphs. Yes, the network graphs look good and interesting; how to put them into action, however, is a bigger challenge[3]. That is why it is important to think first of the biggest problems or questions that your organization is facing. By solving these problems, you could provide a new direction for your organization. If you think of solutions before the problems, you can forget implementing them because you will have a hard time creating the buy-in and "selling" your solutions.

1.7   Mindset

If you're still reading this chapter, I assume that you want to build an analytics team, and I anticipate your next question might be "What type of people do I hire for such positions?" I consider the follow-

---

[3]LinkedIn has one of the largest relationships datasets in the world. Even they put a stop to their network mapping tool in September 2014. These maps did not add anything to our knowledge.

ing qualities, which make up the mindset of analysts, critical for the success of such a team.

1.7.1 Curiosity

Some of the world's biggest inventions happened because someone was curious about something. It would be very nice if we could describe the problems with all the parameters to our analysts and then ask them to find solutions. You know this: it doesn't work that way. What worked in college or graduate school hardly works in the professional world. In a school setting, you **solve** a given problem, whereas, in the professional world, you **interpret** problems.

Your analysts first and foremost must be curious—curious to ask questions, curious to wonder whether there is a better way of doing things, curious to find information, and curious to talk to people and understand their problems.

1.7.2 Balanced Skepticism

To succeed in this type of a role, one needs to have balanced skepticism toward existing practices, available data, current conclusions, and cultural biases[4]. As O'Neil (2013) suggests in her book , "a skeptic is someone who maintains a consistently inquisitive attitude toward facts, opinions, or (especially) beliefs stated as facts."

Skepticism is further helpful in balancing the belief of "data can solve every problem" with "I don't know whether data can support that question, but I will find out."

---

[4]I'm suggesting a careful and objective point of view toward everything and not becoming a "devil's advocate," which I think people use as a shield while bringing down other people's ideas.

12 INTRODUCTION

1.7.3 Persistence

Real-world data is messy. Cleaning and preparing such data takes a lot of time[5]. When you add the learning curve, intricacies, and sheer difficulties of using specialized tools, the whole process no doubt frustrates you. Just when you think you're ready, your underlying question changes, newer data becomes available, or you are asked for something completely different. To survive through this and still succeed, one needs persistence—a lot of it. I have seen many talented professionals quit (not only quit projects, but quit their jobs) because they wanted quick results and did not persist through the messiness of our business.

1.7.4 Hunger to Learn and Improve

As data grows, the tools available to gather, manipulate, and analyze data are changing, too. It is challenging to keep up with the latest technology, but practitioners of data science should willingly give up inefficient tools for better ones. Doing so requires regularly reading and learning about the field and picking up relevant tools.

A good analyst will separate herself from an ordinary analyst with such a mindset. Continuous improvement of processes, tools, methods, and, most importantly, of **oneself** should be the cornerstone of an analyst's mindset.

When you immerse yourself in similar fields and you constantly read and learn about such fields or industries, innovation happens.

When you neglect the other fields, you don't innovate; you repeat.

---

[5]Some comment that 80% of any data analysis project is spent on data preparation.

1.7.5 Motivation

Research shows that an intrinsically motivated person is better at learning than an extrinsically motivated person (Ryan & Deci 2000). People who are intrinsically motivated enjoy their learning, have persistence, and are creative compared to those who are extrinsically motivated.

The extrinsically motivated expect and await rewards. It is hard to keep an extrinsically motivated employee happy in a job requiring nimbleness, curiosity, and continuous improvement.

1.7.6 Portfolio Approach

While tinkering with data and developing various data products, a good approach is the portfolio approach. As Karl Ulrich (a Wharton Business School professor) explained in his talk[6], one must generate many ideas and work on them simultaneously while looking for breakthrough ideas. One of them is likely to be a winner.

1.7.7 Selling

Although you may disagree, it is a fact that at all times, you are selling something. In every conversation, you are explaining your perspective or convincing others to accept your idea. Selling is critical when you want your users to take action on your insights and recommendations. They will not take an action if they can't trust your models and theories, or, worse, you.

 You waste 100% of your analysis that your readers don't take action on.

---

[6]Karl Ulrich's talk: https://youtu.be/ZSZ6WjwB9g8

14 INTRODUCTION

You need to explain your processes using stories or analogies so that you don't have to hard sell, but make them understand that you are solving their problems. Selling becomes easier if you clearly communicate that you are solving your users' problems and that you explain your methods without confusing your listeners. I'll paraphrase Wayne Gretzky: "You waste 100% of your analysis that your readers don't take action on."[7]

1.8   Technical Expertise

You may ask, "Why did you emphasize mindset and softer characteristics over technical expertise second?" "Aren't technical skills more important than soft skills?" Yes, they are important because analysts would be unable to **do** their jobs if they didn't have the technical skills, but they would be unable to **succeed** if they didn't have soft skills. Plus, one can be trained in technical skills, but it is very hard to extrinsically cultivate soft skills.

1.9   Areas of Importance

To do a high level of analytics or use data science, the following areas are of high importance.

1.9.1   Data Mining / Machine Learning / Statistics

Data mining, machine learning, or applied statistics. Whatever you call them, these skills are the foundation of analytics. Data mining is a general name for the process of finding patterns from data.

---

[7]Original: "You miss one hundred percent of the shots you don't take."

Machine learning is a field of computer science that focuses on using various pattern-detection algorithms. Some examples of machine learning algorithms are association rules, nearest neighbors, decision trees, random forests, Bayesian methods, and neural networks. Some methods from applied statistics have also made their way into machine learning. Multiple linear regression, logistic regression, and Bayesian methods are the most used techniques from the applied statistics field.

1.9.1.1 Data Visualization

In this infographic-crazy world, it is easy to dismiss graphics. I know I do.

Bad data visualizations[8] take up the whole space to describe very few data points (think people, flags, buildings, and exploding pie charts), whereas good data visualizations[9] get out of your way and actually show the underlying data (think tables, simple charts, and patterns). If carefully crafted, data visualizations can tell powerful stories. The key is to avoid the trap of making them overly beautiful but hardly actionable.

Noah Iliinsky[10], a data visualization expert, said that "data visualizations are advertisements and not art." Your main objectives are: make the visualizations tell your story, and let the data/patterns stand out and not distract your reader. If you follow the principles of effective data visualizations, you will more than likely make your visualizations actionable and good looking.

---

[8]http://www.infographicdesign.org/projects/the-social-media-landscape/
[9]http://www.nytimes.com/imagepages/2011/03/15/science/15food_graphic.html
[10]http://complexdiagrams.com

16 INTRODUCTION

1.9.1.2 Database Management

Of all the other processes in an analytics project, data gathering and manipulation takes the most time. If you are unable to get the required data in a structure suitable for analysis, you'll spend even more time manipulating the data.

Structured Query Language (SQL) is handy in such cases. Most likely, your data is stored in a database management system such as an Oracle™ or a Microsoft SQL Server®. There are three things you must know to efficiently get the data out of such systems.

1. Database structure: Knowing which data elements are stored in which tables and how the tables are connected to each other.

2. Concepts: Understanding the theory and principles of relational databases will help you get the required data faster and with accuracy.

3. SQL: You'll need to write queries to access the desired data.

1.9.1.3 Programming

You may complete various analytics projects without writing a single piece of code, but programming offers tools to become efficient. The other benefits of using a programming language are reproducibility, repeatability, and readability. Reproducibility helps you track your steps when someone asks you how you arrived at a certain number. Repeatability helps you modify your process when someone asks you to make some changes to your analysis. Readability helps you and others to understand the logic of your analysis.

Open source and free statistical and scientific programming languages such as R[11] and Python[12] are helpful in our analytics pursuit as both languages provide countless libraries for various topics. Plus, they both make data manipulation and analysis very easy, s as you will find out in this book.

1.9.1.4 Communication Skills / Storytelling

Imagine yourself speaking in front of the consumers of your analysis. You want to describe how your predictive models performed. You can show them the "confusion matrix," that is, the errors and accuracy of your model. Or you can describe a single person (and her characteristics) from your data and how those characteristics impact your model. Which version do you think your audience will most likely understand, remember, and trust? I am willing to bet on the second one. Even the most serious scientists enjoy good stories. I take huge inspiration from *The Economist* articles. These often start with the story of one person and later describe a wider phenomenon with detailed statistics.

1.10   Where to Find Them

You may look for one person with all of the above skills, but you may also may be able to build a team with complementary skills. I would like to see organizations create another important position that I call the **insights manager**. Although the analysts themselves can communicate the results to the stakeholders, you will see better results if you have a dedicated person to work with management team members, listen, ask questions, and formulate data questions

---

[11]http://www.r-project.org/
[12]https://www.python.org/

for the analysts. Once the analysts complete their analysis, the insights manager then builds a plan to put the analysis in action and makes sure that the analysis is used in decision making. This person frames the right questions, applies the analysis, and understands that a mediocre analysis that is used is more effective than the excellent analysis that sits on a desk.

 A mediocre analysis that is used is more effective than the excellent analysis that sits on a desk.

Now that you know the technical skills and the required mindset of a sound analytics team, the next logical question you may have is where to find this talent. Two obvious choices are grow or hire the talent.

Growing talent in house would be a good choice if a person interested in this field is interested for the right reason, that is, not to make a quick buck but to learn various tools and their uses. If an employee, in your mind, has already passed all the mindset tests, it is quite easy to put her on the above training or ask her to complete related data science courses[13] at https://www.coursera.org. If you are lucky to work near universities, you could also look for interns who major in computer science or other quantitative fields. Also, you have this book in your hands. :)

Although hiring the almighty data scientist or the measly data analyst may seem like an obvious choice, both are quite hard to find, let alone hire. If you go about hiring, you could look at recent graduates from applied statistics or analytics programs, such as North Carolina State University's MS program, or you could work with a recruiter specializing in analytics. Most likely, your best hires are passive candidates who are already doing well in their current job. Wherever you find them, I recommend testing the technical skills and analytical problem-solving skills of these candidates. The hard-

---

[13]https://www.coursera.org/specializations/jhu-data-science

est qualities to test, I have learned, are perseverance, patience, and hunger to learn. The following job description may help you create your own job posting.

Sample Job Description

Summary

We are looking for an experienced data analyst who enjoys working with messy datasets and finding patterns of business significance from them. An ideal candidate would have a graduate degree or equivalent coursework in a technical and quantitative field along with strong programming skills.

Job Responsibilities

Data Manipulation, Enrichment, and Analysis (80%)

- Manage, acquire, clean, and manipulate data to support analyses and reporting
- Use machine learning and advanced statistical techniques to draw meaningful and actionable recommendations from various data sources
- Use various software and tools (R, SQL, Weka, Python and others) to analyze and present the data analysis

Concept Development and Learning (10%)

- Build and keep up with the knowledge of literature, practices, and techniques in data science, business intelligence, and management communities

20   INTRODUCTION

- Develop product ideas and solutions to increase our operational efficiency

Outreach (10%)

- Promote data-driven culture
- Build and share analytics expertise

Qualifications

- Strong critical thinking and project-management skills along with curiosity, a passion for learning, and balanced skepticism
- Graduate degree or equivalent course work in a technical or quantitative area
- Strong computing and programming expertise

2

ANALYTICS ADOPTION

This is a data-driven world. It's a really exciting time. Industries, both public and private, have been telling us for years that data analytics can make a real difference. With all the buzz around data science and its potential to drive insights and improve outcomes, the role of data analytics has transitioned from backroom operations to having its own seat at the leadership table as a strategic partner.

Before we get into how to use data science, let's explore data analytics adoption, which is a very common challenge we encounter in this type of work.

We will answer three main questions in this chapter.

1. How to translate business pain points into problem-solving opportunities.
2. How to use change management to guide business understanding and stakeholder support.
3. How to use continuous improvement as a framework to drive analytics adoption.

22 ANALYTICS ADOPTION

You can use the answers to these questions to make a case for analytics, start your own program, or take your existing program to the next level.

2.1 Journey from Operations to Strategic Partner

I (Rodger) have worked in higher education for over 15 years on projects ranging from enterprise IT infrastructure and software engineering to financial systems delivery and, most recently, advancement operations, information strategy, and decision support.

My graduate studies were primarily focused on search engine technology, and my main areas of technical expertise are information retrieval, natural language processing, and network analysis. Specifically, I researched document ranking functions and language models used by search engines to return the most relevant document matches relative to a given search query. Examples include Okapi BM25 shown in Figure 2.1, as well as other state-of-the-art retrieval-ranking function variants.

$$\text{score}(D, Q) = \sum_{i=1}^{n} \text{IDF}(q_i) \cdot \frac{f(q_i, D) \cdot (k_1 + 1)}{f(q_i, D) + k_1 \cdot \left(1 - b + b \cdot \frac{|D|}{\text{avgdl}}\right)},$$

Figure 2.1: BM25 document ranking

My additional areas of study and research included the network, structure, and diffusion of information across social systems. Figure 2.2 shows the structure of my social network connections in 2011, as well as four distinct groups of friends or communities I belonged to at that time: **High School**, **Work**, **Ann Arbor**, and **Graduate School**. I applied similar techniques to various kinds of data, ranging from healthcare and disease-symptom networks to research-citation networks, social media activity, and email communication logs to identify information structure, meaningful patterns, and actionable recommendations.

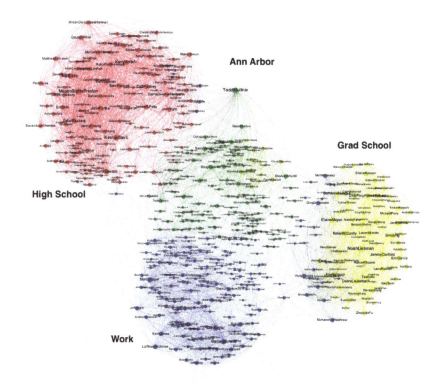

Figure 2.2: Rodger's social network map circa 2011

During graduate school, I also participated in the Ann Arbor Data Dive[1], which is an open platform designed to share data analytics expertise with community partners, organizations, and non-profits. Figure 2.3 is a heat-map calendar visualization I created to summarize resource usage to help a non-profit identify homeless meal-demand planning trends and improve resource-allocation opportunities and programming for the next year.

Prior to working in fundraising analytics and information strategy, I used to work in an office "cube" writing client-server management

---

[1] http://a2datadive.org/

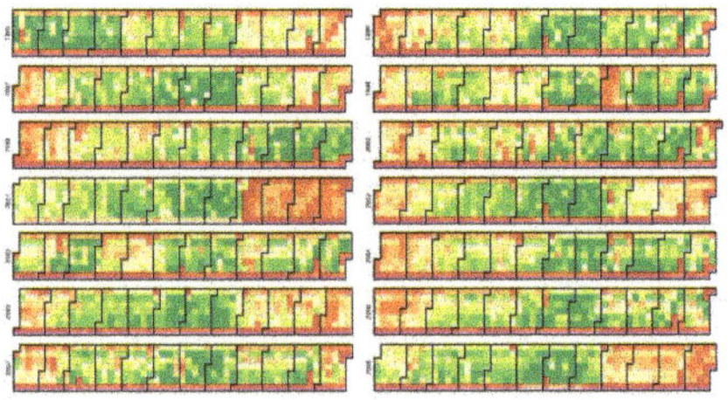

24 ANALYTICS ADOPTION

Figure 2.3: Heat map calendar to help the hungry

tools and accounting software. This work involved storing, analyzing, and moving high volumes of transaction data across different types of financial database systems.

Figure 2.4: Backroom software engineer

During my knitted-hat days in Michigan (OMG, it gets cold!), I created software to store, analyze, distribute, and audit the delivery of accounting information to over 50,000 users in real-time across a diverse set of computing systems, dependencies, and quirks. This infrastructure role required a unique combination of business process mapping, enterprise systems, and software engineering delivery that challenged me to listen, critically think, solve, and translate complex real-world problems into practical and scalable solutions at both the test prototype, staging, and production-ready levels.

I didn't realize it at the time, but I now understand this role is where I learned how to gather, prioritize, and translate business requirements into project road maps or "blueprints" for solution delivery to stakeholders on time and within budget.

Figure 2.5: Business process map

Figure 2.6: Enterprise systems

During my decade of working in IT operations and fixing broken things, I was also responsible for troubleshooting server software onsite in the "backroom." And when I say I was in the "backroom," I was literally working inside server closets to analyze, patch, and keep systems up and running with a high degree of availability (that is, 365 days a year) for faculty, students, and staff.

26 ANALYTICS ADOPTION

Figure 2.7: Hanging out in the server room

I love data analysis, applied statistics, and problem solving. Nowadays, I speak about analytics adoption[2], predictive modeling, and strategic information-management metrics[3] at conferences and workshops to share my knowledge, expertise, and enthusiasm with professional communities of practice, research, and leadership.

My message is that you too can join the exciting field of data analytics right now and discover new ways to solve problems, accomplish your goals and make a real impact on your organization in more creative, innovative, and efficient ways than previously imagined.

2.2 Translating Problems into Opportunities

When we begin any data analytics project, the goal usually is to overcome a challenge, identify an opportunity, or add value to your business. In fact, the problems we encounter in our organizations are often the same drivers that motivate us to create and explore new solutions, tools, or products in the first place.

---

[2]http://www.aprahome.org/p/cm/ld/fid=961&eaid=1075
[3]http://www.aprahome.org/p/cm/ld/fid=961&eaid=1075

Before you jump into data analytics, it is crucial that you identify a key business problem that motivates a solution, recommendation, or decision support for your organization.

Business problems or "pain points" play an important role in defining and shaping the landscape and purpose of our work. Data analytics projects require identifying business problems (inputs), translating them into road maps (means), and delivering solutions (outputs) to your stakeholders.

 What are the current business challenges in your fundraising organization today? Donor retention? Finding prospects? Increasing revenue? Operational efficiencies?

Here are some additional questions to explore and help you get started:

- What are the "pain points" or perpetual obstacles that your organization faces?
- What are some of the key business questions that remain unanswered?
- What kinds of information or analysis would help improve decision making?
- What kind of tools or solutions would help uncover new opportunities or untapped potential?
- What areas would benefit most from increased efficiency and productivity?

2.3 Create a Road map

Now that you've identified a business problem, you will need to begin translating the problem into a solution-oriented road map.

28 ANALYTICS ADOPTION

A road map is a project specification that clearly outlines and defines the following components:

- Goals and objectives (ROI)
- Context and business drivers
- Audience
- Scope, size, and scale
- Deliverable requirements
- Timeline and key milestones
- Dependencies
- Resources (personnel, budget, staff time, systems, tools, and so on)
- Potential risks
- Development plan
- Testing plan
- Communication plan
- Training plan

Road maps will obviously vary in depth and complexity based on the size and scale of your project.

 To avoid analysis paralysis, I recommend first starting with a small project and documenting your current state and desired project outcomes. You can always, and will inevitably have to, go back and refine your original project plan.

Once you have a created your baseline project specification, it's time to find support.

2.4 Identify Your Champions

Data analytics projects of any size, tiny or mighty, need leadership support as these projects require organizational resources, business alignment, and stakeholder buy-in to be successful.

IDENTIFY YOUR CHAMPIONS

So, who can help you convince others that your project is a worthwhile effort?

Ideally, you will be able to quickly identify at least one or two "champions" or individuals who:

1. believe in the problem you are trying to solve,
2. understand what you are doing, and
3. can help promote and socialize your potential solution to others within and/or across your department, organization, or institution.

 If you are currently unable to identify any champions or supporters, it would be advisable to return to the original problem you identified and evaluate whether the problem warrants the investment of time, energy, and resources.

If you determine the problem is still worth exploring, it would be best to identify stakeholders who are most directly affected by the issue since these individuals:

1. are most likely to benefit from a working solution, and, therefore,
2. are most likely to be inclined to discuss requirements, participate in a pilot effort, and offer critical feedback.

Start paying attention to which of your colleagues are "go-to" individuals, domain experts, and data stewards, since these stakeholders are likely well positioned to play an "ambassador" role in driving analytics adoption.

Other factors to keep in mind when seeking potential champions are leadership, managers, and colleagues who are quantitative, inquisitive, and passionate with strong connections across multiple departments as they can help provide valuable organizational insights, as well as promote, advocate, and diffuse solutions within the organization.

When a development officer or a senior leader gets excited about an analytics solution, you're now starting to move the needle on analytics adoption. Three development officers who are excited about a new report or a data analytics tool's ability to work more efficiently will quickly translate to an entire team of development officers who are standing in line to request more solutions.

2.5 Defining Business Purpose

Now that you've identified your champions, let's build on the analytics introduction in the previous chapter and clarify what we mean by "data analytics."

For some, data analytics might refer to a business report or an interactive leadership dashboard. For others, data analytics might refer to trend analyses, data visualization, cluster analysis, or predictive modeling.

All of these are correct answers.

For you, the answer will depend on the current level of analytics maturity within your organization.

2.6 Analytics Maturity

By this point, you've hopefully identified a business problem, outlined a road map draft, and identified some potential supporters. The next step is to assess the current level of analytics maturity within your organization and start where you are.

Analytics maturity refers to the degree to which your organization has invested, implemented, and integrated a set of systems, tools, processes, and technology to solve business problems using data analytics.

As outlined in Section 1.3, Analytics Maturity Model, analytics maturity is a continuum that organizes potential solutions into three main categories:

- Descriptive
- Predictive
- Prescriptive

2.6.1 Descriptive Analytics

Descriptive analytics offers us views of the past. These views, in hindsight, help provide answers to diagnostic questions such as "What happened?" or "When and where did this happen?" and, in some cases, even "Why did this happen?"

2.6.2 Predictive Analytics

Predictive analytics shifts toward future insights and helps answer questions such as "What will happen?" For example, we can use past data to fit a regression model to make educated guesses and predictions about future outcomes using training data and variables with specific parameters.

2.6.3 Prescriptive Analytics

Finally, we have prescriptive analytics. Prescriptive analytics focuses on foresight, scenarios and decision support to help answer questions such as "What should we do right now?" or "Which option would be best if X or Y happens?"

2.6.4 Data Pyramid

The analytics maturity model builds on the foundational concept of the data pyramid[4] (aka wisdom hierarchy), which refers to the systematic process of extracting actionable knowledge from data:

2.6.5 Pathways to Wisdom

Let's explore the pathways to wisdom from a data perspective.

If you're not familiar with database terminology, it might be helpful to think of a spreadsheet (two-dimensional) organized into rows and columns.

First, we begin with collecting and storing data values. This is our raw data.

Next, we transform raw data into information by organizing data values into rows (facts) and columns (features), which provide additional context and meaning.

Subsequently, we analyze information to identify important trends, patterns, and insights to generate knowledge.

---

[4]https://en.wikipedia.org/wiki/DIKW_pyramid

Finally, we evaluate and synthesize knowledge in an organizational context to create wisdom.

Wisdom ultimately helps us understand what makes our organization unique relative to its markets, competitors, assets, capabilities, and opportunities.

2.6.6   Wisdom is Competitive Advantage

Why does wisdom matter?

Because wisdom is a form of competitive advantage.

"The only thing that gives an organization a competitive edge, the only thing that is sustainable, is what it knows, how it uses what it knows and how fast it can know something."

— Larry Prusak, researcher

While your leadership may recognize that wisdom is valuable, we still face many challenges when we seek to introduce new tools, products, and solutions.

Examples include:

- Lack of resources
- Competing priorities
- Change resistance
- Information overload
- Aversion to details
- Preference for big-picture ideas
- Preference for narrative

34 ANALYTICS ADOPTION

In the next section, we will explore adoption challenges in greater detail and some specific ways to approach and overcome them.

2.7 Adoption Barriers

As you prepare to launch your own analytics project or program, it is advisable that you directly ask your stakeholders what kind of adoption barriers they expect to encounter during the launch of your proposed analytics tool, product, or service.

While you solicit feedback, it is important to listen carefully, objectively, and openly as well as documenting any anticipated barriers.

Let's take a look at common adoption barriers you may encounter during the project planning process.

Resources/Support/Buy-In

- Lack of champion support, early adopter participation, and advisers
- Lack of resources to acquire talent and build capacity
- Lack of stakeholder engagement, interest, and commitment

Business Requirements/Specification

- Lack of domain understanding or business context
- Unclear definition of success and requirements
- Failure to define or manage expectations

Planning/Delivery/Testing

- Trying to do too much, too quickly, too soon
- Struggling to translate results into actionable insights
- Fear of failure during the prototype phase and learning process

- Lack of a feedback loop

Trust/Communication/Culture

- Lack of trust required to build, enable, and foster adoption across organization
- Lack of staff training in how to interpret meaning and use of analytics in work context
- Lack of perception of analytics as a strategic partner

2.7.1 Know Your Audience

As you seek to identify, document, and manage analytics adoption barriers, it's also important to understand your audience's preferences (and differences) as you gather requirements, prioritize features, design solutions, and communicate with your stakeholders.

While it is often a useful starting point to divide your audiences into managerial and individual contributors, it is also important to recognize technical versus relational preferences.

Here's a simple and generalized way to think about these different preference types:

- People with technical orientation prefer spreadsheets over people
- People with relationship orientation prefer people over spreadsheets

Our organizations comprise individuals with highly variable and complementary skill sets.

For example, a development officer with exceptional relational skill sets may not find the new database reporting features as intuitive as an operations staff member with highly developed technical skills.

36   ANALYTICS ADOPTION

While some individuals are comfortable with technical details, "nuts and bolts," and "the weeds," others may tend to prefer the "big picture," "takeaways," and "recommended action." Another term for this type of preference is a means orientation (how) versus an ends orientation (what).

For example, if you're working on an analytics project designed for development officers, we advise you to focus on executive summaries, workflow, recommended actions, and relational tasks to help them in the context of their individual portfolio, keeping in mind that the end goal is to help them get out of the spreadsheet and maximize activity and connectivity with prospective donors.

In contrast, an analytics solution for an operations staff member, such as a reporting tool, would likewise benefit from shifting focus from high-level constituent summary information to delving into a high degree of technical detail, granularity, and drill-down such as giving history, pledge payments, pledge balance, and soft credit.

 Keeping your audience in mind is an effective way to (1) ensure your analytics project will be useful, actionable, and well received by your organizational audiences; (2) be aligned with their business needs; and 3) add organizational value.

"Two basic rules of life are: 1) Change is inevitable. 2) Everybody resists change."

— W. Edwards Deming

2.7.2 Adoption is Change

Analytics adoption refers to the process of introducing a new tool, product, or solution to your organization. Simply put, adoption means change. And change is difficult for most individuals, let alone an entire organization.

2.7.3 Competency and Motivation

Adoption requires change, which requires persuasion and stakeholder buy-in. Some of your stakeholders may be very resistant to change and, as you dig deeper, you might uncover various forms of fear (expressed as resistance) such as fear of disruption, fear of job displacement or, simply, fear of the unknown.

> The most common barriers to change are (1) a lack of competency (ability or capacity) and (2) motivation (willingness or inclination).

For example, change barriers may be evident when your users say, "I don't know how to use the new system" (competency) or "I just want to use the old report" (motivation).

So how do we overcome the adoption barriers we encounter in our organization?

Once we identify the adoption barriers and root cause, we need to create an action plan tailored to the specific underlying issue in the context of the users' goals, workflows, and preferences.

> Competency-based barriers may require skills training and professional development, whereas motivational barriers may require a revised clarification of purpose and outcome.

38 ANALYTICS ADOPTION

In either case, elevating staff skills is a recommended strategy for facilitating and accelerating analytics adoption. One immediate suggestion would be to read (or have someone read) this book!

2.7.4 Building Trust

You can inspire your audiences to embrace analytics adoption by winning hearts and minds.

To accomplish this goal, you need to consistently present your stakeholders with solutions with a balanced blend of (1) positivity and enthusiasm and (2) logical thinking and rational problem-solving.

Regardless of the sophistication of your analytics adoption plan, you will need to quickly establish trust and credibility to improve receptivity to your proposed solutions; otherwise, your ideas may get tuned out despite the best of intentions and efforts.

To build trust with stakeholders, you need to build your brand by presenting **results** (proof, facts, data) with **accountability** (plan, action), and **purpose** (objectives).

2.7.5 Quick Wins

Ideally, your quick win, while small in size and scope, will generate immediate positive feedback and good will towards future successes. Moreover, you can use this "quick win" as a discussion point to solicit feedback and elicit requirements for your next analytics project.

 To quickly establish credibility, you need to identify a "quick win," which is a highly visible problem you can quickly solve to build momentum and make the case for additional analytics projects.

Example feedback questions might include, "How did this solution work out for you?" or "Glad we resolved that issue. What else would be useful or helpful?"

2.7.6 Build Your Brand

To build your brand, you need to lead with purpose and socialize your success. You can increase the visibility and exposure of your brand by taking on more of a consulting role in your work, building partnerships, and promoting solutions.

For example, if you currently work in advancement operations, when was the last time you sat down with a development officer to check in and ask what was going well, or which tools could help them be more effective in their roles?

 Questions such as "Do you know how to pull that prospect briefing report?" or "Do you know how to pull giving details for that donor?" can help establish strategic partnerships and build a culture of data-driven decision support.

2.7.7 Purpose

You won't be able to persuade others to adopt analytics without clarity of purpose.

What is the top-priority project that you need to work on? Maybe it's portfolio analysis or building a predictive model to identify new prospects. But ask yourself, "Why does that matter right now? Who are the stakeholders of this work? What will this do for them? And if they don't apply your insights, what will happen?"

All of these questions are focused on the power of purpose. Their thinking is: "What are we going to do? We're going to build an analytic model. How are we going to do that? We're going to find a data analytics minded person, a statistician, or a graduate student. We're going to find consultants."

What's missing is the *why*. However, if you can answer the question of why, you make the value of the proposition more compelling and help guide a more strategic conversation. Your purpose highlights your intention, which should ideally align with your organizational mission. For fundraising professionals, there is a common and shared purpose of trying to increase donors and dollars raised.

Suppose you want to create a best-in-class analytics program and you declare "We're going to hire the best people. We're going to create dashboards." You've articulated the "what" and "how," but there will likely be skepticism and resistance with valid questions such as "What's the return on investment?" or "How will this add value to the organization?"

By clarifying the "why," you can strengthen your proposal and minimize resistance by explaining your purpose:

"We want to use state-of-the-art data analytics as our competitive advantage to maximize our fundraising results and promote learning for the long-term health of the organization."

2.8 People, Talent, and Culture

We need both top-down and bottom-up management, but you have to start where you are.

If you're in an organization in which there's no appetite for analytics, then you have an uphill battle. Maybe you're at an organization that appreciates data analytics, yet they say, "I don't really need that stuff." That's a bottom-up challenge. In both cases, start identifying the people you need to get on board. When I began my new role, my first three development officers said, "I like numbers and want more data" and I said, "I'd like to partner with you on some new data analytics solutions. Would it be OK to circle back with you as an early tester to get your feedback?"

Let's explore how solutions are delivered within your organization.

 How are you building and deploying solutions? How are you collecting feedback? How are you integrating feedback into your analytics projects, tools, and services?

In the next section, we will discuss how to use change management to drive business understanding, audience alignment, and stakeholder support.

2.9 Change Management

Change management provides us with a framework to 1) organize the planning, development, testing, and delivery of solutions; and 2) communicate these changes to our stakeholders in a meaningful way that fosters accountability, transparency, and trust.

Here are some change management questions to guide your analytics adoption planning process:

- Who are your target audience and stakeholders for this project?
- What do you specifically hope to accomplish with this project?

42   ANALYTICS ADOPTION

- How will stakeholders and the organization benefit from this effort?
- What are the business requirements and ROI?
- What is the project deliverable schedule and timeline?
- What does success look like for this project?
- How are the stakeholders supposed to interpret and apply results?
- Who are your project testers for the pilot or testing effort?
- What is the communications and staff training plan?
- Where is the documentation available for self-service or instructor-led support?

2.10   Managing Hype, Priorities, and Expectations

You might often hear "I want a dashboard and I want it on mobile. I want a predictive modeling score." Somebody else says, "I want an engagement score."

All of a sudden you may find yourself pulled in multiple directions at the same time. You might receive requests for a data visualization or RFM tool, but it will be difficult to realize success without sufficient context, business requirements, and feedback.

Even if you deliver the most sophisticated data analytics solutions, your stakeholders are often most concerned with how to interpret these solutions and apply them in the context of their own work.

Just as we are familiar with the importance of being donor centric, we need to keep a similar user-centered focus with solution delivery, as our stakeholders often question "How do I take action on that?" or "You created some nice RFM scores, but what's RFM and why does that matter to me?" While keeping your stakeholders in mind, it's also important to recognize the Hype Cycle, made popular by Gartner®:

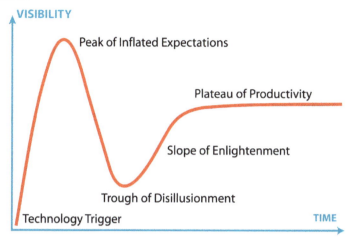

Perhaps you've thought, "I'm excited about this new technology solution!" However, when you go to your leadership, they may not necessarily share the same level of enthusiasm in the product, saying "That technology is limited" or "The platform is still in development, so perhaps we should explore other options". The notable decline in interest in a once-popular technology, platform, or solution is also known as the "trough of disillusionment," which is a common and predictable phase in the development life cycle of any new technology.

2.11 Critical Mass

To survive the Hype Cycle, you must stay focused on the business drivers that motivate your project's innovation, adoption, and solution delivery.

 Most organizations invest in tools such as database systems, CRM applications, and reporting platforms with two primary goals: (1) increasing production or results, and (2) gaining operational efficiencies.

We then expect lift and a boost in dollars, as well as operational efficiency.

To be successful, an analytics project will require organizational investment and buy-in to reach a critical mass of user adoption.

How do you translate the enthusiasm for new tools and technology into user adoption? How do you create an action plan to put some life into your idea or innovation?

2.12   Diffusion of Innovation

The Diffusion of Innovation[5] rule suggests that any major change or innovation needs to be adopted by at least 16% of your target user base. This 16% represents the critical mass required to make a proposed innovation widely adopted and self-sustaining within your organization. In other words, it is critical to reach at least 16% adoption of your potential audience to ensure long-term stakeholder adoption and integration of your solution.

First, you will need to enlist the support of your champion and stakeholders to help identify early adopters, testers, and pilot users.

Key questions to keep in mind when engaging your baseline of pilot users:

- What are the key business drivers (purpose) for implementing this data analytics solution?
- How will this solution or innovation be used in the context of your stakeholder's work?

---

[5]https://en.wikipedia.org/wiki/Diffusion_of_innovations

- How will this solution help make a difference?

2.13 Continuous Improvement

Continuous improvement offers a philosophy of iterative design and user-centered problem-solving that values stakeholder feedback and efficiency.

Awkwardness is the prerequisite of learning.

If you're going to learn how to walk, you're going to fall down. As you deliver analytics solutions within your organization, you will eventually create a model that fails or produces unexpected results. For this reason, it's important to promote a culture of learning with your stakeholders and teach them early on that testing, experimentation, and interpretation are part of the inevitable learning curve and discovery processes associated with data analytics.

But also recognize that there are many different options. If you wait for the perfect tool to come along, five years could go by quickly and you still won't have done anything about it. There's a cost to inaction.

Philosophically we're seeking to create a shift from a **reactive** orientation to a **proactive** one.

Maybe right now in your organization you're creating reports because someone asked you to, but in an organization with analytics maturity, you're also going to be proactively exploring predictive and prescriptive types of questions such as "We analyzed the data and found the top five prospects of interest that you should reach out to right now".

2.14 Wrapping Up

Data analytics is a strategic partner that can provide competitive advantage and solutions that are understandable, memorable and, most importantly, actionable.

To get started, translate your current business problems and questions into opportunities to create an analytics road map. Next, identify your champions, early adopters, and testers to reach critical mass for your proposed analytics project. As you build solutions and implement these changes within or across your organization, you will need a framework to facilitate analytics adoption.

Change management provides a useful framework for developing, testing, delivering, and communicating solutions with your stakeholders. In addition, continuous improvement offers a practical philosophy and approach to managing quality and enhancement requests.

To support analytics adoption, it's important to promote a culture of learning within your organization since analytics frequently generates actionable insights that may challenge conventional or prevailing wisdom.

You do not have to (nor could you ever possibly) know everything. Data analytics is a field that is constantly evolving, so seek to become a learn-it-all instead of a know-it-all. In addition, there are free open-source tools available like R (covered in this book) that can be a powerful asset on your data analytics journey.

Even if you don't consider yourself technically skilled, you can still invite others on your data analytics journey to create solutions and add value to your organization. And who knows, you might be curious and motivated enough to learn R yourself or connect with a colleague who can partner with you to build and deliver data-driven solutions!

3

SUCCESS IN ANALYTICS

There I (Ashutosh) was. The smell of the strawberry slushy sweetened the whole atmosphere. You could feel the heat of the day with your bare toes, but thankfully the water fountains and rides made it fun. Yes, I was at a water park with my kids, of course, because it would be kind of weird to be there by myself. All the kids were having fun except for one little girl with ponytails in a Nemo suit. I overheard her discussion with her mom. The mom looked at the daughter and said, "You cannot play with those water balloons here." And the daughter, without even thinking for a second, looked up at mom and said, "Says who, mom?" I was very puzzled because she wanted to know "who" and not "why?" Is this a problem we face as a society, or even worse at work: that we make our decisions based on authority and not the reasons behind them? That we do not ask "why" but "who" and "how"?

In this chapter, let's talk about the three P's of success — products, people, and passions. If you follow them closely, you'll double your success.

I believe your success is deeply rooted in the three P's, which are deeply rooted in "why". The premise is simple: analytics is not re-

48 SUCCESS IN ANALYTICS

ally about analytics, but it's the action that happens after the analytics. Action must follow analytics, for your success is defined in that action.

Let's look at the first P: Products.

3.1 Products

Products are what people care about. Have you played Minecraft®? If so, you know that it's neither polished nor realistic like, say Call of Duty®, but it's still successful. In fact it is so successful that it has sold more than 121 million copies, and Microsoft purchased the game for $2.5 billion.

What's the reason for its success?

Well, I believe it's successful because it's a product that people care about. It is simple by design, but you can build a world that's truly yours. You can live in your incomplete dreams and fulfill them — and *that* is something people will care about it.

How do you go about building something that your users will care about? There is no doubt that you have to develop your craft.

In his book **Talent is Overrated**, Colvin (2009) talks about a wide receiver from a small school who ran a 40-yard dash in 4.69 seconds. To give you some perspective, most of the NFL prospective recruits complete the 40-yard dash in 4.5 seconds or less. We know that in NFL even 0.01 seconds is a lot and he wasn't even close. It is no wonder that the NFL teams were apprehensive about his performance, but since he was so well known, one NFL team did eventually select him. He then went on to play twenty years of professional football. Can you believe it? Twenty years of professional football and he broke all sorts of records. Do you know who that was?

His name is Jerry Rice.

PRODUCTS **49**

How did he achieve something that seems so humanly impossible?

In the off seasons, he had a six-day workout. He used to run five miles on a hilly trail every day and then come back and do strength training. Others tried to join him but got sick before completing the training by the end of the day.

I have no doubt that with deliberate practice you can build a craft that's way above average.

I have seen many people who say they want to do analytics, but have done nothing deliberate to develop that craft. Why would anyone take you seriously if you are not serious about your own craft? This book will help you sharpen your craft, but we know that most people won't even finish reading it, let alone practice the code in it[1]. Don't be most people.

Let's say you worked hard and developed your craft. What's next?

You build products that solve problems but the problems should be important enough to warrant a solution. An example: the Square™ credit card reader. Square™ credit card readers solve a very important problem and its accessibility and ease of use are what make the product unique. Other people will solve problems which are unimportant and create products that nobody cares about. A good example of a product that didn't solve any real problem is the LinkedIn network map. It didn't provide any new information; LinkedIn realized this and retired the product.

Again, don't try to solve a problem which is not a problem for your users. Only pick problems that you think would have some merit and the users would care about.

Let's say you develop your craft; you know some of the products that you want to develop. Where do you go from there?

---

[1]Using the 80-20 Pareto principle, 20% of the readers will finish this book and even a smaller percentage will actively practice.

50   SUCCESS IN ANALYTICS

Here's a paragraph from **Alice in Wonderland**:

Alice: Would you tell me, please, which way I ought to go from here? The Cheshire Cat: That depends a good deal on where you want to get to. Alice: I don't much care where. The Cheshire Cat: Then it doesn't much matter which way you go.

Don't be a wanderer. Plan and then do. Don't just start walking in the wrong direction. To plan better you can use a tool called an "activity systems map." This tool helps you define your strategy.

I'm kind of finicky about various things. But one particular thing I don't like in particular is when people use buzzwords like "strategy"" and "innovation."

One day I heard that some departments were being named "strategic" something. Why would you name your department 'strategic something'? Would you do anything that is not strategic?

But I really wanted to understand what strategy *is*. I read many books and articles, but I still didn't understand it.

Until one night.

My son, who was 6 years old then, walked into my room and said, "Dad, could I sleep in your room?" And, like any loving parent would do, I sent him back to his room. Then he went to his younger brother, who was 4 years old, and asked him to join in asking me if they could both sleep in my room.

To his disappointment, the younger one said no.

The older one thought for a minute and said, "But what about the dark shadows you see in the window?"

With that, not only did I understand what strategy was, but I also understood that you don't let your kids talk to each other for more than 10 seconds when it's past bedtime. Because then I had to explain to the younger one that he didn't have to worry about any shadows.

What is strategy then? As my son taught me, strategy is planning some deliberate steps to create a sustainable advantage to overcome your competition.

The actions, the steps that you take, are not strategy. They are part of the strategy. Strategy is your "why" and action steps are your "how."

This activity systems map [Note: We can't reproduce the map here due to copyright issues, but you will easily find the map with a simple search] is from Michael Porter's classic paper "What is strategy" (Porter 1996). You can also find this activity systems map in Stadtler (2015)'s paper.

Porter shows how IKEA was able to create its strategic position and align all the actions around it. IKEA's strategic position was to provide affordable furniture to young people. Notice the dark circles. Those are the core pillars of their strategy, providing limited customer service, self-selection by customers, modular design, and low manufacturing cost. Notice the text "suburban locations with ample parking" that's sitting in between "self-selection by customers" and "limited customer service."

That's how you create strategy and a plan.

Using this as an inspiration, you can develop one for your organization.

GG+A shared this idea in a presentation. This is the analytics road map as shown in Table 3.1. The first thing you have to remember is what your are you goals and results. To become the best at something is not a goal; it is a result. Once you identify your goals, you outline all the steps that you have to take to get to that goal, you put

52 SUCCESS IN ANALYTICS

Table 3.1: Analytics road map

Goal	Short term	Long term	Partners	Result
Good data	Standardize addresses	Acquire newer data	Advancement Services and fundraisers	Trust in data
Stable IT/Reporting infrastructure	Produce standard reports	Allow complicated reporting	Advancement Services and IT	Trust in data and reliable reporting
Analytics infrastructure	Run simple models	Combine reporting and modeling	Advancement Services and IT	Start of data driven decision making

a timeline on it, and lastly, you find partners. It could be a short-term goal or a long-term one Don't feel that you don't have all the resources to pull this off. If you start planning right now, in few years, you can go wherever you want to go and create your vision.

People ask me "Why so much emphasis on process? Why so much emphasis on thinking? I've even had some employees who pushed me hard on this. Think about this for a second. If something is easy to do, then it is very likely that it will be replaced by some programs. What organizations cannot afford to lose are thinkers—thinkers who provide valuable actions, valuable insights, and recommendations.

Don't be a commodity.

In Figure 3.1 and 3.2 we have two kickers, Kicker A and Kicker B. Let's say you're the head coach of the team. Which kicker would you choose for your next game and why?

You see that both of kickers are kicking the ball in, but the spread is really high for Kicker B. If you're a leader, you always want Kicker A, who is doing consistent work and hitting the targets all the time.

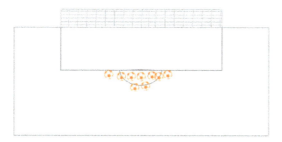

Figure 3.1: Mean and variance of kicks: Kicker A

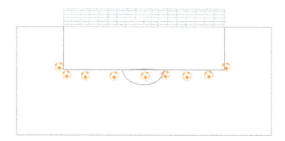

Figure 3.2: Mean and variance of kicks: Kicker B

But if you want innovation, you want variance, and variance is your friend[2].

You have to be at the edge of various fields that give you this inspiration. You try fifteen or twenty different solutions. You will fail 99% of the time, but you will strike gold in one. This can only happen when you are not relying so much on consistency and reliability. You have to give yourself the freedom to innovate.

What do you do once you have your ideas ready, have great products, and have developed your craft? You, of course, go and develop that product, right?

---

[2]Wharton Professor Karl Ulrich on innovation: https://youtu.be/ZSZ6WjwB9g8

No.

You actually develop the most minimal version possible and you test it with your users. See whether they even care about it. See whether they even like those features. Maybe they want the same information but in a different format. But unless they tell you what they want, you will be producing something that nobody cares about.

This is called a Minimally Viable Product (MVP). You develop the smallest version possible that's still workable and demonstrates what you want to do.

Once you have your MVP, you have everything, and everything should go well, right?

Well, no, that's the second P: People.

3.2   People

It doesn't matter how good your models are or how accurate your theories are. If people don't understand you, if they don't trust you, if they don't get you, then your models or your accuracy aren't worth much.

How do you get them to do something? How do you make them take action?

Heath & Heath (2007), in their book **Made to Stick**, compare a CEO directive of "let's maximize shareholder value" to President John F. Kennedy's call of "landing a man on the moon and returning him safely to the earth."

Which one is clearer? Which one provides vision?

As the Heath brothers say (2007), simple ideas stick easier than complicated ideas. They also refer to simple ideas as clearing the path for better adoption, removing all the obstacles so people can take action. Try to remove all the obscurities around the idea and just communicate the core themes.

"Perfection is achieved, not when there is nothing more to add, but when there is nothing left to take away."

— Antoine de Saint-Exupery

That's where data science proves useful. Not only are you creating models that are useful, but you are also creating accessible ways to consume information to drive action.

Here's another example to explain the "stickiness" of a concept:

What do you think of when you think of Einstein? $E = mc^2$? What do you think of when you think of Richard Feynman? Unless you are a student of physics or a Feynman fan, most likely nothing.

Why do we remember Einstein? That equation is simple to remember. Of course, simple doesn't mean trivial.

A good example of how simple performs well is shown in Figure 3.3, which shows a decision tree with the Titanic data. It uses pink boxes to show who did not survive on the Titanic and green boxes to show who did survive. The decision tree model in this case shows with 78% accuracy that boys and females from higher classes survived. This tree is explainable.

But did you know that there is an algorithm called *oner*? As its name implies, it generates only one rule, yet it has 77% accuracy! As Figure 3.4 shows, you can conclude that females survived and males did not survive.

56 SUCCESS IN ANALYTICS

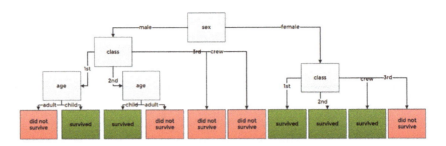

Figure 3.3: Bigger decision tree with 78% accuracy

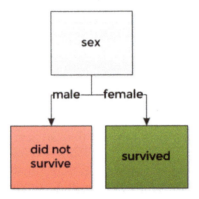

Figure 3.4: Smaller decision tree with 77% accuracy

You may think that this is too simple to perform, but Holte (1993) compared many data sets and many techniques and found that the *oner* algorithm performed equally or slightly worse than other state-of-the-art algorithms.

Even if you don't want to buy into this, that's okay, but at least use this as your baseline to compare and try to outperform this model.

But remember, two to three percentage points of accuracy don't matter much if you are losing all the explanatory power of the model.

What do you do once you simplify your products?

Well, to get people to take some action, you have to understand their needs as well.

One day I asked my then six-year-old son, "Why don't you write the grocery shopping list?" He looked in the fridge and he looked at the fruit basket. He wrote a few things down and gave me a list. I was so proud and I started reading. He had listed "apples, bananas, oranges, milk, juice, toy, and candies."

I realized his needs were completely different from my needs, and his perspective on grocery shopping even more different. Unless we understand the biases, the needs, and the perspectives, what we think could be helping others could actually be hurting them.

But, say, we do everything, but they still don't take action. What do we do?

You may have a better chance if you understand the principles of persuasion and influence. There are two simple techniques that could work really well.

The first is social proof. We all know what social proof looks like: every Amazon® review you read or the canned laughter you hear in the sitcoms (Amblee & Bui 2011, Bore 2011).

Social proof is pretty straightforward. How do you get that into action? You must find a willing partner and provide outstanding results. Then you ask that person to speak about your results. This can create momentum, carrying the message to other people, and removing the inertia. That's social proof.

The second is foot-in-the-door or smaller commitments.

In his book **Influence**, Cialdini (1987) explained the foot in the door principle with an example. A few volunteers went to two groups of homeowners. To one group they said, "We want you to put this huge public service announcement billboard on your lawns."

58   SUCCESS IN ANALYTICS

This idea was so crazy that 86% of the people did not agree to put up a billboard. But in the other group, 76% of the people agreed to that crazy idea.

What do you think was different? Three weeks prior to being asked, another volunteer went to the same homeowners and asked them to put a three-inch sign that said, "Be a safe driver" on their lawns. Because they agreed to this simple idea, three weeks later, they agreed to this crazy idea, 76% of them.

You may ask yourself, "Isn't this book about data science?" Why are we not talking about analysis then?

We will get there, but let's look at one more thing first.

Jerry Allyne, former vice president of strategic planning and analysis at Boeing Commercial Airplanes, spoke[3] about the fantastic Venn diagram seen in Figure 3.5. This is a simple tool, but it has helped me realize that it's not really just about analytics.

Jerry described this diagram further using the change effectiveness equation (see Voehl & Harrington 2016, p. 65). Let's say the quality of analysis is Q and its acceptance is A. The overall effectiveness is the combination of both factors:

$$E = Q \times A$$

He explained this further. Let's say we give a maximum of 10 points to both quality and acceptance. Therefore, the maximum effectiveness is 100.

Say you built a really fantastic model and you said to yourself, "I'm so proud of this model. I deserve a 7 on quality." But while you were working on this, you didn't talk to people, and thus the acceptance was only three points.

Your total effectiveness:

---

[3]https://youtu.be/t2VH_z68jdQ

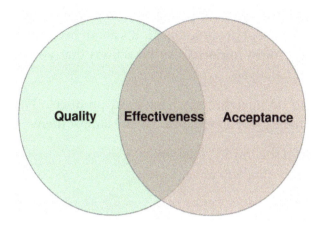

Figure 3.5: Quality, acceptance, and effectiveness (Jerry Allyne, INFORMS presentation)

7 X 3 = 21

Since you were disappointed, you worked harder and built an even better model. You gave yourself an 8 on quality, but the acceptance stayed the same.

The total effectiveness still did not go up.

8 X 3 = 24

Then you realized, "You know what, I'm not going to worry about increasing the quality. I'll meet people for coffee. I'll understand their needs. I'll explain to them how analysis could really be helpful to them."

Now your acceptance went up and you got 6. Since you were meeting people, the quality of the analysis went down to five.

Now your overall effectiveness:

5 X 6 = 30

60 SUCCESS IN ANALYTICS

It's a simple principle, but you have to remember that analytics is really not just about analytics itself. It's about acceptance and effectiveness and, most importantly, the actions that people take after reading your analysis.

That should do it, right? We have great products. We have great ideas. We have great acceptance. We are almost there.

You still need the third P: Passion.

3.3 Passion

It's not only the passion you have about your analysis, but it's the passion you show while communicating your results to others.

Steve Martin once said, "Be so good that they cannot ignore you." In nature, if you stand out, chances are you will get noticed and most likely be eaten. In our world, however, if you get noticed, you will likely get rewarded for your efforts. That will help you sell your analytics and build your authority. Once you have stood out enough times, your consistency and reliability will help build quality and authority. Authority will do wonders for you—whether it's your career or an analytics project.

Have you noticed that when interviewing people you know within the first five minutes if a person is a good candidate? According to a study, the first 20 seconds of an interview decide the outcome (Prickett et al. 2000). Why does this happen? If the technical competence is equal among candidates, interviewers make biased decisions using presentability as a criterion.

One tool that you can use to become really exceptional is given in the book **Innovation You** by DeGraff (2011). When you look at your investments, you're very careful about spreading your risk. But when you look at your own time, you may not be doing so. Lost money may come back, but lost time will never return. DeGraff encourages you to think of your life as an investment portfolio. You diversify your time to learn and do different things. When you diversify your knowledge base, you become exceptional.

Let's say you want to become a stand-up comic. Don't quit your day job yet. You put 5% of your time gaining those qualities and, maybe, after six months you look at what happened: what worked better and what did not. Then you make additions to your portfolio based on your success. DeGraff also describes four C's for better diversified time management.

- Collaborate
- Create
- Compete
- Control

Collaborate is when you are working with other people trying to find something. *Create* is when you are coming up with some new ideas; you are building something and you are learning something for the first time. *Compete* is when you are really going out there and building something new. *Control* is when you give up or reduce something.

Maybe you want to volunteer and so you put 50% of your time volunteering at a local non-profit. Five-percent of your time goes towards your goal of becoming a stand-up comic. After six months, you reevaluate and *control* your choices.

3.4   Storytelling

Storytelling can really show your passion. Think about your own presentations: do you present your analysis in a meaningful way, or do you show off the fact that your model predicted the tenth percentile of your donors with a 93% accuracy?

62 SUCCESS IN ANALYTICS

You have to think about your audiences: what's in it for them? Do they care? Do they want to listen to you?

You should think about all these things before you even open up PowerPoint. Maybe you don't even need PowerPoint.

Smith (2012), in his book **Lead with a Story**, gives an example of when storytelling wins over data:

There was once an advertising manager. He wanted to show that his client's competitors were outperforming his client. He collected all the data and produced beautiful slides and charts, but the night before the meeting, his boss told him not to use any slides.

The manager was really disappointed because he was proud of the hard work that went into creating his branded bar chart. But then he grabbed a newspaper. He got his son's yellow star stickers and put those stickers in front of his client's ads and his competitor's ads. He took this newspaper the next day to the meeting and handed it to an attendee and asked him to count the stars. The attendee counted, "one, two, three," for his own company and, "one, two, three, four, five, six, seven, eight, nine" for his competitor. Three times more ads for their competitor. Do you think a bar chart would have created a better impact? The message of this exercise stuck with this audience—much more so than the bar chart would have.

We like to think that we are rational people, but we make many decisions driven by emotions and biases (Kahneman 2011). If that were not true, we would not purchase more expensive products instead of the generic brand (containing the exact same ingredients) for the hundredth time. Ultimately, you have a better chance at succeeding if you have a good story to tell and can tap into people's emotions. You should consider this before you present your next analysis.

In summary, there are three P's to increase your chances of success in analytics: build great *products*, understand *people*, and show your *passion*.

4

DATA SCIENCE APPLICATIONS FOR FUNDRAISING

4.1   What is Data Science?

"Data science" is a term that describes the systematic process of converting data into actionable insights, decision support and recommendations using computational tools and machine learning techniques. The purpose of data science is to identify trends, confirm intuition, and help us make important predictions about the future using past data.

4.2 How to Use Data Science for Fundraising?

Data science is a tool that can help fundraising professionals understand donor behavior and increase the success of fundraising campaigns. Fundraising analytics creates business value by using data visualization and analysis tools to help identify opportunities, generate leads, guide strategy, prioritize resource allocation, and provide decision support and recommendations relative to campaign goals.

4.3 Problems in Fundraising

Out of the various problems in fundraising, you will agree on the following as the biggest challenges:

- Find prospective donors

- Maximize available resources

If we don't find new donors or don't upgrade existing ones, we won't generate future donations.

Yet sometimes, having too many prospective donors also creates a problem of "little time for a lot work." Organizations with limited resources face this problem disproportionately.

Data science offers answers to both of these problems. But first, let's explore the problems in detail.

4.3.1 Finding Prospective Donors

This is a big and demanding problem. Prospect research professionals spend most of their time on it. It includes finding individuals or organizations who can give, summarizing philanthropic interests, and discovering relationships with their organization:

Finding entities: Typically, we look at the giving history of existing donors as a starting point for further investigation. We also assess the wealth of individuals to put the wealthy ones high on our list for further engagement.

Finding interests: We try to figure out the giving as well as personal interests of individuals to better engage them with our organizations. This approximation of interests helps us create targeted engagement and solicitation opportunities.

Finding relationships: We know that people are willing to act on something if asked by a friend—especially if that something is a request to give. Uncovering relationships among our benefactors and potential donors help us to ask for helps from our friends.

This is our view. This has nothing to do with the individual. What can we do to let them drive the process?

4.4 Maximizing Resources

This is hardly a new problem. Every organization tries to make the most of the available time and people. Fundraising faces the challenge of engaging new potential donors every year with limited staff.

4.5 Are they Really Problems?

Yes: Of course, one would say. Without new donors, our inflow of cash will stop. We need to keep building relationships with the

66 DATA SCIENCE APPLICATIONS FOR FUNDRAISING

prospective donors and work with the ones who are interested in our causes.

If we don't use our time wisely and chase after unlikely donors, we will lose potential revenue.

So, yes, these are real problems and data can help us become more productive.

No: These are not problems if:

- the gift officers already have a lot of people in their portfolios. It doesn't make sense to add more people.
- the practice of systematic qualification is non-existent. If the gift officers don't qualify using a system, what's the point of generating more leads?
- the results using data are marginally better than the current practices. To calculate outcomes, first we need to know what to measure. Let's take the case of events. What's the measure of success? Even if we used data to create a list of invitees, how would we know we improved on the current practice?

Let's see how we can apply data science to solve these fundraising problems.

4.6 How to Use Data Science to Solve These Problems?

Let's divide these problems into two categories: outward and inward looking. When the problems we are trying to solve involve entities outside of our organization, these are outward-looking problems. When we are trying to improve our internal processes, these are looking inward problems.

HOW TO USE DATA SCIENCE TO SOLVE THESE PROBLEMS?

4.6.1 Outward Looking

Figure 4.1 shows some of the outward-facing problems, divided by the donor cycle, as well as the data science techniques we can use to solve these problems.

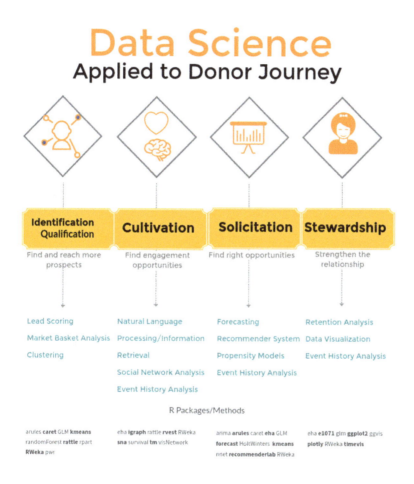

Figure 4.1: Data science applied to the donor journey

68   DATA SCIENCE APPLICATIONS FOR FUNDRAISING

Table 4.1: Inward-looking fundraising problems and data science applications

Challenge	How to solve	Which technique to use
Too many prospects in portfolios	Remove inactive and unlikely-to-give prospects	Predict likelihood of giving
Absent fundraiser activity	Create accountability and ranking reports	Simple activity scoring formula
Shortfall of major gift officer talent	Find talent within annual giving officers	Predict future activity
Limited time to provide information	Automate tasks and reports	Text mining and other programming

4.6.2   Inward Looking

Table 4.1 shows some of the problems that we face within our organizations as we try to improve our productivity and performance.

5

GETTING STARTED WITH R

If you are completely new to all things R, welcome!

If you have a background in computer programming languages or software such as Python, Stata®, SAS®, or Matlab®, you may notice many familiar concepts and terminology such as functions, variables, and operators in the example R code recipes referenced in this book.

5.1 Why R?

R is a free, open source statistical programming language that is powerful, flexible, and evolving. R, which has grown significantly in popularity, is an interactive and object-oriented programming language that offers a variety of data structures, graphical capabilities, functions, packages, documentation, and community support. In addition, it is an evolving ecosystem that can effectively handle different data types and perform complex analysis on individual and distributed computer systems, which are important capabilities to consider when developing data analytics solutions of any size or scale.

5.2 Download R (Required)

R is compatible with Windows™, macOS, and a variety of Unix systems.

The latest version of R is available for download via the Comprehensive R Archive Network (CRAN):

- https://cran.r-project.org/

All of the R code in this book has been tested to work with R version 3.4.3 (2017-11-30). Please check your existing R installation and upgrade to the latest version if needed.

> Remember to download all the R code files and data by visiting http://www.nandeshwar.info/ds4fundraisingcode.

5.3 Install RStudio (Optional)

RStudio is an integrated development environment (IDE), which includes a code editor, debugger, and visualization tools that make R more user friendly.

RStudio Desktop (Open Source Edition) is available for free download via the following links:

- RStudio: https://www.rstudio.com/
- RStudio Desktop: https://www.rstudio.com/products/rstudio/#Desktop

5.4 Install Packages

R is a popular programming language that benefits from community-driven support and ongoing enhancements.

R packages, which you may have already heard about, are bundles of reusable R functions, support documentation, and sample data (if included). As of writing this book, there are currently 12,106 R packages available to download, install, and use. The fact that there are over 12,000 packages of freely available add-on code libraries speaks to the flexibility of the R language and the robust commitment of the R user community. The potential data analytics solutions you can develop using these packages is perhaps only limited by your curiosity, creativity, and willingness to learn R!

We assume you've already downloaded R on your computer, so now it's time to get your feet wet and download two popular R packages, dplyr and ggplot, using the install.packages function to familiarize yourself with the R package installation process.

To run the following code, copy and paste each line into your R console window and click the Enter key. Alternatively, you can copy and paste these commands into a new R script by selecting File > New File > R Script within R Studio.

```r
# Install dplyr package
install.packages("dplyr", repos='http://cran.us.r-project.org')

# Install ggplot2 package
install.packages("ggplot2", repos='http://cran.us.r-project.org')
```

Voila! You successfully ran your first R code, which downloaded and installed two popular R packages for data manipulation and visualization tools. We'll cover these tools later in greater detail.

72   GETTING STARTED WITH R

These lines of R code contain two `install.packages` commands, each of which is preceded by a comment line indicated by the `#` symbol. The `#` symbol is a comment symbol that will not be executed by R. As a good programming practice, comment your code liberally to document it for later reference.

 We strongly recommend you get into the habit of documenting your code with comment lines using the `#` symbol so that you can later reference, check, test, and update your code as needed.

If you create a new R script, you can also highlight all four lines of code in your script with your mouse cursor and then manually select `Code > Run Select Line(s)` from the R Studio menu. Alternatively, you can use the keyboard shortcut `Command + Enter` on a Mac or `Control + Enter` on Windows or Linux to run these lines of code.

For a full list of RStudio keyboard shortcuts, please refer to RStudio's knowledge base[1].

Now that you've installed both R packages, let's load these packages and make them available for use on your system using the `library("package name")` function.

```
# Load dplyr package
library("dplyr")

# Load ggplot2 package
library("ggplot2")
```

To see all of the R packages installed on your system, call the `library` function without any arguments (that is, inputs) or package names.

---

[1] https://support.rstudio.com/hc/en-us/articles/200711853-Keyboard-Shortcuts

```
# List all packages installed
library()
```

In the `library` function output, you should see both the `dplyr` and `ggplot2` packages listed in alphabetically along with the following brief package descriptions.

- `dplyr`: A Grammar of Data Manipulation

- `ggplot2`: Create Elegant Data Visualizations Using the Grammar of Graphics

Congratulations!

You just completed an R package installation process using repeatable and reusable R code, which downloaded, installed, and loaded R packages on your computer.

5.5 Learning R

Although R is a powerful statistical modeling and programming environment, it can take some time to get comfortable using R, especially if you don't have any background in statistics or computer programming. For users with minimal experience in writing code, we encourage you to be patient while you get the hang of working with R. The benefits (flexibility, extensibility, and speed, just to name a few) are well worth the time and effort to overcome the initial learning curve associated with R.

Here are some tips for learning R:

- Do: Many people learn R best through hands-on learning and directly entering R commands within the R console window.
- Review: Check out code samples and retype the commands you find in this book and beyond.

- Experiment: Try modifying R commands and running the code to see what happens to develop a better sense and understanding of how it works.
- Research: You will encounter errors in R. Fortunately, R has excellent error messages that (usually) offer useful diagnostic information to help you figure out the root cause of the issue.

5.6 R Console

Assuming you've already installed R on your computer, the first thing you will encounter when you launch R is the R console window and the command prompt >, which indicates R is ready for your instructions.

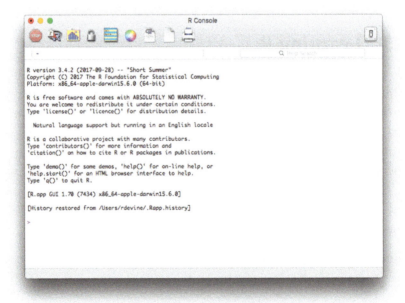

Figure 5.1: Command prompt

As previously mentioned, R is an interactive programming environment, so let's use R as a calculator and enter some basic arithmetic operators to explore it can do.

```
# Addition
1+8
#> [1] 9
# Subtraction
1-7
#> [1] -6
# Division
1/7
#> [1] 0.143
# Multiplication
1*7
#> [1] 7
# Exponentiation
2^3
#> [1] 8
# Order of Operations
1+2*3
#> [1] 7
```

After you enter each command into the R command prompt, each result will be interactively displayed in the R console as shown in Figure 5.2.

If you've installed RStudio, the R Console command prompt and interactive output will be displayed at the bottom of your RStudio session window.

76 GETTING STARTED WITH R

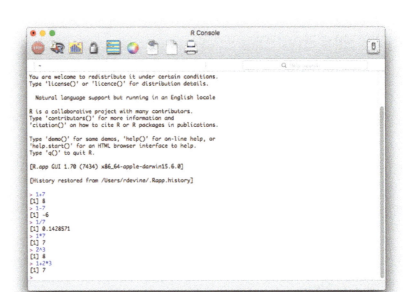

Figure 5.2: Interactive output

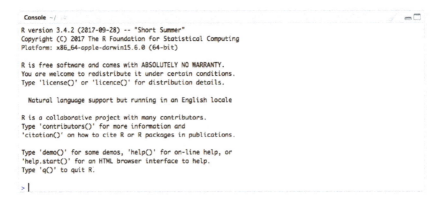

Figure 5.3: RStudio command prompt

```
Console ~/
> 1+7
[1] 8
> 1-7
[1] -6
> 1/7
[1] 0.1428571
> 1*7
[1] 7
> 2^3
[1] 8
> 1+2*3
[1] 7
>
```

Figure 5.4: RStudio interactive output

5.7 Built-in Functions

R has many built-in functions, which are reusable expressions that involve zero or more variables.

```
# Logarithm
log(x = 100)
#> [1] 4.61
# Square Root
sqrt(x = 16)
#> [1] 4
# Round
round(x = 8.3)
#> [1] 8
```

These variables are arguments (inputs or parameters) that are passed to functions in order to perform various types of calculations. For example, the sqrt function takes a single argument of x. We used 16 as our x and the function returned its square root of 4.

Functions can also take more than one parameter, separated by commas.

In the previous example, the round function took the number 8.3 and rounded to the closest integer, which is 8. However, if we pass the round function a number such as pi (3.141592…), we can instruct R to round pi to the nearest hundredth by passing an additional parameter digits the value of 2.

```
# Round
round(x = 3.141592, digits = 2)
#> [1] 3.14
```

The base installation of R includes several built-in constant variables, one of which is pi.

- LETTERS: The 26 upper-case letters of the Roman alphabet
- letters: The 26 lower-case letters of the Roman alphabet
- month.abb: The three-letter abbreviations for the English month names
- month.name: The English names for the months of the year
- pi: The ratio of the circumference of a circle to its diameter

Rather that manually typing the value of pi in the previous example, you could have also used the built-in constant pi.

```
# Round
round(x = pi, digits = 2)
#> [1] 3.14
```

If you want additional information about a function and its parameters, the base R installation comes with useful help pages with function descriptions, usage, arguments, details, and examples.

> You can view a function's help documentation by using the ? operator or help function. Another way is using example(function_name) command. Try example(round) in your console.

To learn more about the `round` function and its usage details, try entering either of the following commands in your R console.

```
# ? Operator Help
?round

# Help Function
help(round)
```

To learn more about built-in constants in the base R namespace, try entering either of the following commands.

```
# ? Operator Help
?Constants

# Help Function
help(Constants)
```

 R also allows you to write your own functions. If you are curious or are already comfortable using built-in functions, we encourage you to explore and try creating your own custom functions. For additional details, you can check out this article[2].

5.8 Variables

Variables allow you to store data in a named object, whose values can later be retrieved and changed as needed. To create a variable in R, use the assignment operator "<-" to assign data to a variable name.

80 GETTING STARTED WITH R

For example, suppose we wanted to store the value of the square root calculation for later use. Here's a code snippet that stores the calculation in a variable.

```
# Calculate square root and assign to "sqroot" variable
sqroot <- sqrt(16)

# Print "sqroot" value
sqroot
#> [1] 4
```

In this example, you will note that we selected sqroot as the variable name to avoid a naming conflict with the sqrt function. To further extend this example, suppose we needed to regularly update the sqrt function input value instead of hard-coding the value "16". We can modify the code to use another variable for the input parameter.

```
# Square Root Function Input (Parameter)
input <- 16

# Calculate square root and assign to "sqroot" variable
sqroot <- sqrt(input)

# Print "sqroot" value
sqroot
#> [1] 4
```

5.9 Conditional Logic

R provides a variety of logical operators that return a value of TRUE or FALSE.

```r
# Less Than
1 < 2
#> [1] TRUE

# Less Than or Equal To
2 <= 2
#> [1] TRUE

# Greater Than
1 > 2
#> [1] FALSE

# Greater Than or Equal to
2 >= 2
#> [1] TRUE

# Exactly Equal to
2 == 2
#> [1] TRUE

# Not Equal To
1 != 1
#> [1] FALSE

# Not X
X <- TRUE
!X
#> [1] FALSE

# X or Y
X <- FALSE
Y <- TRUE
X | Y
```

```
#> [1] TRUE

# X AND Y
X <- FALSE
Y <- TRUE
X & Y
#> [1] FALSE

# Test whether value of X is TRUE
X <- FALSE
isTRUE(X)
#> [1] FALSE
```

5.10 Data Types

Everything in R is an object. R offers a variety of data types such as scalars, vectors, matrices, data frames, and lists.

5.11 Vectors

A vector is an ordered collection of atomic (integer, numeric, character, or logical) values. Vectors are one of the most common and basic data structures in R, so it is useful to familiarize yourself with them.

Vectors can be one of two different types: (1) atomic vectors and (2) lists.

 All of the elements in a vector must have the same data type.

You can manually create a vector by using the c, or combine, function to combine a collection of data values. For example, suppose we needed to create a list of donor ages and store them in a variable called donor_age.

```
# Create donor_age vector
donor_age <- c(28, 32, 77, 57, 52, 41, 42, 49)
```

We can use the c function again to add additional elements to donor_age if needed.

```
# Update donor_age with additional donor age values
donor_age <- c(donor_age, 72, 68)
```

5.12   Sequences

You can also create vectors as a sequence of numbers using the seq function or using the ":" operator.

```
seq(from = 1, to = 10)
#>  [1]  1  2  3  4  5  6  7  8  9 10
series <- 1:10
series
#>  [1]  1  2  3  4  5  6  7  8  9 10
# check whether they give same results
identical(x = seq(1, 10), y = series)
#> [1] TRUE
```

84   GETTING STARTED WITH R

5.13   Matrices

Matrices are a special type of atomic (integer, numeric, character, or logical) vector with dimensional attributes (rows and columns). By default, matrices are filled column wise.

5.14   Lists

A list is a special vector type where elements are not restricted to a single data type. Because the contents of a list can include a mixture of data types, lists are flexible data structures and sometimes referred to as generic vectors.

To create a list, use the list function.

```
# Update donor_age with additional donor age values
donor_name <- "John Smith"
donor_age <- 58
donor_city <- "San Francisco"
donor_lifetimegiving <- 14225
donor_profile <- list(donor_name, donor_age,
                      donor_city, donor_lifetimegiving)
donor_profile
#> [[1]]
#> [1] "John Smith"
#>
#> [[2]]
#> [1] 58
#>
#> [[3]]
#> [1] "San Francisco"
#>
```

FACTORS 85

```
#> [[4]]
#> [1] 14225
```

5.15   Factors

Factors are vectors used to represent categorical data labels.

Factors can be ordered or unordered and are especially useful when organizing and working with categorical data due to their speed and efficiency. Although factors look like character vectors, they are actually stored internally within R as integers, so you need to be careful when treating them like characters to avoid running into errors. It is also important to note that factors can only contain pre-defined label values, also known as levels.

```
donor_ind <- factor(c("no", "no", "yes",
                       "yes", "yes", "no",
                       "no", "yes", "yes",
                       "yes"))
donor_ind
```

Let's use the `table` function to create a two-way frequency table that shows the count of donors versus non-donors using the donor indicator variable `donor_ind` we just created.

```
donor_ind <- factor(c("no", "no", "yes",
                       "yes", "yes", "no",
                       "no", "yes", "yes",
                       "yes"))
table(donor_ind)
#> donor_ind
```

86 GETTING STARTED WITH R

```
#>  no yes
#>   4   6
```

5.16   Data Frame

A data frame is a special kind of list where each element has the same length. Data frames are important in R because they are used frequently for storing tabular data for analysis.

In addition to length, data frames have additional attributes, such as rownames, which can be used to organize and annotate data labels, such as donor_id.

Let's create a data frame using the donor_age and donor_ind vectors we just created.

```r
donor_age <- c(28, 32, 77,
               57, 52, 41, 42,
               49, 72, 68)
donor_ind <- factor(c("no", "no", "yes",
                      "yes", "yes", "no",
                      "no", "yes", "yes",
                      "yes"))
dd <- data.frame(donor_age, donor_ind)
dd
#>     donor_age donor_ind
#> 1          28        no
#> 2          32        no
#> 3          77       yes
#> 4          57       yes
#> 5          52       yes
#> 6          41        no
```

```
#> 7          42          no
#> 8          49          yes
#> 9          72          yes
#> 10         68          yes
```

Let's use the `table` function to display a frequency table of `donor_age` and `donor_ind`.

```
table(dd)
#>            donor_ind
#> donor_age no yes
#>         28  1   0
#>         32  1   0
#>         41  1   0
#>         42  1   0
#>         49  0   1
#>         52  0   1
#>         57  0   1
#>         68  0   1
#>         72  0   1
#>         77  0   1
```

5.17   Data Types

R provides several functions to examine the features of various data types such as:

- `class`: What kind of data object?
- `type`: What kind of data storage type?
- `length`: What is the length of the data object?
- `attributes`: What kind of metadata?
- `str`: What kind of data object and internal structure?

88 GETTING STARTED WITH R

5.18   Additional Support

We encourage you to start where you are and embrace the learning curve you inevitably encounter when learning any type of new language, whether computer or human.

For reference, the following is a link to R manuals provided by the R Development Core Team as a learning resource.

- https://cran.r-project.org/manuals.html

The following is a list of R community support sites with knowledgeable and helpful R user forums, which can be a useful resource when you encounter questions or run into a technical hurdle.

- https://r-dir.com/community/forums.html

```r
# Install dplyr package
#install.packages("dplyr")

# Install ggplot2 package
#install.packages("ggplot2")

# Install tidyverse
#install.packages("tidyverse")

# Load dplyr package
library("dplyr")

# Load ggplot2 package
library("ggplot2")
```

6

LOADING DATA

Before we create visualizations, build models, and extract actionable insights, we need to load data into R.

Data management (which includes finding, loading, cleaning, and manipulating data) plays an integral role in data analytics.

Similar to cooking a meal, you can consider data management the preparation required to set the stage for your analysis. Just like peeling potatoes can be repetitive and tedious, loading and preparing data for analysis isn't usually the most exciting part of the job. Nevertheless, it is important and must be done to lay the groundwork for buttery mashed potatoes or, in your case, delicious data discovery.

First, let's load a sample data set using the built-in R function `read.csv`.

90 LOADING DATA

6.1 Read CSV Files

read.csv is part of the read.table utilities built into R. read.csv reads a comma-separated values (CSV) file, which stores tabular data (numbers and text) in plain text, into a data frame. Each row (or line) of the file is a data record. Each record consists of one or more fields (columns or features) separated by commas.

```
# Load CSV file
data <- read.csv(file = "data/DonorSampleData.csv",
                 header = TRUE, sep = ',')
```

Here we are loading the CSV file using the read.csv function and three arguments (parameters):

- file: The file name along with its path
- header: A logical value indicating whether the file contains the names of the variables as its first line. In this case, we are telling R that the file does contain variable names in its first row.
- sep: A character value that R uses to separate fields.

read.csv loads the DonorSampleData.csv file into a data frame variable called data using the <- assignment operator.

For more details about the read.csv function, enter the following command into your R console:

```
# Display read.csv() help
?read.csv
```

6.2   Read Delimited CSV and TSV Files

You will soon discover there's usually more than one way to accomplish the same task in R. Another popular package for reading flat, delimited files into R is called readr, which includes the read_csv and read_tsv functions, which read comma-separated and tab-separated value files, respectively. These functions do a better job at guessing input file data types and, as an added benefit, they trim excessive whitespace from character data.

```r
# Load readr package
library(readr)

# Load CSV file
data <- read_csv("data/DonorSampleData.csv")
```

6.3   List Session Variables

```r
# Show variables currently loaded in R session
ls()
#> [1] "data"
```

The output of [1] "data" confirms that your CSV file has been loaded into the data frame variable called "data."

6.4   List Data Frame Variable Names

Let's take a look at the field (columns or features) inside the data object we created by loading our CSV file into R.

92 LOADING DATA

```
# List variables stored in "data" object
names(data)
#>  [1] "ID"                  "ZIPCODE"
#>  [3] "AGE"                 "MARITAL_STATUS"
#>  [5] "GENDER"              "MEMBERSHIP_IND"
#>  [7] "ALUMNUS_IND"         "PARENT_IND"
#>  [9] "HAS_INVOLVEMENT_IND" "WEALTH_RATING"
#> [11] "DEGREE_LEVEL"        "PREF_ADDRESS_TYPE"
#> [13] "EMAIL_PRESENT_IND"   "CON_YEARS"
#> [15] "PrevFYGiving"        "PrevFY1Giving"
#> [17] "PrevFY2Giving"       "PrevFY3Giving"
#> [19] "PrevFY4Giving"       "CurrFYGiving"
#> [21] "TotalGiving"         "DONOR_IND"
```

From the `names` function output, we can quickly identify there are 22 different columns or features to this data set.

6.5   Inspect Data Object

Let's inspect our data frame object in greater detail.

```
# Inspect the data object
str(data)
```

`str` is a very useful function that reports a wealth of information. The `str` output tells us we have 34,508 observations of 22 variables and provides a description of each variable, data type, and so on.

6.6 Read Excel files

In addition to CSV files, you will often find data in Excel spreadsheet formats (".xls" and ".xlsx").

To read Excel files directly into R, you can use the readxl function that comes bundled with the popular tidyverse package.

The following is code to download and load the tidverse package so you can use the readxl function to read an Excel file directly into R.

```
# Install tidyverse package
install.packages("tidyverse",
                 repos = "http://cran.us.r-project.org")


# Load tidyverse package
library(tidyverse)

# Load readxl package
library(readxl)

# Load Excel file into "excel" data frame
excel <- read_xlsx("data/DonorSampleData.xlsx")
```

For practice, try using the str function on the excel data frame to examine its structure. Does the excel object have the same number of observations and variables as the CSV file?

94 LOADING DATA

6.7 Read from a Database

Sometimes you need to pull data from a database rather than a CSV file or Excel spreadsheet. There are many different kinds of databases such as SQL, SQLite, and Oracle™. It is best to contact your database administrator to confirm your organization's database details.

In the following example, we will cover how to connect to a SQLite file and introduce you to the general process of how to connect to a database to retrieve data that meets your specific criteria or needs.

```r
# Install DBI
install.packages("DBI",
                 repos = "http://cran.us.r-project.org")


# Install RSQLite
install.packages("RSQlite",
                 repos = "http://cran.us.r-project.org")



# Load DBI package
library(DBI)

# Load RSQLite package
library(RSQLite)

# Connect to SQLite Database File
con <- dbConnect(SQLite(),
                 dbname = "Data/DonorSampleDataSQL.db")

# Build Database Query to Pull Alumni Who Are Also Parents
query <- dbSendQuery(con,
                 "SELECT * FROM data
```

```
                WHERE ALUMNUS_IND = 'Y'
                AND PARENT_IND = 'Y'")

# Fetch Query
db_data <- dbFetch(query)

# Display 10 prospects who are both parent and alumni
head(db_data, n = 10)

# Clear Query from Memory
dbClearResult(query)
```

The dbConnect function will let you connect you to the databases for which you have drivers installed on your system. A typical database management system is Microsoft's SQL Server® (MSSQL). To connect to MSSQL or other databases, follow the syntax of the dbConnect function. You will need to install the odbc package for this code to work. You will also need the ODBC drivers for SQL Server if they are not already installed. On a Windows™ computer, the drivers are already installed, but on a MacOS, you will need to install them manually as well as set up some additional files (not fun or straightforward). RStudio, the maker of the odbc package, provided guidelines on how to install these drivers on its site[1]. The connection to MSSQL may look like:

```
library(odbc)
con <- dbConnect(odbc::odbc(),
                    driver = "SQL Server",
                    server = <your_server_ip_or_address>,
                    database = <your_database_name>,
                    uid = <your_username>,
                    pwd = <your_password>)
```

---

[1]http://db.rstudio.com/best-practices/drivers/

96 LOADING DATA

Once connected, you can list all the tables in your database using this command:

```
dbListTables(con)
```

In this recipe, we connected to a `SQLite` database file (modeled on `DonorSampleData.csv`), built a database query to select prospects who are both alumni and parent constituent type, and displayed 10 sample prospects. We also showed a way to connect to Microsoft SQL Server. To get into the habit of keeping a tidy R workspace, we explicitly cleared the database query from computer memory as best practice. Cleaning up your R programming environment will become increasingly important as you work on larger projects with varied information sources and complex queries across multiple database systems, tables, and so on.

7

CLEANING DATA

Unlike any textbook data, real-world data is messy and hardly ready for analysis. Some common problems with real-world data are incorrect data types and space-padded text. On top of that, R prefers data in a certain way. For example, unknown values are noted as NAs, and for character or factor data types, the plotting order of axis labels depends on the order of underlying data. We'll take a look at some of these cleaning operations, but first let's load the data using the library readr:

```
library(readr)
donor_data <- read_csv("data/DonorSampleData.csv")
```

We will use the dplyr library's glimpse function to peek into the data. You can also see the summary of the data by using the summary(donor_data) command.

```
library(dplyr)
glimpse(donor_data)
#> Observations: 34,508
```

98 CLEANING DATA

```
#> Variables: 22
#> $ ID                   <int> 1, 2, 3, 4, 5, 6,...
#> $ ZIPCODE              <chr> "23187", "77643",...
#> $ AGE                  <int> NA, 33, NA, 31, 6...
#> $ MARITAL_STATUS       <chr> "Married", "Unkno...
#> $ GENDER               <chr> "Female", "Female...
#> $ MEMBERSHIP_IND       <chr> "N", "N", "N", "N...
#> $ ALUMNUS_IND          <chr> "N", "Y", "N", "Y...
#> $ PARENT_IND           <chr> "N", "N", "N", "N...
#> $ HAS_INVOLVEMENT_IND  <chr> "N", "Y", "N", "Y...
#> $ WEALTH_RATING        <chr> NA, NA, NA, NA, N...
#> $ DEGREE_LEVEL         <chr> NA, "UB", NA, NA,...
#> $ PREF_ADDRESS_TYPE    <chr> "HOME", NA, "HOME...
#> $ EMAIL_PRESENT_IND    <chr> "N", "Y", "N", "Y...
#> $ CON_YEARS            <int> 1, 0, 1, 0, 0, 0,...
#> $ PrevFYGiving         <chr> "$0", "$0", "$0",...
#> $ PrevFY1Giving        <chr> "$0", "$0", "$0",...
#> $ PrevFY2Giving        <chr> "$0", "$0", "$0",...
#> $ PrevFY3Giving        <chr> "$0", "$0", "$0",...
#> $ PrevFY4Giving        <chr> "$0", "$0", "$0",...
#> $ CurrFYGiving         <chr> "$0", "$0", "$200...
#> $ TotalGiving          <chr> "$10", "$2,100", ...
#> $ DONOR_IND            <chr> "Y", "Y", "Y", "N...
```

As you see from the glimpse of the data, all columns, except for numeric columns, are character or string type. This is the default setting for the `readr` package, compared to the default setting of the factor using `read.csv` from base R. Reading data as character type helps to clean it easily because factors are stored by their indices compared to the literal string values of the characters.

7.1 Remove Extra Spaces

Often, data-entry errors cause extra spaces around text. For example, "John Smith" might be entered as "John   Smith". The library stringr offers a convenient way to trim all the spaces around text.

```
library(stringr)
str_trim('John Smith ')
#> [1] "John Smith"
str_trim('  John Smith ')
#> [1] "John Smith"
```

Let's remove spaces around the PREF_ADDRESS_TYPE column in our data:

```
donor_data$PREF_ADDRESS_TYPE <- str_trim(
  donor_data$PREF_ADDRESS_TYPE)
```

What if we wanted to trim extra spaces from all character columns? We can use the mutate_if function from the dplyr package. This function will apply any arbitrary function to the selected columns, matched by a condition. For our purposes, we can select all the columns that are of character type using the is.character function.

```
is.character(donor_data$PREF_ADDRESS_TYPE)
#> [1] TRUE
is.character(donor_data$MARITAL_STATUS)
#> [1] TRUE
is.character(donor_data$GENDER)
#> [1] TRUE


donor_data <- mutate_if(donor_data,
```

100 CLEANING DATA

```
                    .predicate = is.character,
                    .funs = str_trim)
```

7.2 Change Data Types

As we saw from the glimpse above, there are a few columns that are indicator variables (with yes or no values). For various types of analyses, it is useful to convert them to factor type variables. We will use the `ends_with` function from the `dplyr` library to select all columns whose names end with "_IND". Then, we will convert these selected columns to factors.

```
donor_data <- mutate_at(donor_data,
                    .vars = vars(ends_with("_IND")),
                    .funs = as.factor)
```

7.3 Replace Values with NA

If your data has text values that denotes missing values, we need to explicitly convert those to `NA` for `R` to treat them as missing values. The `MARITAL_STATUS` column has the value of `Unknown` for a majority of the rows. Let's convert those to `NA` using the `ifelse` function. The `ifelse` function will test for a condition and return some other values based on the result of the test. In this case, we will test whether the `MARITAL_STATUS` column has the value of `Unknown`; if the result is true, then we return `NA`, else we return the original value.

```
donor_data$MARITAL_STATUS <- with(
  donor_data,
```

```
ifelse(MARITAL_STATUS == 'Unknown',
       NA,
       MARITAL_STATUS))
```

7.4 Change Order of Values

For a factor column, the order of the elements in that column matters for various labeling operations. If the order is important to you, you should let R know that order. The following is how to do so.

```
donor_data$WEALTH_RATING <- with(
  donor_data,
  factor(WEALTH_RATING,
         levels = c('$1-$24,999', '$25,000-$49,999',
                    '$50,000-$99,999', '$100,000-$249,999',
                    '$250,000-$499,999', '$500,000-$999,999',
                    '$1,000,000-$2,499,999',
                    '$2,500,000-$4,999,999',
                    '$5,000,000-$9,999,999',
                    '$10,000,000-$24,999,999'),
         ordered = TRUE))
```

7.5 Clean ZIP Codes

ZIP Codes are often problematic in addresses because of data-entry errors or the presence of international ZIP Codes. We will use the zipcode library and the clean.zipcodes function to clean and limit the ZIP Codes to only US ZIP Codes.

The following are some erroneous ZIP Codes.

102   CLEANING DATA

```
#> # A tibble: 6 x 1
#>   ZIPCODE
#>     <chr>
#> 1 NA-1175
#> 2 NA-2179
#> 3 NA-2245
#> 4 NA-4919
#> 5 NA-5419
#> 6 NA-6653
```

And some ZIP Codes in the zip + 4 format.

```
#> # A tibble: 6 x 1
#>      ZIPCODE
#>        <chr>
#> 1 92555-6454
#> 2 90265-5223
#> 3 90265-5785
#> 4 14845-5217
#> 5 33433-3803
#> 6 90265-4485
```

Let's clean them.

```
library(zipcode)
head(donor_data$ZIPCODE)
#> [1] "23187"       "77643"         NA
#> [4] "47141"      "92555-6454" "95191"
donor_data$ZIPCODE <- clean.zipcodes(donor_data$ZIPCODE)
head(donor_data$ZIPCODE)
#> [1] "23187" "77643" NA       "47141" "92555"
#> [6] "95191"
```

7.6   Manipulate Dates

Another common problem with the messy data is incorrect or missing date formats. The `lubridate` library makes it easy to perform various date-based operations.

Let's say we want to add a column for birth dates. We don't have the actual birth date, but only the age in our sample data. Let's look at the wrong way of doing this first.

```r
library(lubridate)
# Wrong Way. Only Subtracted Days
donor_data %>% mutate(BIRTH_DATE = as_date(today() - AGE)) %>%
  select(BIRTH_DATE)
#> # A tibble: 34,508 x 1
#>    BIRTH_DATE
#>        <date>
#> 1          NA
#> 2  2018-01-29
#> 3          NA
#> 4  2018-01-31
#> 5  2017-12-25
#> 6  2018-01-05
#> # ... with 3.45e+04 more rows
```

The correct way is to subtract the age from the current year and then create a date field. We will use random months and days.

```r
# Correct Way
donor_data$BIRTH_DATE <- make_date(
  year = year(today()) - donor_data$AGE,
  month = sample(1:12, replace = TRUE),
  day = sample(1:26, replace = TRUE))
head(donor_data$BIRTH_DATE)
```

```
#> [1] NA            "1985-06-16" NA
#> [4] "1987-12-03" "1950-09-11" "1961-01-23"
```

7.7 Remove Non-Numeric Characters

Often, numeric data columns have non-numeric characters, which create problems in further analysis. A common example is seeing the dollar sign ($) and/or commas in currency columns. The `stringr` library offers the `str_replace_all` function to replace such offending characters with something else.

Let's remove the dollar sign from the `TotalGiving` column.

```
head(donor_data$TotalGiving)
#> [1] "$10"    "$2,100" "$200"   "$0"     "$505"
#> [6] "$0"

donor_data$TotalGiving <- str_replace_all(
  string = donor_data$TotalGiving,
  pattern = "\\$",
  replacement = "")
head(donor_data$TotalGiving)
#> [1] "10"    "2,100" "200"   "0"     "505"
#> [6] "0"
```

Note that we used two backward slashes in front of the dollar sign. We did so because the dollar symbol is a special character in the pattern-matching mechanism known as **regular expressions** or **regex**. We had to tell R that we're looking for a literal symbol by using a backward slash. Unfortunately, a backward slash is a reserved symbol for R but we escaped *that* by using another backward slash.

Let's remove any commas in the `TotalGiving` column.

```
donor_data$TotalGiving <- str_replace_all(
  string = donor_data$TotalGiving,
  pattern = ",",
  replacement = "")
```

Pattern matching and searching using regex is very powerful—think super-charged wildcard matching. Get familiar with regexes to super-charge your searching, finding, and replacing. Here's a good cheat sheet: http://bit.ly/1NgWBbL. You can also test your regular expressions online: http://regexr.com/. Try to combine the two operations above into one single operation. **Hint:** See Section 13.1 to clean multiple columns at the same time.

7.8 Convert from Character to Numeric Data Type

Now that the `TotalGiving` column is clean, let's save it as a numeric column using the `as.numeric` function.

```
donor_data$TotalGiving <- as.numeric(donor_data$TotalGiving)
```

106 CLEANING DATA

7.9 Export Cleaned Data File

In the following chapters, we will use this cleaned version. Let's save this data frame using the `write_csv` function from the `readr` library:

```
write_csv(donor_data, "data/DonorSampleDataCleaned.csv")
```

8

MANIPULATING DATA

Like any analyst, I spend a lot of time manipulating the data to shape it into a desired format. Some say 90% of time spent on any data analysis is spent on data gathering and manipulation. R shines in this category. The `dplyr`, `readr`, and `tidyr` libraries make data manipulation easy.

Before we jump into the actual manipulation of data, let's understand how `dplyr` works.

Let's load the data first.

```
library(readr)
donor_data <- read_csv("data/DonorSampleDataCleaned.csv")
```

`dplyr` offers many helpful functions to make data analysis easy. The following are some functions that I most commonly use.

- `count`: This function automatically groups the categories and returns the number of rows in each category. For example, let's say we want to find out the number of rows in our data

108 MANIPULATING DATA

for each gender type. We can do so with the following simple command.

```
library(dplyr)
count(donor_data, GENDER)
#> # A tibble: 6 x 2
#>    GENDER      n
#>     <chr> <int>
#> 1  Female 16678
#> 2    Male 16233
#> 3       U     1
#> 4  Uknown  1091
#> 5 Unknown    12
#> 6    <NA>   493
```

We can see that we need to clean up the gender column by combining the unknown values. This is very similar to the GROUP BY clause in SQL. The count function wraps the dplyr function group_by to only return the number of rows.

- group_by: You can use this function to perform operations on a subset of data grouped by other columns. We can reproduce the previous count example using group_by and a summary function called tally explicitly.

```
tally(group_by(donor_data, GENDER))
#> # A tibble: 6 x 2
#>    GENDER      n
#>     <chr> <int>
#> 1  Female 16678
#> 2    Male 16233
#> 3       U     1
#> 4  Uknown  1091
#> 5 Unknown    12
```

```
#> 6    <NA>    493
```

- `summarize`: Now that you can group the subsets of data using the `group_by` function, you can calculate any aggregate values for your analysis. Let's say you want to find out average and median giving as well as average and median age by gender. The following is how to do so.

```
summarize(group_by(donor_data, GENDER),
        avg_giving = mean(TotalGiving),
        med_giving = median(TotalGiving),
        avg_age = mean(AGE),
        med_age = median(AGE))
#> # A tibble: 6 x 5
#>     GENDER avg_giving med_giving avg_age med_age
#>     <chr>      <dbl>      <dbl>   <dbl>   <int>
#> 1   Female    3282.6         25      NA      NA
#> 2     Male    1590.1         25      NA      NA
#> 3        U       0.0          0      41      41
#> 4   Uknown     788.0         15      NA      NA
#> 5  Unknown      86.8         20      NA      NA
#> 6     <NA>     286.4         20      NA      NA
```

You will see that the age summary columns show "NA" values. That's because R doesn't remove NA or unknown or NULL values from aggregation. We need to remove those from the calculations by adding the `na.rm = TRUE` argument to the `summarize` function.

```
summarize(group_by(donor_data, GENDER),
        avg_giving = mean(TotalGiving, na.rm = TRUE),
        med_giving = median(TotalGiving, na.rm = TRUE),
        avg_age = mean(AGE, na.rm = TRUE),
        med_age = median(AGE, na.rm = TRUE))
```

110 MANIPULATING DATA

```
#> # A tibble: 6 x 5
#>    GENDER avg_giving med_giving avg_age med_age
#>    <chr>       <dbl>      <dbl>   <dbl>   <dbl>
#> 1  Female     3282.6         25    43.3      39
#> 2    Male     1590.1         25    48.1      46
#> 3       U        0.0          0    41.0      41
#> 4  Uknown      788.0         15    48.4      49
#> 5 Unknown       86.8         20    47.9      53
#> 6    <NA>      286.4         20    44.5      44
```

- mutate: This function adds a column to the provided data frame. This is very convenient when you want to perform some operations and add the result as a column to your data frame. For example, let's say you want to convert the TotalGiving column to its natural logarithmic value.

```
d1 <- mutate(donor_data, log_totalgiving = log(TotalGiving))
summary(d1$log_totalgiving)
#>    Min. 1st Qu.  Median    Mean 3rd Qu.    Max.
#>    -Inf    -Inf    3.22    -Inf    4.97   16.32
```

- arrange: This function orders the data by the values in the given column. This is similar to the ORDER BY clause in SQL. Let's say you want to order the data frame by total giving. The following is one way to do so.

```
arrange(donor_data, TotalGiving)
```

If you want to order the data in descending order, you need to add the desc function.

```
arrange(donor_data, desc(TotalGiving))
```

- `select`: This is exactly like the SELECT clause in SQL. This function will select only the columns you choose and return that subset of the data. You can also rename the columns while selecting.

For example, let's say you want to select only `TotalGiving` and also want to rename it to `TOTAL_GIVING`. You can do so like this.

```
select(donor_data, TOTAL_GIVING = TotalGiving)
#> # A tibble: 34,508 x 1
#>   TOTAL_GIVING
#>          <dbl>
#> 1           10
#> 2         2100
#> 3          200
#> 4            0
#> 5          505
#> 6            0
#> # ... with 3.45e+04 more rows
```

- `filter`: This function is similar to the WHERE clause in SQL. You can filter the data by providing various criteria. For example, let's say you want the subset of donors who gave more than $10,000 and have a valid email address.

```
filter(donor_data, TotalGiving > 10000 &
       EMAIL_PRESENT_IND == 'Y')
#> # A tibble: 117 x 23
#>      ID ZIPCODE   AGE MARITAL_STATUS GENDER
#>   <int>   <chr> <int>          <chr>  <chr>
#> 1    72   47708    83        Married   Male
#> 2   187   06359    32           <NA> Female
#> 3   416   46604    NA           <NA>   Male
#> 4   619   90265    59           <NA> Female
```

```
#> 5    782   39479   54           <NA> Female
#> 6   1046   99019   NA           <NA>   Male
#> # ... with 111 more rows, and 18 more variables:
#> #   MEMBERSHIP_IND <chr>, ALUMNUS_IND <chr>,
#> #   PARENT_IND <chr>, HAS_INVOLVEMENT_IND <chr>,
#> #   WEALTH_RATING <chr>, DEGREE_LEVEL <chr>,
#> #   PREF_ADDRESS_TYPE <chr>,
#> #   EMAIL_PRESENT_IND <chr>, CON_YEARS <int>,
#> #   PrevFYGiving <chr>, PrevFY1Giving <chr>,
#> #   PrevFY2Giving <chr>, PrevFY3Giving <chr>,
#> #   PrevFY4Giving <chr>, CurrFYGiving <chr>,
#> #   TotalGiving <dbl>, DONOR_IND <chr>,
#> #   BIRTH_DATE <date>
```

 Note the two equals signs (==) in the code to compare the column values. You will get an error if you use a single equals (=) sign, which is reserved for assigning values.

8.1 Chaining Operations

Many of the `dplyr` functions are useful by themselves, but the power of `dplyr` is in chaining various functions together. Just like how you can extend a chain by adding a link, you can continue to operate on a data set by adding functions. This will be easy to see with an example. Let's say you want to find out the number of donors, who have given over $10,000 and have an email address. You will use the "%>%" symbol to continue the chain.

```
donor_data %>% filter(TotalGiving > 10000 &
                      EMAIL_PRESENT_IND == 'Y') %>%
```

CHAINING OPERATIONS   113

```
  tally()
#> # A tibble: 1 x 1
#>        n
#>    <int>
#> 1    117
```

But then you think you'd like to see the distribution of donors by gender. Easy-peasy.

```
donor_data %>% filter(TotalGiving > 10000 &
                      EMAIL_PRESENT_IND == 'Y') %>%
  count(GENDER)
#> # A tibble: 4 x 2
#>    GENDER      n
#>     <chr> <int>
#> 1 Female     58
#> 2   Male     56
#> 3 Uknown      2
#> 4   <NA>      1
```

How about calculating the aggregates on these donors?

```
donor_data %>%
  filter(TotalGiving > 10000 &
         EMAIL_PRESENT_IND == 'Y') %>%
  group_by(GENDER)  %>%
  summarize(avg_giving = mean(TotalGiving, na.rm = TRUE),
         med_giving = median(TotalGiving, na.rm = TRUE),
         avg_age = mean(AGE, na.rm = TRUE),
         med_age = median(AGE, na.rm = TRUE))
#> # A tibble: 4 x 5
#>   GENDER avg_giving med_giving avg_age med_age
#>    <chr>      <dbl>      <dbl>   <dbl>   <dbl>
```

114 MANIPULATING DATA

```
#> 1 Female      49303     17260    42.8     40
#> 2   Male     113929     23412    56.0     55
#> 3 Uknown      57354     57354    58.0     58
#> 4   <NA>      40788     40788     NaN     NA
```

Let's see further examples of data manipulation.

8.2   Selecting Columns

Let's say that you want to create a new data set with a few columns from existing data. Say you want to select the IDs, wealth ratings, and total giving. You also want to rename the ID column to PROSPECT_ID and the TotalGiving column to TOTAL_GIVING to help your readers. You'd start with this.

```
donor_data %>%
  select(PROSPECT_ID = ID,
         WEALTH_RATING,
         TOTAL_GIVING = TotalGiving)
```

To see the changes, you can chain the glimpse function.

```
donor_data %>%
  select(PROSPECT_ID = ID,
         WEALTH_RATING,
         TOTAL_GIVING = TotalGiving) %>%
  glimpse()
#> Observations: 34,508
#> Variables: 3
#> $ PROSPECT_ID   <int> 1, 2, 3, 4, 5, 6, 7, 8,...
#> $ WEALTH_RATING <chr> NA, NA, NA, NA, NA, NA,...
#> $ TOTAL_GIVING  <dbl> 10, 2100, 200, 0, 505, ...
```

SELECTING COLUMNS   **115**

But you need to save the results in a different data set.

```
donor_data_new <- donor_data %>%
  select(PROSPECT_ID = ID,
         WEALTH_RATING,
         TOTAL_GIVING = TotalGiving)
```

You can also reorder columns by changing the order of the columns listed in the `select` function.

```
donor_data %>%
  select(PROSPECT_ID = ID,
         TOTAL_GIVING = TotalGiving, WEALTH_RATING) %>%
  glimpse()
#> Observations: 34,508
#> Variables: 3
#> $ PROSPECT_ID   <int> 1, 2, 3, 4, 5, 6, 7, 8,...
#> $ TOTAL_GIVING  <dbl> 10, 2100, 200, 0, 505, ...
#> $ WEALTH_RATING <chr> NA, NA, NA, NA, NA, NA,...
```

You can also deselect a column by using a minus operation.

```
donor_data %>%
  select(PROSPECT_ID = ID,
         TOTAL_GIVING = TotalGiving,
         -WEALTH_RATING) %>%
  glimpse()
#> Observations: 34,508
#> Variables: 2
#> $ PROSPECT_ID  <int> 1, 2, 3, 4, 5, 6, 7, 8, ...
#> $ TOTAL_GIVING <dbl> 10, 2100, 200, 0, 505, 0...
```

116 MANIPULATING DATA

If you want to move the ID column to the end, you could use the `everything` function.

```
donor_data %>%
  select(-ID, everything(), ID) %>%
  glimpse()
#> Observations: 34,508
#> Variables: 23
#> $ ZIPCODE             <chr> "23187", "77643",...
#> $ AGE                 <int> NA, 33, NA, 31, 6...
#> $ MARITAL_STATUS      <chr> "Married", NA, "M...
#> $ GENDER              <chr> "Female", "Female...
#> $ MEMBERSHIP_IND      <chr> "N", "N", "N", "N...
#> $ ALUMNUS_IND         <chr> "N", "Y", "N", "Y...
#> $ PARENT_IND          <chr> "N", "N", "N", "N...
#> $ HAS_INVOLVEMENT_IND <chr> "N", "Y", "N", "Y...
#> $ WEALTH_RATING       <chr> NA, NA, NA, NA, N...
#> $ DEGREE_LEVEL        <chr> NA, "UB", NA, NA,...
#> $ PREF_ADDRESS_TYPE   <chr> "HOME", NA, "HOME...
#> $ EMAIL_PRESENT_IND   <chr> "N", "Y", "N", "Y...
#> $ CON_YEARS           <int> 1, 0, 1, 0, 0, 0,...
#> $ PrevFYGiving        <chr> "$0", "$0", "$0",...
#> $ PrevFY1Giving       <chr> "$0", "$0", "$0",...
#> $ PrevFY2Giving       <chr> "$0", "$0", "$0",...
#> $ PrevFY3Giving       <chr> "$0", "$0", "$0",...
#> $ PrevFY4Giving       <chr> "$0", "$0", "$0",...
#> $ CurrFYGiving        <chr> "$0", "$0", "$200...
#> $ TotalGiving         <dbl> 10, 2100, 200, 0,...
#> $ DONOR_IND           <chr> "Y", "Y", "Y", "N...
#> $ BIRTH_DATE          <date> NA, 1985-06-16, ...
#> $ ID                  <int> 1, 2, 3, 4, 5, 6,...
```

Note that `select` can perform renaming and selecting of columns at the same time. But if you just want to rename certain columns and still keep the rest of the data, you should use `select`'s cousin function, `rename`.

```
donor_data %>%
  rename(PROSPECT_ID = ID, TOTAL_GIVING = TotalGiving) %>%
  glimpse()
#> Observations: 34,508
#> Variables: 23
#> $ PROSPECT_ID         <int> 1, 2, 3, 4, 5, 6,...
#> $ ZIPCODE             <chr> "23187", "77643",...
#> $ AGE                 <int> NA, 33, NA, 31, 6...
#> $ MARITAL_STATUS      <chr> "Married", NA, "M...
#> $ GENDER              <chr> "Female", "Female...
#> $ MEMBERSHIP_IND      <chr> "N", "N", "N", "N...
#> $ ALUMNUS_IND         <chr> "N", "Y", "N", "Y...
#> $ PARENT_IND          <chr> "N", "N", "N", "N...
#> $ HAS_INVOLVEMENT_IND <chr> "N", "Y", "N", "Y...
#> $ WEALTH_RATING       <chr> NA, NA, NA, NA, N...
#> $ DEGREE_LEVEL        <chr> NA, "UB", NA, NA,...
#> $ PREF_ADDRESS_TYPE   <chr> "HOME", NA, "HOME...
#> $ EMAIL_PRESENT_IND   <chr> "N", "Y", "N", "Y...
#> $ CON_YEARS           <int> 1, 0, 1, 0, 0, 0,...
#> $ PrevFYGiving        <chr> "$0", "$0", "$0",...
#> $ PrevFY1Giving       <chr> "$0", "$0", "$0",...
#> $ PrevFY2Giving       <chr> "$0", "$0", "$0",...
#> $ PrevFY3Giving       <chr> "$0", "$0", "$0",...
#> $ PrevFY4Giving       <chr> "$0", "$0", "$0",...
#> $ CurrFYGiving        <chr> "$0", "$0", "$200...
#> $ TOTAL_GIVING        <dbl> 10, 2100, 200, 0,...
#> $ DONOR_IND           <chr> "Y", "Y", "Y", "N...
#> $ BIRTH_DATE          <date> NA, 1985-06-16, ...
```

118 MANIPULATING DATA

`dplyr` also offers various helper functions to select columns by conditions. Run `?select_helpers` in your console to see all the functions.

The following are a few examples.

- Select all indicator columns.

```
donor_data %>%
  select(ends_with('IND')) %>%
  glimpse()
#> Observations: 34,508
#> Variables: 6
#> $ MEMBERSHIP_IND      <chr> "N", "N", "N", "N...
#> $ ALUMNUS_IND         <chr> "N", "Y", "N", "Y...
#> $ PARENT_IND          <chr> "N", "N", "N", "N...
#> $ HAS_INVOLVEMENT_IND <chr> "N", "Y", "N", "Y...
#> $ EMAIL_PRESENT_IND   <chr> "N", "Y", "N", "Y...
#> $ DONOR_IND           <chr> "Y", "Y", "Y", "N...
```

- Select all columns containing `Giving`.

```
donor_data %>%
  select(contains('Giving')) %>%
  glimpse()
#> Observations: 34,508
#> Variables: 7
#> $ PrevFYGiving  <chr> "$0", "$0", "$0", "$0",...
#> $ PrevFY1Giving <chr> "$0", "$0", "$0", "$0",...
#> $ PrevFY2Giving <chr> "$0", "$0", "$0", "$0",...
#> $ PrevFY3Giving <chr> "$0", "$0", "$0", "$0",...
#> $ PrevFY4Giving <chr> "$0", "$0", "$0", "$0",...
#> $ CurrFYGiving  <chr> "$0", "$0", "$200", "$0...
#> $ TotalGiving   <dbl> 10, 2100, 200, 0, 505, ...
```

SELECTING COLUMNS **119**

- Select all columns saved in a character vector.

```
select_these_cols <- c('DEGREE_LEVEL',
                       'PREF_ADDRESS_TYPE',
                       'ZIPCODE')
donor_data %>%
  select(one_of(select_these_cols)) %>%
  glimpse()
#> Observations: 34,508
#> Variables: 3
#> $ DEGREE_LEVEL      <chr> NA, "UB", NA, NA, N...
#> $ PREF_ADDRESS_TYPE <chr> "HOME", NA, "HOME",...
#> $ ZIPCODE           <chr> "23187", "77643", N...
```

- Select columns 1 through 6.

```
donor_data %>%
  select(1:6) %>% #can also be written as select(num_range())
  glimpse()
#> Observations: 34,508
#> Variables: 6
#> $ ID             <int> 1, 2, 3, 4, 5, 6, 7, 8...
#> $ ZIPCODE        <chr> "23187", "77643", NA, ...
#> $ AGE            <int> NA, 33, NA, 31, 68, 57...
#> $ MARITAL_STATUS <chr> "Married", NA, "Marrie...
#> $ GENDER         <chr> "Female", "Female", "F...
#> $ MEMBERSHIP_IND <chr> "N", "N", "N", "N", "N...
```

120 MANIPULATING DATA

8.3 Filtering Rows

We've already learned how to filter rows, but let's check out an example of chaining `select` and `filter`. Let's say you want to select the IDs, wealth ratings, and total giving, but only those donors who gave more than $10,000 and have a valid email address.

```
donor_data %>%
  filter(TotalGiving > 10000 &
         EMAIL_PRESENT_IND == 'Y') %>%
  select(PROSPECT_ID = ID,
         WEALTH_RATING,
         TOTAL_GIVING = TotalGiving) %>%
  glimpse()
#> Observations: 117
#> Variables: 3
#> $ PROSPECT_ID   <int> 72, 187, 416, 619, 782,...
#> $ WEALTH_RATING <chr> NA, NA, "$100,000-$249,...
#> $ TOTAL_GIVING  <dbl> 125805, 17971, 20690, 1...
```

The order of chaining is important for the operations to succeed. For example, if you use `filter` after `select`, what do you think will happen? Yes, exactly: The code won't work because the `TotalGiving` and `EMAIL_PRESENT_IND` columns won't exist after selecting only the `ID`, `WEALTH_RATING`, and `TotalGiving` columns.

```
##This code will give you 'object not found' error.
donor_data %>%
  select(PROSPECT_ID = ID,
         WEALTH_RATING,
         TOTAL_GIVING = TotalGiving) %>%
  #the data set now has only these columns:
  # PROSPECT_ID, WEALTH_RATING, TOTAL_GIVING
```

CREATING COLUMNS **121**

```r
filter(TotalGiving > 10000 &
        EMAIL_PRESENT_IND == 'Y') %>%
#you can't filter what doesn't exist.
glimpse()
```

8.4 Creating Columns

Often you will need to compute new values or add explanatory
fields to your data sets. While `select` lets you rename fields, it
doesn't permit calculations on the fields. To do so, you can use the
`mutate` function. Let's say you want to add the natural log of value
of the value of total giving as a column.

```r
donor_data %>%
  select(PROSPECT_ID = ID,
        WEALTH_RATING,
        TOTAL_GIVING = TotalGiving) %>%
  mutate(TOTAL_GIVING_log = log(TOTAL_GIVING))  %>%
  glimpse()
#> Observations: 34,508
#> Variables: 4
#> $ PROSPECT_ID      <int> 1, 2, 3, 4, 5, 6, 7,...
#> $ WEALTH_RATING    <chr> NA, NA, NA, NA, NA, ...
#> $ TOTAL_GIVING     <dbl> 10, 2100, 200, 0, 50...
#> $ TOTAL_GIVING_log <dbl> 2.30, 7.65, 5.30, -I...
```

You also want to create a column that shows whether the wealth rating is over $500,000. You can either modify the earlier `mutate` com-
mand or chain another `mutate`. For clarity's sake, let's add another
`mutate` command.

122 MANIPULATING DATA

But first, you want to see all the available values in the `WEALTH_RATING` column. You can either use the `distinct` function or just use 'count. With a larger data set, finding unique values will be costlier on the CPU than summarizing.

```
donor_data %>%
  count(WEALTH_RATING)
#> # A tibble: 9 x 2
#>              WEALTH_RATING      n
#>                      <chr> <int>
#> 1              $1-$24,999    580
#> 2 $1,000,000-$2,499,999     59
#> 3        $100,000-$249,999   511
#> 4 $2,500,000-$4,999,999      4
#> 5          $25,000-$49,999   564
#> 6         $250,000-$499,999  265
#> # ... with 3 more rows
```

```
donor_data %>%
  select(WEALTH_RATING) %>%
  distinct(WEALTH_RATING)
#> # A tibble: 9 x 1
#>         WEALTH_RATING
#>                 <chr>
#> 1                <NA>
#> 2    $50,000-$99,999
#> 3 $100,000-$249,999
#> 4    $25,000-$49,999
#> 5 $250,000-$499,999
#> 6         $1-$24,999
#> # ... with 3 more rows
```

We know that to create our indicator column for the wealth rating over $500,000, we need to check for these wealth ratings: $500,000–

CREATING COLUMNS **123**

$999,999; $1,000,000–$2,499,999; and $2,500,000–$4,999,999. We do so by placing these values in a vector and using `ifelse` and the "%in%" operator as follows.

```r
donor_data %>%
  select(PROSPECT_ID = ID,
         WEALTH_RATING,
         TOTAL_GIVING = TotalGiving) %>%
  mutate(TOTAL_GIVING_log = log(TOTAL_GIVING))  %>%
  mutate(IS_OVER_500K = ifelse(
    WEALTH_RATING %in% c('$500,000-$999,999',
                         '$1,000,000-$2,499,999',
                         '$2,500,000-$4,999,999'),
    'Yes', 'No')) %>%
  glimpse()
#> Observations: 34,508
#> Variables: 5
#> $ PROSPECT_ID     <int> 1, 2, 3, 4, 5, 6, 7,...
#> $ WEALTH_RATING   <chr> NA, NA, NA, NA, NA, ...
#> $ TOTAL_GIVING    <dbl> 10, 2100, 200, 0, 50...
#> $ TOTAL_GIVING_log <dbl> 2.30, 7.65, 5.30, -I...
#> $ IS_OVER_500K    <chr> "No", "No", "No", "N...
```

We can also get a quick count of prospects rated over $500,000.

```r
donor_data %>%
  select(PROSPECT_ID = ID,
         WEALTH_RATING,
         TOTAL_GIVING = TotalGiving) %>%
  mutate(TOTAL_GIVING_log = log(TOTAL_GIVING))  %>%
  mutate(IS_OVER_500K = ifelse(
    WEALTH_RATING %in% c('$500,000-$999,999',
                         '$1,000,000-$2,499,999',
                         '$2,500,000-$4,999,999'),
```

124 MANIPULATING DATA

```
  'Yes', 'No')) %>%
  count(IS_OVER_500K)
#> # A tibble: 2 x 2
#>   IS_OVER_500K       n
#>          <chr> <int>
#> 1           No 34364
#> 2          Yes   144
```

8.5 Creating Aggregate Data Frames

Let's say that we want to calculate the giving statistics for alumni and non-alumni as well as the parent and non-parent population. How would we do so? We can group the data set by ALUMNUS_IND and PARENT_IND and then calculate the summary stats, like this.

```
alum_parent_summary <- donor_data %>%
  group_by(ALUMNUS_IND, PARENT_IND) %>%
  summarize(avg_giving = mean(TotalGiving, na.rm = TRUE),
          med_giving = median(TotalGiving, na.rm = TRUE),
          min_giving = min(TotalGiving, na.rm = TRUE),
          max_giving = max(TotalGiving, na.rm = TRUE))
```

```
alum_parent_summary
#> # A tibble: 4 x 6
#> # Groups:   ALUMNUS_IND [?]
#>   ALUMNUS_IND PARENT_IND avg_giving med_giving
#>          <chr>      <chr>      <dbl>      <dbl>
#> 1           N          N       1377         25
#> 2           N          Y       1460         20
#> 3           Y          N       5543         25
#> 4           Y          Y       1529         35
```

```
#> # ... with 2 more variables: min_giving <dbl>,
#> #   max_giving <dbl>
```

8.6   Creating Joins

Aggregation is fun, but sometimes you need to combine your data with some other external data. For me, often, it is the ZIP Code-level data. The `zipcode` library provides the city, state, latitude, and longitude of each ZIP Code. So how do you integrate this data into your donor data? You use joins. The set operations dictate joins between two data sets. The most common data-manipulation and aggregation mistakes happen because of incorrect joins[1]. I recommend studying this topic in detail if you are not familiar with joins (here's one resource for practitioners[2]; and read Maier (1983) for theory.). But for completeness' sake, here's a quick overview.

Let's say we have two data sets.

- Set A: This data contains the address and names of all our constituents, donors and non-donors
- Set B: This data contains total giving for every donor

Both the sets have a prospect ID, which we will use for joining. As donors are a subset of all of our constituents, set B is a subset of set A.

Here are some ways we can join set A and set B.

---

[1]The joins by themselves are rarely incorrect; the mistakes happen because of poor understanding of what happens after joining two sets. If one data set has multiple rows for a field used for joining another data set, the resulting join will have multiple rows.

[2]https://www.sqlshack.com/mathematics-sql-server-fast-introduction-set-theory/

126   MANIPULATING DATA

- Inner join: This join will return rows from both the sets only where the IDs are the same. That means all the non-donors will be excluded from the resulting set. The following is how you would write this in SQL.

```
SELECT A.*, B.*
FROM A
INNER JOIN B on A.ID = B.ID
```

- Outer join: Depending on which set is considered outer in the join, the returning result will contain all the rows from one set and only matching rows from the other set. For example, let's say that we want to see all the constituents from set A along with their total giving. In this case, set B is the outer set. Here's the SQL code for such a join.

```
SELECT A.*, B.*
FROM A
LEFT OUTER JOIN B on A.ID = B.ID
```

Since set B is a subset of set A, the outer join between sets B and A will result in the same data as an inner join between them.

- Cross join: This join results in a set with the number of rows equal to the number of rows in the first set times the number of rows in the second set. This is a Cartesian product[3]. This is the basis of joins, but we apply conditions to reduce the resulting set. The inner join is a Cartesian product with the criteria that the values of the two joining fields should match, resulting in a smaller set. Use cases of a cross join are limited and unless you have a good reason to use this type of join, find another way to get your results.

---

[3]https://en.wikipedia.org/wiki/Cartesian_product

CREATING JOINS   **127**

How do we use these joins, then? Let's say that you want to get latitude and longitude values for each ZIP Code in your data. You can join your data with a `zipcode` data set. If we want the result set to contain only the ZIP Codes with a latitude and longitude in the `zipcode` data set, use an inner join. But if you want all the rows back from your original data set, use an outer join. Let's see how to do both using `dplyr`.

```r
library(zipcode)
data(zipcode)
glimpse(zipcode)
#> Observations: 44,336
#> Variables: 5
#> $ zip       <chr> "00210", "00211", "00212", ...
#> $ city      <chr> "Portsmouth", "Portsmouth",...
#> $ state     <chr> "NH", "NH", "NH", "NH", "NH...
#> $ latitude  <dbl> 43.0, 43.0, 43.0, 43.0, 43....
#> $ longitude <dbl> -71.0, -71.0, -71.0, -71.0,...

inner_join(donor_data, zipcode, by = c("ZIPCODE" = "zip")) %>%
  glimpse()
#> Observations: 34,417
#> Variables: 27
#> $ ID                 <int> 1, 2, 4, 5, 6, 7,...
#> $ ZIPCODE            <chr> "23187", "77643",...
#> $ AGE                <int> NA, 33, 31, 68, 5...
#> $ MARITAL_STATUS     <chr> "Married", NA, NA...
#> $ GENDER             <chr> "Female", "Female...
#> $ MEMBERSHIP_IND     <chr> "N", "N", "N", "N...
#> $ ALUMNUS_IND        <chr> "N", "Y", "Y", "N...
#> $ PARENT_IND         <chr> "N", "N", "N", "N...
#> $ HAS_INVOLVEMENT_IND <chr> "N", "Y", "Y", "N...
#> $ WEALTH_RATING      <chr> NA, NA, NA, NA, N...
#> $ DEGREE_LEVEL       <chr> NA, "UB", NA, NA,...
```

128   MANIPULATING DATA

```
#> $ PREF_ADDRESS_TYPE    <chr> "HOME", NA, "HOME...
#> $ EMAIL_PRESENT_IND    <chr> "N", "Y", "Y", "Y...
#> $ CON_YEARS            <int> 1, 0, 0, 0, 0, 3,...
#> $ PrevFYGiving         <chr> "$0", "$0", "$0",...
#> $ PrevFY1Giving        <chr> "$0", "$0", "$0",...
#> $ PrevFY2Giving        <chr> "$0", "$0", "$0",...
#> $ PrevFY3Giving        <chr> "$0", "$0", "$0",...
#> $ PrevFY4Giving        <chr> "$0", "$0", "$0",...
#> $ CurrFYGiving         <chr> "$0", "$0", "$0",...
#> $ TotalGiving          <dbl> 10, 2100, 0, 505,...
#> $ DONOR_IND            <chr> "Y", "Y", "N", "Y...
#> $ BIRTH_DATE           <date> NA, 1985-06-16, ...
#> $ city                 <chr> "Williamsburg", "...
#> $ state                <chr> "VA", "TX", "IN",...
#> $ latitude             <dbl> 37.3, 30.0, 38.5,...
#> $ longitude            <dbl> -76.7, -93.9, -85...
```

The vector used in the `by` argument, `c("ZIPCODE" = "zip")`, tells `dplyr`
the columns to use for the join. If you didn't want to see the city and
state from the `zipcode` data, you could deselect those columns, like
so.

```
inner_join(donor_data,
           select(zipcode, -city, -state),
           by = c("ZIPCODE" = "zip")) %>%
  glimpse()
#> Observations: 34,417
#> Variables: 25
#> $ ID              <int> 1, 2, 4, 5, 6, 7,...
#> $ ZIPCODE         <chr> "23187", "77643",...
#> $ AGE             <int> NA, 33, 31, 68, 5...
#> $ MARITAL_STATUS  <chr> "Married", NA, NA...
#> $ GENDER          <chr> "Female", "Female...
```

```
#> $ MEMBERSHIP_IND        <chr> "N", "N", "N", "N...
#> $ ALUMNUS_IND           <chr> "N", "Y", "Y", "N...
#> $ PARENT_IND            <chr> "N", "N", "N", "N...
#> $ HAS_INVOLVEMENT_IND   <chr> "N", "Y", "Y", "N...
#> $ WEALTH_RATING         <chr> NA, NA, NA, NA, N...
#> $ DEGREE_LEVEL          <chr> NA, "UB", NA, NA,...
#> $ PREF_ADDRESS_TYPE     <chr> "HOME", NA, "HOME...
#> $ EMAIL_PRESENT_IND     <chr> "N", "Y", "Y", "Y...
#> $ CON_YEARS             <int> 1, 0, 0, 0, 0, 3,...
#> $ PrevFYGiving          <chr> "$0", "$0", "$0",...
#> $ PrevFY1Giving         <chr> "$0", "$0", "$0",...
#> $ PrevFY2Giving         <chr> "$0", "$0", "$0",...
#> $ PrevFY3Giving         <chr> "$0", "$0", "$0",...
#> $ PrevFY4Giving         <chr> "$0", "$0", "$0",...
#> $ CurrFYGiving          <chr> "$0", "$0", "$0",...
#> $ TotalGiving           <dbl> 10, 2100, 0, 505,...
#> $ DONOR_IND             <chr> "Y", "Y", "N", "Y...
#> $ BIRTH_DATE            <date> NA, 1985-06-16, ...
#> $ latitude              <dbl> 37.3, 30.0, 38.5,...
#> $ longitude             <dbl> -76.7, -93.9, -85...
```

To see all the rows from the donor data, but only matching rows
from the zipcode data, you can use the left outer join.

```
left_join(donor_data,
          select(zipcode, -city, -state),
          by = c("ZIPCODE" = "zip")) %>%
  glimpse()
#> Observations: 34,508
#> Variables: 25
#> $ ID                    <int> 1, 2, 3, 4, 5, 6,...
#> $ ZIPCODE               <chr> "23187", "77643",...
#> $ AGE                   <int> NA, 33, NA, 31, 6...
```

```
#> $ MARITAL_STATUS      <chr> "Married", NA, "M...
#> $ GENDER              <chr> "Female", "Female...
#> $ MEMBERSHIP_IND      <chr> "N", "N", "N", "N...
#> $ ALUMNUS_IND         <chr> "N", "Y", "N", "Y...
#> $ PARENT_IND          <chr> "N", "N", "N", "N...
#> $ HAS_INVOLVEMENT_IND <chr> "N", "Y", "N", "Y...
#> $ WEALTH_RATING       <chr> NA, NA, NA, NA, N...
#> $ DEGREE_LEVEL        <chr> NA, "UB", NA, NA,...
#> $ PREF_ADDRESS_TYPE   <chr> "HOME", NA, "HOME...
#> $ EMAIL_PRESENT_IND   <chr> "N", "Y", "N", "Y...
#> $ CON_YEARS           <int> 1, 0, 1, 0, 0, 0,...
#> $ PrevFYGiving        <chr> "$0", "$0", "$0",...
#> $ PrevFY1Giving       <chr> "$0", "$0", "$0",...
#> $ PrevFY2Giving       <chr> "$0", "$0", "$0",...
#> $ PrevFY3Giving       <chr> "$0", "$0", "$0",...
#> $ PrevFY4Giving       <chr> "$0", "$0", "$0",...
#> $ CurrFYGiving        <chr> "$0", "$0", "$200...
#> $ TotalGiving         <dbl> 10, 2100, 200, 0,...
#> $ DONOR_IND           <chr> "Y", "Y", "Y", "N...
#> $ BIRTH_DATE          <date> NA, 1985-06-16, ...
#> $ latitude            <dbl> 37.3, 30.0, NA, 3...
#> $ longitude           <dbl> -76.7, -93.9, NA,...
```

8.7   Transforming Data

Often you see the need to transform or pivot the data so that it becomes easier to perform further computations. You can do so in SQL using complicated CASE, PARTITION, or PIVOT statements. But the tidyr package makes the whole process easy in R.

Let's consider two types of data layouts. The most typical data layout is the *wide* (a.k.a. *flat*) layout, which is one row per ID and all other descriptive information in columns as shown in Figure 8.1. The other common layout is the *long* layout, which is multiple rows per ID with different information in each row as shown in Figure 8.2. The donor sample file we have been using so far has the wide layout, and a typical gift transaction table has a long layout.

ID	GENDER	AGE	ALUM_IND	GIVING
1	M	50	Y	$100
2	F	70	N	$5,000
3	U	55	Y	$0

Figure 8.1: Wide layout

ID	FISCAL YEAR	GIVING
1	2015	$50
1	2016	$50
2	2017	$5,000
4	2014	$10
4	2015	$10
4	2016	$10

Figure 8.2: Long layout

8.7.1 Transforming from Wide to Long Layout

Let's say you want to transform the donor data file so that all the indicator column types are in one column and the resulting values in another column. Let's get started by loading the `tidyr` library.

132 MANIPULATING DATA

```r
library(tidyr)
```

We will then use the `gather` function to combine the columns.

```r
donor_data %>%
  select(ID, ends_with("IND")) %>%
  gather(key = "WHICH_IND", value = "IND_VALUE", -ID) %>%
  #just to show different values in the resulting data set
  sample_n(size = 15)
#> # A tibble: 15 x 3
#>       ID           WHICH_IND IND_VALUE
#>    <int>               <chr>     <chr>
#> 1   4388 EMAIL_PRESENT_IND         N
#> 2  32892         PARENT_IND         N
#> 3   2439         PARENT_IND         N
#> 4  33481          DONOR_IND         Y
#> 5   5919 EMAIL_PRESENT_IND         N
#> 6   2216     MEMBERSHIP_IND         N
#> # ... with 9 more rows
```

We provided the value of WHICH_IND to the key argument. This lets tidyr know to create a column named WHICH_IND housing all the different indicator column names. We also provided the value of IND_VALUE to the value argument. By doing this, tidyr created a column named IND_VALUE to house all the various values from the indicator columns. The last argument of -ID was to remove the ID column from the combination and instead use it as another column.

Another more meaningful example: Let's say that you want to combine all the previous years' giving columns together into one column.

```r
donor_data %>%
  select(ID, starts_with("PrevFY")) %>%
```

```
  gather(key = "WHICH_FY", value = "GIVING", -ID) %>%
  #just to show different values in the resulting data set
  sample_n(size = 15)
#> # A tibble: 15 x 3
#>      ID     WHICH_FY GIVING
#>   <int>        <chr>  <chr>
#> 1 17928  PrevFYGiving     $0
#> 2  3159 PrevFY2Giving     $0
#> 3 11649 PrevFY4Giving     $0
#> 4 26287 PrevFY1Giving     $0
#> 5 32751 PrevFY1Giving     $0
#> 6 31136 PrevFY1Giving     $0
#> # ... with 9 more rows
```

8.7.2 Transforming Data from Long to Wide Layout

Let's say that you want to transform the giving data file so that all
the fiscal years are column names and the values under each column
show the giving in that fiscal year. This is a typical pivot table example. For this example, we will use the RFM data file. Let's load
this file and see the contents.

```
giving_data <- read_csv("data/SampleDataRFM.csv")
glimpse(giving_data)
#> Observations: 6,973
#> Variables: 3
#> $ ID          <int> 1, 1, 2, 2, 2, 2, 2, 3, 3...
#> $ FISCAL_YEAR <int> 2015, 2016, 2012, 2013, 2...
#> $ Giving      <chr> "$1,000", "$600", "$100",...
```

134 MANIPULATING DATA

Now, let's create new columns with the fiscal years as column names and fill them with the giving of that respective year and donor. We will use the `spread` function.

```
giving_data %>%
  spread(key = FISCAL_YEAR, value = Giving, fill = 0) %>%
  head()
#> # A tibble: 6 x 6
#>      ID `2012` `2013` `2014` `2015` `2016`
#>   <int>  <chr>  <chr>  <chr>  <chr>  <chr>
#> 1     1      0      0      0 $1,000   $600
#> 2     2   $100    $55   $160   $135 $1,135
#> 3     3 $1,750      0 $1,065    $80    $35
#> 4     4      0   $555      0   $285   $885
#> 5     5 $1,000   $555      0      0      0
#> 6     7 $1,000   $250      0      0      0
```

R doesn't take column names that start with a number; therefore, `tidyr` automatically puts the column names in back ticks ("'"). This creates a problem when you want to select this type of column.

You can't use this.

```
#don't run
giving_data %>%
  spread(key = FISCAL_YEAR, value = Giving, fill = 0) %>%
  select(2012)
```

Because the `select` function expects a column at the "2012" position. You can select that column by surrounding it in back ticks. It becomes cumbersome quickly.

You have two options.

TRANSFORMING DATA **135**

- Change the value of the column before applying `spread`. I prefer this option because I know I need to modify only one column.
- Rename the columns after applying `spread`. This is not a bad option, but you do need to provide names for all the columns at their respective positions. This is not repeatable.

But let's try both.

Changing the values of the column by prefixing the year values with FY.

```
giving_data %>%
  mutate(FISCAL_YEAR = paste0("FY", FISCAL_YEAR)) %>%
  spread(key = FISCAL_YEAR, value = Giving, fill = 0) %>%
  head()
#> # A tibble: 6 x 6
#>      ID FY2012 FY2013 FY2014 FY2015 FY2016
#>   <int>  <chr>  <chr>  <chr>  <chr>  <chr>
#> 1     1      0      0      0 $1,000   $600
#> 2     2   $100    $55   $160   $135 $1,135
#> 3     3 $1,750      0 $1,065    $80    $35
#> 4     4      0   $555      0   $285   $885
#> 5     5 $1,000   $555      0      0      0
#> 6     7 $1,000   $250      0      0      0
```

Renaming the resulting columns.

```
giving_data %>%
  spread(key = FISCAL_YEAR, value = Giving, fill = 0) %>%
  setNames(., c('ID', 'FY2012', 'FY2013',
                'FY2014', 'FY2015', 'FY2016')) %>%
  head()
#> # A tibble: 6 x 6
#>      ID FY2012 FY2013 FY2014 FY2015 FY2016
```

136 MANIPULATING DATA

```
#>     <int>   <chr>    <chr>    <chr>    <chr>    <chr>
#> 1       1       0        0        0  $1,000     $600
#> 2       2    $100      $55     $160    $135   $1,135
#> 3       3  $1,750        0  $1,065     $80      $35
#> 4       4       0    $555        0    $285     $885
#> 5       5  $1,000    $555        0       0        0
#> 6       7  $1,000    $250        0       0        0
```

 As a challenge, try replacing the hard-coded values for each fiscal year using code. **Hint:** use the `rep` function.

If you're enjoying this book, consider sharing it with your network by running `source("http://arn.la/shareds4fr")` in your R console.

— Ashutosh and Rodger

9

EXPLORATORY DATA ANALYSIS

Exploratory data analysis (also known as EDA[1]) describes a broad set of statistical and graphical techniques that summarize information to guide further analysis and data collection processes. Exploratory data analysis lays the foundation for more formal analyses such as model building and statistical hypothesis testing. Since exploratory data analysis is somewhat loosely defined, it may also be useful to think of it as an intermediate or staging process that involves a variety of data analysis and visualization techniques that you can use to evaluate, guide, and refine your analyses, data collection, and model building.

John W. Tukey[2], a prominent American mathematician best known for creating the box plot data visualization (and perhaps less well known for coining the term "bit" while developing computational statistical methods at Bell Labs[3]), is the author of **Exploratory Data**

---

[1]https://en.wikipedia.org/wiki/Exploratory_data_analysis
[2]https://en.wikipedia.org/wiki/John_Tukey
[3]https://en.wikipedia.org/wiki/Bell_Labs

138 EXPLORATORY DATA ANALYSIS

Analysis (Tukey 1977). Tukey cautioned against jumping headfirst into statistical hypothesis testing without first exploring and analyzing data beforehand.

Tukey's contributions to statistical computing and EDA are especially significant because they inspired the development of the S programming language at Bell Labs, which is the precursor of the R programming language used in this book. S, which was launched in 1976 and evolved into S-PLUS (1988) and eventually R (1993), accelerated the course of statistical computing by introducing revolutionary graphical capabilities to identify outliers, trends, and insights.

EDA includes many graphical techniques that will be covered extensively in the Data Visualization chapter. In this chapter, we will provide a few graphical methods to introduce you to statistical thinking and inspire you to think about how you can use R to identify outliers, trends, and meaningful patterns in your data.

Let's take a dive into our sample donor file and introduce you to some exploratory data analysis concepts.

```r
# Load readr and dplyr libraries
library(readr)
library(dplyr)

# Load CSV file
donor_data <- read_csv("data/DonorSampleDataCleaned.csv")
```

9.1   Heads or Tails

You can use the `head` or `tail` function to select the first or last `n` rows of data, where `n` specifies the *number* of rows.

```r
# Show first 10 rows
head(donor_data, n = 10)

# Show last 10 rows
tail(donor_data, n = 10)
```

9.2 Glimpse

Since we loaded the `dplyr` library, let's use the `glimpse` function to take a look at the features in our sample donor file:

```r
# Show loaded data
glimpse(donor_data)
```

9.3 Slice and Dice

The following are two additional ways to select and display the first 10 rows of data using either manual row selection or the `slice` function from `dplyr`.

```r
# Select first 10 rows
donor_data[1:10, ]

# Select first 10 rows using dplyr
slice(donor_data, 1:10)
```

140 EXPLORATORY DATA ANALYSIS

9.4 Indexing Notation

In addition to selecting rows, you can select specific columns in data frame indexing [rows, columns] notation.

```r
# Select first 10 rows of the first 3
# columns: [rows, columns]
donor_data[1:10, 1:3]

# Select first 3 columns of the first 10 rows using
# dplyr
select(donor_data, 1:3) %>% slice(1:10)
```

9.5 Deselect Rows and Columns

You can also use the "-" character to indicate all rows or columns *except* those meeting certain criteria. The following command selects the first three rows and excludes columns 1–6 and 9–23, which leaves only columns 7 and 8 (Alumnus and Parent Indicators).

```r
# Select first 3 rows of all columns except columns
# 1-6 and columns 9-23
donor_data[1:3, -c(1:6, 9:23)]
#> # A tibble: 3 x 2
#>   ALUMNUS_IND PARENT_IND
#>         <chr>      <chr>
#> 1           N          N
#> 2           Y          N
#> 3           N          N
```

9.6 Select Columns by Name

In addition to column (or feature) selection by column number, you can also specify the column name using the $ operator.

```
# Select by column name, calculate sum and store
# into TotalGivingSum
TotalGivingSum <- sum(donor_data$TotalGiving)

# Print TotalGivingSum
TotalGivingSum
#> [1] 81560838
```

9.7 Summary

Another useful way to explore your data is to invoke the summary function, which produces summary statistics for each variable within your data object. The output displayed will depend on the type of data object. This function is especially useful when working with numeric data because the output displays the following summary statistics for each variable: minimum, maximum, first quartile (25th percentile), median (50th percentile), mean, and third quartile (75th percentile) values. Give summary a try within the R console using the following command.

```
# Summarize "data" by individual variable
summary(donor_data)
```

142 EXPLORATORY DATA ANALYSIS

9.8 Average Gift Size

Let's use some statistical measures of central tendency to identify average gift size.

```
# Print average, median, standard deviation and
# quantiles of giving
mean(donor_data$TotalGiving)
#> [1] 2364
median(donor_data$TotalGiving)
#> [1] 25
```

It's the tale of two averages. Using the `mean` function, we can see that the average gift size (mean) in our donor file is $2,364, and the median is $25. Let's further explore and compare both statistical measures of average gift size in this example.

While both calculations report the "average" gift size, the mean value of $2,364 is significantly larger than the median value of $25, which indicates there are some large gifts (outliers) strongly influencing the overall average (mean) gift size. The median value ($25), by contrast, is calculated by arranging all of the gift size values in order from smallest to largest and selecting the middle (or median) value.

In cases where there are a few extremely low or high values (outliers) in your data, the median value is useful because it is robust against outlier values and may offer a better way to represent what is a typical value in your data set. In this example, the median value of $25 likely provides a better sense of the average gift size.

9.9 Measures of Spread

Let's use some additional statistical methods to explore the distribution (spread) of this data.

```
# Print average, median, standard deviation and
# quantiles of giving
sd(donor_data$TotalGiving)
#> [1] 113801
quantile(donor_data$TotalGiving)
#>        0%       25%       50%       75%      100%
#>         0         0        25       144  12221854
```

Using the quantile function, we learn that 75% of the donors in our synthetic data set are giving $144 or below.

You can also use the quantile function to determine the 90th, 95th, and 99th percentiles of giving levels in the donor file.

```
# Print average, median, standard deviation and
# quantiles of giving
quantile(donor_data$TotalGiving,
         probs = c(0.9, 0.95, 0.99))
#>  90%  95%  99%
#>  525 1309 9599
```

Using the quantile function with an additional array of probability parameters, we determine that 90% of donors gave $525 or below, 95% of donors gave $1,309 or below, and that 99% of donors gave below $10,000 in this data set.

9.10 Two-Way Contingency Table

One useful strategy to summarize data is to select a particular column (feature) and count (tally) the number of values meeting this criterion. For example, suppose we want to explore the number of donors by gender. Using the `table` function, we can quickly create a contingency table (also known as a cross-tabulation or crosstab) that displays the frequency distributions of these variables for comparative insight.

```
# Create cross-tab of donor count by gender
table(donor_data$GENDER, donor_data$DONOR_IND)
#>
#>               N      Y
#>    Female   6433  10245
#>    Male     5990  10243
#>    U           1      0
#>    Uknown    461    630
#>    Unknown     4      8
```

Based on this output, there does not appear to be a significant difference in giving as a function of gender. Let's use the `table` function again to explore whether giving varies between alumni and non-alumni.

```
# Create cross-tab of donor count by alumnus
# indicator
table(donor_data$ALUMNUS_IND, donor_data$DONOR_IND)
#>
#>          N      Y
#>    N  10001  16085
#>    Y   3074   5348
```

Yes, alumni are giving (donor = Y) more on average than their non-alumni counterparts.

Now, let's similarly explore whether parents tend to give more than non-parents.

```
# Create cross-tab of donor count by parent
# indicator
table(donor_data$PARENT_IND, donor_data$DONOR_IND)
#>
#>          N      Y
#>   N  12008  19799
#>   Y   1067   1634
```

Yes, parents, like alumni, are giving more than non-parents in this data set. Let's keep these constituent variables in mind when we further explore and measure the relative strength (association) of these variables with giving behavior in our data set.

9.11   Group By

Similar to using the GROUP BY clause in SQL, you can use the `group_by` function in the `dplyr` package for data analysis tasks using the "split-apply-combine" paradigm introduced in Hadley Wickham's influential paper "The Split-Apply-Combine Strategy for Data Analysis" (Wickham 2011). As you may have inferred from the name, "split-apply-combine" describes a systematic process where you split data into groups, apply analysis to each group and combine the results. In the following example, you will use the `dplyr` function to split the donor file into groups by gender (M or F) and apply the `top_n` function to tally the `TotalGiving` results for each group:

146 EXPLORATORY DATA ANALYSIS

```
# select top 5 by giving and gender
group_by(donor_data, GENDER) %>%
  top_n(n = 5, wt = TotalGiving)
#> # A tibble: 27 x 23
#> # Groups:   GENDER [6]
#>      ID ZIPCODE   AGE MARITAL_STATUS  GENDER
#>   <int>   <chr> <int>          <chr>   <chr>
#> 1  1059   46794    NA           <NA>  Uknown
#> 2  1325   90231    89        Married  Female
#> 3  2173   47175    99        Married  Female
#> 4  2929   12438    NA           <NA>    Male
#> 5  4142   45385    NA         Single Unknown
#> 6  9475   90265    81       Divorced    Male
#> # ... with 21 more rows, and 18 more variables:
#> #   MEMBERSHIP_IND <chr>, ALUMNUS_IND <chr>,
#> #   PARENT_IND <chr>, HAS_INVOLVEMENT_IND <chr>,
#> #   WEALTH_RATING <chr>, DEGREE_LEVEL <chr>,
#> #   PREF_ADDRESS_TYPE <chr>,
#> #   EMAIL_PRESENT_IND <chr>, CON_YEARS <int>,
#> #   PrevFYGiving <chr>, PrevFY1Giving <chr>,
#> #   PrevFY2Giving <chr>, PrevFY3Giving <chr>,
#> #   PrevFY4Giving <chr>, CurrFYGiving <chr>,
#> #   TotalGiving <dbl>, DONOR_IND <chr>,
#> #   BIRTH_DATE <date>
```

9.12   Histograms and Bar plots

In addition to statistical methods, exploratory data analysis uses graphic capabilities to visually explore and summarize relationships in the data to identify trends and emergent patterns. Let's use the `barplot` function to explore giving by fiscal year.

```r
# Load CSV file
donor_data <- read.csv("data/DonorSampleDataCleaned.csv",
    header = TRUE, sep = ",")

# Load ggplot2 package
library(ggplot2)

# Load RColorBrewer package
library(RColorBrewer)

# Attach data set to R namespace
attach(donor_data)

# Prepare vector of total giving by fiscal year
GivingByFY <- cbind(PrevFY4Giving, PrevFY3Giving, PrevFY2Giving,
    PrevFY1Giving, PrevFYGiving, CurrFYGiving)

# Aggregate total giving by fiscal year
GivingByFYTotal <- colSums(GivingByFY)

# Create histogram of total giving by fiscal year
barplot(GivingByFYTotal,
        main = "Giving by Fiscal Year",
        xlab = "Fiscal Year",
        ylab = "Total Giving",
        space = 0.2,
        cex.axis = .3,
        cex = 0.2,
        cex.names = 0.5)
```

148 EXPLORATORY DATA ANALYSIS

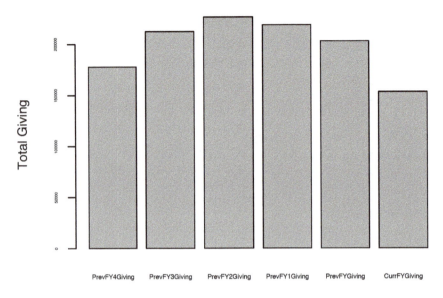

For comparison, let's use ggplot to create a histogram of average total giving by gender rather than using the built-in barplot function included with the base installation of R.

```
# Create dataframe for ggplot
df <- data.frame(donor_data)

# Create Histogram
p <- ggplot(df)
p + stat_summary_bin(
  aes(y = TotalGiving, x = GENDER),
  fun.y = "mean", geom = "bar")
```

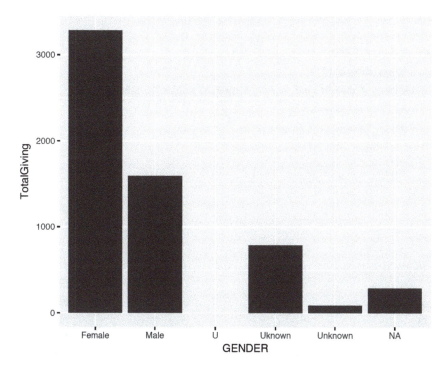

As you may notice, the histogram created using the `ggplot` function includes a background grid. Let's continue using `ggplot` to visually explore patterns and relationships in our data.

9.13 Boxplots with Outliers

We previously used statistical measures of `mean`, `median`, and `quantile` to identify the presence of outlier giving activity in our data set. Let's use the `ggplot` function to create a `boxplot` to see if we can further visualize these outliers.

```
# Create Boxplot
p <- ggplot(df)
p <- p + geom_boxplot(aes(y = TotalGiving, x = GENDER))
```

150 EXPLORATORY DATA ANALYSIS

```r
# Detect outliers
p + geom_boxplot(
  aes(y = TotalGiving, x = GENDER, fill = GENDER),
  outlier.colour = "red",
  outlier.shape = 1, outlier.size = 0.25)
```

Due to the outliers in our giving data, it is difficult to see any clear patterns from this visualization. In this situation, it can be useful to transform the outcome (dependent) variable to see if we can discern any more important information or trends. Let's revise the boxplot to include a `scale_y_log10` parameter, which will log transform the "TotalGiving" variable.

```r
# Create Boxplot
p <- ggplot(df)
p <- p + geom_boxplot(aes(y = TotalGiving, x = GENDER))



# Detect outliers + Brewer Divergent Color Palette

# Detect outliers + Brewer Divergent Color Palette
# + Log Transformation

p <- p + geom_boxplot(
  aes(y = TotalGiving,
      x = GENDER,
      fill = GENDER),
  outlier.colour = "red",
  outlier.shape = 1,
  outlier.size = 0.25) +
  scale_y_log10()

# Add Color Brewer Color Palette
p + scale_fill_brewer(palette = "RdYlBu")
#> Warning: Transformation introduced infinite values
#> in continuous y-axis

#> Warning: Transformation introduced infinite values
#> in continuous y-axis
#> Warning: Removed 13075 rows containing non-finite values
#> (stat_boxplot).

#> Warning: Removed 13075 rows containing non-finite values
#> (stat_boxplot).
```

152 EXPLORATORY DATA ANALYSIS

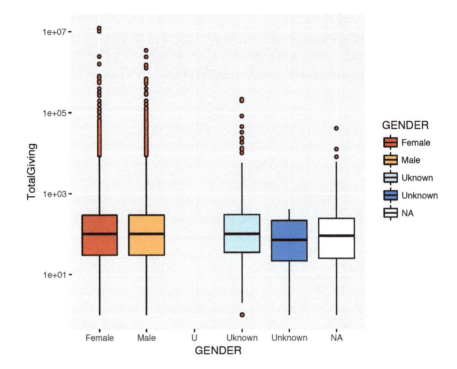

The `boxplot` visualization (also known as the box-and-whisker plot or diagram), with the addition of the log transformation parameter, reveals a wealth of information all at once. The boxplot shows numerical data (TotalGiving) and their respective quantiles by group (gender). The "whiskers" represent the minimum and maximum values, and the box shows the first and third quartiles (also known as the interquartile range or IQR); the line inside the boxplot depicts the `median` value, and the values located outside the perimeter (range) of the whiskers are `outlier` values. In this example, the boxplot reveals that there are indeed some extreme levels of donation activity in our data set and highlights the outlier values in red to distinguish them from other values.

 You may have noticed there are duplicate genders in the boxplot: Female, Male, U, Uknown, Unknown, and NA. When working with real-world data, you will often encounter these types of data-integrity issues. Based on what you learned in the Cleaning Data and Manipulating Data chapters, can you create a new boxplot with only 3 gender groups (Female, Male, and Other) and use a different Brewer color palette?

Let's use some additional built-in statistical functions within R to explore whether there is any potential association between the total giving and the constituent age variables in our donor file.

9.14   Correlation Matrix

The cor function calculates the correlation or measure of the strength between input variables. However, if we try running the following command, we get the value "NA".

```
cor(donor_data$TotalGiving, donor_data$AGE)
#> [1] NA
```

Let's take a further look at the TotalGiving and AGE variables using the summary function.

```
# Summary of TotalGiving
summary(donor_data$TotalGiving)
#>     Min.  1st Qu.   Median    Mean  3rd Qu.
#>        0        0       25    2364      144
#>     Max.
#> 12221854


# Summary of AGE
```

154 EXPLORATORY DATA ANALYSIS

```
summary(donor_data$AGE)
#>    Min. 1st Qu.  Median    Mean 3rd Qu.    Max.
#>       1      31      42      46      58     110
#>    NA's
#>   21190
```

The output of summary(donor_data$AGE) shows there are 21,190 records with missing age values.

Before we proceed with our analysis, we need to deal with these missing age values. One approach would be to exclude "NA" values, but this would severely restrict the number of records available for our analysis. Another preliminary strategy would be to contact your database administrator to see if there's other constituent age data available in another database table.

Let's suppose there is no other age data available in our database. One approach would be to impute (or estimate) constituent age by creating a new age variable using degree year as a proxy for age. For example, if a constituent graduated 20 years ago with a B.A. in 1997 and you assume he or she was 22 at the time, then we could translate degree year into an estimated age of 42 by using the following formula:

Current Year - Graduation Year + 22 (presumed age for B.A. degree completion)

If we don't have the degree year available and we want to guess the age, we could use the existing age information. Let's explore how to replace missing age values in our data set using the median age.

9.15   Missing Values (NA)

```
# Calculate average (median) age
median(donor_data$AGE)
#> [1] NA
```

The result "NA" tells us we need to add an additional parameter to tell the `median` function to skip missing values before calculating the average.

```
# Calculate average (median) age
median(donor_data$AGE, na.rm = TRUE)
#> [1] 42
```

```
# Store average age
median_age <- median(donor_data$AGE, na.rm = TRUE)
```

Now that we know the average donor is 42 years old, let's use this value to replace the missing age values using the `ifelse` function:

```
# Replace missing age with imputed (guessed) values
# using median (average) age
ifelse(is.na(donor_data$AGE), median_age, donor_data$AGE)
```

The following is a snapshot that shows the first 10 records of the original data set and the insertion of the imputed (guessed) age for missing values (NA).

```
head(donor_data$AGE, n = 10)
#>  [1] NA 33 NA 31 68 57 NA NA NA NA
head(ifelse(is.na(donor_data$AGE),
          median_age,
```

156 EXPLORATORY DATA ANALYSIS

```
            donor_data$AGE),
    n = 10)
#>   [1] 42 33 42 31 68 57 42 42 42 42
```

Let's store the imputed age values into the data set and show the summary.

```
# Store missing age values with imputed (guessed)
# values using median (average) age
donor_data$AGE <- ifelse(is.na(donor_data$AGE),
                         median_age,
                         donor_data$AGE)


# Summary of age variable with missing value
# imputation
summary(donor_data$AGE)
#>    Min. 1st Qu.  Median    Mean 3rd Qu.    Max.
#>     1.0    42.0    42.0    43.4    42.0   110.0


# Write CSV file
write_csv(donor_data, "data/DonorSampleDataCleaned2.csv")
```

9.16   Correlation Matrix Revisited

Now that we have dealt with the missing age values, let's try creating the correlation matrix again.

```
cor(donor_data$TotalGiving, donor_data$AGE)
#> [1] 0.0312
```

The correlation matrix shows there is a small (0.03) positive association between total giving and imputed age.

Now, let's use R's built-in graphical capabilities to visually examine if there are any patterns between selected variables in our donor file.

9.17   Scatter Plot Matrix

We can use the `pairs` function to create a scatter plot matrix to explore relationships between total giving and other selected variables such as age, wealth rating, and degree level.

```
# Create scatter plot matrix
pairs(~AGE + MARITAL_STATUS + DEGREE_LEVEL +
    WEALTH_RATING + CON_YEARS + TotalGiving,
    col = donor_data$MARITAL_STATUS,
    data = donor_data,
    main = "Donor Scatter Plot Matrix")
```

158 EXPLORATORY DATA ANALYSIS

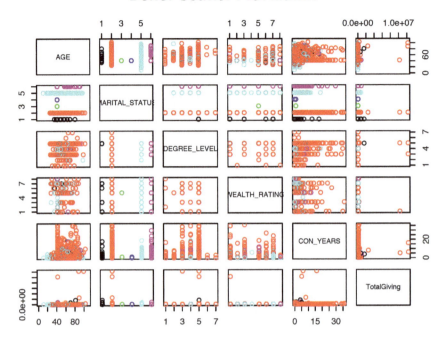

Based on the scatter plot matrix, we can observe the variation in total giving relative to variables such as age and marital status.

Let's take a look at how total giving varies by the feature (variable) of marital status.

```r
# Load caret
library(caret)

# Load donor data
donor_data <- read_csv("data/DonorSampleDataCleaned2.csv")

# Remove Donor ID, Zip, etc.
donor_data <- donor_data[-c(1:2,5:13,23)]

donor_data$MARITAL_STATUS <- as.factor(donor_data$MARITAL_STATUS)
```

```r
# Convert from character to numeric data type
convert_fac2num <- function(x){
  as.numeric(as.factor(x))
}

donor_data <- mutate_at(donor_data,
                     .vars = c(4:9),
                     .funs = convert_fac2num)

# Create feature plot
featurePlot(x=donor_data$TotalGiving,
  y=donor_data$MARITAL_STATUS,
  jitter = TRUE)

# Create feature plot
featurePlot(log(donor_data$TotalGiving),
  donor_data$MARITAL_STATUS, plot = "box",
  jitter = TRUE)
```

160 EXPLORATORY DATA ANALYSIS

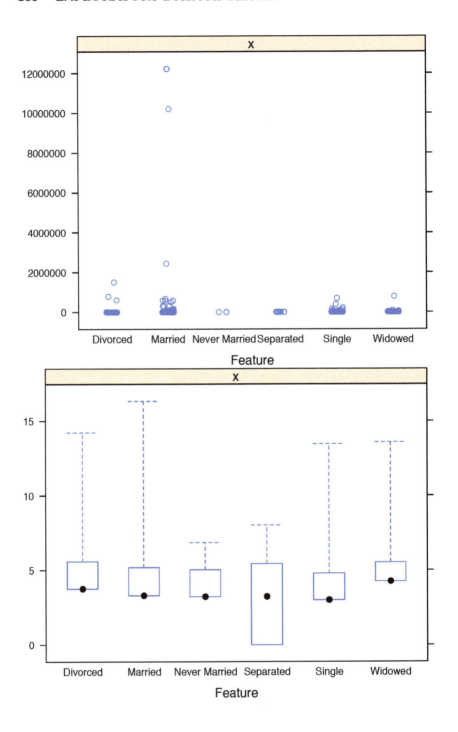

Based on the feature plot, we can visually identify that the top donors in the example data file happen to be married.

Let's explore potential relationships between age, past giving, and total giving.

```r
# Load corrplot
library(corrplot)

# Load donor data
donor_data <- read_csv("data/DonorSampleDataCleaned2.csv")

# Remove Donor ID, Zip, etc.
donor_data <- donor_data[-c(1:2,4:13,23)]

# Convert from character to numeric data type
convert_fac2num <- function(x){
  as.numeric(as.factor(x))
}

donor_data <- mutate_at(donor_data,
                        .vars = c(1:10),
                        .funs = convert_fac2num)

# Create correlation matrix
cd_cor <- cor(donor_data)

# Create correlation plot
col <- colorRampPalette(c("#BB4400", "#EE9990",
  "#FFFFFF", "#77AAEE", "#4477BB"))
corrplot(cd_cor, method="color", col=col(100),
  type="lower", addCoef.col = "black",
  tl.pos="lt", tl.col="black",
  tl.cex=0.7, tl.srt=45,
  number.cex=0.7,
```

162 EXPLORATORY DATA ANALYSIS

```
diag=FALSE)
```

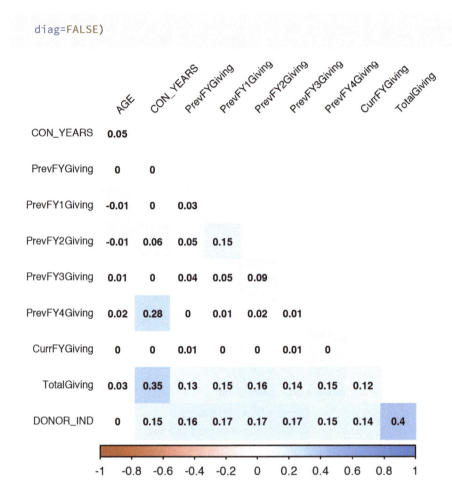

9.18 Summary

In this chapter, we introduced the broad concept of exploratory data analysis and how you can use a variety of statistical and graphical methods to identify trends, patterns, and insights. As you continue your data analytics journey using R, you will soon discover that real-world data is messy, and therefore, requires a variety of tools and techniques to effectively manage and overcome challenges, such as dealing with missing values in your data.

In the next chapter, we will dive further into data visualization, which can serve as a platform to tell stories, share knowledge, and inspire action within your organization.

164 EXPLORATORY DATA ANALYSIS

10

DATA VISUALIZATION

10.1 Creating Better Charts

Data is the most critical aspect of any project: It's with data that decisions get made. It's hard to make sense of a heap of data, and in that form, it is useless. No matter how technology shapes the data that we collect and analyze, we will make decisions based on simple, understandable data points.

Nobody, except you, cares that your predictive models have 99% accuracy, but your boss does care when you say, "Product X will lose 83% of sales in the next six months unless we increase activity A by 23%." Data visualization gives such information quickly. That's why creating effective data visualizations is a must.

With careful planning, you can provide decision-makers clear and understandable information that tells a story and also make them remember the objective.

166 DATA VISUALIZATION

Key elements include accessibility and using the right type of chart as well as not getting distracted by colors or crazy formats. It's easy to confuse pretty with useful.

Too much information is rarely useful: Strive for simplicity.

10.2 Understanding Perception

Because data visualization tools make creating charts easy, we may create charts that manipulate the understanding of the data or trends. A dramatic rise or shift in the chart will trigger a response from the reader. That is the whole point of data visualization, to either increase the understanding of the data or raise questions about it. Incorrect chart types or scales can manipulate this perception.

For example, consider the two graphs shown in Figure 10.1 from a study on graph interpretation (Zacks & Tversky 1999). Some participants in the study saw data represented as a bar graph and others saw the data as a trend-line graph. In both charts, two variables were compared: Age and height.

The age variable was broken in two groups, shown on the X axis, and the average height was shown on the Y axis.

The participants were asked to record their observations. By studying these observations, the researchers concluded that the chart type influenced readers' understanding of the data.

Some observations of the bar chart observations were:

- Males' height is higher than that of females'
- The average male is taller than the average female
- Twelve-year-olds are taller than ten-year-olds

Some observations of the trend assessments are listed below.

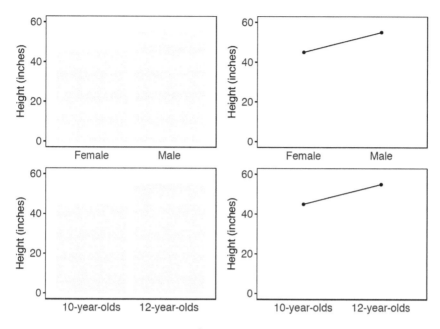

Figure 10.1: Bar and line graphs testing (Zacks and Tversky 1999)

- The graph shows a positive correlation between a child's increases in age and height between the ages of 10 and 12
- Height increases with age (from about 46 inches at 10 to 55 inches at 12)
- The more male a person is, the taller he/she is

Read the last one again: The more male a person is, the taller he/she is.

What difference do you notice between the two assessments?

The trend-line is unsuitable for numeric values on the X axis, while bar graphs make sense for these types of data. And, because the trend-line chart type is unsuitable for this data, it leads to wrong and hilarious conclusions.

168   DATA VISUALIZATION

In a similar study, researchers gave participants various frames with data on the risk of gum disease using the current toothpaste and an improved formula (Chua et al. 2006).

The participants saw two frames: A graphical one and a numeric one, as shown in Figure 10.2.

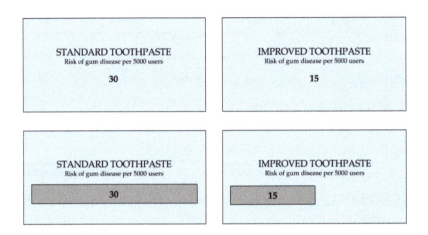

Figure 10.2: Bar and line graphs testing (Chua, Yates, and Shah 2006)

The participants were then asked to enter the price they were willing to pay for the improved toothpaste.

Some were shown the graphical frame and some were shown the numerical frame.

Can you guess in which frame the participants were willing to pay a higher price?

The participants were willing to pay significantly more for the safer product when the chances of harm were displayed graphically than when they were displayed numerically.

That's a big conclusion, and worth repeating: **People were willing to pay more when the chances of risk were shown graphically instead of numerically.**

People's tolerance for assessing and avoiding risk is heavily influenced by whether they're seeing information graphically or numerically. Seeing data presented in graphical format can make people less likely to take risks (Chua et al. 2006).

Another very popular example, Anscombe's quartet[1], is perhaps the one that gave birth to the idea of modern statistical data visualization.

Anscombe's quartet is made up of four data sets that have nearly identical mean, variance, and linear regression equations, yet they appear very different when graphed. Each data set consists of eleven (x, y) points. The statistician Anscombe constructed these sets in 1973 to show both the importance of graphing data before analyzing it and the effect of outliers on statistical properties. See the box plots shown in the Figure 10.3. Although the median values for both the variables look similar, you can notice the outliers.

When you plot the variables as a scatter plot, as shown in Figure 10.4, you can clearly see that the correlation between the two variables is very different, but the linear regression equation lines are exactly the same.

Matejka & Fitzmaurice (2017) extended the Anscombe principle further and created a dataset with similar statistical properties, but very different looking shapes. Figure 10.5 shows three of those shapes and Table 10.1 shows the statistical properties.

This should settle the "why data visualization is important" question. Let's see what makes data visualization effective.

---

[1]https://en.wikipedia.org/wiki/Anscombe%27s_quartet

170 DATA VISUALIZATION

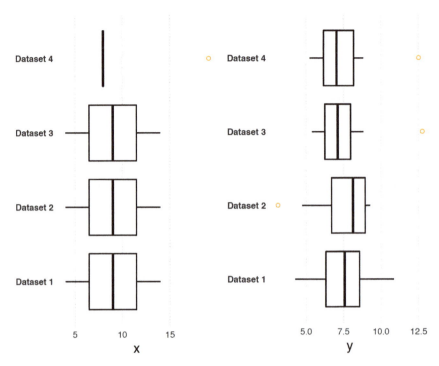

Figure 10.3: Anscombe's quartet: four different data sets with similar statistical distributions

Table 10.1: Same statistical properties datasets but different shapes (Matejka et al. 2017)

dataset	meanx	meany	sdx	sdy	cor
bullseye	54.3	47.8	16.8	26.9	-0.069
dino	54.3	47.8	16.8	26.9	-0.064
star	54.3	47.8	16.8	26.9	-0.063

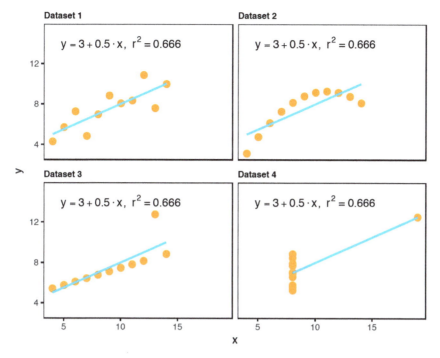

Figure 10.4: Anscombe's quartet: four different data sets with similar statistical properties

10.3 Process

We can understand charts by measuring the distance of a shape from the origin.

Think of the number line.

We know that the number five is five "units" away from zero.

Now, think of a bar chart: It is a rectangle that shows the distance in units between its origin and the observation.

You can replace the rectangle with a line or a dot and you will get the exact same information, but the speed of grasping the information might be different.

172   DATA VISUALIZATION

Figure 10.5: Same statistical properties datasets but different shapes (Matejka et al. 2017)

Often, we want to compare multiple "distances"—but there's perhaps no best way to show these distances.

Statisticians and scientists, therefore, devised various ways to show this comparison.

If there are various ways to show the same information, what makes a visualization effective?

It is simple: A visualization is effective when it helps the viewer speed up his or her understanding of the presented information.

 A visualization is effective when it helps the viewer speed up his or her understanding of the presented information.

Many times, analysts get stuck in thinking about the "how" of data visualization. They may see a cool chart and immediately they ask, "How do I create such a chart?" This distracts them from thinking whether this chart shows the patterns or insights they want to share.

PROCESS **173**

Worse, it can distract them from considering whether this chart is actually needed.

Noah Iliinsky[2], a data visualization expert and author of Beautiful Visualization[3] (Steele & Iliinsky 2010), says this about the process:

1. What do I care about?
2. What actions do I need to inform?
3. What questions need answering?
4. What data matters?
5. What graph do I use?

10.3.1   Chart Junk

When a chart is not thought out carefully, we create "chart junk."

Ask yourself: Do you add unnecessary parts to a machine? Then why add unnecessary pieces to a graphic?

Sometimes graphics take up a lot of space but give very little information.

For example, check out the graphic on this page[4]. It shows the top 10 and bottom 10 states according to the expenditure. It shows this information by including a flagpole of each state, and the height of the flagpole represents the dollar amount. Imagine how much time a designer spent placing all those flags, captions, and more. This information can easily be shown by a simple dot chart as seen in Figure 10.6.

Sure, infographics can be cute, but as Edward Tufte encouraged, we need to maximize the information-to-pixel ratio (Tufte 2001).

---

[2]http://complexdiagrams.com
[3]http://amzn.to/2rtTa8J
[4]http://aol.it/2hHX8tT

174   DATA VISUALIZATION

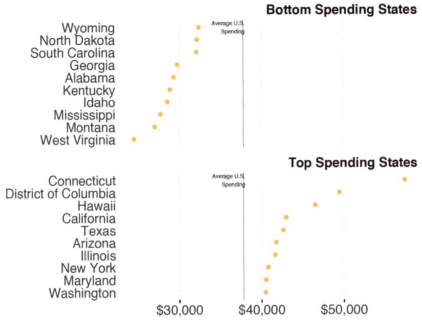

Figure 10.6: Redesigned chart on state spending

Tufte also said, "Show data variation, not design variation." Similarly, when performing data visualization work, our objective is not to show our craftsmanship but, as Noah Iliinsky[5] said, "to inform or persuade."

10.3.2 Critical Thinking

Critical thinking is essential when creating visualizations or conducting analysis based upon them. When coming up with ideas, delay your judgment. There's a neat trick from design thinking that applies well here: diverge and converge.

---

[5]www.complexdiagrams.com

The approach is this: First, come up with as many ideas as possible (diverge), then select a few that make the most sense (converge).

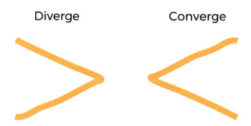

Figure 10.7: Idea-generation framework

My process for creating new graphs or reports starts with a blank piece of paper. I draw approximate versions of visualizations I would like to see based on my data.

At times I get excited about illustrating some trends that would show gaps, but when I create the visualization using real-world data, I realize that the data doesn't support such trends. I grab some more paper and start again.

As you evaluate ideas, decide and remember the objective of your graphic: To inform or to persuade, like Noah Iliinsky suggests.

Does the audience care? Is the information required?

Instead of applying the prettiest graph in your toolbox, remember: you must use the most effective graph for your data. Don't lose sight of the objective of the graphic (inform or persuade).

And as important it is to maximize the information-to-pixel ratio, you should pay special attention to **maximizing the information-to-time ratio** and lead the reader to actionable insights.

In analysis and in data visualization, the process is more important than the result. Progress without process leads to collapse. Remember to kick-off with why and begin with "so what."

176 DATA VISUALIZATION

You will improve your visualizations by asking yourself the following questions:

- What do you want to show?
- Why is it important?
- What does your audience know?
- What's the best way to represent that information?
- Are you hoping to inform or persuade?
- What type of data do you need?

10.4 Improving Effectiveness of Visuals

You can make your charts more effective using four C's: Clarity, context, concision, and compression.

- **Clarity** lets the readers understand the charts quicker. When you remove all distractions, you achieve clarity.
- **Context** lets the readers compare. When you add key information using reference lines or legends, you provide context to the single graph.
- **Concision** keeps the readers focused. When you show something using as few pixels as possible, you don't lose the reader's attention.
- **Compression** makes the visualizations smaller but not smaller than they need to be. When you achieve all the three C's above and can still make the graphs smaller, you make the graphs accessible.

10.4.1 Design Principles

Golombisky & Hagen (2016), in their book **White Space is Not Your Enemy**, describe four main graphic design principles. Every aspiring data analyst should become familiar with these principles. They are easy to understand and will improve your charts dramatically. They are easy to remember also as the acronym is actually the opposite of the results they achieve: CRAP.

- **C**: Contrast
- **R**: Repetition
- **A**: Alignment
- **P**: Proximity

Here's a short summary of these principles. Read their book for more information.

Contrast lets us see and compare. Good contrast between the foreground and the background makes the foreground stand out and/or readable. White and black forms the best contrast, but reading a white text on a black background causes eye strain. I prefer black or light foreground objects on a white background. Try these tools to find colors with good contrast: https://webaim.org/resources/contrastchecker/ and https://app.contrast-finder.org.

Repetition trains the reader to quickly get used to the design and find things easily.

Alignment creates order in your graphic. As you see particular objects aligned with each other, you assume some relationship.

Proximity of the objects, like the other principles, lets your mind know to expect some sort of relationship between those objects and provides a structure.

10.4.2   Clarity

To help readers draw appropriate conclusions from your charts, you must provide clarity. If you are very careful with the process, chances are you are creating something useful.

178 DATA VISUALIZATION

Noah Iliinsky said, "Data visualizations are not art, they're advertisements."

A good example of clarity is the Wall Street Journal graphic[6] on the story of Chick-fil-A and its opposition to gay marriage. This graphic works because it is neutral and removes anything that could distract the reader, including excessive grid lines, labels, background colors, and axis tick-marks.[7]

It focuses on the message.

In the graph, the size of the circle denotes the number of restaurants. The circles are color coded for regions. You can further explore the regions and the general opinions on gay marriage in that area, as shown in very simple pie charts.

10.4.3 Format

As you think of clarity, choose the right format for your data, and encode your data accurately.

An infamous example is an old Fox News pie chart. All the parts of a pie chart should add up to 100%, but instead, this one showed what percentage of the population supported each candidate. The pieces of the pie added up to more than 100%.

---

[6]http://bit.ly/2FeSief
[7]Follow this tutorial to create this graphic in R: http://arn.la/WSJCfA

IMPROVING EFFECTIVENESS OF VISUALS 179

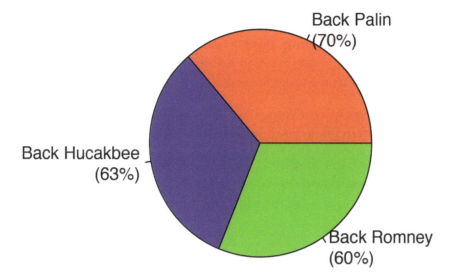

The appropriate format for presenting this information is a bar chart.

The right format is directly dependent on your objective.

Some chart components work better for certain projects. For example, color is useful for showing categories of data but not so effective for illustrating relationships.

Charts where changes in size or position of an element are good for demonstrating relationships don't work so well for quantitative data.

10.4.4 Color

Although colors often make graphics come alive, it's important to avoid excessive use of color. Use color for distinguishing and not for "prettifying."

As Dona Wong, Edward Tufte's student and the Wall Street Journal's graphics editor, wrote in her book, "Admit colors into charts gracefully, as you would receive in-laws into your home." (Wong 2013)

180   DATA VISUALIZATION

If you want to use color in your charts, use a single color with different gradients. Also, important to note is to avoid light text on a dark background. This combination results in a good contrast; however, it also proves challenging to read.

Here's a quick test for your chart: Print a black-and-white copy. Can you still differentiate your data points?

Online tools like ColorBrewer[8] can be useful in developing effective color palettes. Based on data type and color scheme, users can get an idea of good choices for adding color appropriately to charts.

10.4.5   Distractions

Visual distractions like legends, 3D, shadow, too many grid lines, or a busy background can interfere with a viewer's ability to accurately view and assess information in graphical form.

While it is important to highlight key trends or areas, it's vital to make the information on the chart very accessible to the reader. One caveat—legends may sometimes be necessary and, in those cases, be sure to place them right next to the data item. If that's not possible, place them below the chart.

10.4.6   Accessibility

It is our duty to make visuals easy to read and understand.

Two quick ways to do so are:

1. Don't make your reader guess or calculate.
2. Don't cause neck pain: turn the axis labels.

---

[8]www.ColorBrewer2.org

When planning your data visualization, it helps the reader when you provide labels when needed, remove background, add captions explaining key items about the graphic, and highlight key trends or areas.

A good example of creating accessible data visualizations is from *Time* magazine. The magazine published a story on why medical bills are killing us. Although healthcare costs are hard to understand, they made all the numbers very accessible[9]. Here's how they did it:

- They provided context with their graphs.
- They added descriptions and captions explaining key things about the graph.
- They added reference lines to help the reader understand the graph.

10.4.7 Incorrect Encoding

When the *Washington Post* blog posted a chart using circles of different sizes to compare WhatsApp's acquisition by Facebook for $19 billion, it included the acquisition costs for Snapchat ($3 billion) and Instagram ($1 billion). All the radii of the circles were proportionate to the acquisition value. Then somebody commented on Twitter that the proportion should be by area and not by radii.

I confess that when I looked at this the first time I thought the proportions, whether by radius or by area, should still be the same. But when you actually calculate the ratio by radius, $19 billion is 39% bigger than $1 billion, and when you look by area, $19 billion is 5.33% bigger than $1 billion, as shown in Figure 10.8.

Tufte called this "lying with charts." You take this risk when you encode data incorrectly.

---

[9]http://ti.me/1A7IQU0

182 DATA VISUALIZATION

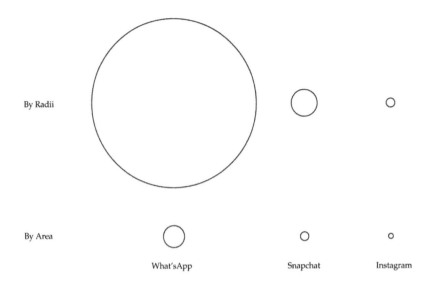

Figure 10.8: Encoding of circle sizes by radius and area

10.4.8 Aspect Ratio and Axis Values

The aspect ratio, which is the ratio of width to height, of a chart can significantly alter reader's conclusions. If the aspect ratio is large, we risk squishing the trends. And if it is small, we risk overstating the trends. Similarly, adjusting the minimum and maximum values of axes can alter the perspective of the data. For example, take a look at the different aspect ratios shown in the Figures 10.9, 10.10, and 10.11. Doesn't the rise look more dramatic with an aspect ratio of 5? With an aspect ratio of 0.4, the growth doesn't look as dramatic. Similarly, when you start the Y axis at zero as in Figure 10.12, the growth doesn't look as dramatic compared to Figure 10.13.

IMPROVING EFFECTIVENESS OF VISUALS   183

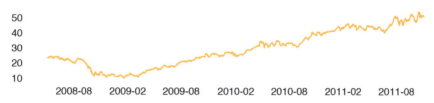

Figure 10.9: Apple performance with an aspect ratio of 5

Figure 10.10: Apple performance with an aspect ratio of 1

Figure 10.11: Apple performance with an aspect ratio of 0.4

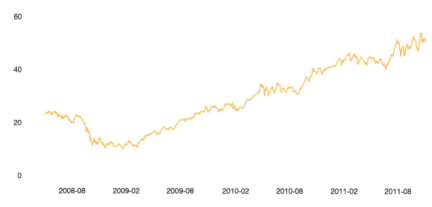

Figure 10.12: Apple performance with the Y axis starting at 0

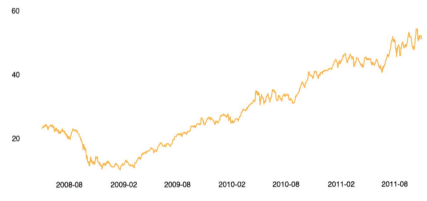

Figure 10.13: Apple performance with the Y axis starting at 10

10.4.9 Context

After creating your graph, you should provide context. Compare items or provide information. Use labels or other descriptive tools to offer viewers some framework for understanding what you're trying to tell them.

10.5 Choosing the Right Chart Types

Now that we've seen some principles of effective data visualizations, let's look at various chart types to visualize our data.

10.5.1 Tables

People are very familiar with tables where data is presented in rows and columns. Headers along the top or side provide context. Tables can accommodate both small and large data sets.

- **Pros**: Tables report information with precision and clarity. Tables can also show variables from multiple dimensions. Imagine trying to show multiple variables, such as population, income, and education levels, about U.S. states using a graph. We can achieve that, but the readers will have to spend a good amount of time understanding everything that's shown on the graph. Placing that same information in a table can make it easier for the reader to view and use the data.

- **Cons**: Although tables do show data with the greatest accuracy, people just don't get excited over tables (that is, tables don't get shared over social media). Tables also sometimes hide the magnitude of differences. Sure, we can know that $100 million is larger than $50 million, but a graph just makes that difference look "real."

186 DATA VISUALIZATION

Alternatives: If your data has only two variables, a bar chart (for discrete values), a line chart (for time series), or a scatter plot (to show relationships) are good choices. If you have multiple related variables, faceted plots, or plots by group will be effective.

10.5.2 Simple Bar Charts

A simple bar chart presents data graphically, with a series of lines standing in for a series of numbers—either horizontally or vertically. Bar charts enable quick comparison among data points.

- **Pros**: Because of their similarity to number lines, bar charts are easy to create and understand. Horizontal bar charts are typically easier to assess than vertical bar charts, a.k.a. column charts.
- **Cons**: There is a risk of misrepresentation of information when vertical bar charts don't start at zero.

Alternatives: Instead of a simple bar graph, information can be presented through a dot plot or dot chart. A dot chart will show the exact same information as a bar chart, but will take up less space. Circle plots are an option, but there is a risk of losing the main advantage of a bar graph—the ability to easily compare data elements. Depending on the size of the data set, a table may be a good choice, too.

10.5.3 Line Charts

Line charts are often used for trends and time-series data. Data is plotted along the X and Y axes. A line is drawn that connects data points from left to right.

- **Pros**: Line charts are very helpful in understanding trends or data that reflects changes over time. They are also simple by design. Line charts can accommodate multiple concurrent data sets.

- **Cons**: Overlapping data series can make it harder to study trends. Individual data points are hidden. Line charts with discrete scales can result in wrong conclusions. Labeling data points runs the risk of making the chart look very busy; the same can happen when attempting to highlight key data points through content boxes. Be mindful, however, of the aspect ratio. Instead of legends, clearly place labels over lines. Avoid too many lines. If appropriate, use panels or facets while comparing data.

Alternatives: Depending on the data set, a simple bar chart may be a usable alternative. It could be possible to plot multiple data sets as long as there's no overlap and data sets are layered carefully to avoid confusion. Also, remember our good friend, the table.

10.5.4 Pie Charts

There may be no other chart type more disputed than the pie chart. In fact, the debate over its efficacy goes back decades (Croxton & Stryker 1927), yet they remain very popular and commonplace—so commonplace that I saw the banner shown in Figure 10.14 in a hotel elevator.

You may disagree on the efficacy of a pie chart, but everyone will agree that pie charts are only for showing proportions, and the pieces of the pie should always add up to 100%.

According to Wong (2013), pie charts are often read like a clock, so in order to be most effective, the largest slice goes to the *right* of 12 o'clock, followed by the second-largest slice to the *left* of 12 o'clock, and progressing by ever-smaller slices in a counterclockwise direction.

188 DATA VISUALIZATION

Figure 10.14: Meeting = pie chart

- **Pros**: Very recognizable. Many managers actually prefer pie charts. If your data distribution is simple, you can explain the proportions very quickly.
- **Cons**: Pie charts with too many slices can be difficult to read. Also, some slices may be so thin compared to others that they're barely visible.

Alternatives: Like a pie chart, a sorted bar chart will show the proportion of each category as well as letting you compare the proportions. You can convert the raw values to percentages if you would like. This is a good alternative as you don't need to use multiple colors for each category.

CHOOSING THE RIGHT CHART TYPES **189**

A tree map is an alternative, but it faces the same challenges as a pie chart. The biggest difference is the proportions are shown with a rectangle rather than a slice of pie. Some may argue that rectangles are more effective.

A dot chart is a great alternative because the magnitude of differences is clearly visible.

And, of course, our trusted hombre, the table.

10.5.5 Stacked Bar Charts

Stacked bar charts are similar to line charts, except instead of individual lines, data points are measured by rectangles that are stacked on top of/adjacent to each other, making a longer vertical or horizontal bar.

- **Pros**: It shows the total as well as the distribution of categories in a bar, allowing us to compare the totals and individual areas. Stacked bar charts can also help the viewer determine proportions for a given element.

- **Cons**: If you have too many categories, you really can't figure out the differences. We try to overcome these problems by using different colors or placing text labels, but that actually worsens the problem. If we do need to place text labels, why should we use the graph in the first place? Worse, we can't compare one rectangle of one bar to another rectangle of a different bar. While these types of charts are helpful in seeing the proportions of each category better than a pie chart, we really don't see the difference in proportions if there are too many categories or the proportions are too small or too similar. These charts become worse when you have to compare two or more stacked bar charts. Can you really compare one category from a stacked bar to another category from another bar? Most likely, no.

190 DATA VISUALIZATION

Alternatives: Dot plots with groups are a great alternative. They achieve the same goals with greater efficacy by showing individual proportions as well as allowing us to compare with other categories.

Pie charts are also a satisfactory alternative. You can try side-by-side bar charts as groups, and that may work better than a stacked bar chart. But, you still have too many colors and labels to compare.

May I mention our cool, but shy friend, the table?

10.5.6 Scatter Plots

Scatter plots show the correlation between two variables. Typically, we use a dot as the shape for the data points. But dots can be replaced with text or other shapes for better readability and comparison.

Here's a story of scatter plots gone wrong:

In Happisburgh (pronounced "haze-bruh", a village in the English county of Norfolk), some scientists discovered fossilized hominin footprints in a newly uncovered sediment layer on a beach. These fossils were destroyed by the tide shortly afterwards.

Luckily for us, though, the scientists took 3D scans and models. They found approximately 50 footprints; 12 were largely complete and 2 showed details of the toes. The footprints of approximately 5 individuals have been identified, including adults and children. Here's the best part: They are more than 800,000 to 1 million years old, making them the oldest known hominin footprints outside Africa.

Such an amazing discovery, but in their research paper, Ashton et al. (2014) included the scatter plot shown in Figure 10.15. Now you try mapping every foot number to the picture above the plot.

CHOOSING THE RIGHT CHART TYPES 191

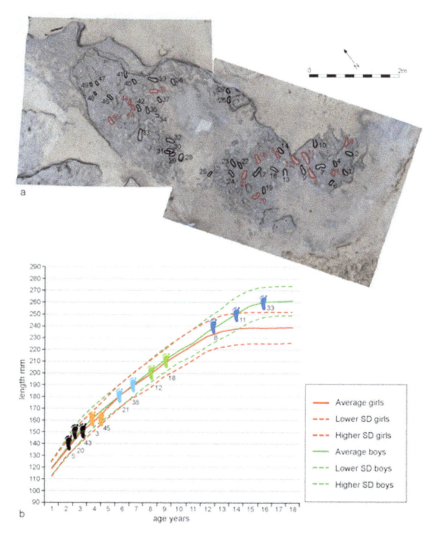

Figure 10.15: Scatter plot of age and length (Ashton et al. 2014)

192 DATA VISUALIZATION

- **Pros**: After bar plots, scatter plots are perhaps the easiest to understand. As long as the variables and scales on the axes make sense, the chart should come out A-OK. This is the best plot for understanding any relationship between two variables. With a scatter plot, we get many properties to play with: colors of the dots, sizes and shapes of the dots, and text labels.

- **Cons**: If you have too many data points, then learning about one single data point becomes harder. If you do want to show a point, then you can use the principles of contrast and direct labeling. So, you may want to make all the other data points a lighter color and the point of interest a darker color. Of course, with great power comes great responsibility. If you use too many variations, you risk losing the reader. It is best to high-light one or two plot properties with care.

Alternatives: If you are trying to show a lot of data, you risk losing the reader. It is best to create separate, multiple charts, whether it's multiple scatter plots or another kind of chart.

10.5.7 Maps

Data on maps is very powerful. There are a few ways to show data on a map. Individual points of interest are represented as dots or circles. They could be as granular as an address level or as big as a country level. Alternatively, data could be represented by filled maps with different colors, a.k.a. choropleth maps. These could go from a zipcode level to a country or continent level.

- **Pros**: Maps are easy to understand if created carefully. They are very useful for looking at big trends or patterns.

- **Cons**: If there are too many colors or patterns, they are hard to see. We don't gain any benefit from showing the data on a map.

Alternatives: A sorted bar graph or a dot chart is a good alternative to a map, depending on the data.

10.6 Creating Data Visualizations with `ggplot`

Wickham (2009) completely changed the way R users plotted graphs. Although base R graphics are very customizable, finding all the right options can be challenging. Wickham used the principles of grammar of graphics (Wilkinson 2006) to create the `ggplot` library. Like the grammar of a language, charts can be broken into individual components. We can use these components to add or remove layers on a chart. Using a consistent way of referencing these components, you can create great-looking charts in minutes. You can create a graph using `ggplot` like this:

```
ggplot(data = <your_data>,
       aes(x = <your_x_var>,
           y = <your_y_var>,
           size = <your_size_var>,
           color = <your_color_var>)) + geom_<of_your_choice>
```

Here are the main components that you need to learn before you begin your journey to awesomeness.

10.6.1 `geom`

A geometric object or `geom` tells `ggplot` which plot we want to see. Some of the most common `geom` objects are:

194 DATA VISUALIZATION

- `geom_bar`: Adds a frequency bar graph layer by default, unless you pass an already calculated column and specify `identity = TRUE`
- `geom_line`: Adds a line graph layer.
- `geom_point`: Adds a scatter plot layer in which the X-axis variable doesn't need to be a continuous variable.
- `geom_text`: Adds a text layer, which is very useful for annotation or name plots.

See the full list of `geom` objects on the `ggplot`'s documentation site[10].

10.6.2 Aesthetics (`aes`) Mapping

The aesthetics mapping tells `ggplot` which variable to use for plotting on the axes and for choosing colors, sizes, and shapes. There are two ways to assign the variable: in the `ggplot` function or in the `geom_*` function. If you assign the aesthetics in the `ggplot` function, the code following the initial `ggplot` call will use those same mappings unless you explicitly supply other values. However, if you assign the aesthetics in the `geom_*` function, you can limit the mappings to that `geom`. Mapping the aesthetics in the `geom_*` call becomes very useful when you have multiple `geom` objects. Figures 10.16 and 10.17 show examples of mapping both ways resulting in the same graph.

```
require(ggplot2)
require(dplyr)
#We will use the mpg dataset that comes with the ggplot package
?mpg #see the documentation for this dataset
glimpse(mpg) #see the data
#> Observations: 234
#> Variables: 11
```

---

[10]http://ggplot2.tidyverse.org/reference/#section-layer-geoms

CREATING DATA VISUALIZATIONS WITH GGPLOT 195

```
#> $ manufacturer <chr> "audi", "audi", "audi", ...
#> $ model        <chr> "a4", "a4", "a4", "a4", ...
#> $ displ        <dbl> 1.8, 1.8, 2.0, 2.0, 2.8,...
#> $ year         <int> 1999, 1999, 2008, 2008, ...
#> $ cyl          <int> 4, 4, 4, 4, 6, 6, 6, 4, ...
#> $ trans        <chr> "auto(l5)", "manual(m5)"...
#> $ drv          <chr> "f", "f", "f", "f", "f",...
#> $ cty          <int> 18, 21, 20, 21, 16, 18, ...
#> $ hwy          <int> 29, 29, 31, 30, 26, 26, ...
#> $ fl           <chr> "p", "p", "p", "p", "p",...
#> $ class        <chr> "compact", "compact", "c...
ggplot(data = mpg, aes(x = cyl, y = hwy, color = manufacturer)) +
  geom_point()
```

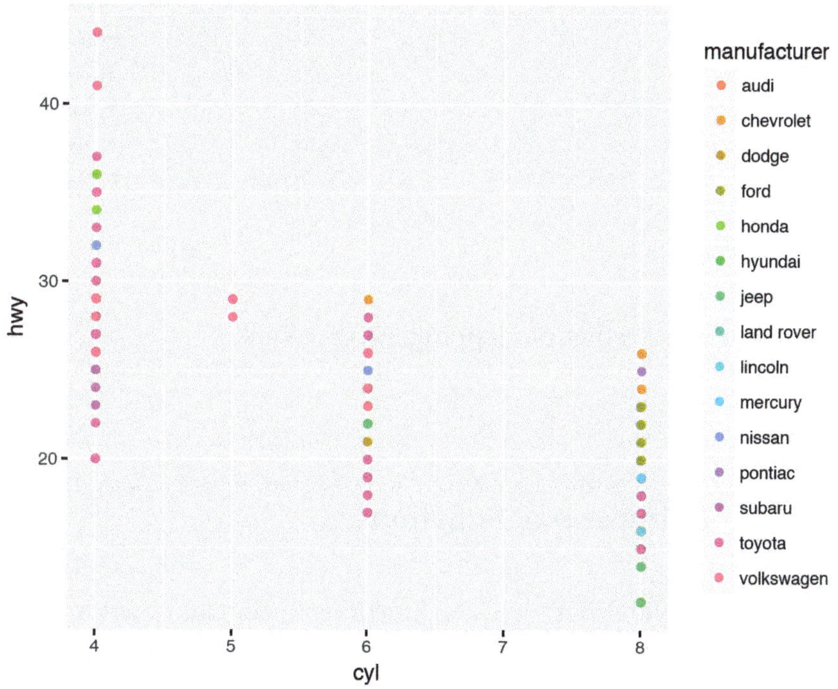

Figure 10.16: Aesthetics mapping using 'ggplot'

```
ggplot() +
  geom_point(data = mpg, aes(x = cyl, y = hwy, color = manufacturer))
```

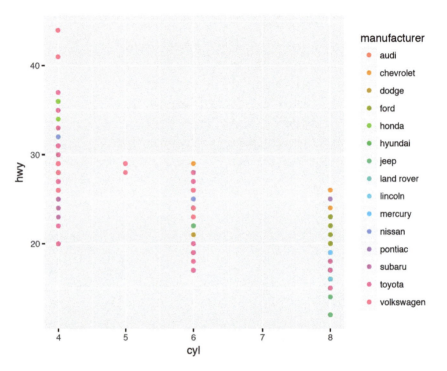

Figure 10.17: Aesthetics mapping using 'geom'

10.6.3 Using `scales` Functions

You can use the different `scale` functions to control how you want the axes and data points on the graphics to look. You can change the format of the axes to discrete, continuous, date, or other transformed axes. Similarly, you can change the look and feel of the graphed data points by changing the colors, sizes, or shapes. There are many options, which are best explored by going through the documentation[11]. The following are some common scales:

- `scale_x_continuous` or `scale_y_continuous`: This tells `ggplot` that the variable plotted on the axis is a continuous variable. We can specify the position of the gridlines, axis tic kmark labels, range of possible values of the axis, and other controls.
- `scale_color_*` or `scale_fill_*`: This tells `ggplot` how and which color schemes to use for the plotted data points. You use `scale_color_*` for coloring unfillable `geom` objects such as `geom_line` and `geom_text`. You use `scale_fill_*` for filling other fillable `geom` objects such as `geom_bar` and `geom_area`.

Figure 10.18 shows how to limit the Y-axis range, whereas Figure 10.19 shows the Y-axis gridlines by breaking the axis at every 10 units.

```
ggplot(data = mpg, aes(x = cyl, y = hwy, color = manufacturer)) +
  geom_point() + scale_y_continuous(limits = c(0, 60))
```

```
ggplot(data = mpg, aes(x = cyl, y = hwy, color = manufacturer)) +
  geom_point() +
  scale_y_continuous(limits = c(0, 60),
                     breaks = seq(from = 0, to = 60, by = 10))
```

We can also transform the axis value by supplying a transform function. `ggplot` provides convenient function wrappers for the most common transformations, such as `scale_*_log10` and `scale_*_sqrt`. Figure 10.20 shows the Y axis transformed using the square root of the Y values.

```
ggplot(data = mpg, aes(x = cyl,
                       y = hwy,
```

---

[11]http://ggplot2.tidyverse.org/reference/#section-scales

198 DATA VISUALIZATION

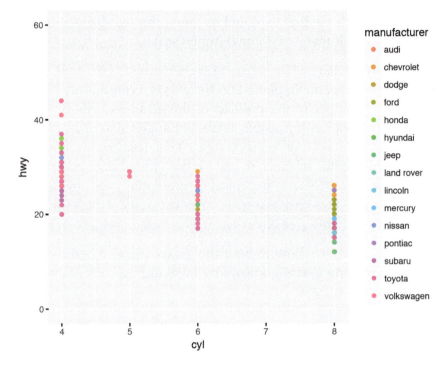

Figure 10.18: Y-axis limits changed

```
                          color = manufacturer)) +
geom_point() +
scale_y_sqrt(limits = c(0, 60),
             breaks = seq(from = 0, to = 60, by = 10))
```

10.6.4 Use `theme` to Control the Look and Feel

The `theme` option provides the user with great flexibility to control various plot elements. You can change the axis text sizes, colors, angle, justification, and more. You can change the panel and plot fill, color, and size options. You can also change the appearance of the axis lines. You use the `theme` function like this:

CREATING DATA VISUALIZATIONS WITH GGPLOT 199

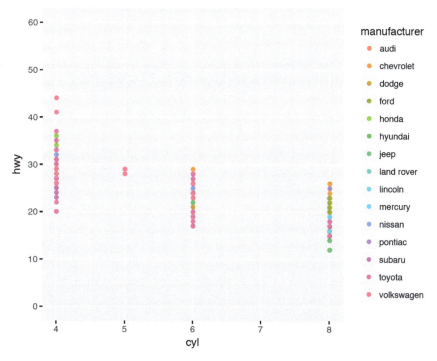

Figure 10.19: Y-axis gridlines changed

```
theme(<element_to_control> = element_*(<specify_properties>))
```

Depending on the plot element you're trying to change, use the appropriate `element_*` function. These functions are: `element_rect`, `element_line`, `element_text`, and `element_blank`. The only common element function, regardless of what you're trying to change, is `element_blank()`. This function removes the specified plot element. For example, Figure 10.21 shows the plot by removing the Y-axis label.

```
ggplot(data = mpg, aes(x = cyl, y = hwy, color = manufacturer)) +
  geom_point() +
```

200 DATA VISUALIZATION

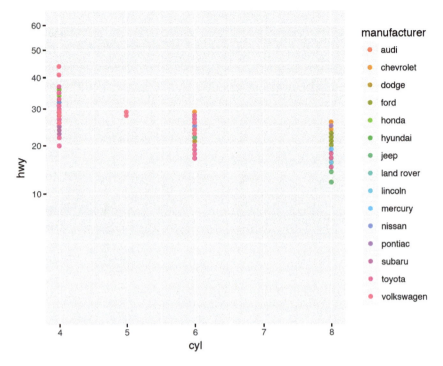

Figure 10.20: Y axis transformed with a square root

```
scale_y_continuous(limits = c(0, 60),
                   breaks = seq(from = 0, to = 60, by = 10)) +
theme(axis.title.y = element_blank())
```

Figure 10.22 shows the increased font sizes for both axis labels.

```
ggplot(data = mpg, aes(x = cyl, y = hwy, color = manufacturer)) +
  geom_point() +
  scale_y_continuous(limits = c(0, 60),
                     breaks = seq(from = 0, to = 60, by = 10)) +
  theme(axis.text = element_text(size = rel(1.2), face = "bold"))
```

CREATING DATA VISUALIZATIONS WITH GGPLOT

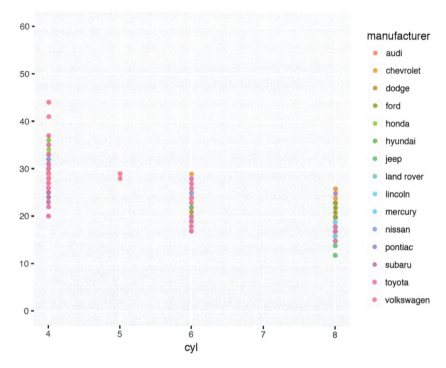

Figure 10.21: Y-axis label removed

Check out the complete list of arguments for the `theme` function on the `ggplot` site[12] or by running `?theme` in your console after loading the `ggplot2` library.

These arguments and options will become clearer when you see real examples of modifications.

---

[12] http://ggplot2.tidyverse.org/reference/theme.html

202 DATA VISUALIZATION

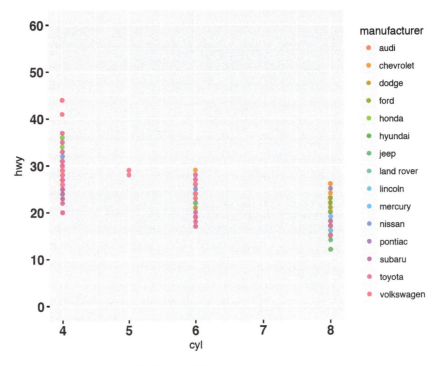

Figure 10.22: Axis labels modified

10.7 Creating Bar Charts

Creating bar charts is straightforward using ggplot. Let's say, using our sample donor data, we want to plot how many prospects we have at each of the wealth ratings. Figure 10.23 shows this count.

```
require(readr)
require(ggplot2)

donor_data <- read_csv('data/DonorSampleData.csv')
ggplot(data = donor_data, aes(x = WEALTH_RATING)) + geom_bar()
```

CREATING BAR CHARTS

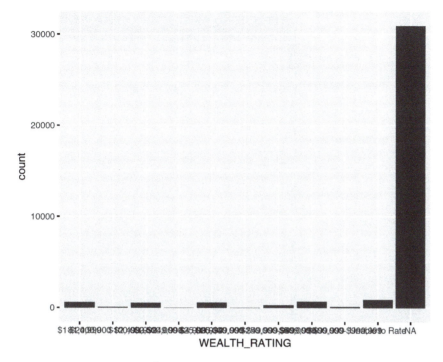

Figure 10.23: Bar graph of number of prospects by wealth ratings

Pretty easy, right? Not very pretty though. Let's change a few things:

Flip the bar: Since the X-axis labels are hard to read, let's flip the axes and make the bars horizontal.

```
ggplot(data = donor_data, aes(x = WEALTH_RATING)) +
  geom_bar() + coord_flip()
```

Change the axis tick label format: Let's add commas to the axis tick labels. For this you would need the scales library installed.

```
require(scales)
ggplot(data = donor_data, aes(x = WEALTH_RATING)) +
```

204 DATA VISUALIZATION

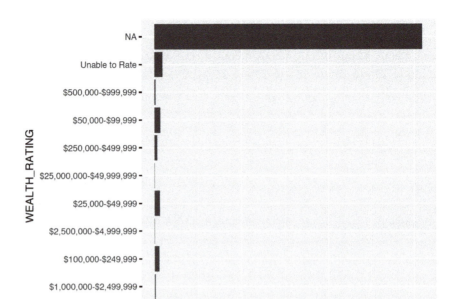

Figure 10.24: Horizontal bar graph of number of prospects by wealth ratings

```
geom_bar() + coord_flip() +
scale_y_continuous(labels = comma)
```

Although the axes are flipped, ggplot still remembers the original Y axis. If you were to use scale_x_continuous instead, you would get this error: Error: Discrete value supplied to continuous scale.

Reorder the wealth ratings: We would like to see the wealth ratings in decreasing order. For discrete variables, ggplot requires the underlying data to be in the same order as you would like to it be plotted. Let's adjust the WEALTH_RATING column by assigning ordered levels, as seen in Figure 10.26

CREATING BAR CHARTS 205

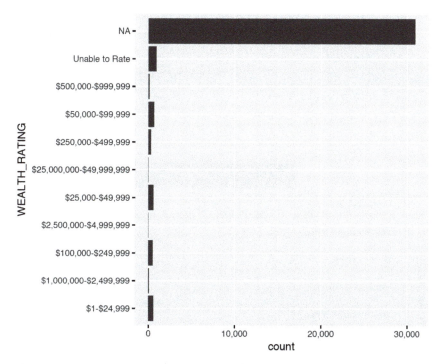

Figure 10.25: Horizontal bar graph of number of prospects by wealth ratings with commas

```
donor_data$WEALTH_RATING <- with(
  donor_data,
  factor(x = WEALTH_RATING,
         levels = c('Unable to Rate',
                    '$1-$24,999',
                    '$25,000-$49,999',
                    '$50,000-$99,999',
                    '$100,000-$249,999',
                    '$250,000-$499,999',
                    '$500,000-$999,999',
                    '$1,000,000-$2,499,999',
                    '$2,500,000-$4,999,999',
```

206 DATA VISUALIZATION

```
                '$25,000,000-$49,999,999'),
         ordered = TRUE))
ggplot(data = donor_data, aes(x = WEALTH_RATING)) +
  geom_bar() + coord_flip() +
  scale_y_continuous(labels = comma)
```

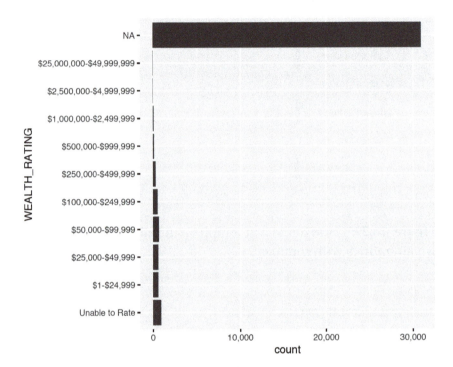

Figure 10.26: Horizontal bar graph of number of prospects by ordered wealth ratings

Remove unknown (NA) values: Since the unknown values are the most common, it is hard to see the other wealth ratings. Let's remove the unknown (NA) values from this plot. Figure 10.27 shows the bar graph with the unknown values removed from the chart.

CREATING BAR CHARTS   207

```
ggplot(data = subset(donor_data, !is.na(WEALTH_RATING)),
       aes(x = WEALTH_RATING)) +
  geom_bar() + coord_flip() +
  scale_y_continuous(labels = comma)
```

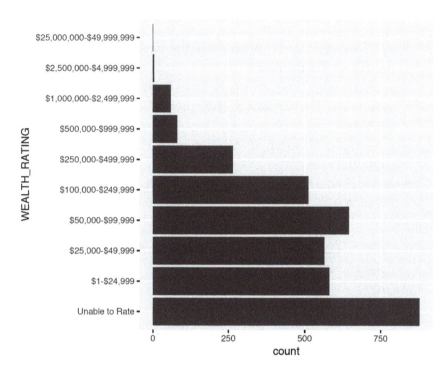

Figure 10.27: Horizontal bar graph of number of prospects with unknown values removed

Make the plot cleaner: I like to keep the non-data plot elements to a minimum. I either remove those elements or change the color to a light gray. Since we will be using this configuration for other plots too, let's define our own theme called theme_bare.

```
theme_bare <- theme(panel.background = element_blank(),
                    panel.border = element_blank(),
```

208 DATA VISUALIZATION

```
            axis.title = element_blank(),
            axis.ticks = element_blank(),
            panel.grid = element_blank())
```

Let's look at these items one by one.

- `panel.background`: This controls the background behind the panel and not the plot
- `panel.border`: This defines the lines bordering the panel
- `axis.title`: This defines the text properties of the title for both the axes
- `axis.ticks`: This defines the line properties of the tick marks along the axes
- `panel.grid`: This defines the line properties of the gridlines of the plot

```
ggplot(data = subset(donor_data, !is.na(WEALTH_RATING)),
       aes(x = WEALTH_RATING)) +
  geom_bar() + coord_flip() +
  scale_y_continuous(labels = comma) + theme_bare
```

Once I get to a clean, minimal design (Figure 10.28), I start tinkering with the plot to make it more helpful for the reader. You'll also see that the code becomes longer. You can reduce code repetition by assigning the code to a variable. Since all the additions will still return a `ggplot` object, we can add more options to the same object. Let's save the plotting commands to a variable called g.

```
g <- ggplot(data = subset(donor_data, !is.na(WEALTH_RATING)),
            aes(x = WEALTH_RATING)) +
  geom_bar() + coord_flip() +
  scale_y_continuous(labels = comma) + theme_bare
```

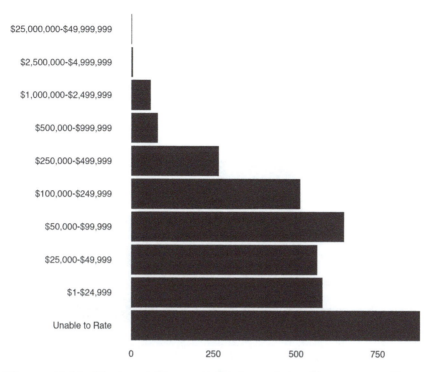

Figure 10.28: Horizontal bar graph of number of prospects. Cleaning up

Add plot titles and caption: It is always a good idea to let a chart speak for itself. Let's add a title, subtitle, and caption to the chart, as seen in Figure 10.29.

```
g <- g + labs(title = "Number of Prospects by Wealth Rating",
              subtitle = "Using the highest available ratings",
              caption = paste0("Data as of ", Sys.Date()))

g <- g + theme(plot.title = element_text(hjust = 1),
               plot.subtitle = element_text(hjust = 1),
               plot.caption = element_text(colour = "grey60"))
print(g)
```

210   DATA VISUALIZATION

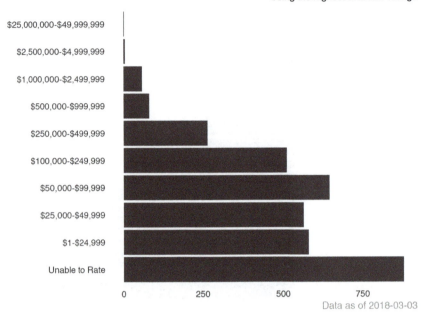

Figure 10.29: Horizontal bar graph of number of prospects with added titles

Add light gridlines: Since we removed all the gridlines, we can add light-colored gridlines over the graph, as recommended by Few (2006). We will use geom_hline for this approach, as shown in Figure 10.30.

```
g <- g + geom_hline(yintercept = c(250, 500, 750),
                    color = "grey96",
                    size = rel(0.2))
print(g)
```

Make the axis labels bigger: We can use the theme function and supply values to the axis.text argument to change the formatting of the axis labels, as seen in Figure 10.31.

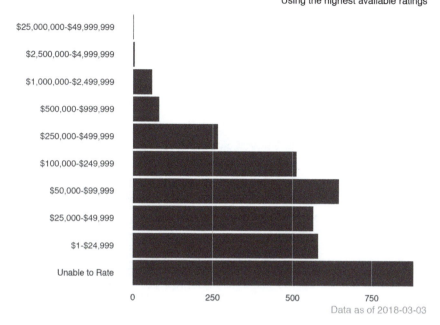

Figure 10.30: Horizontal bar graph of number of prospects with vertical gridlines

```
g + theme(axis.text = element_text(size = rel(0.9),
                                   face = "bold"))
```

To save all your changes, ggplot provides a convenient wrapper function called ggsave. You can save a plot in various formats, including the popular ones: PNG, JPEG, and PDF. Run ?ggsave in your console to see more details about the function.

212 DATA VISUALIZATION

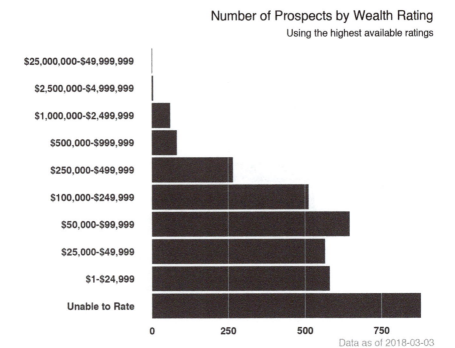

Figure 10.31: Horizontal bar graph of number of prospects with axis labels reformatted

10.8 Creating Dot Charts

Dot charts are similar to bar charts, but show information with a point or dot rather than a bar. You saw an example of this chart earlier in Figure 10.6. Cleveland & Cleveland (1985) advocated this chart as a superior alternative to circles/shapes or stacked bar graphs. The dotchart function in base R has an advantage over ggplot as it lets you group and color variables to create a nice compact chart. In ggplot, it becomes a little busy. Let's see this with an example. Let's recreate the wealth rating prospect count graph from Figure 10.31 using ggplot first. Figure 10.32 shows the dot plot created using ggplot.

CREATING DOT CHARTS   213

```r
require(dplyr)
wealth_rating_cnt <- filter(donor_data, !is.na(WEALTH_RATING)) %>%
  count(WEALTH_RATING)
g <- ggplot(data = wealth_rating_cnt,
            aes(x = WEALTH_RATING, y = n)) +
  geom_point() + coord_flip() +
  scale_y_continuous(labels = comma)
g <- g + theme_bare +
  theme(panel.grid.major.y = element_line(linetype = 2,
                                          size = 0.2))
g <- g + labs(title = "Number of Prospects by Wealth Rating",
              subtitle = "Using the Highest Available Ratings",
              caption = paste0("Data as of ", Sys.Date()))
g + theme(plot.title = element_text(hjust = 1),
          plot.subtitle = element_text(hjust = 1),
          plot.caption = element_text(colour = "grey60"))
```

Let's create the same plot using the built-in `dotchart` function, as shown in Figure 10.33.

```r
dotchart(x = wealth_rating_cnt$n,
         labels = wealth_rating_cnt$WEALTH_RATING,
         main = "Number of Prospects by Wealth Rating" )
```

214   DATA VISUALIZATION

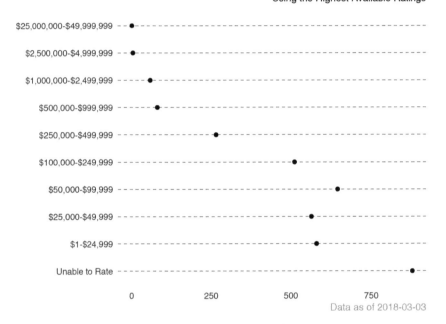

Figure 10.32: Wealth rating count. A dot chart example using 'ggplot'

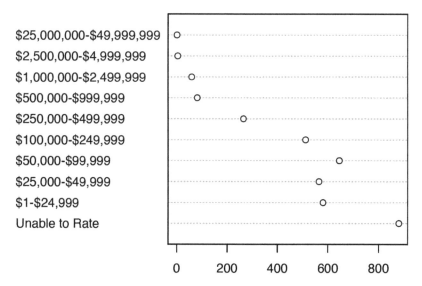

Figure 10.33: Wealth rating count. A dot chart example using 'dotchart'

216 DATA VISUALIZATION

Now, let's say that we want to see the wealth ratings by the giving status (donor/non-donor). Figure 10.34 shows the dot chart of wealth ratings for donor and non-donor population.

```r
#calculate the summary.
#using base R instead of dplyr to get the 0 values
wealth_rating_cnt <- as.data.frame(xtabs(~WEALTH_RATING +
                                            DONOR_IND,
                                          donor_data))
g <- ggplot(data = wealth_rating_cnt,
            aes(x = WEALTH_RATING, y = Freq)) +
  geom_point() + coord_flip() +
  scale_y_continuous(labels = comma) + facet_wrap(~DONOR_IND)
g <- g + theme_bare +
  theme(panel.grid.major.y = element_line(linetype = 2, size = 0.2))
g <- g + labs(
  title = "Number of Prospects by Wealth Rating and Giving Status",
  subtitle = "Using the Highest Available Ratings",
  caption = paste0("Data as of ", Sys.Date()))
g + theme(plot.title = element_text(hjust = 1),
          plot.subtitle = element_text(hjust = 1),
          plot.caption = element_text(colour = "grey60"))
```

Now let's see the simplicity and elegance of the built-in `dotchart` function, seen in Figure 10.35.

```r
donor_colors <- c("Y" = "#FF993F", "N" = "#5870C0")
dotchart(
  x = wealth_rating_cnt$Freq,
  groups = as.factor(wealth_rating_cnt$DONOR_IND),
  labels = wealth_rating_cnt$WEALTH_RATING,
  main = "Number of Prospects by Wealth Rating\nand Giving Status",
  gcolor = donor_colors,
  color = donor_colors[as.factor(wealth_rating_cnt$DONOR_IND)])
```

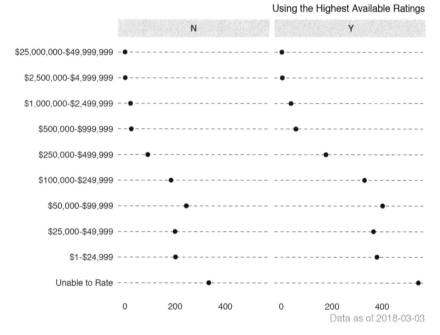

Figure 10.34: Wealth rating count. A dot chart example using 'ggplot'

218   DATA VISUALIZATION

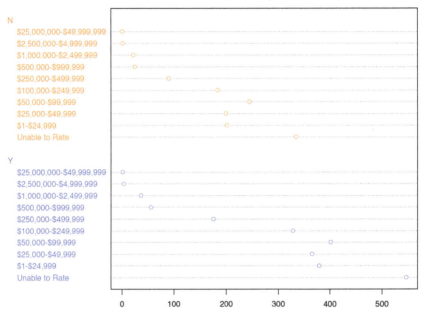

Figure 10.35: Wealth rating count. A dot chart example using the 'dotchart' function

10.9 Creating Line Charts

Line charts are best suited for time-series type of data, in which we expect to see trends and changes over time. Let's say we want to compare the stock performance of Amazon, Google, and Microsoft stocks as shown in Figure 10.36.

```r
require(quantmod)
require(dplyr)

amzn_data <- getSymbols(Symbols = "AMZN",
                        auto.assign = FALSE,
                        from = '2008-05-01',
                        to = Sys.Date())
googl_data <- getSymbols(Symbols = "GOOG",
                         auto.assign = FALSE,
                         from = '2008-05-01',
                         to = Sys.Date())
msft_data <- getSymbols(Symbols = "MSFT",
                        auto.assign = FALSE,
                        from = '2008-05-01',
                        to = Sys.Date())

combined_close <- data.frame(date = index(amzn_data),
                             amzn_data,
                             row.names = NULL) %>%
  select(date, close = AMZN.Close) %>%
  mutate(ticker = 'AMZN') %>%
  bind_rows(.,
            data.frame(date = index(googl_data),
                       googl_data,
                       row.names = NULL) %>%
              select(date, close = GOOG.Close) %>%
```

220 DATA VISUALIZATION

```r
            mutate(ticker = 'GOOG')) %>%
    bind_rows(.,
              data.frame(date = index(msft_data),
                         msft_data,
                         row.names = NULL) %>%
              select(date, close = MSFT.Close) %>%
                mutate(ticker = 'MSFT'))


g <- ggplot(data = combined_close,
            aes(x = date, y = close, color = ticker)) +
  geom_line()
g <- g + theme_bare + coord_fixed(ratio = 2) +
  theme(axis.text = element_text(face = "bold", size = rel(1)))
g <- g + labs(title = "Stock Values at Closing",
              caption = "Source: Yahoo Finance")
print(g)
```

We can make this line chart better by removing the legend and placing it directly next to the line. We can use the `annotate` function
to add the labels. Figure 10.37 shows this modification. I picked
branded colors using the https://brandcolors.net/ site.

```r
stock_colors <- c("MSFT" = "#00188F",
                  "AMZN" = "#ff9900",
                  "GOOG" = "#34a853")
g <- ggplot(data = combined_close,
            aes(x = date, y = close, color = ticker)) +
  geom_line() + scale_color_manual(values = stock_colors)
g <- g + theme_bare + coord_fixed(ratio = 2) +
  theme(axis.text = element_text(face = "bold", size = rel(1)),
        legend.position = "none")
g <- g + labs(title = "Stock Values at Closing",
              caption = "Source: Yahoo Finance")
```

CREATING LINE CHARTS   221

Figure 10.36: Comparing stock values with a line chart

```
g + annotate("text",
             x = as.Date('01/01/2014', "%m/%d/%Y"),
             y = c(80, 420, 650),
             label = c("MSFT", "AMZN", "GOOG"),
             color = stock_colors)
```

222 DATA VISUALIZATION

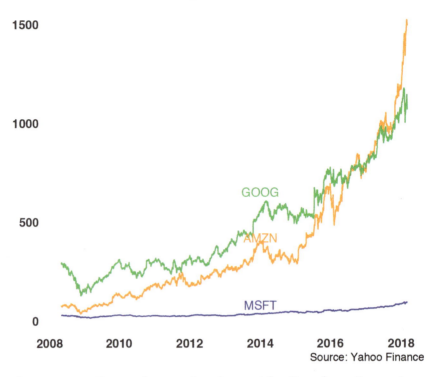

Figure 10.37: Comparing stock values with a line chart. Legends on the line.

You may have noticed two new elements, scale_color_manual and annotate, in the code.

How do they work?

- scale_color_manual: When a color variable is assigned, ggplot selects its internal color palette, which is not the most visually appealing. We can override those colors using the scale_color_* function, which automatically creates another color palette or manually providing one. In this code, we've provided the color palette manually by creating a named

CREATING SCATTER/TEXT PLOTS   **223**

vector. `ggplot` then knows to match the variable value with the name in the vector.

- `annotate`: You can provide different `geom` values to this function, but we used `text`. We need to provide the `x` and `y` values to position the text labels. We also provided the colors for the text labels.

10.10   Creating Scatter/Text Plots

Scatter plots are typically used with two continuous variables. Let's create a graph with age on the X axis and total giving on the Y axis, as shown in Figure 10.38.

```
library(dplyr)
library(stringr)
donor_data <- mutate(donor_data,
                  TotalGiving = as.double(
                     str_replace_all(TotalGiving, '[$,]', '')))

g <- ggplot(data = donor_data,
            aes(x = AGE, y = TotalGiving)) +
  geom_point()
g <- g + theme(axis.text = element_text(size = rel(1.2)),
               axis.title = element_text(size = rel(1.2),
                                         face = "bold"),
               axis.title.y = element_text(angle = 0,
                                           vjust = 0.5),
               panel.background = element_blank(),
               axis.ticks = element_blank())
g <- g + labs(x = "Age", y = "Total\nGiving")
print(g)
#> Warning: Removed 21190 rows containing missing values
```

```
#> (geom_point).
```

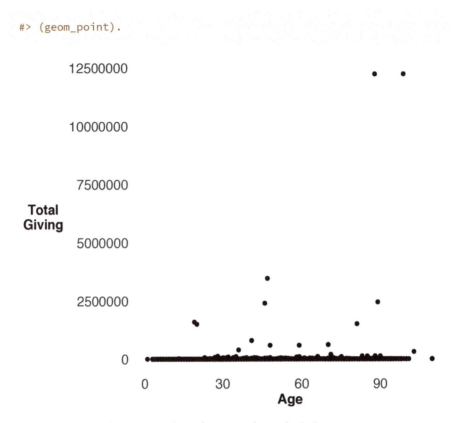

Figure 10.38: A scatter plot of age and total giving

We can make the graph in Figure 10.38 a little better by formatting the Y axis to currency, changing its scale to see more data, and adding transparency to the data points.

Format Y axis to currency: Since the data on the Y axis shows the dollar amounts, it makes sense to change the axis labels to currency format. We need to use the scales library to do so. See Figure 10.39 for the changed format.

```
require(scales)
g <- g + scale_y_continuous(labels = dollar)
```

```
print(g)
#> Warning: Removed 21190 rows containing missing values
#> (geom_point).
```

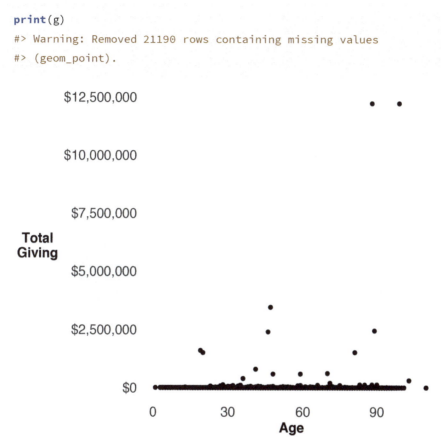

Figure 10.39: A scatter plot of age and total giving with currency format

Transform Y axis: Since most of the entities in this sample data file have given zero dollars, all the data points are crowded at the bottom of the X axis. We can't see any pattern between age and total giving. Let's try to two different transformations: square root and log. Figures 10.40a and 10.40b show both of these transformations.

```
g + scale_y_sqrt(labels = dollar)
#> Warning: Removed 21190 rows containing missing values
```

226   DATA VISUALIZATION

```
#> (geom_point).
g + scale_y_log10(labels = dollar)
#> Warning: Transformation introduced infinite values in continuous y-axis

#> Warning: Removed 21190 rows containing missing values
#> (geom_point).
```

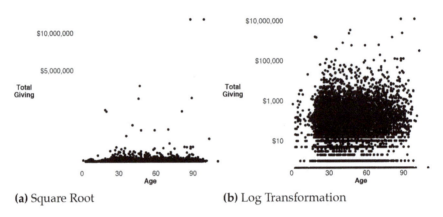

(a) Square Root **(b)** Log Transformation

Figure 10.40: Scatter plot of age and total giving

Although the log transformation makes more data visible, it hides all the non-donors. This is because `log(0)` returns `-Inf`, and you can't plot infinity!

Add transparency: Since there is an overlap of data, we can add transparency to add visibility to the hidden data points, as seen in Figure 10.41.

```
g <- ggplot(data = donor_data, aes(x = AGE, y = TotalGiving)) +
  geom_point(alpha = 0.5, size = 4)
g <- g + theme(axis.text = element_text(size = rel(1.2)),
               axis.title = element_text(size = rel(1.2),
                                         face = "bold"),
```

```
                 axis.title.y = element_text(angle = 0,
                                             vjust = 0.5),
                 panel.background = element_blank(),
                 axis.ticks = element_blank())
g <- g + scale_y_log10(labels = dollar) +
  labs(x = "Age", y = "Total\nGiving")
print(g)
#> Warning: Transformation introduced infinite values
#> in continuous y-axis
#> Warning: Removed 21190 rows containing missing values
#> (geom_point).
```

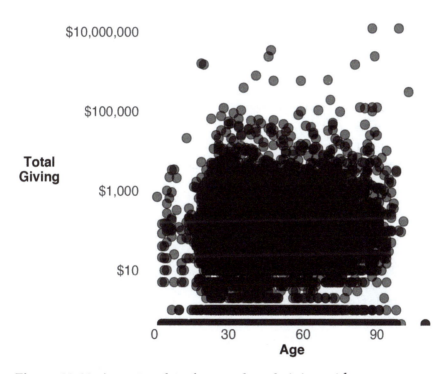

Figure 10.41: A scatter plot of age and total giving with transparency

10.10.1   Text Plots

When we replace the points of scatter plots with text, we create text plots. These are useful when you want to see the labels associated with individual data points. Of course, they work best when you have a limited number of data points on the plot. Let's say that we want to see all the names of all the people who have a wealth rating of $1,000,000–$2,499,999, along with their likelihood of making a major gift. Since we don't have the likelihood stored as a data point, we will create some random probabilities. Also, since we don't have any names stored in the sample data set, we will create some fake names using the randomNames library! You can see the results in Figure 10.42.

```r
require(randomNames)
require(dplyr)
require(ggplot2)
require(scales)

donor_data_ss <- filter(
  donor_data,
  WEALTH_RATING == '$1,000,000-$2,499,999') %>%
  mutate(major_giving_likelihood = runif(nrow(.)),
         prospect_name = randomNames(
           nrow(.),
           name.order = 'first.last',
           name.sep = " ",
           sample.with.replacement = FALSE))

g <- ggplot(data = donor_data_ss,
            aes(x = ID,
                y = major_giving_likelihood,
                label = prospect_name)) +
  geom_text()
g <- g + theme_bare +
```

```r
  theme(axis.text.x = element_blank(),
        axis.text.y = element_text(size = rel(1.3),
                                   face = "bold"),
        axis.line.y = element_line(size = 0.5,
                                   arrow = arrow())))
g <- g + scale_y_continuous(labels = percent) +
  ggtitle(
    label = "Major Giving Likelihood of Rated Prospects",
    subtitle = "Wealth rating between $1,000,000 and $2,499,999")
print(g)
```

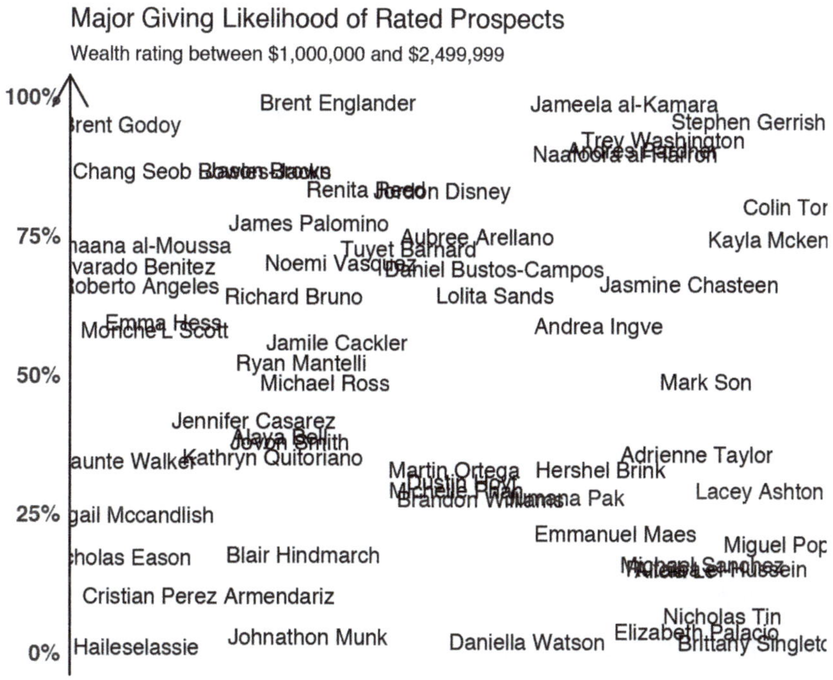

Figure 10.42: Fictional name plot

Since there are some overlapping names, we can remove them by adding the optional argument of `check_overlap = TRUE` to `geom_text`. We can also add color with a gradient, making it so the names with

230 DATA VISUALIZATION

darker colors have a higher likelihood of giving a major gift, and those with lighter colors have a lower likelihood. You can see the results of using the `scale_color_gradient` function in Figure 10.43. I selected the colors from the site https://uigradients.com. You can find a better selection of colors for graphs at Cynthia Brewer's color brewer[13].

```r
g <- ggplot(data = donor_data_ss,
            aes(x = ID, y = major_giving_likelihood,
                label = prospect_name,
                color = major_giving_likelihood)) +
  geom_text(check_overlap = TRUE)
g <- g + theme_bare +
  theme(axis.text.x = element_blank(),
        axis.text.y = element_text(size = rel(1.3),
                                   face = "bold"),
        axis.line.y = element_line(size = 0.5,
                                   arrow = arrow())))
g <- g + scale_y_continuous(labels = percent) +
  ggtitle(
    label = "Major Giving Likelihood of Rated Prospects",
    subtitle = "Wealth rating between $1,000,000 and $2,499,999")
g + scale_color_gradient(low = "#fffbd5",
                         high = "#b20a2c",
                         guide = "none")
```

10.10.1.1   Another Example of a Text Plot

Sometimes you have to view data differently to see and notice patterns. My employer, the University of Southern California (USC), has had a high undergraduate participation rate (~40%) for the past

---

[13]http://colorbrewer2.org/

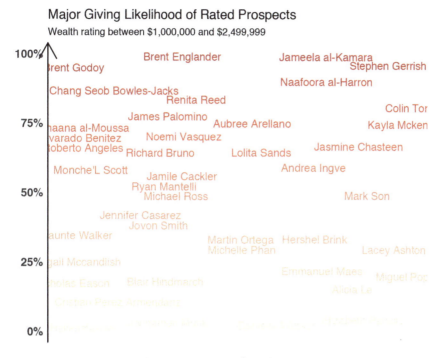

Figure 10.43: Fictional name plot with colors

three years. You could show this rate by comparing various institutions by line graphs or bubble graphs. But as we found out while developing these charts at USC, when you show the participation rates by institution and its solicitable alumni base, you can clearly see how remarkable USC's participation rate is. Can you see it in Figure 10.44?

```
library(readr)
library(dplyr)
library(ggplot2)
library(scales)
library(ggrepel)
alumni_participation <- read_csv(
    file = "data/AlumniParticipationFY11_FY15.csv")
```

232 DATA VISUALIZATION

```r
alumni_participation_fy15 <- filter(alumni_participation,
                                    FY == 2015) %>%
  mutate(ugalumnibrks = cut(
    noofugalumni,
    breaks = c(1,10^4,5*10^4,10^5, 10^6),
    labels = c('<10,000','10,000-50,000',
               '50,000-100,000','100,000+'),
    include.lowest = TRUE))

label_colors <- rep("black",
                    length(alumni_participation_fy15$instshortname))
names(label_colors) <- alumni_participation_fy15$instshortname
label_colors["USC"] <- "#990000"

g <- ggplot(data = alumni_participation_fy15,
            aes(x = ugalumnibrks,
                y = ugparticpation,
                label = instshortname,
                color = instshortname)) +
  geom_text_repel(segment.size = 0,
                  force = 0.2,
                  size = 4,
                  point.padding = NA)
g <- g + scale_color_manual(values = label_colors,
                            guide = "none") +
  scale_y_continuous(labels = percent, limits = c(0, 0.7)) +
  scale_x_discrete(expand = c(0, .15))
g <- g + xlab("Number of Undergrad Solicitable Alumni")
g <- g + theme(text = element_text(family = 'sans',
                                   size = 12,
                                   face = "bold"),
               axis.line = element_blank(),
               axis.text = element_text(size = rel(1), colour = NULL),
```

```
                axis.ticks = element_blank(),
                panel.grid.major.y = element_line(color = "black",
                                                 linetype = 3),
                panel.grid.major.x = element_blank(),
                panel.background = element_rect(fill = '#f8f2e4'),
                plot.background = element_rect(fill = '#f8f2e4'),
                panel.ontop = FALSE,
                axis.title.y = element_blank(),
                plot.title = element_blank(),
                plot.margin = unit(c(1, 1, 1, 1), "lines"))
g
```

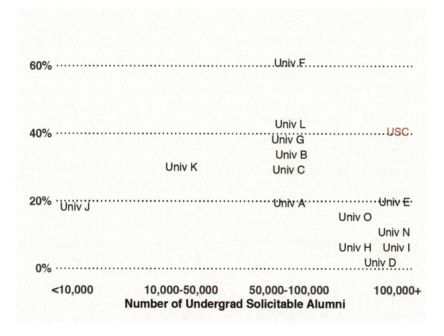

Figure 10.44: Alumni size and participation rates (FY15)

234 DATA VISUALIZATION

10.10.2 Creating Bubble Plots

When you replace the individual data points in a scatter plot with circles proportional to some measure, you create bubble plots. Hans Rosling gave the most wonderful example of a bubble plot in his video[14]. Thanks to the gapminder[15] library we can use the data set to create our own bubble plot, as seen in Figure 10.45.

```r
library(gapminder)
library(dplyr)
library(ggplot2)

plot_data <- filter(gapminder, year == '2007')
g <- ggplot(data = plot_data,
            aes(x = gdpPercap,
                y = lifeExp,
                size = pop,
                color = continent)) +
  geom_point(alpha = 0.4) + theme_bare
print(g)
```

We need to make some changes to make this chart better.

Increase the size of the circles: We can increase the size of the circles by adding the scale_size function, as seen in Figure 10.46.

```r
g <- g + scale_size(range = c(2, 15))
print(g)
```

Adjust Legends: The plot area is small because of the legends on the right. We can remove the circle size legend and place the color legend at the bottom. Jennifer Bryan, the author of this R package,

---

[14]https://www.youtube.com/watch?v=jbkSRLYSojo
[15]https://github.com/jennybc/gapminder

CREATING SCATTER/TEXT PLOTS 235

Figure 10.45: Gapminder bubble plot

even provided the continent colors to use in this plot. Let's use those colors.

```
g <- g + scale_color_manual(values = continent_colors) +
  guides(size = "none") +
  theme(legend.position = "bottom")
print(g)
```

These colors don't look pretty. I selected the following colors from gapminder's website[16]. As you can see in Figure 10.48, I also tweaked the legend size and removed the size legend and background color on the legend keys.

---

[16]http://bit.ly/2qo6rOT

236 DATA VISUALIZATION

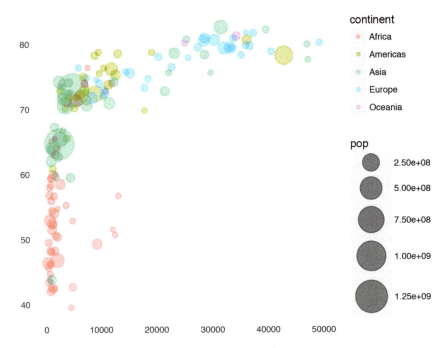

Figure 10.46: Gapminder bubble plot with increased size

```
continent_colors <- c('Africa' = '#00d5e9',
                      'Americas' = '#7feb00',
                      'Asia' = '#ff5872',
                      'Europe' = '#ffe700',
                      'Oceania' = '#ff5872')
g <- g + scale_color_manual(
  values = continent_colors,
  guide = guide_legend(title = NULL,
                       override.aes = list(size = 5))) +
  guides(size = "none") +
  theme(legend.position = "bottom",
        legend.key = element_rect(fill = "white", colour = NA))
print(g)
```

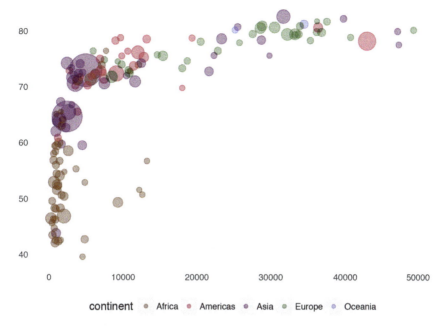

Figure 10.47: Gapminder bubble plot with colors

Increase Visibility of Data Points: Since many countries have low GDP per capita, they are all bunched up in the corner. We will add the log scale with the scale breaks as given in the gapminder chart to the Y axis. We will also add limits to the X axis and fix the aspect ratio using the `coord_fixed` function.

```
library(scales)
g <- g + scale_x_log10(breaks = 500*2^(0:8),
                       limits = c(200, 130000), label = dollar) +
  scale_y_continuous(limits = c(20, 90)) +
  coord_fixed(ratio = .02)
print(g)
```

Add essential non-plot information: Let's add axis labels as well as country labels. As you can see in Figure 10.50, the country labels

238 DATA VISUALIZATION

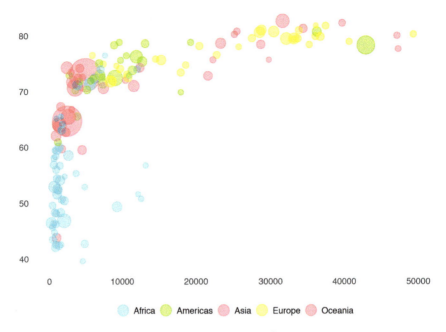

Figure 10.48: Gapminder bubble plot with better colors

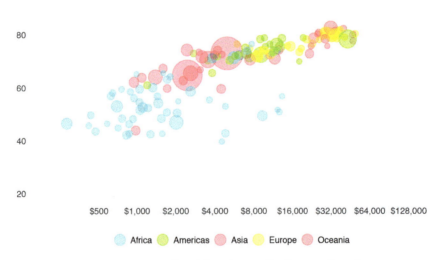

Figure 10.49: Gapminder bubble plot with changed scale

add more clutter, but are necessary for a better understanding of the data. An interactive version, like the one on the gapminder site, is a better choice.

```
g <- g + labs(x = "GDP per capita", y = "Life\nexpectancy") +
  theme(axis.title = element_text(face = "bold", hjust = 1))
g <- g + theme(axis.title.y = element_text(angle = 0),
               axis.text = element_text(face = "bold"))
g <- g + geom_text(aes(label = country),
                   size = 3,
                   check_overlap = TRUE,
                   show.legend = FALSE)
print(g)
```

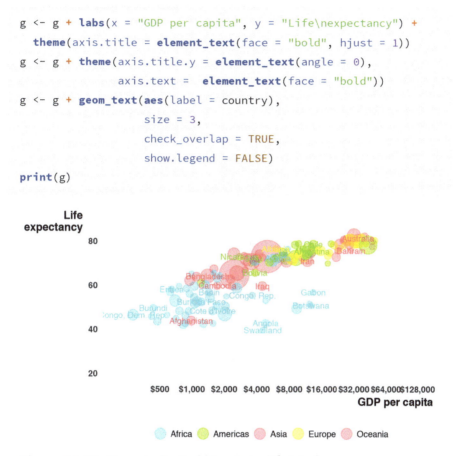

Figure 10.50: Gapminder bubble plot with labels

10.11 Creating Slopegraphs

"Slopegraphs" are line graphs with two vertical axes. These are vertical axes that don't show two different measures. Although using

240   DATA VISUALIZATION

two different measures on two y-axes is somewhat debated (Few 2008), slopegraphs let you see the change of a measure in two different time periods. For example, using the alumni participation data, let's see the changes in the participation ranking (Figure 10.51).

```r
library(readr)
library(dplyr)
library(ggthemes)
library(directlabels)

alumni_participation <- read_csv(
  file = "data/AlumniParticipationFY11_FY15.csv")

#exclude institutions with only one participation
insts_both <- count(alumni_participation, instshortname) %>%
  filter(n == 2) %>% select(instshortname)

alumni_participation_both <- filter(
  alumni_participation,
  instshortname %in% insts_both$instshortname) %>%
  group_by(FY) %>%
  mutate(partranking = row_number(-ugparticpation),
         revpartranking = row_number(ugparticpation)) %>%
  ungroup()

label_colors <- rep(
  "gray80",
  length(alumni_participation_both$instshortname))
names(label_colors) <- alumni_participation_both$instshortname
label_colors["USC"] <- "#990000"

g <- ggplot(data = alumni_participation_both,
            aes(x = FY,
                y = revpartranking,
```

CREATING SLOPEGRAPHS   241

```r
                        color = instshortname)) +
   geom_line(size = 1.2, alpha = 0.7) + geom_point()
g <- g + scale_color_manual(values = label_colors)
g <- g + scale_x_continuous(breaks = c(2011, 2015),
                            limits = c(2010.9, 2015.5)) +
   theme_wsj()
g <- g + scale_y_continuous(breaks = c(1, 10, 15))
g <- g + theme(axis.text.y = element_blank(),
               panel.grid.major.y = element_blank())
g <- g + theme(legend.position = "none",
               plot.background = element_rect(fill = "white"),
               panel.background = element_rect(fill = "white"))
g <- g + geom_dl(aes(label = instshortname, x = FY + 0.1),
                 method = "last.points",
                 cex = 1)
g <- g + geom_dl(aes(label = partranking, x = 2010.9),
                 method = "first.points",
                 cex = 1,
                 color = "grey90")
g <- g + theme(axis.ticks.x = element_line(size = 1),
               axis.ticks.length=unit(0.2,"cm"))
g <- g + ggtitle("Alumni Participation Ranking Change") +
   theme(plot.title = element_text(size = 14,
                                   face = "bold",
                                   colour = "#990000",
                                   hjust = 0,
                                   family = "Helvetica"))
g
```

242   DATA VISUALIZATION

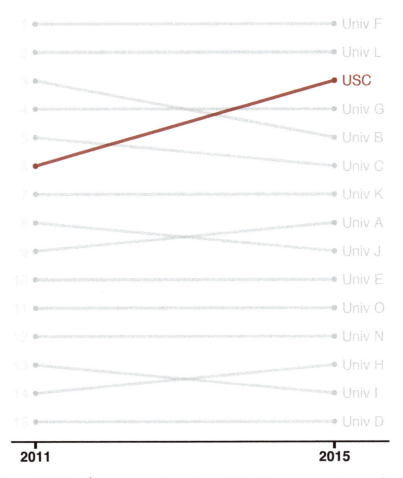

Figure 10.51: Changes in alumni participation seen using a slopegraph

10.12 Creating Heat Maps

Heat maps let us see a lot of data quickly using small rectangles and colors. Usually the color changes from light to dark as the measure shown in the plot increases. Let's say we want to see the visit activity of a fundraiser for the past three years by month. Since we don't have this data, we will create a data set. You can see the resulting heat map in Figure 10.52.

```r
library(ggplot2)
library(dplyr)
contact_activity <- data.frame(
  month = rep(1:12, 3),
  month_abb = rep(month.abb, 3),
  year = c(rep(2015, 12),
           rep(2016, 12),
           rep(2017, 12)),
  contacts = round(abs(sin(x = 1:36))*10),
  stringsAsFactors = FALSE)

contact_activity <- mutate(contact_activity,
                           date = as.Date(paste(month,
                                                1,
                                                year,
                                                sep = "/"),
                                          "%m/%d/%Y"),
                           month_abb = factor(month_abb,
                                              levels = month.abb))

min_max_activity <- bind_rows(top_n(contact_activity,
                                    n = 1,
                                    wt = contacts),
                              top_n(contact_activity,
```

244 DATA VISUALIZATION

```
                                   n = 1,
                                   wt = -contacts))

g <- ggplot(data = contact_activity,
            aes(x = month_abb, y = year, fill = contacts)) +
  geom_tile(color = "white")
g <- g + scale_fill_gradient(low = "white", high = "orange") +
  scale_y_continuous(expand = c(0, 0), breaks = 2015:2017)
g <- g + theme(axis.ticks = element_blank(),
          panel.background = element_rect(fill = "white"),
          axis.title = element_blank(),
          legend.position = "none",
          axis.text = element_text(size = rel(1.2)))
print(g)
```

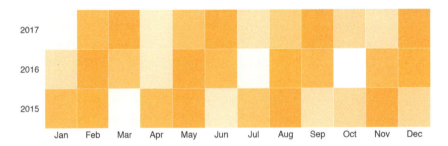

Figure 10.52: Contact activity heat map

If we want to show the lowest and highest contact values, we can easily show them by adding geom_text, as seen in Figure 10.53.

```
g <- g + geom_text(data = min_max_activity,
                   aes(x = month_abb, y = year, label = contacts))
print(g)
```

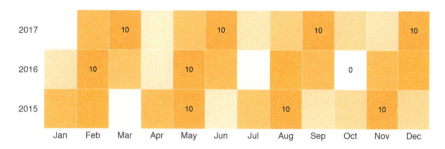

Figure 10.53: Contact activity heat map with labels

10.13 Creating Panels/Facets

With a lot of data on a graph, it's harder for us to distinguish among various data trends. To avoid overcrowding the graph, we can use panels, also known as facets, to study each trend separately. You saw an example of this graph in Figure 10.34, in which we created two panels: one for donors and another for non-donors. Once you have created your plot, you need to pass the faceting variable to one of the `facet_*` functions. See Figure 10.54 for an example.

```r
library(ggplot2)
library(dplyr)
plot_data <- filter(donor_data,
                    GENDER %in% c('Male', 'Female') &
                    !(is.na(PREF_ADDRESS_TYPE)))
ggplot(data = plot_data,
       aes(x = GENDER, y = TotalGiving)) +
  geom_boxplot() + scale_y_log10() +
  facet_wrap(~ PREF_ADDRESS_TYPE + PARENT_IND,
             labeller = label_both)
#> Warning: Transformation introduced infinite values
#> in continuous y-axis
#> Warning: Removed 10923 rows containing non-finite values
#> (stat_boxplot).
```

246 DATA VISUALIZATION

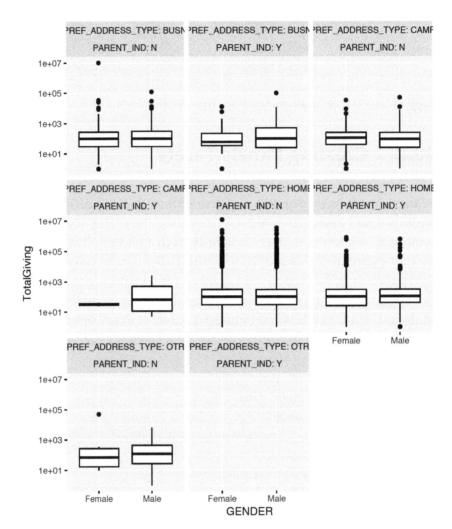

Figure 10.54: A faceted box plot

You can supply the optional `nrow` and `ncol` arguments to specify the number of rows and columns you would like to see in your plot.

10.14 Geographic Mapping

For reasons unknown, people get excited about maps just like kids get excited about ice cream. We, as data practitioners, can use this excitement to our advantage. Although I dislike creating "interesting" stuff, to increase the adoption of analytics, I am flexible about audience preferences. Also, creating maps in R has become easier. Let's go through a couple of ways in which we can create maps.

10.14.1 Points on a map

The simplest way of mapping is showing data points on a map. For example, you can show the exact location of prospects on the U.S. map, or you can show the number of prospects in each ZIP code. Let's show the latter.

First, let's count all the prospects in each ZIP code and clean them up using the `zipcode` library:

```
require(dplyr)
require(zipcode)
zipcode_counts <- count(donor_data, ZIPCODE) %>%
  mutate(ZIPCODE = clean.zipcodes(ZIPCODE))
```

Now, let's pull the latitude and longitude for each ZIP code using the data provided in the `zipcode` package:

```
data("zipcode")
zipcode_counts_coords <- inner_join(zipcode_counts,
                                    zipcode,
                                    by = c("ZIPCODE" = "zip"))
```

Now for the fun part. Get the map data from the `maps` package.

248 DATA VISUALIZATION

```r
require(maps)
require(ggplot2)
us_map <- map_data(map = "state")
glimpse(us_map)
#> Observations: 15,537
#> Variables: 6
#> $ long      <dbl> -87.5, -87.5, -87.5, -87.5,...
#> $ lat       <dbl> 30.4, 30.4, 30.4, 30.3, 30....
#> $ group     <dbl> 1, 1, 1, 1, 1, 1, 1, 1, 1, ...
#> $ order     <int> 1, 2, 3, 4, 5, 6, 7, 8, 9, ...
#> $ region    <chr> "alabama", "alabama", "alab...
#> $ subregion <chr> NA, NA, NA, NA, NA, NA, NA,...
```

We have two options: either we join the counts data frame with the map coordinates data, or we draw the map first and then pass the counts as a separate layer. Let's explore the second option so we can see the power of ggplot's layering.

```r
ggplot() + geom_polygon(data = us_map,
                        aes(x = long, y = lat, group = group)) +
  coord_quickmap()
```

GEOGRAPHIC MAPPING 249

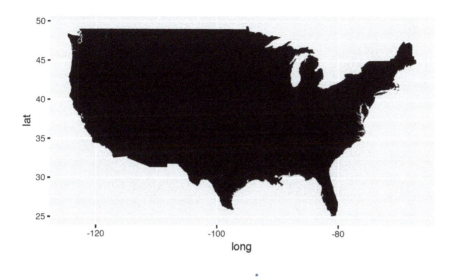

You will see we added the coord_quickmap() function to the plot call. We won't delve into all the inner workings or uses of this function, but it can be used to preserve the aspect ratio of the map so that the U.S. will look like the U.S.

Since the map is filled with a dark gray color, it is not exactly pleasing to the eye. Also, it will be harder to see the data points once we plot them. Let's change the background color as well as the border color. Let's also remove all the extra, non-data related items from the plot using theme_bare.

```
g <- ggplot() + geom_polygon(data = us_map,
                             aes(x = long, y = lat, group = group),
                             fill = "gray97",
                             color = "#FF993F",
                             size = 0.5) +
  coord_quickmap() + theme_bare +
  theme(axis.text = element_blank())
g
```

250 DATA VISUALIZATION

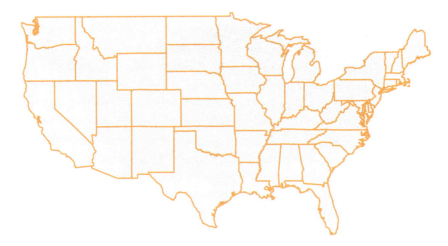

Let's add a layer of all the counts using geom_point, with the size of the point reflecting the number of prospects in that ZIP code.

```
g + geom_point(data = zipcode_counts_coords,
               aes(x = longitude, y = latitude, size = n))
#> Warning: Removed 303 rows containing missing values
#> (geom_point).
```

A couple of things happened.

- We plotted data points that are not in the lower 48 states.
- The point size overwhelmed the map.

Let's remove the ZIP codes outside of the lower 48 states.

```
g <- g + geom_point(data = filter(zipcode_counts_coords,
                                  between(longitude, -125,-66),
```

GEOGRAPHIC MAPPING   251

```
                         between(latitude, 25,50)),
             aes(x = longitude, y = latitude, size = n),
             alpha = 0.4)
g
```

Much better. But the size of the points is still overcrowding the map. Let's change the size scale. First, let's see the distribution of the number of prospects in each ZIP code.

```
summary(zipcode_counts_coords$n)
#>    Min. 1st Qu.  Median    Mean 3rd Qu.    Max.
#>       1       1       1       2       2    5835
```

It looks like the majority of prospects are spread around the country with the exception of one zip code, (90265. Find out why here[17]). Let's make the individual data points smaller. The final map is shown in Figure 10.55.

```
g <- g + scale_size_area(breaks = c(1, 4000),
                         max_size = 8,
```

---

[17]https://www.quora.com/Iron-Man-3-2013-movie-What-address-did-Tony-Stark-give-out-as-his-home-address

```
                                    guide = "none")
g
```

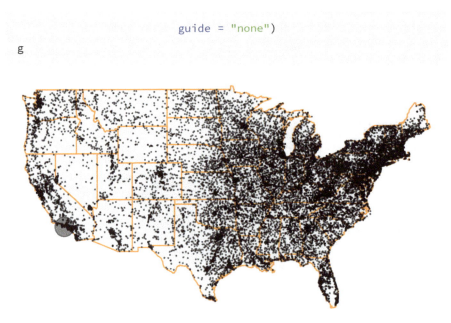

Figure 10.55: Number of prospects by ZIP code on the US map

Much better!

We can change the color of points based on the number of prospects in each ZIP code, but we will have to change our initial call to `geom_point`. We need to add the "color = n" argument. Then we can use the `scale_colour_gradient` function. You can see the resulting map in Figure 10.56. Since most of the prospects are located in one place, the gradient is really not helping us see anything different. You may want to change the color based on the wealth ratings and explore different patterns. But that's an exercise for you.

```
g <- ggplot() + geom_polygon(data = us_map,
                             aes(x = long,
                                 y = lat,
                                 group = group),
                             fill = "gray97",
```

GEOGRAPHIC MAPPING   253

```r
                            color = "grey80",
                            size = 0.5) +
    coord_quickmap() + theme_bare +
    theme(axis.text = element_blank())
g <- g + geom_point(data = filter(zipcode_counts_coords,
                            between(longitude, -125,-66),
                            between(latitude, 25,50)),
                    aes(x = longitude,
                        y = latitude,
                        size = n,
                        color = n),
                alpha = 0.4)
g <- g + scale_size_area(breaks = c(1, 4000),
                    max_size = 8,
                    guide = "none") +
    scale_colour_gradient(low = "#fc9272",
                    high = "#de2d26",
                    guide = "none")
g
```

What if we want to explore only one specific region, say, the Bay Area in San Francisco. We can use another useful library called ggmap. This library will allow you to download and plot Google Maps®, Stamen Maps®, and OpenStreetMap® maps. See the library's code and documentation[18] for more details.

This package is very easy to use. For example, let's download and plot the Bay Area as seen in Figure 10.57.

```r
require(ggmap)
ggmap(get_map("San Francisco Bay Area",
            zoom = 11,
```

---

[18]https://github.com/dkahle/ggmap

254 DATA VISUALIZATION

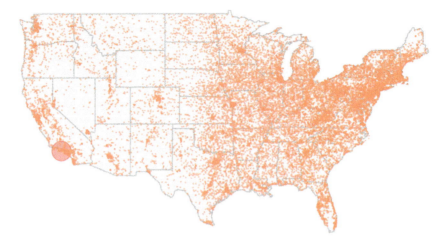

Figure 10.56: Number of prospects by ZIP code on the U.S. map, colored by density

```
                    source = "google"))
```

You can change various aspects of the map with the get_map function. You can change the zoom level, map types (satellite, watercolor), the source of map, and many other things. Figure 10.58 shows various versions of the Los Angeles map.

```
require(gridExtra)
g0 <- ggmap(get_map("los angeles", zoom = 10, source = "google"),
           extent = "device") +
  ggtitle(label = 'g0')
g1 <- ggmap(get_map("los angeles", zoom = 10, source = "google"),
           extent = "device", darken = 0.5) +
  ggtitle(label = 'g1')
g2 <- ggmap(get_map("los angeles", zoom = 10, source = "stamen",
                    maptype = "toner"), extent = "device") +
  ggtitle(label = 'g2')
```

GEOGRAPHIC MAPPING 255

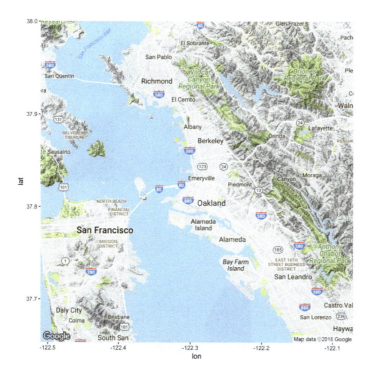

Figure 10.57: Bay Area map

```
g3 <- ggmap(get_map("los angeles", zoom = 10, source = "stamen",
                    maptype = "toner-lite"), extent = "device") +
  ggtitle(label = 'g3')
g4 <- ggmap(get_map("los angeles", zoom = 10, source = "stamen",
                    maptype = "toner-background"),
           extent = "device") +
  ggtitle(label = 'g4')
g5 <- ggmap(get_map("los angeles", zoom = 10, source = "stamen",
                    maptype = "watercolor"), extent = "device") +
  ggtitle(label = 'g5')
grid.arrange(g0, g1, g2, g3, g4, g5, nrow = 2)
```

Let's plot the prospects in the Bay Area, as seen in Figure 10.59.

256 DATA VISUALIZATION

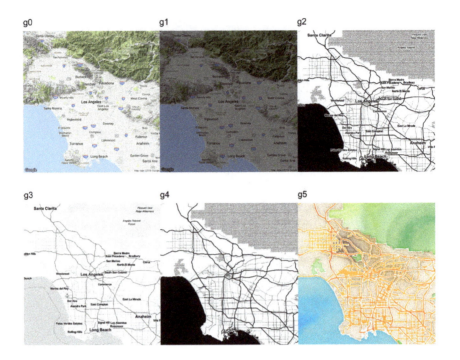

Figure 10.58: Various maps of Los Angeles

```
require(dplyr)
require(zipcode)
data("zipcode")
bay_area_prospects <- mutate(donor_data,
                             ZIPCODE = clean.zipcodes(ZIPCODE)) %>%
  select(ZIPCODE) %>%
  inner_join(., zipcode, by = c("ZIPCODE" = "zip")) %>%
  filter(between(longitude, -122.391821, -122.2984824),
         between(latitude, 37, 38))

bay_area_map <- get_map(location = "San Fransico Bay Area",
                        maptype = "toner",
```

```
                   source = "stamen",
                   zoom = 10)

ggmap(bay_area_map, extent = "device") +
  geom_point(data = bay_area_prospects,
             aes(x = longitude, y = latitude),
             color = "red",
             size = 3)
```

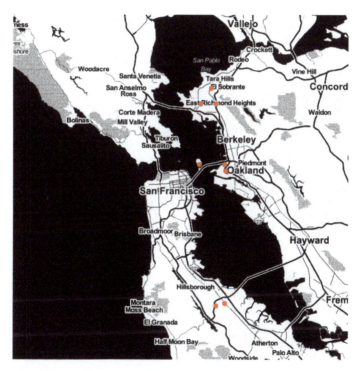

Figure 10.59: Prospects in the Bay Area

What if you didn't have the ZIP code but some malformed address? The `ggmap` library offers a useful function called `mutate_geocode()`, which uses Google's API to give you the longitude and latitude of the address. If you plan to geocode thousands of addresses, get

258 DATA VISUALIZATION

an API key and associate a payment method with your account. You can find more details on Google's developer pages[19]. I once geocoded more than 50,000 addresses. I believe it was less than $20.

Let's say we know three prospects who live in a wealthy neighborhood. We want to show them on a map for a meeting. But the addresses are malformed. Note that I just picked these addresses randomly using Google Maps. You can see two addresses have spaces and one doesn't have the full city name spelled out.

```
30166 Via Victoria Rancho Palos CA
30288 Via Victoria     Rancho Palos Verdes, CA
30233 Via     Victoria Rancho Palos Verdes
```

```r
library(ggmap)
rpv_addr <- data.frame(
  addr = c('30166 Via Victoria Rancho Palos CA',
           '30288 Via Victoria     Rancho Palos Verdes, CA',
           '30233 Via     Victoria Rancho Palos Verdes'),
  name = c('Elizabeth Brown', 'Jeremy Kim', 'Largo Tyler'),
  stringsAsFactors = FALSE)

rpv_addr <- mutate_geocode(rpv_addr, addr)
glimpse(rpv_addr)
#> Observations: 3
#> Variables: 4
#> $ addr <chr> "30166 Via Victoria Rancho Palos...
#> $ name <chr> "Elizabeth Brown", "Jeremy Kim",...
#> $ lon  <dbl> -118.4106738, -118.4093515, -118...
#> $ lat  <dbl> 33.7604252, 33.7588896, 33.7594908
```

---

[19]https://developers.google.com/maps/documentation/geocoding/get-api-key

GEOGRAPHIC MAPPING 259

You can see that Google geocoded all the addresses and returned the coordinates.

Now the easy part. Let's map the area.

```
rpv_coords <- c(lon = -118.4113781, lat = 33.7586502)
rpv_map <- ggmap(get_map(location = rpv_coords,
                         zoom = 16,
                         maptype = "hybrid"),
                 extent = "device")
rpv_map
```

260 DATA VISUALIZATION

Next, let's show the houses along with the names of the prospects, as seen in Figure 10.60.

```r
rpv_map + geom_point(data = rpv_addr,
                     aes(x = lon, y = lat),
                     shape = 21,
                     size = 5,
                     stroke = 2,
                     color = "#FF993F") +
   geom_text(data = rpv_addr,
             aes(x = lon, y = lat, label = name),
             hjust = -0.1,
             size = rel(5),
             color = "#FF993F")
```

GEOGRAPHIC MAPPING   261

Figure 10.60: Prospects mapped on a street

10.14.2   Filled a.k.a. Choropleth Maps

Filled maps, also known as choropleth maps, are perhaps the best-known data-layer added maps. The U.S. general election maps with the red color[20], for the Republican party and blue for the Democratic party for the state won by the party, is a common example of a filled map. Filled maps quickly let the reader see any big pattern shift.

---

[20]http://www.smithsonianmag.com/history/when-republicans-were-blue-and-democrats-were-red-104176297/

262 DATA VISUALIZATION

These maps aren't meant to be read to find micro-patterns, but just to show overall patterns. The key in creating these maps is the availability of the shapes or polygons to be filled in. For example, if you want to fill all the ZIP codes in the state of California by population using colors (darker for dense ZIP codes and lighter for less-dense ZIP codes), you will need a matrix with the location of all the lines of the shape of each ZIP code. The `maps` library provides these polygons for all the U.S. states, counties within each state, and for the world.

Let's create a filled map with the number of prospects for each state.

First, let's count the number of prospects in each state. Let's also get the state's full name using the `base R` data sets `state.abb` and `state.name`. We will use the state names to join with the state map polygon data frame.

```r
state_counts <- group_by(zipcode_counts_coords, state) %>%
  summarize(n = sum(n)) %>%
  ungroup() %>%
  left_join(., data.frame(st_abb = state.abb,
                          st_full = tolower(state.name),
                          stringsAsFactors = FALSE),
            by = c("state" = "st_abb"))
```

Let's join the counts data frame with the `us_map` data frame that we defined in Section 10.14.1. We need to make sure that the order of lines and groups is preserved, and thus, after joining, we use the `arrange` function to sort those two columns.

```r
filled_states_df <- left_join(us_map,
                              state_counts,
                              by = c("region" = "st_full")) %>%
  arrange(group, order)
```

Let's map.

GEOGRAPHIC MAPPING

```r
g <- ggplot(data = filled_states_df,
            aes(x = long, y = lat, group = group, fill = n)) +
  geom_polygon(size = 0.3, color = "grey95") + coord_quickmap()
g
```

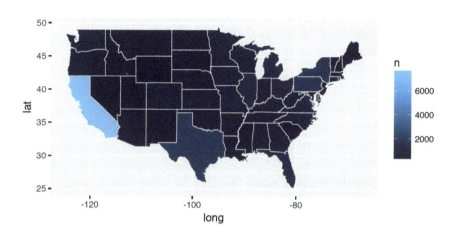

We need to adjust the color scale to better reflect the data, as shown in Figure 10.61.

```r
g <- g + scale_fill_distiller(type = "seq",
                              palette = "Oranges",
                              direction = 1,
                              breaks = c(1, 100, 500, 1000,
                                         5000, 10000),
                              guide = "none") +
  theme_bare + theme(axis.text = element_blank())
g + labs(
  title = 'Number of prospect by each state',
  caption = 'Dark orange color shows states with the most prospects.') +
  theme(plot.caption = element_text(hjust = 0))
```

264   DATA VISUALIZATION

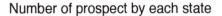

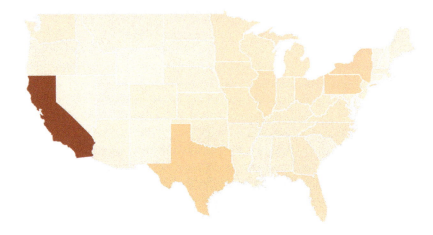

Dark orange color shows states with the most prospects.

Figure 10.61: State filled map

Similarly, we can create a filled map for each county. Since we don't have data for each county, for learning's sake, let's create some fake data.

```r
us_county_map <- map_data("county")

us_county_counts <- distinct(us_county_map, region, subregion) %>%
  mutate(n = rbeta(n = nrow(.), shape1 = 5, shape2 = 2)) %>%
  mutate(n = round(n*100))

us_county_map <- inner_join(us_county_map, us_county_counts) %>%
  arrange(group, order)
```

Now plot this fake count data by county, as shown in Figure 10.62.

```
g <- ggplot(data = us_county_map,
            aes(x = long, y = lat, group = group, fill = n)) +
  geom_polygon(size = 0.3, color = "grey95") + coord_quickmap()
g <- g + scale_fill_distiller(type = "seq",
                              palette = "Oranges",
                              direction = 1,
                              guide = "none") +
  theme_bare + theme(axis.text = element_blank())
g + labs(
  title = 'Number of prospects by county',
  caption = 'Dark orange color shows counties
  with the most prospects.') +
  theme(plot.caption = element_text(hjust = 0))
```

Number of prospects by county

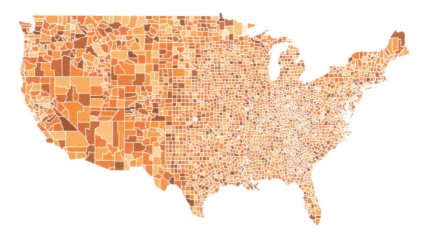

Dark orange color shows counties
with the most prospects.

Figure 10.62: County filled map

266 DATA VISUALIZATION

10.15   Creating Dashboards

Dashboards or scorecards show the key measures you like to track regularly. I started on the path to better data visualization when I had to create a dashboard for the first time. Few (2006) gave me the start I needed. Before you can decide the approach for your dashboard design, you need to ask these questions:

- Does the dashboard need to be interactive?
- How frequently do I need to update it?
- Does it need to be print-ready?
- How much time do I need to spend editing?
- Is this an "infographic"?

If you want to create an infographic type of dashboard, you will be better off by selecting online tools, or even PowerPoint or Keynote. If you want the dashboard to be interactive, you can use JavaScript libraries such as `D3.js`, `highcharts`, or http://variancecharts.com/. RStudio also offers a package called flexdashboard[21] that lets you create interactive dashboards using `rmarkdown`. See flexdashboard's documentation[22] for more details.

In this section, we will see how to create a high-quality, almost print-ready dashboard.

A dashboard is an arrangement of various important measures. Two popular options of arranging such measures are the `cowplot` package's `plot_grid` function and `gridExtra` package's `arrangeGrob` function. The `arrangeGrob` function offers more flexibility in combining text with plots, whereas, with `plot_grid`, you can arrange various plots.

Before you jump into the "hows""", you should figure out the"what" and "why". What do you want to show? Why does it belong there?

---

[21]http://rmarkdown.rstudio.com/flexdashboard/
[22]http://rmarkdown.rstudio.com/flexdashboard/using.html

What graphical representation do you want for your data? Always start with a few pieces of paper and a pencil. Draw what you would like to see, and then work on the code to get closer to what you have in mind.

For this dashboard example, let's say we want to see the number of donors, dollar amount, annual giving amount, number of prospects by wealth rating, and ZIP code map. We will draw a grid of two rows. In the first row, we have two columns and, in the second row, we have three. You can see my (really bad) draft sketch in Figure 10.63.

Figure 10.63: A quick and dirty mockup of a dashboard

Here's my attempt seen in Figure 10.64 with the `gridExtra` package and the `grid.arrange` function.

First, load all the libraries.

```
require(grid)
require(gridExtra)
require(ggplot2)
require(scales)
require(dplyr)
```

Next, prepare the header text.

268 DATA VISUALIZATION

```r
g1 <- textGrob("Stark\nUniversity",
               gp = gpar(fontsize = 30,
                         col = "#F3790C",
                         fontface = "bold"))
g2 <- textGrob("$250M", gp = gpar(fontsize = 20))
g3 <- textGrob("2,538", gp = gpar(fontsize = 20))

g4 <- textGrob("")
g5 <- textGrob("dollars raised", gp = gpar(fontsize = 10))
g6 <- textGrob("number of donors", gp = gpar(fontsize = 10))
```

Prepare the "cumulative dollars raised" chart.

```r
g7 <- ggplot(data = data.frame(
  date = seq.Date(from = as.Date("2010-1-1"),
                  to = as.Date("2017-1-1"),
                  by = "year"),
  dollars_raised = c(32, 34, 28, 24, 26, 22, 36, 35)),
  aes(x = date, y = cumsum(dollars_raised))) +
  geom_line(color = "#FF993F") +
  theme_bare +
  theme(axis.text = element_text(size = rel(1.2))) +
  scale_y_continuous(labels = dollar) +
  coord_fixed(ratio = 10)
```

Get the prospect count by wealth rating. I used a Stackoverflow tip[23] to format the table.

```r
my_table_settings <- ttheme_default(
  base_size = 10,
  core = list(
    fg_params = list(hjust = 1, x = 1),
```

---

[23]https://stackoverflow.com/a/31798975

CREATING DASHBOARDS 269

```r
      bg_params = list(fill = c("grey95", "white")))),
   colhead = list(
      fg_params = list(col = "black"),
      bg_params = list(fill = "white")))

wealth_rating_counts <- count(donor_data, WEALTH_RATING) %>%
  arrange(desc(WEALTH_RATING)) %>%
  mutate(n = comma(n))


g8 <- tableGrob(wealth_rating_counts,
                rows = NULL,
                cols = c("Rating", "#"),
                theme = my_table_settings)
```

Prepare the map showing the prospect locations by ZIP.

```r
g9 <- ggplot() +
  geom_polygon(data = us_map,
               aes(x = long, y = lat, group = group),
               fill = "gray97",
               color = "grey80",
               size = 0.5) +
  coord_quickmap() + theme_bare +
  theme(axis.text = element_blank())
g9 <- g9 + geom_point(data = filter(zipcode_counts_coords,
                             between(longitude, -125,-66),
                             between(latitude, 25,50)),
                      aes(x = longitude,
                          y = latitude,
                          size = n,
                          color = n),
                   alpha = 0.4)
g9 <- g9 + scale_size_area(breaks = c(1, 4000),
```

270   DATA VISUALIZATION

```
                            max_size = 8,
                            guide = "none") +
       scale_colour_gradient(low = "#fc9272",
                            high = "#de2d26",
                            guide = "none")
```

Prepare the footer text.

```
g10 <- textGrob("Cumulative dollars raised (in millions)",
                gp = gpar(fontsize = 10))
g11 <- textGrob("number of prospects", gp = gpar(fontsize = 10))
g12 <- textGrob("prospect location", gp = gpar(fontsize = 10))
```

Now, let's put everything together. The `grid.arrange` function provides a `layout_matrix` parameter to control the location of each of the elements. We simply divided the layout into nine cells, but we adjusted the relative heights of each of the rows using the `heights` parameter. The header text has 20% of the vertical space, the graphs have 60%, and the other text labels get 10% each. Check out more layout options in the `gridExtra` documentation[24].

```
grid_layout <- rbind(c(1,2,3),
                     c(4,5,6),
                     c(7,8,9),
                     c(10,11,12))
```

```
grid.arrange(g1,g2,g3,g4,g5,g6,g7,g8,g9,g10,g11,g12,
             layout_matrix = grid_layout,
             heights = c(0.2, 0.1, 0.6, 0.1),
             padding = unit(0.01, "line"))
```

---

[24]https://cran.r-project.org/web/packages/gridExtra/vignettes/arrangeGrob.html

CREATING DASHBOARDS 271

Figure 10.64: Dashboard using gridextra

You may say, "This seems really complicated. Why should I go through this hassle?" The short answer is: When you get used to this code, you gain control over highly dynamic, repeatable, and reproducible documents. Your manager asks for a change, you change the code, and future documents are ready. The dashboard itself may not be worth the effort, but when you combine your analysis with your programming to create documents (also known as literate programming[25]), you unleash the power of R.

 You can create amazing documents, like this book, using LaTeX, rmarkdown, and knitr in R. Follow Yihui Xie's examples to create your own dynamic, reproducible analysis: https://yihui.name/knitr/demo/minimal/

---

[25]https://en.wikipedia.org/wiki/Literate_programming

272 DATA VISUALIZATION

10.16   Creating Animated Charts

Animated charts are fun and sometimes tell stories that static charts can't. In this section, we will see an example of such charts through the growth of Walmart locations across the U.S. You clearly see the explosion of stores in this animated version. Once you can run this code without R giving you headaches, you can adapt it to show prospect or giving data across the U.S.

Let's get started by loading the necessary libraries.

```r
library(ggplot2) #for plotting, of course
library(ggmap) #to get the US map
library(dplyr) #for data manipulation like a ninja
library(readr) #to read the data in csv
library(lubridate) #to play with dates
library(scales) #for number labeling
library(stringr) #to play with strings
library(Cairo) #for anti-aliasing images on Windows
library(zipcode) #to clean up and geocode zipcodes
```

10.16.1   Gathering, Cleaning-Up, and Summarizing Data

Let's load the ZIP code data using the following command.

```r
data(zipcode)
```

Next, use the `ggmap` library to get the US map. Here, I'm using the toner-lite type of map from Stamen Maps, a great resource for fantastic maps.

CREATING ANIMATED CHARTS   273

```
us_map <- get_stamenmap(c(left = -125,
                          bottom = 25.75,
                          right = -67,
                          top = 49),
                        zoom = 5,
                        maptype = "toner-lite")
```

10.16.2   Get the Store Openings Data

Holmes (2011) has provided Walmart data used in their paper. We will load the store openings data set, which has the opening dates as well as the zipcode of the location.

```
walmart_op_data <- read_csv(
  "http://users.econ.umn.edu/~holmes/data/WalMart/store_openings.csv")
```

Let's wrap up with a couple of cleanup items.

- Convert the date column data to date format
- Create opening year and month columns.

I also created another date column to loop through and create maps for each month. You may ask, "Why did you not use the opening date?" Good question. I am not using the opening date because after creating a map, I am saving the map using the date as the filename. We are using ffmpeg to create a movie out of the map images, and ffmpeg likes sequential numbering of files. If we were to use the opening date, the maps would be out of order. For macOS, the file name is irrelevant because we can use the glob argument of ffmpeg.

```
walmart_op_data <- walmart_op_data %>%
                   mutate(
                       OPENDATE = as.Date(OPENDATE, '%m/%d/%Y'),
```

274 DATA VISUALIZATION

```
                              OpYear = year(OPENDATE),
                              OpMonth = month(OPENDATE),
                              ZIPCODE = clean.zipcodes(ZIPCODE))
```

Now, calculate the number of monthly openings and cumulative openings by month and year.

```
wm_op_data_smry <- walmart_op_data %>%
                  count(OpYear, OpMonth) %>% ungroup() %>%
                  arrange(OpYear, OpMonth) %>%
                  mutate(cumm_n = cumsum(n),
                        OpDate = as.Date(paste(.$OpMonth,
                                              1,
                                              .$OpYear,
                                              sep = "/"),
                                    '%m/%d/%Y'))
```

Join the data with the ZIP code data to pull the latitude and longitude for each one.

```
walmart_op_data <- left_join(walmart_op_data,
                            select(zipcode,
                                  zip,
                                  latitude,
                                  longitude),
                        by = c("ZIPCODE" = "zip"))
```

Get all the ZIP codes for each month's Walmart opening.

```
wm_op_data_smry <- inner_join(wm_op_data_smry,
                            select(walmart_op_data, ZIPCODE,
                                  latitude, longitude,
```

CREATING ANIMATED CHARTS   275

```
                      OpYear, OpMonth),
         by = c("OpYear" = "OpYear",
                "OpMonth" = "OpMonth"))
```

10.16.3   Creating Maps

Now the fun part: To actually see the data on the U.S. map. Since
we have to create a map for each month, we are using a function for
repetition and ease of use.

```r
#this function has three arguments.
#' df: a dataframe used for plotting
#' plotdate: date used for splitting the data frame
# into before and after
#' mapid: a number for naming the final map file
my_zip_plot <- function(df, plotdate, mapid){
  # create the background map.
  # using the darken argument to make the map filled with black color.
  g <- ggmap(us_map, darken = c("0.8", "black"))
  # split the data frame for all Walmarts
  # before a plot date i.e. a month
  old_df <- filter(df, OpDate < plotdate)
  # split the data frame for all Walmarts for the plot date
  # i.e. during a month
  new_df <- filter(df, OpDate == plotdate)
  # plot all the Walmarts before the current opening month.
  # Make all the older store locations as shown in circles smaller
  g <- g + geom_point(data = old_df,
                    aes(x = longitude, y = latitude),
                    size = 5,
                    color = "dodgerblue",
                    alpha = 0.4)
```

276   DATA VISUALIZATION

```r
#plot all the Walmarts during the current opening month.
# Make all the newer store locations as shown in
# circles bigger to get the "pop" effect
g <- g + geom_point(data = new_df,
                    aes(x = longitude, y = latitude),
                    size = 8,
                    color = "dodgerblue",
                    alpha = 0.4)
# remove axis marks, labels, and titles
g <- g + theme(axis.ticks = element_blank(),
               axis.title = element_blank(),
               axis.text = element_blank(),
               plot.title = element_blank())
# place the label for year
g <- g + annotate("text",
                  x = -75,
                  y = 34,
                  label = "YEAR:",
                  color = "white",
                  size = rel(5),
                  hjust = 0)
# place the value of for year
g <- g + annotate("text",
                  x = -75,
                  y = 33,
                  label = unique(new_df$OpYear),
                  color = "white",
                  size = rel(6),
                  fontface = 2,
                  hjust = 0)
# place the label for stores opened
g <- g + annotate("text",
                  x = -75,
```

CREATING ANIMATED CHARTS 277

```r
                   y = 32,
                   label = "STORE COUNT:",
                   color = "white",
                   size = rel(5),
                   hjust = 0)
# place cumulative store openings
g <- g + annotate("text",
                   x = -75,
                   y = 31,
                   label = comma(unique(new_df$cumm_n)),
                   color = "white",
                   size = rel(6),
                   fontface = 2,
                   hjust = 0)
# generate the file name for the map.
# Using str_pad to make the filename same length and prefixed with zeroes.
# create a maps directory inside the directory of this script.
#browser()

#create the maps directory if doesn't exist
if (!dir.exists("maps")) {dir.create("maps")}
filename <- paste0("maps/img_" ,
                   str_pad(mapid, 7, pad = "0"),
                   ".png")
# save the map as a png using Cairo for anti-aliasing on Windows.
ggsave(filename = filename,
       plot = g,
       width = 13,
       height = 7,
       dpi = 150,
       type = "cairo-png")
}
```

278 DATA VISUALIZATION

A note about color: I played with a few tools, such as paletton[26], to find good contrasting colors for the individual dots. After spending a lot of time trying different combinations, I picked one of the blue shades from the named colors in R.

Loop through the data frame for each month and create a map for that month. **Warning:** these commands will take about 5 minutes and create a lot of maps (see Figure 10.65 for an example). Make sure that you've created a directory named maps inside the directory of this file and that you have enough space to store all the maps.

```
wm_op_data_smry %>%
  mutate(id = row_number()) %>%
  group_by(OpDate) %>%
  # create a group id for each group defined using OpDate i.e. a month
  mutate(mapid = max(id)) %>%
  # note when you are using user-defined functions in dplyr,
  # you have to use do
  ## pass the summary data frame, the date, and map number to the function
  do(pl = my_zip_plot(wm_op_data_smry,
                      unique(.$OpDate),
                      unique(.$mapid)))
```

10.16.4 Creating the Walmart Growth Movie

This is the fun part in which we put all the images together to make a "motion picture." For this to work, you will need ffmpeg[27] installed on your computer. On Windows, for ease of use, install it on the c drive.

---

[26]http://paletton.com/
[27]https://www.ffmpeg.org/

CREATING ANIMATED CHARTS 279

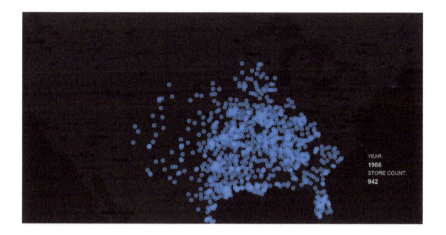

Figure 10.65: Walmart locations

```
# prepare the command for execution
# the framerate argument controls how many frames per second
# we want to see.
# Increase that number for a faster transition between months.
# since we used 7 digits as the fixed length of filenames,
# %7d pattern will match those filenames.
makemovie_cmd <- paste0("C:/ffmpeg/bin/ffmpeg -framerate 5 -y -i ",
                       paste0(getwd(), "/maps/img_%7d.png"),
                       " -c:v libx264 -pix_fmt yuv420p ",
                       paste0(getwd(), "/maps/"), "
                       movie.mp4")
# for mac os, you can use the glob argument
# and obviate the need for sequential numbering of files.
# uncomment for mac
# makemovie_cmd <- paste0("ffmpeg -framerate 5 -y -pattern_type glob -i '",
```

```
#                           paste0(getwd(), "/maps/"),
#                           "*.png'",
#                           " -c:v libx264 -pix_fmt yuv420p '",
#                           paste0(getwd(), "/maps/"),
#                           "movie.mp4'")
system(makemovie_cmd)
# the system command will execute the ffmpeg command and create the final m
```

Watch the final video on YouTube: https://youtu.be/adm3RB4ieXU.

10.17   Summary

In this chapter, we explored many design principles of effective data visualizations, learned their importance, and executed recipes to create them. We learned different types of charts and when to use them. We saw `ggplot`'s various chart creation and customization options. We hope that your charts look elegant and guide readers to insight.

If you're enjoying this book, consider sharing it with your network by running `source("http://arn.la/shareds4fr")` in your R console.

— Ashutosh and Rodger

11

RFM MODELING

Recency, Frequency, Monetary (RFM) modeling has its root in direct marketing. Although many sophisticated statistical techniques were developed after the initial use of RFM, it remains a top choice for marketers to segment their population (McCarty & Hastak 2007). The ease of use of RFM models is the primary reason for its widespread use (Verhoef et al. 2003). Secondly, as we saw in Section 3.2, since the decision-makers understand the segments based on RFM easily, they are more likely to use them. Some researchers have argued that its simplicity goes against the efficiency of other models (Yang 2004). Taking note of that argument, we will look into how to develop our own RFM models.

11.1 Calculate RFM Values

Let's review the definitions of RFM.

- Recency measures how recently the customers (in our case, donors) made a transaction.

- **F**requency measures how often the customers make transactions.
- **M**onetary measures how much money that the customers spent on their transactions.

As you can guess, a donor who made a recent gift, has been giving frequently, and makes large gifts is likely to make further gifts. Of course, there are quite a few parameters at play here. Let's denote the low values for each of the measures with a negative sign and the high values with a positive sign.

What do you think of the following donors?

- $R^-\ F^+\ M^+$: It has been a while since they gave but they gave frequently and gave a lot. Did we lose them?
- $R^+\ F^-\ M^-$: They gave recently but have not given frequently and not a whole lot. Are these new donors?
- $R^+\ F^-\ M^+$: They gave recently but have not given frequently. They made some big gifts. Did we get lucky with these donors?

If you just use two values (that is, high or low), you will have eight combinations of RFM to go through—many opportunities for segmentation! How you use these scores depend on your objective: Do you want to upgrade donors or do you want to save mailing costs? Before you compute these scores, you must decide what *recent* means. Is it the last month or last year?

 How you use these scores depends on your objective: Do you want to upgrade donors or do you want to save mailing costs?

All right. Let's write some code to get our RFM values. Most likely you will pull the data for this analysis from a transactional table. The common format of such a table includes multiple rows per donor per gift. Table 11.1 shows an example:

CALCULATE RFM VALUES **283**

Table 11.1: Sample gift transaction table

DONOR_ID	GIFT_DATE	GIFT_AMOUNT
3	2017-01-30	$5,803.17
4	2017-03-04	$6,602.89
6	2017-01-02	$7,327.90
6	2017-02-12	$8,662.71
8	2017-06-18	$5,947.82

We need to transform this data to summarize recency, frequency, and monetary data for each donor, creating one row per donor. You will find the sample data file with gift transactions in the code bundle for this book. Let's read this data first.

```
library(readr)

rfm_data <- read_csv("data/SampleDataRFM.csv")

head(rfm_data)
#> # A tibble: 6 x 3
#>        ID FISCAL_YEAR Giving
#>     <int>       <int> <chr>
#> 1   1        2015 $1,000
#> 2   1        2016   $600
#> 3   2        2012   $100
#> 4   2        2013    $55
#> 5   2        2014   $160
#> 6   2        2015   $135
summary(rfm_data)
#>        ID         FISCAL_YEAR      Giving
#>  Min.   :   1   Min.   :2012   Length:6973
#>  1st Qu.: 901   1st Qu.:2013   Class :character
#>  Median :1773   Median :2014   Mode  :character
```

284 RFM MODELING

```
#>  Mean    :1788    Mean    :2014
#>  3rd Qu.:2679    3rd Qu.:2015
#>  Max.    :3575    Max.    :2016
```

As you can see, this sample data has a fiscal year column and not an actual gift date. If you had the actual gift date (with the column name of GIFT_DATE and in date format), you could write something like this:

```
library(lubridate)

rfm_data <- rfm_data %>%
  mutate(DaysSinceGift = as.numeric(Sys.Date() - GIFT_DATE,
                                    units = "days"))
```

In this example, we will use one-year periods to calculate recency. Since 2016 is the latest year in the data, we will use it to calculate the time since the last gift.

First, let's clean up the $ signs from the giving column. We will use the stringr library to do a simple find and replace.

```
library(dplyr)
library(stringr)

rfm_data <- rfm_data %>%
  mutate(Giving = as.double(str_replace_all(Giving,
                                            pattern = "[$,]",
                                            replacement = "")))
glimpse(rfm_data)
#> Observations: 6,973
#> Variables: 3
#> $ ID          <int> 1, 1, 2, 2, 2, 2, 2, 3, 3...
#> $ FISCAL_YEAR <int> 2015, 2016, 2012, 2013, 2...
```

CALCULATE RFM VALUES **285**

```
#> $ Giving        <dbl> 1000, 600, 100, 55, 160, ...
```

Now that the data is cleaned up, let's create a summary data frame.

```
rfm_counts <- rfm_data %>%
  group_by(ID) %>%
  summarize(Recency = min(2016 - FISCAL_YEAR),
            Frequency = n(),
            Monetary = sum(Giving))
```

```
glimpse(rfm_counts)
#> Observations: 3,058
#> Variables: 4
#> $ ID        <int> 1, 2, 3, 4, 5, 7, 8, 9, 10,...
#> $ Recency   <dbl> 0, 0, 0, 0, 3, 3, 2, 0, 0, ...
#> $ Frequency <int> 2, 5, 4, 3, 2, 2, 2, 4, 2, ...
#> $ Monetary  <dbl> 1600, 1585, 2930, 1725, 155...
summary(select(rfm_counts, -ID))
#>     Recency        Frequency        Monetary
#>  Min.   :0.00   Min.   :1.00   Min.   :     0
#>  1st Qu.:0.00   1st Qu.:1.00   1st Qu.:   150
#>  Median :1.00   Median :2.00   Median :   496
#>  Mean   :1.13   Mean   :2.28   Mean   :  4104
#>  3rd Qu.:2.00   3rd Qu.:3.00   3rd Qu.:  1851
#>  Max.   :4.00   Max.   :5.00   Max.   :400000
```

What's the code doing, you ask?

- `min(2016 - FISCAL_YEAR)` calculates the time between 2016 and the fiscal year of the gift, and the `min` function takes the lowest value. If a donor gave in 2013 and 2014, before taking the minimum, we would get two values: 3 and 2. But the latest gift was in 2014, so the minimum would be 2. If you have the gift date, you will replace this code with `min(DaysSinceGift)`.

286 RFM MODELING

- `n()` calculates the number of gifts by a donor.
- `sum(Giving)` totals the donor's giving.

So, what do we learn from this aggregation? We can see from Figure 11.1 that the majority of donors gave recently, many of them gave one or two gifts, and a very small percentage gave more than $2,000.

```
#> Warning: Transformation introduced infinite values
#> in continuous x-axis
#> Warning: Removed 2 rows containing non-finite values
#> (stat_density).
```

11.2 Create Quintiles

Once you have the summary data, you would like to put these donors in bins. Typically, each measure is divided into five bins. The top 20% of each measure go in bin number five and the bottom 20% go in bin number one. If a donor is in the top 20% for each of the measures, then his or her RFM score will be *555*. Similarly, if a donor is in the bottom 20% for each of the measures, then his or her RFM score will be *111*. We can use the `ntile` function from the `dplyr` library to compute these percentile bins.

```
rfm_ranks <- rfm_counts %>%
  mutate_at(.funs = funs(rank = ntile(., n = 5)),
            .vars = vars(Frequency, Monetary)) %>%
  mutate(Recency_rank = 5 - Recency) %>%
  mutate(RFM_score = as.integer(paste0(Recency_rank,
                                       Frequency_rank,
                                       Monetary_rank)))


glimpse(rfm_ranks)
#> Observations: 3,058
```

CREATE QUINTILES 287

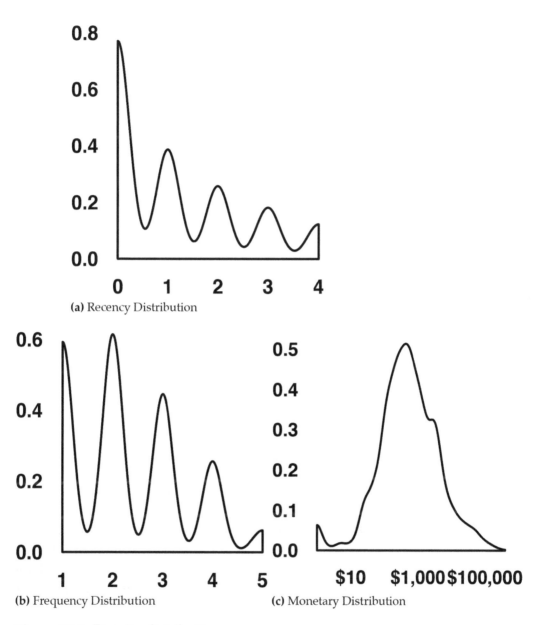

Figure 11.1: Density distribution

288 RFM MODELING

```
#> Variables: 8
#> $ ID             <int> 1, 2, 3, 4, 5, 7, 8, 9...
#> $ Recency        <dbl> 0, 0, 0, 0, 3, 3, 2, 0...
#> $ Frequency      <int> 2, 5, 4, 3, 2, 2, 2, 4...
#> $ Monetary       <dbl> 1600, 1585, 2930, 1725...
#> $ Frequency_rank <int> 2, 5, 5, 4, 2, 2, 2, 5...
#> $ Monetary_rank  <int> 4, 4, 5, 4, 4, 4, 3, 4...
#> $ Recency_rank   <dbl> 5, 5, 5, 5, 2, 2, 3, 5...
#> $ RFM_score      <int> 524, 554, 555, 544, 22...
head(rfm_ranks)
#> # A tibble: 6 x 8
#>       ID Recency Frequency Monetary Frequency_rank
#>    <int>   <dbl>     <int>    <dbl>          <int>
#> 1     1       0         2     1600              2
#> 2     2       0         5     1585              5
#> 3     3       0         4     2930              5
#> 4     4       0         3     1725              4
#> 5     5       3         2     1555              2
#> 6     7       3         2     1250              2
#> # ... with 3 more variables: Monetary_rank <int>,
#> #   Recency_rank <dbl>, RFM_score <int>
```

Here's what the code is doing.

- The `mutate_at` function is creating five bins for the Frequency and Monetary variables in the data. It is also creating a new variable using those variables with `_rank` as a suffix.
- `Recency_rank = 5 - Recency` is creating a new variable by subtracting the current recency value from 5. We are doing so because the recency of a gift from 2016 will be zero, but it also needs the highest rank. What if you had actual gift dates? In that case, you would simply use the `ntile` function to create five bins, but you would have to use `desc` because the latest gift date will have the lowest value and we want

Table 11.2: Median giving by recency bins

Recency_rank	median(Monetary)
1	100
2	222
3	330
4	506
5	755

that value to have the highest bin number. You would use:
`mutate(Recency_rank = ntile(desc(Recency), 5))`.

- The last `mutate` call is simply concatenating the individual RFM bin numbers.

Let's see what the giving looks like for the recency and frequency bins.

```
rfm_ranks %>% group_by(Recency_rank) %>%
  summarize(median(Monetary))
rfm_ranks %>% group_by(Frequency_rank) %>%
  summarize(median(Monetary))
```

As you can see from Table 11.2 and 11.3, for the top 20% of most recent and frequent donors, the median giving is higher than the other bins.

11.3   Plot Ranks

We can uncover various patterns when we visualize the RFM scores and ranks. Kohavi & Parekh (2004) shared different ways to look at these scores and ranks. Let's look at a few, but please note that these

290 RFM MODELING

Table 11.3: Median giving by frequency bins

Frequency_rank	median(Monetary)
1	114
2	200
3	432
4	836
5	1605

visualizations are exploratory, thus I'm spending minimal time to make them pretty.

Let's look at simple counts first. How many donors do we have in each of the bins? Figure 11.2 shows that a majority of the donors are in the *555* bin and some are in *111*.

```
ggplot(rfm_ranks, aes(x = RFM_score)) +
  geom_bar() +
  theme_bw(base_size = 12)
```

Figure 11.3 shows, as suspected, that the donors with scores above 500 have higher giving. But some donors in the 300 range also have relatively higher giving. We should study this population because, although they have not given recently, they still have good frequency and have made large gifts.

```
library(ggplot2)
library(scales)

ggplot(rfm_ranks, aes(x = RFM_score,
                      y = Monetary,
                      size = Monetary,
                      color = factor(Monetary_rank))) +
```

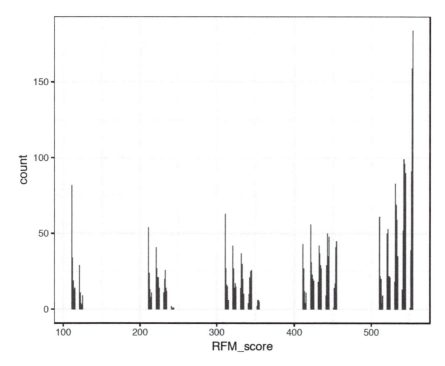

Figure 11.2: RFM scores and counts

```
geom_jitter() + scale_colour_brewer() +
scale_y_sqrt(labels = dollar) + theme_bw(base_size = 12) +
theme(legend.position = "bottom")
```

Figure 11.4 shows the recency and frequency ranks and the giving values with circle sizes and color changes. You can see that the donors who don't have recent gifts have not made frequent gifts either, although the gift size could be bigger.

```
ggplot(rfm_ranks, aes(x = Recency_rank,
                     y = Frequency_rank,
                     size = Monetary,
                     color = factor(Monetary_rank))) +
```

292   RFM MODELING

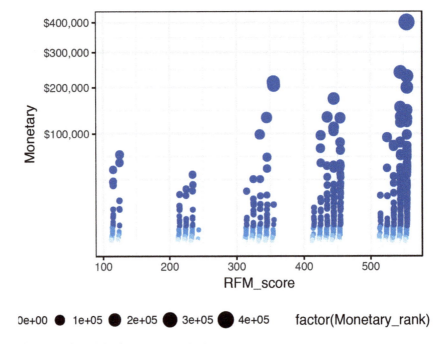

Figure 11.3: RFM scores and giving

```
geom_jitter() + scale_colour_brewer() +
theme_bw(base_size = 12) +
theme(legend.position = "bottom")
```

Figure 11.5 shows that donors who have given more frequently or recently tend to have slightly more giving (using median or 75th percentile as a measure).

```
ggplot(rfm_ranks, aes(x = factor(Frequency_rank), y = Monetary)) +
  geom_boxplot() + scale_y_sqrt(labels = dollar) +
  theme_bw(base_size = 12)
ggplot(rfm_ranks, aes(x = factor(Recency_rank), y = Monetary)) +
  geom_boxplot() + scale_y_sqrt(labels = dollar) +
  theme_bw(base_size = 12)
```

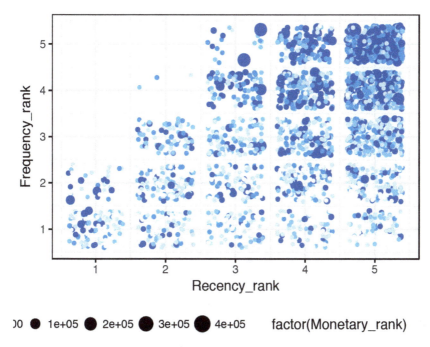

Figure 11.4: Recency rank, frequency rank, and giving

We can modify one of the plots used by Kohavi & Parekh (2004). In this plot, we show recency ranks on the X axis and frequency ranks on the Y axis. We then show the number of donors in each of the bins by changing the size of the points (shown as squares) and show the average giving by changing the color scale. Figure 11.6 shows the result of such a plot. It is clear from this plot that donors with a recency rank of three and frequency rank of five have the highest average giving as a group.

```
rfm_ranks %>%
  group_by(Recency_rank, Frequency_rank) %>%
  summarize(n = n(), avg_giving = mean(Monetary)) %>%
  ggplot(., aes(x = Recency_rank,
                y = Frequency_rank,
```

294   RFM MODELING

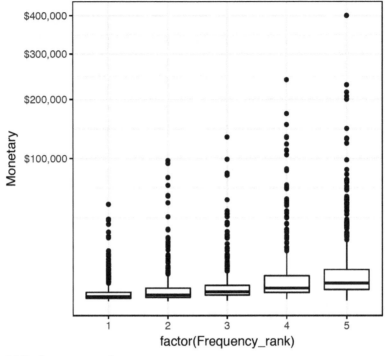

(a) By frequency rank

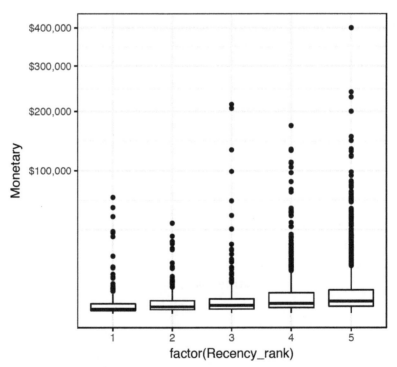

(b) By recency rank

Figure 11.5: Box plot of giving

```r
                    fill = n))  +
  geom_tile(color = "white") +
  scale_fill_gradient(low = "#fed98e", high = "#993404") +
  theme_bw(base_size = 12) +
  theme(legend.position = "bottom")

rfm_ranks %>%
  group_by(Recency_rank, Frequency_rank) %>%
  summarize(n = n(), avg_giving = mean(Monetary)) %>%
  ggplot(., aes(x = Recency_rank,
                y = Frequency_rank,
                color = avg_giving,
                size = n))  + geom_point(shape = 15) +
  scale_color_gradient(low = "#fed98e", high = "#993404") +
  theme_bw(base_size = 12) + scale_size(range = c(5, 13)) +
  theme(legend.position = "bottom")
```

As a variation of Figure 11.6, in Figure 11.7, we can see the percentage of total donors that fall in each of these bins.

```r
rfm_ranks %>%
  count(Recency_rank, Frequency_rank) %>%
  ungroup() %>%
  mutate(pct_donors = n / sum(n)) %>%
  ggplot(., aes(x = Recency_rank,
                y = Frequency_rank,
                fill = pct_donors,
                label = percent(pct_donors)))  +
  geom_tile(color = "white") +
  scale_fill_gradient(low = "white", high = "lightblue") +
  geom_text() + theme_bw(base_size = 12) +
  theme(legend.position = "bottom")
```

296 RFM MODELING

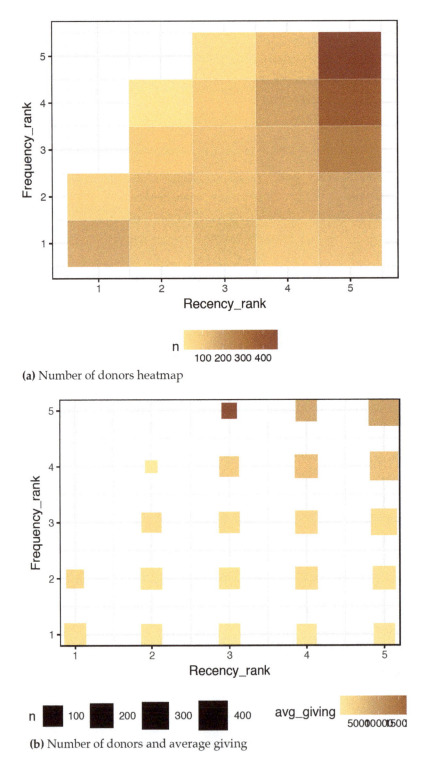

(a) Number of donors heatmap

(b) Number of donors and average giving

Figure 11.6: Recency and frequency rank along with giving

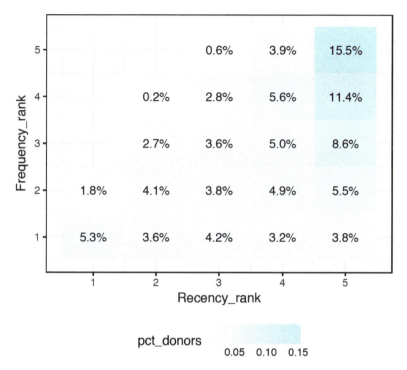

Figure 11.7: Recency and frequency rank along with giving

11.4 Use Cases

Let's see some of the use cases of RFM scores and ranks:

- **Find the future big donors**: We can filter the *554* or *555* bins for any donors who have not given above a certain threshold. Since some donors in these bins have given large amounts, there's a good likelihood that other donors may too. Let's consider the average giving in these bins as the threshold.

```
avg_giving_555_554 <- mean(filter(
  rfm_ranks,
  RFM_score %in% c(555, 554))$Monetary)
```

298 RFM MODELING

```
filter(rfm_ranks, RFM_score %in% c(555, 554) &
         Monetary < avg_giving_555_554)
#> # A tibble: 280 x 8
#>      ID Recency Frequency Monetary Frequency_rank
#>   <int>   <dbl>     <int>    <dbl>          <int>
#> 1     2       0         5     1585              5
#> 2     3       0         4     2930              5
#> 3     9       0         4     1740              5
#> 4    19       0         5     4882              5
#> 5    22       0         4     3436              5
#> 6    32       0         4     3420              5
#> # ... with 274 more rows, and 3 more variables:
#> #   Monetary_rank <int>, Recency_rank <dbl>,
#> #   RFM_score <int>
```

- **Upgrade donors**: We can find the donors who have given recently and frequently but have not made large gifts. We can find such donors by looking at the *551* or *552* bins.

```
filter(rfm_ranks, RFM_score %in% c(551, 552))
#> # A tibble: 40 x 8
#>      ID Recency Frequency Monetary Frequency_rank
#>   <int>   <dbl>     <int>    <dbl>          <int>
#> 1   715       0         4      270              5
#> 2   736       0         4      229              5
#> 3   764       0         4      270              5
#> 4   852       0         4      192              5
#> 5  1003       0         4      136              5
#> 6  1283       0         4      276              5
#> # ... with 34 more rows, and 3 more variables:
#> #   Monetary_rank <int>, Recency_rank <dbl>,
#> #   RFM_score <int>
```

- **Find cheaper channels for appeals**: We don't need to waste resources on donors who are not very likely to respond or make bigger gifts. We can find these donors by looking at bins *111, 112, 121, 122, 211, 212, 221,* and *222*.

```
filter(rfm_ranks, RFM_score <= 222 &
        !(substr(RFM_score, start = 3, stop = 3) %in% 4:5))
#> # A tibble: 338 x 8
#>       ID Recency Frequency Monetary Frequency_rank
#>    <int>   <dbl>     <int>    <dbl>          <int>
#> 1     33       3         1      500              1
#> 2     34       4         1        1              1
#> 3     35       4         1      150              1
#> 4     41       3         1       20              1
#> 5     78       4         1      320              1
#> 6     88       4         1      100              1
#> # ... with 332 more rows, and 3 more variables:
#> #   Monetary_rank <int>, Recency_rank <dbl>,
#> #   RFM_score <int>
```

- **Re-acquire lapsed donors**: Lapsed donors are very hard to re-acquire, but we may try reaching out to lapsed donors (recency rank < 4) who used to give frequently.

```
filter(rfm_ranks, RFM_score < 400 &
        (substr(RFM_score, start = 2, stop = 2) %in% 4:5))
#> # A tibble: 110 x 8
#>       ID Recency Frequency Monetary Frequency_rank
#>    <int>   <dbl>     <int>    <dbl>          <int>
#> 1     21       2         3      307              4
#> 2     45       2         3      871              4
#> 3     64       2         3     3887              4
#> 4     76       2         3     2260              4
#> 5    157       2         3   131303              4
```

300 RFM MODELING

```
#> 6    215       2        3     1345           4
#> # ... with 104 more rows, and 3 more variables:
#> #   Monetary_rank <int>, Recency_rank <dbl>,
#> #   RFM_score <int>
```

 Figure out why and how we're using the `substr` function. Write, test and run code in your console to find out the last letter of Iron Man.

If you're enjoying this book, consider sharing it with your network by running `source("http://arn.la/shareds4fr")` in your R console.

— Ashutosh and Rodger

12

MACHINE LEARNING RECIPES

Machine learning is the study of computer-based algorithms to build models that learn and make predictions using data.

George Box, a noted statistician, is often credited for saying "all models are wrong" in his paper **Science and Statistics** (Box 1976). Box's quote expanded to "all models are wrong, but some are useful" in the popular text **Model Selection and Multimodel Inference: A Practical Information-Theoretic Approach** (Burnham 2002).

All models are wrong, but some are useful.

— George Box

Many machine learning tasks draw from pattern-recognition concepts in artificial intelligence (AI), which is a discipline focused on enabling computers to learn concepts and functions without explicit programming. In terms of real-world applications, machine learning is widely used to design and build models that can solve a variety of complex computing tasks and make useful predictions using data. Examples you might recognize include spam filtering, fraud detection, and optical character recognition (OCR).

As you explore the following recipes, keep in mind that the models you build will be imperfect, but can still offer useful insights.

12.1 Feature Selection

As you build your own models, it is important to first identify the specific types of problems you are trying to solve with your model and its outputs. It is also important to think about what kinds of data you will need to find, use, and test with your models.

Most of the recipes in this chapter focus on building models that predict whether a constituent is a donor or non-donor. By design, we are focusing on the same donor modeling problem so you can develop a sense of the similarities and differences between various machine learning methods. We also selected this modeling problem due to the fundamental and pressing need in non-profits to identify potential donors. Fortunately, many of you reading this book already have access to heaps of institutional data and, by following the recipes in this chapter, you will hopefully be inspired to take a fresh look at your data and modify these recipes to generate actionable insights.

Feature selection is the process of choosing input variables or relevant attributes for your model. To quickly introduce you to multiple machine learning methods, we opted to simplify this process and preselect some features (variables) from our test data set, such as age, constituent type, involvement indicators, and communication preferences.

The `caret` package includes tools that you can use to rank the importance of your data variables and automatically select the most important features (variables) to potentially incorporate into your models. One popular automatic method for feature selection provided by the `caret` package is **Recursive Feature Elimination** (RFE). To read more about using RFE, check out this tutorial[1].

In addition to the `caret` package, the `mlr` package also offers methods to calculate feature importance and guide your feature selection process. To read more about using `mlr`'s filtering and wrapper methods to identify the most relevant feature, check out this article[2].

12.2   Supervised Learning

The purpose of supervised learning is to make accurate predictions using labeled data.

Typically, there are two types of predictions: categorical (classification) and numeric (regression).

---

[1]http://ml-tutorials.kyrcha.info/rfe.html

[2]https://mlr-org.github.io/mlr-tutorial/release/html/feature_selection/index.html

12.2.1 Classification

Classification, which is a type of supervised learning, uses labeled input (training) data to predict categorical (or discrete) values on new (test) data. The classification model is built with training data containing known categorical labels, which are used to predict the unknown category values of new (test) observations.

12.2.2 Instance-Based Learning

Instance-based learning is a machine learning method that constructs a hypothesis directly from an entire training dataset. Instance-based learning, also known as **memory-based** or **lazy** learning, is one of the simplest types of machine learning algorithms.

Instance-based learning models store training data, compute similarities (that is, distance measurements such as Euclidean, Manhattan, Canberra, and Minkowski) between training and test instances, and decide (predict) the value or class for a new observation of test data.

For more documentation on available distance metrics and usage details in R, write the command ?dist into the R console.

The primary advantage of instance-based (or memory-based) models over other machine learning methods is the ability to instantly adapt learning models to new data. The key disadvantage is that instance-based learning methods require significant computational resources to store entire training datasets into memory all at once, which can present limitations when working with large datasets with many attributes or variables (also known as **features**). In addition, instance-based models are prone to overfitting noise (error) in training data, which is important to keep in mind as you

SUPERVISED LEARNING 305

dive further into building models and exploring various machine learning techniques.

12.2.2.1 K-Nearest Neighbor

The K-nearest neighbor (KNN) algorithm is a commonly used instance-based learning method and one of the simplest machine learning algorithms available.

The KNN algorithm can be used for both classification (categorical) and regression (numeric) prediction problems. In KNN classification, the output is a categorical (discrete) value such as gender, constituent type, or marital status. In KNN regression, the output is a numerical (continuous) value of an object attribute.

KNN is a non-parametric learning method, which means that it does not make any assumptions about your input data or its distribution. Because KNN stores its entire training dataset into memory, it does not require an explicit learning phase like other machine learning algorithms. Instead, KNN seeks to identify patterns within your input data (**k** closest observations) using a distance measurement (Euclidean, by default) and majority vote to classify (predict) each data point rather than fitting your data to a particular model or function.

Let's begin preparing our data to build a KNN classification model:

```
# Load dplyr package
library(dplyr)
library(readr)

# Load string package
library(stringr)

# Load Data
donor_data <- read_csv("data/DonorSampleDataML.csv")
```

306   MACHINE LEARNING RECIPES

Using the `glimpse` function from the `dplyr` library, we can see that the donor data file is structured with 34,508 examples (observations) and 23 features (variables).

```
# Glimpse donor_data
glimpse(donor_data)
```

Before building our classification model, we should drop the "ID" variable since it is not appropriate to use as a classification feature.

```
# Drop 'ID' variable
donor_data <- select(donor_data, -ID)
```

The `DONOR_IND` variable, which indicates Y or N, is the variable (feature) we seek to classify (predict) based on input (training) data. Let's use the `table` function to count the distribution of donors and non-donors in the example data file.

```
# Table of Donor Count
table(donor_data$DONOR_IND)
#>
#>     N     Y
#> 13075 21433
```

Based on the table output, there are 13,075 non-donors and 21,433 donors. Even though the majority (62%) of constituents are donors in this dataset, it is important to note that this is an artificially generated dataset and that your mileage (that is, donors per constituent record) will vary based on your institutional activity and transactional record.

Now let's use the `CrossTable` function, from the `gmodels` library (Warnes et al. 2015), to produce a two-way contingency table (also known as **cross-tabulation**) that compares donor and parent constituent type indicators (Y or N) to identify the relative proportion of overall donor parents in the data file.

```r
# Install gmodels package
install.packages("gmodels",
  repos = "http://cran.us.r-project.org")



# Load gmodels
library(gmodels)

# Use CrossTable
CrossTable(x = donor_data$ALUMNUS_IND,
           y = donor_data$DONOR_IND,
           chisq = FALSE)
#>
#>
#>    Cell Contents
#> |-----------------------|
#> |                     N |
#> | Chi-square contribution |
#> |           N / Row Total |
#> |           N / Col Total |
#> |         N / Table Total |
#> |-----------------------|
#>
#>
#> Total Observations in Table:  34508
#>
#>
#>                     | donor_data$DONOR_IND
#> donor_data$ALUMNUS_IND |         N |         Y | Row Total |
#> ----------------------|-----------|-----------|-----------|
#>                    N |    10800 |       297 |     11097 |
```

```
#>                             | 10345.493 |  6311.171 |           |
#>                             |     0.973 |     0.027 |     0.322 |
#>                             |     0.826 |     0.014 |           |
#>                             |     0.313 |     0.009 |           |
#> ----------------------|-----------|-----------|-----------|
#>                     Y |      2275 |     21136 |     23411 |
#>                             |  4903.846 |  2991.545 |           |
#>                             |     0.097 |     0.903 |     0.678 |
#>                             |     0.174 |     0.986 |           |
#>                             |     0.066 |     0.612 |           |
#> ----------------------|-----------|-----------|-----------|
#>          Column Total |     13075 |     21433 |     34508 |
#>                             |     0.379 |     0.621 |           |
#> ----------------------|-----------|-----------|-----------|
#>
#>
```

Based on the relative proportions in the cross-table output, it appears that alumni (68%) tend to give much more frequently on average than their non-alumni (32%) counterparts. Specifically, the cross-table reveals that 90% of alumni give and 10% do not give in this example dataset.

Now, let's explore how to use the KNN algorithm to build a classification model that predicts whether a constituent is a donor or non-donor using input (training) data features such as age, constituent type, involvement indicators, and communication preferences.

First let's install the `class` library, which provides various classification functions (Ripley 2015). We will also use the `caret` library for model evaluation (from Jed Wing et al. 2017).

```
# Install class package
install.packages("class",
```

```r
                    repos = "http://cran.us.r-project.org")


# Load dplyr
library(dplyr)

# Load class package
library(class)

# Load caret package
library(caret)

# Set Seed for Repeatable Results
set.seed(777)
```

Since the function expects numeric columns, let's convert some of the factors to numeric.

```r
# Convert from character to numeric data type
convert_fac2num <- function(x){
  as.numeric(as.factor(x))
}

# Convert features from factor to numeric
donor_data <- mutate_at(donor_data,
                    .vars = c('MARITAL_STATUS', 'GENDER',
                      'ALUMNUS_IND', 'PARENT_IND',
                      'HAS_INVOLVEMENT_IND', 'DEGREE_LEVEL',
                      'PREF_ADDRESS_TYPE', 'EMAIL_PRESENT_IND'),
                    .funs = convert_fac2num)

# Convert feature to factor
donor_data$DONOR_IND <- as.factor(donor_data$DONOR_IND)
```

310   MACHINE LEARNING RECIPES

Next, let's split 70% of the data into training data and 30% into test data.

```r
dd_index <- sample(2, nrow(donor_data),
                   replace = TRUE,
                   prob = c(0.7, 0.3))
dd_trainset <- donor_data[dd_index == 1, ]
dd_testset <- donor_data[dd_index == 2, ]

# Confirm size of training and test
# datasets
dim(dd_trainset)
dim(dd_testset)

# Store class labels
dd_trainset_labels <- dd_trainset$DONOR_IND[1:5000]
dd_testset_labels <- dd_testset$DONOR_IND[1:5000]
```

Since we need only numeric columns for this function, let's select the numeric variables.

```r
dd_trainset <- select_if(dd_trainset[1:5000, ], is.numeric)
dd_testset <- select_if(dd_testset[1:5000, ], is.numeric)
```

We need to convert the numeric values to a range between 0 and 1. Let's do so by defining a min-max normalization function.

```r
min_max <- function(x) {
    return((x - min(x))/(max(x) - min(x)))
}
```

Next, let's apply this function to all the columns.

```
dd_trainset_n <- mutate_all(dd_trainset_n,
                            min_max)
dd_testset_n <- mutate_all(dd_testset_n,
                           min_max)
```

Now, let's train multiple KNN models using different cluster sizes, where k specifies the size of each cluster.

```
dd_test_pred_k1 <- knn(train = dd_trainset_n,
    test = dd_testset_n, cl = dd_trainset_labels[1:5000],
    k = 1)
dd_test_pred_k5 <- knn(train = dd_trainset_n,
    test = dd_testset_n, cl = dd_trainset_labels[1:5000],
    k = 5)
dd_test_pred_k10 <- knn(train = dd_trainset_n,
    test = dd_testset_n, cl = dd_trainset_labels[1:5000],
    k = 10)
dd_test_pred_k32 <- knn(train = dd_trainset_n,
    test = dd_testset_n, cl = dd_trainset_labels[1:5000],
    k = 32)
```

Let's see how the models performed using the confusion matrix.

```
confusionMatrix(table(dd_test_pred_k1,
    dd_testset_labels), positive = "Y")
confusionMatrix(table(dd_test_pred_k5,
    dd_testset_labels), positive = "Y")
confusionMatrix(table(dd_test_pred_k10,
    dd_testset_labels), positive = "Y")
confusionMatrix(table(dd_test_pred_k32,
    dd_testset_labels), positive = "Y")
```

Instead of normalizing all the values between 0 and 1, let's scale all the values that are centered at 0 using the `scale` function.

312   MACHINE LEARNING RECIPES

```
# Apply z-score standardization to
# training and test datasets
dd_trainset_zscore <- as.data.frame(scale(dd_trainset))
dd_testset_zscore <- as.data.frame(scale(dd_testset))
```

Let's build models using these scaled values.

```
dd_test_pred_zs_k1 <- knn(
  train = dd_trainset_zscore,
  test = dd_testset_zscore,
  cl = dd_trainset_labels[1:5000],
  k = 1)
dd_test_pred_zs_k5 <-  knn(
  train = dd_trainset_zscore,
  test = dd_testset_zscore,
  cl = dd_trainset_labels[1:5000],
  k = 5)
dd_test_pred_zs_k10 <-  knn(
  train = dd_trainset_zscore,
  test = dd_testset_zscore,
  cl = dd_trainset_labels[1:5000],
  k = 10)
dd_test_pred_zs_k32 <-  knn(
  train = dd_trainset_zscore,
  test = dd_testset_zscore,
  cl = dd_trainset_labels[1:5000],
  k = 32)
```

Let's see whether the scaling helped.

```
confusionMatrix(table(dd_test_pred_zs_k1,
    dd_testset_labels), positive = "Y")
confusionMatrix(table(dd_test_pred_zs_k5,
```

```
        dd_testset_labels), positive = "Y")
confusionMatrix(table(dd_test_pred_zs_k10,
    dd_testset_labels), positive = "Y")
confusionMatrix(table(dd_test_pred_zs_k32,
    dd_testset_labels), positive = "Y")
```

Using the KNN algorithm, we were able to predict whether a constituent was a donor or non-donor with 92% accuracy using a k (neighbors) value of 10, which produced 141 false negatives and 263 false positives.

To improve the results of the KNN model, we alternatively used the scale function to rescale our numerical input data values into z-scores and built a second classifier with 93% accuracy using a k (neighbors) value of 10, which produced 120 false negatives and 239 false positives.

> We selected this model and its corresponding features (variables) to introduce you to the concept and process of building a model. While the other machine learning recipes in this chapter build on this example, we encourage you to think about your own institutional data and the kinds of problems you need to solve. Please refer to the Feature Selection section for more details.

12.2.3 Probabilistic Machine Learning

Probabilistic machine learning uses statistical metrics to classify (predict) test values based on input (training) data about prior events.

314 MACHINE LEARNING RECIPES

12.2.3.1 Naive Bayes

Naive Bayes is one of the most commonly used machine learning methods for classification tasks such as spam filtering, and fraud detection

As suggested by its name, the naive Bayes algorithm makes a couple of "naive" assumptions about your input data. Specifically, naive Bayes assumes that all of the features in your data are independent and equally important. Despite these rather unrealistic set of assumptions, the naive Bayes algorithm is useful and performs relatively well in many kinds of real-world applications and contexts. Naive Bayes is an especially popular choice for text-classification learning problems, which we will further explore in the Text Mining chapter.

Since we changed the underlying data in the previous example, going forward we will reload the data and manipulate it so that the format works for the technique used in the following examples.

```r
# Load readr
library(readr)

# Load dplyr
library(dplyr)

# Load e1071
library(e1071)

# Load caret package
library(caret)

# Set Seed for Repeatable Results
set.seed(123)
```

SUPERVISED LEARNING 315

```r
# Load Data
donor_data <- read_csv("data/DonorSampleDataML.csv")
```

Let's select the variables (features) we need for this example.

```r
pred_vars <- c('MARITAL_STATUS', 'GENDER',
                'ALUMNUS_IND', 'PARENT_IND',
                'HAS_INVOLVEMENT_IND', 'DEGREE_LEVEL',
                'PREF_ADDRESS_TYPE', 'EMAIL_PRESENT_IND',
                'DONOR_IND')
donor_data <- select(donor_data,
                pred_vars,
                AGE)
```

Next, let's convert the character variables to factor type.

```r
donor_data <- mutate_at(donor_data,
                .vars = pred_vars,
                .funs = as.factor)
```

Similar to the example above, let's split the data into test and training.

```r
dd_index <- sample(2, nrow(donor_data),
                replace = TRUE,
                prob = c(0.7, 0.3))
dd_trainset <- donor_data[dd_index == 1, ]
dd_testset <- donor_data[dd_index == 2, ]

# Confirm size of training and test
# datasets
dim(dd_trainset)
#> [1] 24287     10
```

316   MACHINE LEARNING RECIPES

```r
dim(dd_testset)
#> [1] 10221    10
```

Now, the easy part. Let's build the naive Bayes classification model
from the e1071 library (Meyer et al. 2017).

```r
dd_naivebayes <- naiveBayes(
  DONOR_IND ~ MARITAL_STATUS + GENDER
  + ALUMNUS_IND + PARENT_IND + HAS_INVOLVEMENT_IND
  + DEGREE_LEVEL + EMAIL_PRESENT_IND + AGE,
  data = dd_trainset)
```

Let's see how the model performed.

```r
dd_naivebayes
#>
#> Naive Bayes Classifier for Discrete Predictors
#>
#> Call:
#> naiveBayes.default(x = X, y = Y, laplace = laplace)
#>
#> A-priori probabilities:
#> Y
#>     N      Y
#> 0.377 0.623
#>
#> Conditional probabilities:
#>    MARITAL_STATUS
#> Y   Divorced  Married Never Married Separated
#>   N 2.62e-03 1.74e-01     1.09e-04  1.09e-04
#>   Y 2.05e-03 1.97e-01     6.61e-05  3.30e-04
#>    MARITAL_STATUS
#> Y    Single  Unknown  Widowed
```

```
#>    N 1.00e-01 7.19e-01 4.15e-03
#>    Y 8.70e-02 7.08e-01 5.62e-03
#>
#>    GENDER
#> Y    Female    Male Unknown
#>    N 0.4876 0.4600   0.0524
#>    Y 0.4761 0.4796   0.0443
#>
#>    ALUMNUS_IND
#> Y         N        Y
#>    N 0.8276 0.1724
#>    Y 0.0136 0.9864
#>
#>    PARENT_IND
#> Y         N        Y
#>    N 0.9825 0.0175
#>    Y 0.9246 0.0754
#>
#>    HAS_INVOLVEMENT_IND
#> Y        N        Y
#>    N 0.782 0.218
#>    Y 0.750 0.250
#>
#>    DEGREE_LEVEL
#> Y    Graduate Non-Alumni Undergrad
#>    N   0.0000     0.8337    0.1663
#>    Y   0.1130     0.0136    0.8734
#>
#>    EMAIL_PRESENT_IND
#> Y        N        Y
#>    N 0.687 0.313
#>    Y 0.659 0.341
#>
```

318 MACHINE LEARNING RECIPES

```
#>      AGE
#> Y   [,1] [,2]
#>   N 31.4 11.8
#>   Y 43.7 11.2
```

Let's make predictions on the test data set using the `predict` function.

```
donor_prediction <- predict(
  dd_naivebayes, select(dd_testset,
                        pred_vars,
                        AGE))
```

Did the predictions work? Let's check out the confusion matrix.

```
naivebayes.crosstab <- table(donor_prediction, dd_testset$DONOR_IND)

confusionMatrix(naivebayes.crosstab, positive = "Y")
#> Confusion Matrix and Statistics
#>
#>
#> donor_prediction    N     Y
#>                N 3241    91
#>                Y  677  6212
#>
#>                Accuracy : 0.925
#>                  95% CI : (0.92, 0.93)
#>     No Information Rate : 0.617
#>     P-Value [Acc > NIR] : <2e-16
#>
#>                   Kappa : 0.836
#>   Mcnemar's Test P-Value : <2e-16
#>
#>             Sensitivity : 0.986
```

```
#>             Specificity : 0.827
#>          Pos Pred Value : 0.902
#>          Neg Pred Value : 0.973
#>              Prevalence : 0.617
#>          Detection Rate : 0.608
#>    Detection Prevalence : 0.674
#>       Balanced Accuracy : 0.906
#>
#>        'Positive' Class : Y
#>
```

Using the naive Bayes algorithm, we predicted whether a constituent was a donor or non-donor with 92.49% accuracy, which produced 648 false negatives and 85 false positives.

Instead of using the naive Bayes algorithm with out-of-the-box parameters, try experimenting with different `laplace` values in your `naiveBayes()` function. Can you increase the accuracy of the model using different `laplace` values? Write the `?naiveBayes` command in your R console for additional documentation details.

We will explore how to use the naive Bayes machine learning method to build a text classifier, make predictions, and evaluate results in the Text Mining chapter.

For now, let's continue exploring different types of machine learning algorithms to increase your overall exposure, familiarity, and understanding of various algorithms you will likely encounter and/or use in your data analytics journey.

320 MACHINE LEARNING RECIPES

12.2.4 Decision Trees

Decision trees are fundamental machine learning tools that help explore the structure of input (training) data by providing visual decision rules that predict classification (categorical) or regression (continuous) outcomes.

Decision trees (also known as **tree-based models**) use a split condition method to classify (predict) class or group membership based on one or more input variables. The classification process begins at the root node of the decision tree and repeatedly checks whether it should proceed to the right or left sub-branch node based on the split condition criteria, evaluating the input variable value at each node. The decision tree (also known as a **recursive partitioning tree**) is built once this recursive splitting process is completed.

For additional details about decision trees, you may refer to the Decision Tree Learning[3] article.

12.2.4.1 CART

Classification and Regression Tree (also known as **CART**) models can be generated using the `rpart` package.

Suppose you are preparing for an upcoming fundraising campaign and need to identify, prioritize, and engage various constituents (for example, alumni, parents, and friends) to support your institution. Using example data and the `rpart` package (Therneau et al. 2017), let's train a classification model that predicts whether a constituent is a donor or non-donor based on available input (training) data such as demographic factors, educational level, involvement indicators, and communication preferences.

---

[3]https://en.wikipedia.org/wiki/Decision_tree_learning

12.2.4.2 `rpart`

First, let's install the `rpart` and `rpart.plot` libraries (Therneau et al. 2017, Milborrow 2017).

```
# Install rpart.plot
install.packages(c("rpart", "rpart.plot"),
                 repos = 'http://cran.us.r-project.org')
```

Next, let's load the data, select model variables, and change the column types.

```
# Load readr
library(readr)

# Load rpart
library(rpart)

# Load rpart.plot
library(rpart.plot)

# Load caret library
library(caret)

# Load Data
donor_data <- read_csv("data/DonorSampleDataML.csv")

pred_vars <- c('MARITAL_STATUS', 'GENDER',
               'ALUMNUS_IND', 'PARENT_IND',
               'HAS_INVOLVEMENT_IND', 'DEGREE_LEVEL',
               'PREF_ADDRESS_TYPE', 'EMAIL_PRESENT_IND',
               'DONOR_IND')

donor_data <- select(donor_data,
```

322 MACHINE LEARNING RECIPES

```r
                          pred_vars,
                          AGE)

# Set Seed for Repeatable Results
set.seed(777)

# Convert features to factor
donor_data <- mutate_at(donor_data,
                        .vars = pred_vars,
                        .funs = as.factor)
```

Let's divide the data into test and training data sets.

```r
dd_index <- sample(2,
                   nrow(donor_data),
                   replace = TRUE,
                   prob = c(0.7, 0.3))
dd_trainset <- donor_data[dd_index == 1, ]
dd_testset <- donor_data[dd_index == 2, ]

# Confirm size of training and test
# datasets
dim(dd_trainset)
#> [1] 24195     10
dim(dd_testset)
#> [1] 10313     10
```

Now, let's build the decision tree using the rpart function.

```r
dd.rp <- rpart(
  DONOR_IND ~ .,
  method = "class",
  control = rpart.control(minsplit = 2,
```

```
                    minbucket = 2,
                    cp = 0.001),
  data = dd_trainset)
```

You will notice that I provided control parameters such as `minsplit`, `minbucket`, and `cp` to the `rpart` function. These parameters help us decide how the tree is constructed. You should try different settings to test whether you obtain different results.

Now, the easy part. Let's see what the tree looks like.

```
dd.rp
#> n= 24195
#>
#> node), split, n, loss, yval, (yprob)
#>       * denotes terminal node
#>
#>  1) root 24195 9200 Y (0.3801 0.6199)
#>    2) DEGREE_LEVEL=Non-Alumni 7856  212 N (0.9730 0.0270) *
#>    3) DEGREE_LEVEL=Graduate,Undergrad 16339 1550 Y (0.0950 0.9050)
#>      6) AGE< 25.5 1568  590 N (0.6237 0.3763)
#>       12) AGE>=22.5 1263  313 N (0.7522 0.2478)
#>         24) PREF_ADDRESS_TYPE=BUSN,HOME,OTR,Unknown 1191  256 N (0.7851 0.2149) *
#>         25) PREF_ADDRESS_TYPE=CAMP 72   15 Y (0.2083 0.7917) *
#>       13) AGE< 22.5 305   28 Y (0.0918 0.9082) *
#>      7) AGE>=25.5 14771  575 Y (0.0389 0.9611) *
```

Let's look at the complexity of the tree.

```
printcp(dd.rp)
#>
#> Classification tree:
#> rpart(formula = DONOR_IND ~ ., data = dd_trainset, method = "class",
#>     control = rpart.control(minsplit = 2, minbucket = 2, cp = 0.001))
```

```
#> 
#> Variables actually used in tree construction:
#> [1] AGE               DEGREE_LEVEL
#> [3] PREF_ADDRESS_TYPE
#> 
#> Root node error: 9197/24195 = 0.4
#> 
#> n= 24195
#> 
#>       CP nsplit rel error xerror  xstd
#> 1 0.808      0       1.0    1.0 0.008
#> 2 0.042      1       0.2    0.2 0.004
#> 3 0.027      2       0.1    0.1 0.004
#> 4 0.005      3       0.1    0.1 0.004
#> 5 0.001      4       0.1    0.1 0.004
```

We can also visualize the complexity and model performance using the `plotcp` function.

```
plotcp(dd.rp)
```

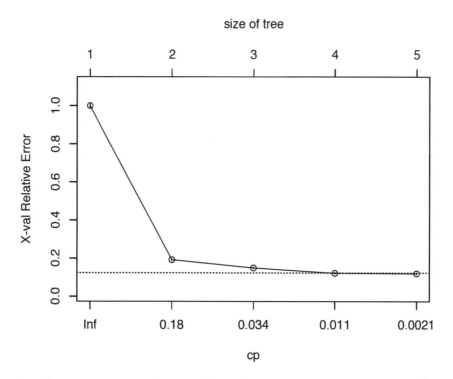

Another way to see the model performance is to simply use the summary function.

```
summary(dd.rp)
#> Call:
#> rpart(formula = DONOR_IND ~ ., data = dd_trainset, method = "class",
#>     control = rpart.control(minsplit = 2, minbucket = 2, cp = 0.001))
#>   n= 24195
#>
#>         CP nsplit rel error xerror    xstd
#> 1 0.80809      0     1.000  1.000 0.00821
#> 2 0.04219      1     0.192  0.192 0.00440
#> 3 0.02707      2     0.150  0.150 0.00392
#> 4 0.00457      3     0.123  0.123 0.00357
#> 5 0.00100      4     0.118  0.120 0.00353
#>
```

```
#> Variable importance
#> DEGREE_LEVEL   ALUMNUS_IND          AGE
#>           39             39           22
#>
#> Node number 1: 24195 observations,    complexity param=0.808
#>   predicted class=Y  expected loss=0.38  P(node) =1
#>     class counts:  9197 14998
#>    probabilities: 0.380 0.620
#>    left son=2 (7856 obs) right son=3 (16339 obs)
#>    Primary splits:
#>        DEGREE_LEVEL       splits as  RLR,      improve=8180.0, (0 missing
#>        ALUMNUS_IND        splits as  LR,       improve=8090.0, (0 missing
#>        AGE                < 25.5 to the left,  improve=4910.0, (0 missing
#>        PARENT_IND         splits as  LR,       improve= 182.0, (0 missing
#>        HAS_INVOLVEMENT_IND splits as  LR,      improve=  22.5, (0 missing
#>    Surrogate splits:
#>        ALUMNUS_IND splits as  LR,       agree=0.998, adj=0.993, (0 split)
#>        AGE         < 25.5 to the left,  agree=0.813, adj=0.424, (0 split)
#>
#> Node number 2: 7856 observations
#>   predicted class=N  expected loss=0.027  P(node) =0.325
#>     class counts:  7644    212
#>    probabilities: 0.973 0.027
#>
#> Node number 3: 16339 observations,    complexity param=0.0422
#>   predicted class=Y  expected loss=0.095  P(node) =0.675
#>     class counts:  1553 14786
#>    probabilities: 0.095 0.905
#>    left son=6 (1568 obs) right son=7 (14771 obs)
#>    Primary splits:
#>        AGE                < 25.5 to the left,  improve=970.000, (0 missi
#>        DEGREE_LEVEL       splits as  R-L,      improve= 33.400, (0 missi
#>        PARENT_IND         splits as  LR,       improve= 19.600, (0 missi
```

```
#>       HAS_INVOLVEMENT_IND splits as  LR,        improve=  2.790, (0 missing)
#>       MARITAL_STATUS      splits as  RRRRLLR,  improve=  0.846, (0 missing)
#>
#> Node number 6: 1568 observations,    complexity param=0.0271
#>   predicted class=N  expected loss=0.376  P(node) =0.0648
#>     class counts:   978    590
#>    probabilities: 0.624 0.376
#>   left son=12 (1263 obs) right son=13 (305 obs)
#>   Primary splits:
#>       AGE               < 22.5 to the right, improve=214.0, (0 missing)
#>       MARITAL_STATUS    splits as  LL--LRL,  improve= 86.5, (0 missing)
#>       PREF_ADDRESS_TYPE splits as  LRLLL,    improve= 39.5, (0 missing)
#>       EMAIL_PRESENT_IND splits as  LR,       improve= 15.4, (0 missing)
#>       DEGREE_LEVEL      splits as  R-L,      improve= 10.2, (0 missing)
#>
#> Node number 7: 14771 observations
#>   predicted class=Y  expected loss=0.0389  P(node) =0.61
#>     class counts:   575 14196
#>    probabilities: 0.039 0.961
#>
#> Node number 12: 1263 observations,    complexity param=0.00457
#>   predicted class=N  expected loss=0.248  P(node) =0.0522
#>     class counts:   950    313
#>    probabilities: 0.752 0.248
#>   left son=24 (1191 obs) right son=25 (72 obs)
#>   Primary splits:
#>       PREF_ADDRESS_TYPE   splits as  LRLLL,    improve=45.20, (0 missing)
#>       MARITAL_STATUS      splits as  LL--LRL,  improve=41.20, (0 missing)
#>       EMAIL_PRESENT_IND   splits as  LR,       improve=19.70, (0 missing)
#>       DEGREE_LEVEL        splits as  R-L,      improve=13.70, (0 missing)
#>       HAS_INVOLVEMENT_IND splits as  LR,       improve= 6.47, (0 missing)
#>
#> Node number 13: 305 observations
```

```
#>    predicted class=Y   expected loss=0.0918   P(node) =0.0126
#>       class counts:    28    277
#>      probabilities: 0.092 0.908
#>
#> Node number 24: 1191 observations
#>    predicted class=N   expected loss=0.215   P(node) =0.0492
#>       class counts:   935    256
#>      probabilities: 0.785 0.215
#>
#> Node number 25: 72 observations
#>    predicted class=Y   expected loss=0.208   P(node) =0.00298
#>       class counts:    15    57
#>      probabilities: 0.208 0.792
```

Using the `rpart.plot` function, we can visualize the tree.

```
rpart.plot(dd.rp, extra = 2, tweak = 1,
           main = "Donor decision tree using the rpart package")
```

Donor decision tree using the rpart package

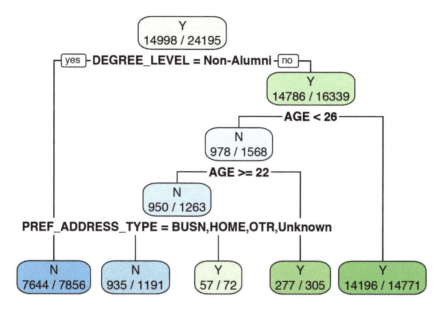

Let's see how the model performed on the test data set. First, let's store all the predictions.

```
predictions <- predict(dd.rp, dd_testset,
                       type = "class")
```

Then, let's create a cross-table of actual donors and non-donors and the predictions.

```
table(dd_testset$DONOR_IND, predictions)
#>    predictions
#>       N    Y
#>    N 3635  243
#>    Y  199 6236
```

Finally, let's create a confusion matrix using the caret library.

330 MACHINE LEARNING RECIPES

```r
confusionMatrix(
  table(predictions, dd_testset$DONOR_IND),
  positive = "Y")
#> Confusion Matrix and Statistics
#>
#>
#> predictions    N    Y
#>           N 3635  199
#>           Y  243 6236
#>
#>                Accuracy : 0.957
#>                  95% CI : (0.953, 0.961)
#>     No Information Rate : 0.624
#>     P-Value [Acc > NIR] : <2e-16
#>
#>                   Kappa : 0.908
#>   Mcnemar's Test P-Value : 0.0408
#>
#>             Sensitivity : 0.969
#>             Specificity : 0.937
#>          Pos Pred Value : 0.962
#>          Neg Pred Value : 0.948
#>              Prevalence : 0.624
#>          Detection Rate : 0.605
#>    Detection Prevalence : 0.628
#>       Balanced Accuracy : 0.953
#>
#>        'Positive' Class : Y
#>
```

The decision tree created using the example donor data observes 95.71% accuracy with primary node splits using features such as educational level (DEGREE_LEVEL), alumni type (ALUM-

NUS_IND), AGE, parent (PARENT_IND), and involvement indicator (HAS_INVOLVEMENT_IND).

Decision trees are widely used for building classification models based on their training flexibility, output readability, and ease of interpretation. The disadvantage of using decision trees is that they tend to be biased and over-fitted to noise (error) in your training data. To deal with this you can explore tree pruning, as well as other machine learning algorithms such as conditional inference trees, random forests, etc.

12.2.4.3 Conditional Inference Tree

The `party` package provides non-parametric classification (categorical) and regression (continuous) tree-based models. The specific type of tree created will depend on the outcome variable type (for example, nominal, ordinal, or numeric.), and the tree growth will be determined by statistical metrics.

Use the following command to install the `party` package (Hothorn et al. 2017):

```
# Install party
install.packages("party",
  repos = 'http://cran.us.r-project.org')
```

Let's explore how to build a conditional inference tree using the `party` and `caret` library. Let's load the libraries and prepare the data.

```
# Load party
library(party)

# Load caret library
library(caret)
```

332   MACHINE LEARNING RECIPES

```r
# Load Data
donor_data <- read_csv("data/DonorSampleDataML.csv")

pred_vars <- c('MARITAL_STATUS', 'GENDER',
                  'ALUMNUS_IND', 'PARENT_IND',
                  'HAS_INVOLVEMENT_IND', 'DEGREE_LEVEL',
                  'PREF_ADDRESS_TYPE', 'EMAIL_PRESENT_IND',
                  'DONOR_IND')

donor_data <- select(donor_data,
                  pred_vars,
                  AGE)
# Set Seed for Repeatable Results
set.seed(777)

# Convert features to factor
donor_data <- mutate_at(donor_data,
                  .vars = c('MARITAL_STATUS', 'GENDER',
                  'ALUMNUS_IND', 'PARENT_IND',
                  'HAS_INVOLVEMENT_IND', 'DEGREE_LEVEL',
                  'PREF_ADDRESS_TYPE', 'EMAIL_PRESENT_IND',
                  'DONOR_IND'),
                  .funs = as.factor)

# Split 70% of donor_data into training
# data and 30% into test data
dd_index <- sample(2,
                  nrow(donor_data),
                  replace = TRUE,
                  prob = c(0.7, 0.3))
dd_trainset <- donor_data[dd_index == 1, ]
dd_testset <- donor_data[dd_index == 2, ]
```

```r
# Confirm size of training and test datasets
dim(dd_trainset)
dim(dd_testset)
```

Now, let's use the `ctree` function to build a conditional inference tree.

```r
dd.cit <- ctree(DONOR_IND ~ .,
                data = dd_trainset)
```

What does the conditional inference tree look like?

```r
dd.cit
```

Let's also see the summary of the mode.

```r
summary(dd.cit)
```

Next, let's plot the conditional inference tree.

```r
plot(dd.cit, main = "Donor Conditional Inference Tree")
```

Now, let's store the predictions and create a confusion matrix.

```r
predictions <- predict(dd.cit, dd_testset)

# Generate cross-table for conditional inference tree
table(dd_testset$DONOR_IND, predictions)

# Create confusion matrix
confusionMatrix(
  table(predictions, dd_testset$DONOR_IND),
  positive = "Y")
```

334 MACHINE LEARNING RECIPES

The `ctree` algorithm built a model with 95.71% accuracy with our test data.

12.2.4.4 `C50`

The `C50` package is another popular tool for building decision trees (Kuhn & Quinlan 2017).

Let's explore how to use the `C50` algorithm to build a decision tree, but first, we should install the library.

```
# Install C50 package
install.packages("C50",
                 repos = 'http://cran.us.r-project.org')
```

Next, let's load and prep the data.

```
# Load readr
library(readr)

# Load dplyr
library(dplyr)

# Load lubridate
library(lubridate)

# Load C50 package
library(C50)

# Load caret library
library(caret)

# Set Seed for Repeatable Results
set.seed(123)
```

```r
# Load Data
donor_data <- read_csv("data/DonorSampleDataML.csv")

# Drop 'ID', 'MEMBERSHIP_ID', etc.
pred_vars <- c('MARITAL_STATUS', 'GENDER',
                    'ALUMNUS_IND', 'PARENT_IND',
                    'HAS_INVOLVEMENT_IND', 'DEGREE_LEVEL',
                    'PREF_ADDRESS_TYPE', 'EMAIL_PRESENT_IND')
donor_data <- select(donor_data,
                    pred_vars,
                    DONOR_IND)

# Convert from character to numeric data type
convert_fac2num <- function(x){
  as.numeric(as.factor(x))
}

# Convert features from factor to numeric

donor_data <- mutate_at(donor_data,
                    .vars = pred_vars,
                    .funs = convert_fac2num)

# Convert feature to factor
donor_data$DONOR_IND <- as.factor(donor_data$DONOR_IND)

# Split 70% of donor_data into training
# data and 30% into test data
dd_index <- sample(2,
                    nrow(donor_data),
                    replace = TRUE,
                    prob = c(0.7, 0.3))
dd_trainset <- donor_data[dd_index == 1, ]
```

336 MACHINE LEARNING RECIPES

```r
dd_testset <- donor_data[dd_index == 2, ]

# Confirm size of training and test
# datasets
dim(dd_trainset)
#> [1] 24287      9
dim(dd_testset)
#> [1] 10221      9

# Create prop table
prop.table(table(dd_trainset$DONOR_IND))
#>
#>     N     Y
#> 0.377 0.623
prop.table(table(dd_testset$DONOR_IND))
#>
#>     N     Y
#> 0.383 0.617
```

Using the `prop.table` function reveals there are about 62% donors and 38% non-donors in both the training and test datasets.

Now, let's build the model using the `c50` algorithm.

```r
# Use C50 to build a decision tree model
donor_model <- C5.0(x = select(dd_trainset, -DONOR_IND),
                    y = dd_trainset$DONOR_IND)
```

What does the tree look like?

```r
donor_model
#>
#> Call:
#> C5.0.default(x = select(dd_trainset,
```

```
#>   -DONOR_IND), y = dd_trainset$DONOR_IND)
#>
#> Classification Tree
#> Number of samples: 24287
#> Number of predictors: 8
#>
#> Tree size: 3
#>
#> Non-standard options: attempt to group attributes
```

Let's see the summary of the model.

```
summary(donor_model)
#>
#> Call:
#> C5.0.default(x = select(dd_trainset,
#>   -DONOR_IND), y = dd_trainset$DONOR_IND)
#>
#>
#> C5.0 [Release 2.07 GPL Edition]      Sat Mar  3 21:20:37 2018
#> -------------------------------
#>
#> Class specified by attribute `outcome'
#>
#> Read 24287 cases (9 attributes) from undefined.data
#>
#> Decision tree:
#>
#> DEGREE_LEVEL <= 1: Y (1710)
#> DEGREE_LEVEL > 1:
#> :...DEGREE_LEVEL <= 2: N (7840/206)
#>     DEGREE_LEVEL > 2: Y (14737/1523)
#>
```

338   MACHINE LEARNING RECIPES

```
#>
#> Evaluation on training data (24287 cases):
#>
#>        Decision Tree
#>      ----------------
#>      Size      Errors
#>
#>         3 1729( 7.1%)    <<
#>
#>
#>     (a)    (b)      <-classified as
#>     ----   ----
#>     7634   1523     (a): class N
#>      206 14924      (b): class Y
#>
#>
#>  Attribute usage:
#>
#>  100.00% DEGREE_LEVEL
#>
#>
#> Time: 0.0 secs
```

Now, let's store the predictions and create a confusion matrix.

```
donor_predictions <- predict(donor_model,
   dd_testset)

# Create confusion matrix
confusionMatrix(table(donor_predictions,
  dd_testset$DONOR_IND),
  positive = "Y")
#> Confusion Matrix and Statistics
```

```
#> 
#> 
#> donor_predictions    N    Y
#>                  N 3242    91
#>                  Y  676 6212
#> 
#>                 Accuracy : 0.925
#>                   95% CI : (0.92, 0.93)
#>      No Information Rate : 0.617
#>      P-Value [Acc > NIR] : <2e-16
#> 
#>                    Kappa : 0.837
#>   Mcnemar's Test P-Value : <2e-16
#> 
#>              Sensitivity : 0.986
#>              Specificity : 0.827
#>           Pos Pred Value : 0.902
#>           Neg Pred Value : 0.973
#>               Prevalence : 0.617
#>           Detection Rate : 0.608
#>     Detection Prevalence : 0.674
#>        Balanced Accuracy : 0.907
#> 
#>         'Positive' Class : Y
#> 
```

The `c50` algorithm built a model with 92.50% accuracy with our test data. Let's explore if we can improve the performance of the decision tree model using ensemble methods.

340 MACHINE LEARNING RECIPES

12.2.4.5 Ensemble Learning

Ensemble learning is a machine learning method that uses a combination of learning algorithms to improve predictive results. Boosting is a popular ensemble learning technique that reduces model bias by adding models that learn from the misclassification errors generated by other models.

Let's explore how to use the boosting parameters within the C5.0 library to increase the performance of your decision tree models by adding multiple trials (models) with adaptive boosting.

12.2.4.6 Adaptive Boosting

We can create ensemble models by simply adding the number of boosting iterations to the `trials` parameter of the `C50` function. Note that this code may take a long time to run.

```r
# Set Seed for Repeatable Results
set.seed(123)

# Use C5.0 to build a decision tree model
# with n=20 trials of adaptive boosting
donor_model_boost20 <- C5.0(
  x = select(dd_trainset, -DONOR_IND),
  y = dd_trainset$DONOR_IND,
  trials = 20)
```

After the model is trained, we can see how well it performed by printing the model details and summary and looking at the confusion matrix.

```r
# Show C5.0 decision tree with adaptive boosting
donor_model_boost20
```

```
# Examine C5.0 decision tree model with
# adaptive boosting
summary(donor_model_boost20)

# Apply decision tree to test data
donor_predictions_boost20 <- predict(donor_model_boost20,
                                     dd_testset)

# Create confusion matrix
confusionMatrix(
  table(donor_predictions_boost20, dd_testset$DONOR_IND),
positive = "Y")
```

With our test data, the addition of 20 trials of adaptive boosting did not significantly increase the performance of the decision tree beyond 92.5%.

Try different adaptive boosting parameters to determine whether you can improve the accuracy of the model. Does the accuracy always improve as you increase the number of trials?

12.2.4.7 Random Forests

Random forests (also known as **random decision forests**) is an ensemble learning method that builds a collection of decision tree models and uses its output to correct any observed overfitting encountered during the training process.

The following example outlines how to use the `randomForest` library to build a random forest model to predict donor classification (Liaw et al. 2002, Breiman et al. 2015).

342 MACHINE LEARNING RECIPES

```r
# Install randomForest
install.packages("randomForest",
  repos = 'http://cran.us.r-project.org')
```

Let's load the library and prep the data.

```r
# Load randomForest
library(randomForest)

# Load Data
donor_data <- read_csv("data/DonorSampleDataML.csv")

# Drop 'ID', 'MEMBERSHIP_ID', etc.
pred_vars <- c('MARITAL_STATUS', 'GENDER',
               'ALUMNUS_IND', 'PARENT_IND',
               'HAS_INVOLVEMENT_IND', 'DEGREE_LEVEL',
               'PREF_ADDRESS_TYPE', 'EMAIL_PRESENT_IND')
donor_data <- select(donor_data,
                     pred_vars,
                     DONOR_IND)
# Set Seed for Repeatable Results
set.seed(777)

# Convert features to factor
donor_data <- mutate_at(donor_data,
                        .vars = c(pred_vars,
                                  'DONOR_IND'),
                        .funs = as.factor)

# Split 70% of donor_data into training
# data and 30% into test data
dd_index <- sample(2, nrow(donor_data), replace = TRUE,
    prob = c(0.7, 0.3))
```

SUPERVISED LEARNING **343**

```
dd_trainset <- donor_data[dd_index == 1, ]
dd_testset <- donor_data[dd_index == 2, ]

# Confirm size of training and test
# datasets
dim(dd_trainset)
dim(dd_testset)
```

Now let's use the `randomForest` function to build a model.

```
dd.rf <- randomForest(DONOR_IND ~ .,
                      data = dd_trainset)

# Show randomForest details
dd.rf

# Examine model summary
summary(dd.rf)

# Print results
print(dd.rf)

# Measure predictor importance
importance(dd.rf)
```

12.2.4.8 `xgboost`

Extreme gradient boosting (`xgboost`) is another ensemble learning method for classification and regression tasks. The `xgboost` library builds upon gradient boosting, which is an ensemble machine learning method that generates predictions using a collection of decision tree learners. `xgboost` is a popular machine learning tool in data mining competitions due to its speed and ability to execute parallel computations on a single machine (Chen et al. 2017).

To learn more about gradient boosting, you can refer to this article[4].

 Download the xgboost library and build an ensemble learning model to predict whether a constituent is a donor or nondonor based on available training (input) data.

12.2.5 Rule-Based Classification

Rule-based classification, similar to decision tree classification, is a machine learning method you can use to identify actionable patterns in your data. Rule-based models (also known as **separate-and-conquer** rule learners) select test conditions that help identify useful relationships in your data.

12.2.5.1 OneR

As seen in Section 3.2, the OneR (also known as **One Rule**) algorithm can be used to build a simple, yet accurate, model that strikes a balance between accuracy and interpretability (Holte 1993). OneR generates one rule for each predictor in your training data and then selects the rule with the smallest total error as its "one rule".

Let's explore how to build a classification model using the OneR algorithm. We will use the R version of the Weka machine learning package called RWeka (Witten & Frank 2005, Hornik et al. 2009).

```
install.packages("RWeka",
                 repos = 'http://cran.us.r-project.org')
```

---

[4]https://en.wikipedia.org/wiki/Gradient_boosting

```
# Load RWeka
library(RWeka)

# Set Seed for Repeatable Results
set.seed(777)
```

Let's build the OneR model using the OneR function from the RWeka library.

```
donor_OneR <- OneR(DONOR_IND ~ AGE + MARITAL_STATUS +
                   GENDER + ALUMNUS_IND + PARENT_IND +
                   HAS_INVOLVEMENT_IND + PREF_ADDRESS_TYPE +
                   EMAIL_PRESENT_IND,
                data = donor_data)
```

Let's see what the model looks like.

```
donor_OneR
```

We can also see the summary of model performance using the summary function.

```
summary(donor_OneR)
```

The OneR model observed an accuracy of 92.5%.

Let's try another rule learning method to see if we can increase accuracy.

346 MACHINE LEARNING RECIPES

12.2.5.2 `JRip`

The `JRip` library implements a propositional rule learner, "Repeated Incremental Pruning to Produce Error Reduction" (RIPPER), as proposed in the article **Fast Effective Rule Induction** (Cohen 1995).

```r
# Load RWeka
library(RWeka)

# Set Seed for Repeatable Results
set.seed(777)
```

Let's build the `JRip` model.

```r
donor_JRip <- JRip(DONOR_IND ~ AGE + MARITAL_STATUS +
                     GENDER + ALUMNUS_IND + PARENT_IND +
                     HAS_INVOLVEMENT_IND +
                     PREF_ADDRESS_TYPE + EMAIL_PRESENT_IND,
                   data = donor_data)
```

Let's see what the `JRIP` rules look like.

```r
donor_JRip
```

And, finally, let's see the model evaluation.

```r
summary(donor_JRip)
```

The `JRip` model generated 10 rules which correctly classified 95.6% of the test instances.

Let's explore some other advanced machine learning methods that are used in various real-world applications.

12.2.5.3 Neural Networks

A neural network is a powerful machine learning technique that uses a network of computational models to provide iterative feedback and make predictions using input data. Neural networks, which simulate the interconnected signaling processes and activities of the human brain, are composed of input layers (training data), hidden layers (backpropagation layers that optimize input variable weights to improve predictive power), and output layers (predicted outcomes based on iterative feedback from input and hidden layers) (Nandeshwar 2006). A typical representation of a neural network is shown in Figure 12.1. Due to the complexity of neural network (NN) algorithms, they are often referred to as black box methods.

Let's explore how to build and implement an NN model using our synthetic donor data file. First, let's load the libraries and prep the data.

```
# Load readr
library(readr)

# Load dplyr
library(dplyr)

# Load neuralnet package
library(neuralnet)

# Load caret package
library(caret)

# Set Seed for Repeatable Results
set.seed(123)

# Load Data
```

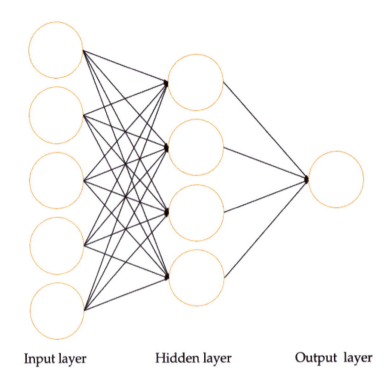

Figure 12.1: A neural network representation

```
donor_data <- read_csv("data/DonorSampleDataML.csv")

# Drop 'ID' variable
pred_vars <- c('MARITAL_STATUS', 'GENDER',
               'ALUMNUS_IND', 'PARENT_IND',
               'HAS_INVOLVEMENT_IND', 'DEGREE_LEVEL',
               'PREF_ADDRESS_TYPE', 'EMAIL_PRESENT_IND')
donor_data <- select(donor_data,
                     pred_vars,
                     DONOR_IND)
```

```r
# Convert from character to numeric data type
convert_fac2num <- function(x){
  as.numeric(as.factor(x))
}


# Convert features from factor to numeric
donor_data <- mutate_at(donor_data,
                    .vars = pred_vars),
                    .funs = convert_fac2num)


# Convert feature to factor
donor_data$DONOR_IND <- as.factor(donor_data$DONOR_IND)
```

Then let's divide 70% of the `donor_data` file into training data and 30% into test data.

```r
dd_index <- sample(2,
                    nrow(donor_data),
                    replace = TRUE,
                    prob = c(0.7, 0.3))
dd_trainset <- donor_data[dd_index == 1, ]
dd_testset <- donor_data[dd_index == 2, ]


# Confirm size of training and test
# datasets
dim(dd_trainset)
dim(dd_testset)


# Select data variable predictors
dd_trainset <- select(dd_trainset[1:5000,],
                    pred_vars)
dd_testset <- select(dd_testset[1:5000,],
                    pred_vars)
```

350 MACHINE LEARNING RECIPES

```r
# Define min-max normalization function
min_max <- function(x) {
    return((x - min(x))/(max(x) - min(x)))
}


# Apply min-max normalization to training
# and test datasets except DONOR_IND
dd_trainset_n <- mutate_at(dd_trainset,
                            .vars = pred_vars,
                            .funs = min_max)
dd_testset_n <- mutate_at(dd_testset,
                            .vars = pred_vars,
                            .funs = min_max)


# Recombine and prepare datasets for Neural Network (NN)
dd_trainset_n <- cbind(dd_trainset_n, dd_trainset[9])
dd_trainset_n <- cbind(dd_trainset_n,
                    dd_trainset_n$DONOR_IND == 'Y')
dd_trainset_n <- cbind(dd_trainset_n,
                    dd_trainset_n$DONOR_IND == 'N')
names(dd_trainset_n)[10] <- 'donor'
names(dd_trainset_n)[11] <- 'non_donor'


# Remove DONOR_IND for NN
dd_trainset_n <- dd_trainset_n[-c(9)]


# Prepare testset for NN
dd_testset_n <- cbind(dd_testset_n,dd_testset[9])

# Build NN model
dd_pred_nn <- neuralnet(donor + non_donor ~ AGE + MARITAL_STATUS
  + GENDER + ALUMNUS_IND + PARENT_IND + HAS_INVOLVEMENT_IND +
    DEGREE_LEVEL  + EMAIL_PRESENT_IND,
```

```
  data = dd_trainset_n, hidden = 1, threshold = 0.01)

# Examine NN model
dd_pred_nn$result.matrix

# Plot NN model
plot(dd_pred_nn)

# Make predictions using NN model
donor_prediction <- compute(dd_pred_nn, dd_testset_n[-9])$net.result

# Measure correlation predicted giving and true value
cor(donor_prediction[,1], as.numeric(dd_testset_n$DONOR_IND))
```

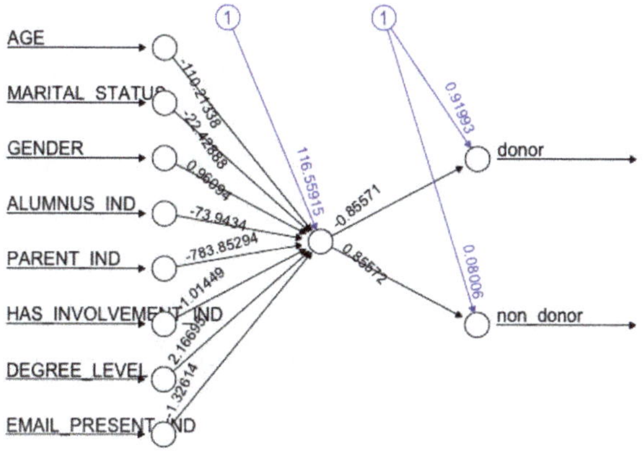

Figure 12.2: Donor neural network using neuralnet

In this example, we covered how to build an NN model, which performed relatively well with an 82% correlation between the predicted classification (donor versus non-donor) outcomes and true values relative to our test donor data.

Overall, NN models perform well with learning non-linear functions and handling multiple output variables at the same time. As

352 MACHINE LEARNING RECIPES

you might have already figured out, the primary disadvantages of NNs are that they (1) require additional training time and (2) can be more difficult to interpret than some of the other traditional and less complex machine learning algorithms previously covered.

Let's take a look at another powerful machine learning method you will likely encounter on your data science journey.

12.2.5.4 Support Vector Machines

Support vector machines (SVM) (also known as **support vector networks**) is another powerful black box[5] algorithm commonly used with supervised learning tasks such as classification and regression.

SVM uses kernel functions to map input data into high-dimensional feature (variable) spaces to efficiently perform non-linear classification. Machine learning algorithms capable of operating with kernel functions and statistical learning parameters include SVM, principal components analysis (PCA), ridge regression, spectral clustering, linear adaptive filters, and many others.

While the inner workings of NN and SVM algorithms are beyond the scope of this book, we will provide an SVM recipe you can use and test while exploring other machine learning methods and applications with your data.

```
# Load readr
library(readr)

# Load dplyr
library(dplyr)

# Load e1071
```

---

[5]https://en.wikipedia.org/wiki/Black_box

```r
library(e1071)

# Load caret package
library(caret)

# Set Seed for Repeatable Results
set.seed(123)

# Load Data
donor_data <- read_csv("data/DonorSampleDataML.csv")

# Drop 'ID', 'MEMBERSHIP_ID', etc.
pred_vars <- c('MARITAL_STATUS', 'GENDER',
                        'ALUMNUS_IND', 'PARENT_IND',
                        'HAS_INVOLVEMENT_IND', 'DEGREE_LEVEL',
                        'PREF_ADDRESS_TYPE', 'EMAIL_PRESENT_IND',
                        'DONOR_IND')
donor_data <- select(donor_data,
                    pred_vars,
                    AGE)

# Convert features to factor
donor_data <- mutate_at(donor_data,
                        .vars = pred_vars,
                        .funs = as.factor)

# Split 70% of donor_data into training
# data and 30% into test data
dd_index <- sample(2, nrow(donor_data), replace = TRUE,
    prob = c(0.7, 0.3))
dd_trainset <- donor_data[dd_index == 1, ]
dd_testset <- donor_data[dd_index == 2, ]
```

354 MACHINE LEARNING RECIPES

```
# Confirm size of training and test
# datasets
dim(dd_trainset)
dim(dd_testset)
```

Finally, let's build the model.

```
dd_svm <- svm(DONOR_IND ~ MARITAL_STATUS + GENDER +
                ALUMNUS_IND + PARENT_IND +
                HAS_INVOLVEMENT_IND + DEGREE_LEVEL +
                EMAIL_PRESENT_IND + AGE,
            data = dd_trainset,
            kernel = "radial",
            cost = 1,
            gamma = 1/ncol(dd_trainset))
```

Let's see what the model looks like.

```
dd_svm
```

Next, let's store the predictions and create a confusion matrix.

```
donor_prediction <- predict(dd_svm,
                        select(dd_testset,
                            pred_vars))

# Create SVM crosstab
svm.crosstab <- table(donor_prediction, dd_testset$DONOR_IND)

# Confusion Matrix
confusionMatrix(svm.crosstab, positive = "Y")
```

In this example, we built an SVM model using the `e1071` package and our donor file. The SVM model predicted donor versus non-donor classification with an accuracy of 94%, which suggests it is a useful machine learning algorithm to keep in mind for future predictive modeling projects.

SVMs, similar to neural networks, can efficiently handle non-linear classification problems, which makes it useful with text categorization, image segmentation, and other science-based applications. You can refer to this article[6] if you would like to learn more.

Now, let's turn our attention to another exciting topic in machine learning concepts: deep learning.

12.2.5.5 Deep Learning with `TensorFlow`

The field of data analytics is dynamic, so it is important to recognize that the machine learning algorithms we are using today will continue to improve and evolve in terms of efficiency and capability.

Deep learning (also known as **deep structured learning** or **hierarchical learning**) is a type of machine learning focused on learning data representations and feature learning rather than individual or specific tasks. Feature learning (also known as representation learning) can be supervised, semi-supervised, or unsupervised.

Deep learning architectures include deep neural networks, deep belief networks, and recurrent neural networks. Real-world applications using deep learning include computer vision, speech recognition, machine translation, natural language processing, image recognition, and so on.

The following recipe introduces how to implement a deep neural network using TensorFlow[7], which is an open source software li-

---

[6]https://en.wikipedia.org/wiki/Support_vector_machine
[7]https://www.tensorflow.org/

356   MACHINE LEARNING RECIPES

brary (originally developed at Google) for complex computation by constructing network graphs of mathematical operations and data (Abadi et al. 2016, Cheng et al. 2017). Tang et al. (2017) developed an R interface to the TensorFlow API for our use.

Before we use this library, we need to install it. Since this is a very recent library, we will install it from GitHub directly.

```
devtools::install_github("rstudio/tfestimators")
library(tfestimators)
```

Although we've installed the library, we don't have the actual compiled code for TensorFlow, which we need to install using the install_tensorlfow() command that came with the tfestimators package.

```
install_tensorflow()
```

When you try to run it, you may face an error like the following:

```
#> Error: Prerequisites for installing
#> TensorFlow not available.  Execute the
#> following at a terminal to install the
#> prerequisites: $ sudo
#> /usr/local/bin/pip install --upgrade
#> virtualenv
```

I was able to fix the error by running the above command on a Mac or Linux machine. On Windows, you may need further troubleshooting. After installing the prerequisites, you can try installing TensorFlow again.

```
install_tensorflow()
```

Next, let's load the data.

```r
library(readr)
library(dplyr)

donor_data <- read_csv("data/DonorSampleDataCleaned.csv")
```

The TensorFlow library doesn't tolerate missing values; therefore, we will replace missing factor values with modes and missing numeric values with medians.

```r
# function copied from
# https://stackoverflow.com/a/8189441/934898
my_mode <- function(x) {
    ux <- unique(x)
    ux[which.max(tabulate(match(x, ux)))]
}

donor_data <- donor_data %>%
  mutate_if(is.numeric,
            .funs = funs(
              ifelse(is.na(.),
                     median(., na.rm = TRUE),
                     .))) %>%
  mutate_if(is.character,
            .funs = funs(
              ifelse(is.na(.),
                     my_mode(.),
                     .)))
```

Next, we need to convert the character variables to factors.

```r
predictor_cols <- c("MARITAL_STATUS", "GENDER",
                    "ALUMNUS_IND", "PARENT_IND",
                    "WEALTH_RATING", "PREF_ADDRESS_TYPE")
```

358 MACHINE LEARNING RECIPES

```
# Convert feature to factor
donor_data <- mutate_at(donor_data,
                        .vars = predictor_cols,
                        .funs = as.factor)
```

Now, we need to let `TensorFlow` know about the column types. For factor columns, we need to specify all the values contained in those columns using the `column_categorical_with_vocabulary_list` function. Then, using the `column_indicator` function, we convert each of the factor values in a column to its own column with 0s and 1s — this process is known as **one hot encoding**. For example, for the GENDER column say, we have two possible values of male and female. The one hot encoding process will create two columns, one for male and the other for female. Each of these columns will contain either 0 or 1, depending on the data value the GENDER column contained.

```
feature_cols <- feature_columns(
  column_indicator(
    column_categorical_with_vocabulary_list(
      "MARITAL_STATUS",
      vocabulary_list = unique(donor_data$MARITAL_STATUS))),
    column_indicator(
      column_categorical_with_vocabulary_list(
        "GENDER",
        vocabulary_list = unique(donor_data$GENDER))),
    column_indicator(
      column_categorical_with_vocabulary_list(
        "ALUMNUS_IND",
        vocabulary_list = unique(donor_data$ALUMNUS_IND))),
    column_indicator(
      column_categorical_with_vocabulary_list(
        "PARENT_IND",
```

```
            vocabulary_list = unique(donor_data$PARENT_IND))),
    column_indicator(
      column_categorical_with_vocabulary_list(
        "WEALTH_RATING",
        vocabulary_list = unique(donor_data$WEALTH_RATING))),
    column_indicator(
      column_categorical_with_vocabulary_list(
        "PREF_ADDRESS_TYPE",
        vocabulary_list = unique(donor_data$PREF_ADDRESS_TYPE))),
    column_numeric("AGE"))
```

After we've created the column types, let's partition the data set into train and test datasets.

```
row_indices <- sample(1:nrow(donor_data),
                      size = 0.8 * nrow(donor_data))
donor_data_train <- donor_data[row_indices, ]
donor_data_test <- donor_data[-row_indices, ]
```

The TensorFlow package then requires that we create an input function with the listing of input and output variables.

```
donor_pred_fn <- function(data) {
    input_fn(data,
             features = c("AGE", "MARITAL_STATUS",
                          "GENDER", "ALUMNUS_IND",
                          "PARENT_IND", "WEALTH_RATING",
                          "PREF_ADDRESS_TYPE"),
             response = "DONOR_IND")
}
```

Finally, we can use the prepared data set as well as the input function to build a deep-learning classifier. We will create three hidden layers with 80, 40, and 30 nodes, respectively.

360 MACHINE LEARNING RECIPES

```
classifier <- dnn_classifier(
  feature_columns = feature_cols,
  hidden_units = c(80, 40, 30),
  n_classes = 2,
  label_vocabulary = c("N", "Y"))
```

Using the `train` function we will build the classifier.

```
train(classifier,
      input_fn = donor_pred_fn(donor_data_train))
```

We will next predict the values using the model for the test data set as well as the full data set.

```
predictions_test <- predict(
  classifier,
  input_fn = donor_pred_fn(donor_data_test))
predictions_all <- predict(
  classifier,
  input_fn = donor_pred_fn(donor_data))
```

Similarly, we will evaluate the model for both the test data and the full data set. You can see the evaluation using the test data in Table 12.1 and using the full data sets in Table 12.2.

```
evaluation_test <- evaluate(
  classifier,
  input_fn = donor_pred_fn(donor_data_test))
evaluation_all <- evaluate(
  classifier,
  input_fn = donor_pred_fn(donor_data))
```

Table 12.1: 'TensorFlow' evaluation using test data

Measure	Value
accuracy	84.34
accuracy_baseline	0.63
auc	216.00
auc_precision_recall	0.51
average_loss	0.62
global_step	0.63
label/mean	0.66
loss	0.63
prediction/mean	0.63

Table 12.2: 'TensorFlow' evaluation using full data

Measure	Value
accuracy	84.87
accuracy_baseline	0.62
auc	216.00
auc_precision_recall	0.51
average_loss	0.62
global_step	0.62
label/mean	0.66
loss	0.62
prediction/mean	0.62

362 MACHINE LEARNING RECIPES

12.2.6 Regression

Regression is a supervised machine learning method that analyzes and estimates the relationships among variables. Regression is widely used for prediction and forecasting tasks. Regression models are used to make numerical predictions of a continuous variable or can be used to make classification (categorical) predictions of a discrete response (dependent) variable.

12.2.6.1 Linear Regression

Linear regression is the simplest type of regression and is suitable if there is a linear relationship between the predictor (independent) and response (dependent) variables in your data. Otherwise, you should consider and explore other approaches (quadratic, polynomial, logistic, and so on).

Let's explore how to fit a linear model using the example donor file. We will use the age variable to predict the total giving of a donor. Let's load the data.

```r
# Load readr
library(readr)

# Load dplyr
library(dplyr)

# Load Data
donor_data <- read_csv("data/DonorSampleDataML.csv")

# Set Seed for Repeatable Results
set.seed(777)
```

SUPERVISED LEARNING 363

Let's look at the relationship between age and total giving by plotting that data.

```
with(donor_data, plot(AGE, TotalGiving))
```

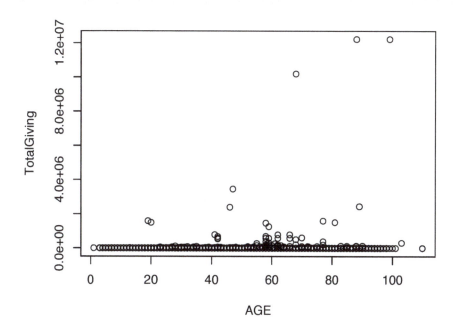

To create the linear regression model, we will use the in-built lm function.

```
giving_model <- lm(TotalGiving ~ AGE,
                   data = donor_data)
```

Next, to see the fit of the model, we will plot the regression line using the abline function.

```
with(donor_data, plot(AGE, TotalGiving))
abline(giving_model, col = "red")
```

364 MACHINE LEARNING RECIPES

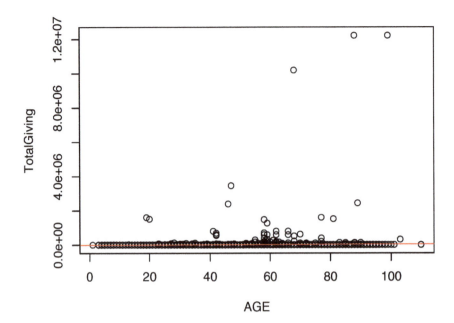

Finally, we will see the model performance using the summary function.

```
summary(giving_model)
#> 
#> Call:
#> lm(formula = TotalGiving ~ AGE, data = donor_data)
#> 
#> Residuals:
#>     Min      1Q  Median      3Q     Max
#>  -31428   -3579   -3379    3382 12199436
#> 
#> Coefficients:
#>              Estimate Std. Error t value Pr(>|t|)
#> (Intercept) -13620.8     1944.5   -7.00  2.5e-12
#> AGE            409.5       47.3    8.66  < 2e-16
#> 
#> (Intercept) ***
```

```
#> AGE            ***
#> ---
#> Signif. codes:
#> 0 '***' 0.001 '**' 0.01 '*' 0.05 '.' 0.1 ' ' 1
#>
#> Residual standard error: 114000 on 34506 degrees of freedom
#> Multiple R-squared:  0.00217,    Adjusted R-squared:  0.00214
#> F-statistic:    75 on 1 and 34506 DF,  p-value: <2e-16
```

The `summary(giving_model)` command produces various types of information you can use to evaluate the model's performance in greater detail.

The residuals provide summary statistics for the predictions errors. For example, the inter-quartile range (IQR) of the prediction errors (residuals) in this model range between -3,578 over the true value and 3,382 under the true value.

The "***" next to the AGE coefficient indicates that the AGE feature (variable) is extremely unlikely to be unrelated to the "TotalGiving" response variable, which suggests we should keep this variable in mind for feature selection when building other models.

The `R-squared` value (also known as the **coefficient of determination**) describes the proportion of variance in `TotalGiving` (dependent variable) that is explained by the model. Broadly speaking, the closer that value is to 1.0, the better the model explains the observed variance in the input data. In this instance, the adjusted `R-squared` value is 0.002, which indicates that only 0.2% of the variance is explained by the model and suggests we should try a different approach. Most real-world applications using regression models include more than one independent variable for numeric prediction tasks, which we will further explore in the next recipe.

366 MACHINE LEARNING RECIPES

12.2.6.2 Multiple Linear Regression

Multiple linear regression models the relationships between two or more independent (explanatory) variables and a numerical dependent (response) variable by fitting a linear equation to observed data.

Let's build on the previous example and explore how to use multiple independent variables to fit a multiple linear regression model to predict the current fiscal year's giving.

```r
# Load readr
library(readr)

# Load dplyr
library(dplyr)

# Load Data
donor_data <- read_csv("data/DonorSampleDataML.csv")

# Drop 'ID', 'MEMBERSHIP_ID', etc.
pred_vars <- c('MARITAL_STATUS', 'GENDER',
               'ALUMNUS_IND', 'PARENT_IND',
               'HAS_INVOLVEMENT_IND', 'DEGREE_LEVEL',
               'PREF_ADDRESS_TYPE', 'EMAIL_PRESENT_IND')
donor_data <- select(donor_data,
                     pred_vars,
                     AGE,
                     PrevFYGiving,
                     PrevFY1Giving,
                     PrevFY2Giving,
                     PrevFY3Giving,
                     PrevFY4Giving,
                     CurrFYGiving)
# Set Seed for Repeatable Results
```

```r
set.seed(777)

# Convert features to factor
donor_data <- mutate_at(donor_data,
                        .vars = pred_vars,
                        .funs = as.factor)
```

Now that our data is loaded and prepared, let's build the multiple linear regression model.

```r
# Fit multiple linear regression model
giving_mlg_model <- lm(CurrFYGiving ~ .,
                       data = donor_data)
```

Let's see what the model performance looks like.

```r
summary(giving_mlg_model)
#>
#> Call:
#> lm(formula = CurrFYGiving ~ ., data = donor_data)
#>
#> Residuals:
#>     Min       1Q  Median       3Q      Max
#> -402697     -83      62      150  1147081
#>
#> Coefficients:
#>                              Estimate Std. Error
#> (Intercept)                  2.42e+02   1.35e+03
#> MARITAL_STATUSMarried       -6.95e+02   9.07e+02
#> MARITAL_STATUSNever Married -3.84e+02   4.80e+03
#> MARITAL_STATUSSeparated     -2.06e+03   2.87e+03
#> MARITAL_STATUSSingle        -8.57e+02   9.19e+02
#> MARITAL_STATUSUnknown       -9.45e+02   9.08e+02
```

```
#> MARITAL_STATUSWidowed        -9.16e+02   1.12e+03
#> GENDERMale                    4.82e+00   9.04e+01
#> GENDERUnknown                -4.09e+00   2.23e+02
#> ALUMNUS_INDY                 -2.00e+00   9.39e+02
#> PARENT_INDY                  -3.76e+02   2.15e+02
#> HAS_INVOLVEMENT_INDY          9.58e+01   1.08e+02
#> DEGREE_LEVELNon-Alumni        3.26e+02   9.53e+02
#> DEGREE_LEVELUndergrad         1.61e+02   1.81e+02
#> PREF_ADDRESS_TYPECAMP         1.87e+02   4.18e+02
#> PREF_ADDRESS_TYPEHOME         1.09e+01   2.67e+02
#> PREF_ADDRESS_TYPEOTR         -1.21e+02   1.00e+03
#> PREF_ADDRESS_TYPEUnknown      8.57e+01   2.92e+02
#> EMAIL_PRESENT_INDY           -1.98e+01   9.67e+01
#> AGE                           9.47e+00   3.73e+00
#> PrevFYGiving                 -8.50e-02   8.83e-04
#> PrevFY1Giving                 3.09e-03   4.21e-03
#> PrevFY2Giving                 4.48e+00   1.46e-02
#> PrevFY3Giving                 1.60e-03   2.55e-02
#> PrevFY4Giving                -2.28e-02   6.56e-03
#>                             t value Pr(>|t|)
#> (Intercept)                    0.18   0.8581
#> MARITAL_STATUSMarried         -0.77   0.4432
#> MARITAL_STATUSNever Married   -0.08   0.9362
#> MARITAL_STATUSSeparated       -0.72   0.4728
#> MARITAL_STATUSSingle          -0.93   0.3513
#> MARITAL_STATUSUnknown         -1.04   0.2984
#> MARITAL_STATUSWidowed         -0.82   0.4121
#> GENDERMale                     0.05   0.9575
#> GENDERUnknown                 -0.02   0.9854
#> ALUMNUS_INDY                   0.00   0.9983
#> PARENT_INDY                   -1.75   0.0802 .
#> HAS_INVOLVEMENT_INDY           0.89   0.3750
#> DEGREE_LEVELNon-Alumni         0.34   0.7321
```

```
#> DEGREE_LEVELUndergrad              0.89    0.3737
#> PREF_ADDRESS_TYPECAMP              0.45    0.6542
#> PREF_ADDRESS_TYPEHOME              0.04    0.9674
#> PREF_ADDRESS_TYPEOTR              -0.12    0.9037
#> PREF_ADDRESS_TYPEUnknown           0.29    0.7695
#> EMAIL_PRESENT_INDY               -0.21    0.8375
#> AGE                               2.54    0.0111 *
#> PrevFYGiving                    -96.22    <2e-16 ***
#> PrevFY1Giving                     0.73    0.4627
#> PrevFY2Giving                   307.64    <2e-16 ***
#> PrevFY3Giving                     0.06    0.9499
#> PrevFY4Giving                    -3.48    0.0005 ***
#> ---
#> Signif. codes:
#> 0 '***' 0.001 '**' 0.01 '*' 0.05 '.' 0.1 ' ' 1
#>
#> Residual standard error: 8160 on 34483 degrees of freedom
#> Multiple R-squared:  0.735,  Adjusted R-squared:  0.735
#> F-statistic: 3.99e+03 on 24 and 34483 DF,  p-value: <2e-16
```

Let's also plot the model.

```
par(mfrow = c(2, 2))
plot(giving_mlg_model)
#> Warning in sqrt(crit * p * (1 - hh)/hh): NaNs
#> produced

#> Warning in sqrt(crit * p * (1 - hh)/hh): NaNs
#> produced
```

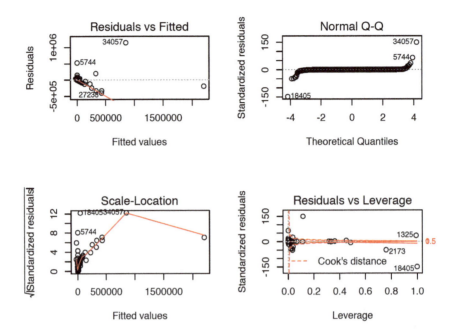

Based on the summary(giving_mlg_model) output, the multiple linear regression model does a much better job of predicting current fiscal year giving than our previous linear regression model, which predicted total giving. Specifically, the inter-quartile range (IQR) of the prediction errors (residuals) in this multiple linear regression model range between $83 over the true value and $150 under the true value. It makes sense that the Age and PrevFY*Giving variables are correlated with current FY's giving.

The R-squared value (coefficient of determination) describes the proportion of variance in CurrFYGiving (dependent variable) that is explained by the model. As previously mentioned, the closer that value is to 1.0, the better the model explains the observed variance in the input data. In this instance, the adjusted R-squared value is 0.735, which indicates that approximately 74% of the observed variance in CurrFYGiving is explained by this model.

SUPERVISED LEARNING **371**

In the Predicting Gift Size and [Finding Prospects for Mail Solicitations] chapters, we will further explore how to use regression analysis to predict gift size and select prospects for mailing solicitations.

12.2.6.3 Logistic Regression

Logistic regression models the relationships between one or more independent (explanatory) variables and a dependent (outcome) variable that is categorical. Binary logistic regression is a common type of logistic regression where the dependent (response) variable is binary or dichotomous (that is, takes only one of two values such as giving/not giving to attended/not attended).

Let's explore how to create a logistic regression model to predict whether a constituent will be a donor or non-donor based on input data. Let's load and prep the data.

```
# Load readr
library(readr)

# Load dplyr
library(dplyr)

# Load caret package
library(caret)

# Load Data
donor_data <- read_csv("data/DonorSampleDataML.csv")

# Drop 'ID', 'MEMBERSHIP_ID', etc.
pred_vars <- c('MARITAL_STATUS', 'GENDER',
               'ALUMNUS_IND', 'PARENT_IND',
               'HAS_INVOLVEMENT_IND', 'DEGREE_LEVEL',
               'PREF_ADDRESS_TYPE', 'EMAIL_PRESENT_IND',
```

372   MACHINE LEARNING RECIPES

```r
                    'DONOR_IND')
donor_data <- select(donor_data,
                     pred_vars,
                     AGE)


# Set Seed for Repeatable Results
set.seed(777)


# Convert features to factor
donor_data <- mutate_at(donor_data,
                        .vars = pred_vars,
                        .funs = as.factor)
```

Let's split 70% of the data into training and the rest into test data.

```r
dd_index <- sample(2,
                   nrow(donor_data),
                   replace = TRUE,
                   prob = c(0.7, 0.3))
dd_trainset <- donor_data[dd_index == 1, ]
dd_testset <- donor_data[dd_index == 2, ]


# Confirm size of training and test
# datasets
dim(dd_trainset)
#> [1] 24195     10
dim(dd_testset)
#> [1] 10313     10
```

Now, let's fit the logistic regression model.

```r
giving_lr_model <- glm(DONOR_IND ~ .,
                       data = dd_trainset,
```

```
                                         family = "binomial")
```

Let's see how the model performed.

```
summary(giving_lr_model)
#>
#> Call:
#> glm(formula = DONOR_IND ~ ., family = "binomial", data = dd_trainset)
#>
#> Deviance Residuals:
#>     Min      1Q  Median      3Q     Max
#> -3.499  -0.093   0.144   0.419   3.774
#>
#> Coefficients:
#>                               Estimate Std. Error
#> (Intercept)                   29.54367  759.25367
#> MARITAL_STATUSMarried         -0.72166    0.72249
#> MARITAL_STATUSNever Married   -1.06711    5.42223
#> MARITAL_STATUSSeparated        3.18970    2.45027
#> MARITAL_STATUSSingle          -0.44973    0.72734
#> MARITAL_STATUSUnknown         -0.35620    0.72183
#> MARITAL_STATUSWidowed         -0.47427    0.81945
#> GENDERMale                    -0.12138    0.05532
#> GENDERUnknown                 -0.20367    0.13083
#> ALUMNUS_INDY                 -14.80159  743.91015
#> PARENT_INDY                    2.34458    0.21162
#> HAS_INVOLVEMENT_INDY           0.20372    0.06838
#> DEGREE_LEVELNon-Alumni       -37.01917  759.25330
#> DEGREE_LEVELUndergrad        -16.04282  151.86597
#> PREF_ADDRESS_TYPECAMP          1.09975    0.26711
#> PREF_ADDRESS_TYPEHOME          0.04452    0.17423
#> PREF_ADDRESS_TYPEOTR           0.60209    0.79611
#> PREF_ADDRESS_TYPEUnknown      -0.23205    0.18866
```

```
#> EMAIL_PRESENT_INDY            0.07867     0.05961
#> AGE                           0.09819     0.00252
#>                           z value Pr(>|z|)
#> (Intercept)                   0.04   0.9690
#> MARITAL_STATUSMarried        -1.00   0.3179
#> MARITAL_STATUSNever Married  -0.20   0.8440
#> MARITAL_STATUSSeparated       1.30   0.1930
#> MARITAL_STATUSSingle         -0.62   0.5364
#> MARITAL_STATUSUnknown        -0.49   0.6217
#> MARITAL_STATUSWidowed        -0.58   0.5627
#> GENDERMale                   -2.19   0.0282 *
#> GENDERUnknown                -1.56   0.1195
#> ALUMNUS_INDY                 -0.02   0.9841
#> PARENT_INDY                  11.08   < 2e-16 ***
#> HAS_INVOLVEMENT_INDY          2.98   0.0029 **
#> DEGREE_LEVELNon-Alumni       -0.05   0.9611
#> DEGREE_LEVELUndergrad        -0.11   0.9159
#> PREF_ADDRESS_TYPECAMP         4.12   3.8e-05 ***
#> PREF_ADDRESS_TYPEHOME         0.26   0.7983
#> PREF_ADDRESS_TYPEOTR          0.76   0.4495
#> PREF_ADDRESS_TYPEUnknown     -1.23   0.2187
#> EMAIL_PRESENT_INDY            1.32   0.1869
#> AGE                          38.99   < 2e-16 ***
#> ---
#> Signif. codes:
#> 0 '***' 0.001 '**' 0.01 '*' 0.05 '.' 0.1 ' ' 1
#>
#> (Dispersion parameter for binomial family taken to be 1)
#>
#>     Null deviance: 32136.9  on 24194  degrees of freedom
#> Residual deviance:  9839.7  on 24175  degrees of freedom
#> AIC: 9880
#>
```

```
#> Number of Fisher Scoring iterations: 17
```

Next, let's make predictions and store them.

```
predictions <- predict(giving_lr_model,
                       newdata = dd_testset,
                       type = "response")
preds <- as.factor(ifelse(predictions > 0.5,
                          "Y",
                          "N"))
```

Finally, let's see the confusion matrix.

```
confusionMatrix(table(preds, dd_testset$DONOR_IND),
                positive = "Y")
#> Confusion Matrix and Statistics
#>
#>
#> preds    N    Y
#>     N 3198  106
#>     Y  680 6329
#>
#>               Accuracy : 0.924
#>                 95% CI : (0.918, 0.929)
#>    No Information Rate : 0.624
#>    P-Value [Acc > NIR] : <2e-16
#>
#>                  Kappa : 0.833
#>  Mcnemar's Test P-Value : <2e-16
#>
#>            Sensitivity : 0.984
#>            Specificity : 0.825
#>         Pos Pred Value : 0.903
```

```
#>         Neg Pred Value : 0.968
#>            Prevalence : 0.624
#>        Detection Rate : 0.614
#>  Detection Prevalence : 0.680
#>     Balanced Accuracy : 0.904
#>
#>        'Positive' Class : Y
#>
```

Logistic regression performs with an accuracy of 92.4%, which is on par with the performance of the KNN, C50, and OneR algorithms we previously explored.

Now that we have covered supervised learning algorithms, let's explore another machine learning method that does not require labeled input (training) data.

12.3   Unsupervised Learning

Unsupervised learning is a type of machine learning that draws inferences and extracts hidden structure from unlabeled input data. In contrast to supervised learning, unsupervised learning does not require labeled data for training because there is no predicted outcome. Instead, unsupervised learning algorithms rely on the similarity (distance) metrics between data features (variables) to organize data into groupings known as clusters.

The de facto unsupervised learning method is cluster analysis, which can be used to find emergent patterns in your data. There are many different types of clustering methods, including hierarchical clustering, k-means clustering, model-based clustering, and density-based clustering.

K-means is one of the most popular and widely used clustering algorithms, which randomly assigns each observation (data point) to a cluster and calculates the centroid (that is, cluster center) of each cluster. The kmeans algorithm continues to reassign data points to the cluster with the closest centroid value and iteratively updates cluster centroid values until the cluster variation cannot be further minimized.

In the following recipe, we will explore how to use the kmeans algorithm to perform cluster analysis and reveal hidden groupings in the donor data file.

12.3.1 K-Means

Let's load and prep the data first.

```r
# Load readr
library(readr)

# Load dplyr
library(dplyr)

# Load ggplot2
library(ggplot2)
library(scales)
# Set Seed for Repeatable Results
set.seed(123)

# Load Data
donor_data <- read_csv("data/DonorSampleDataML.csv")

pred_vars <- c('MARITAL_STATUS', 'GENDER',
               'ALUMNUS_IND', 'PARENT_IND',
               'HAS_INVOLVEMENT_IND', 'DEGREE_LEVEL',
```

378 MACHINE LEARNING RECIPES

```
                    'PREF_ADDRESS_TYPE', 'EMAIL_PRESENT_IND')

# Convert from character to numeric data type
convert_fac2num <- function(x){
  as.numeric(as.factor(x))
}


# Convert features from factor to numeric
donor_data <- mutate_at(donor_data,
                        .vars = pred_vars,
                        .funs = convert_fac2num)


# Convert feature to factor
donor_data$DONOR_IND <- as.factor(donor_data$DONOR_IND)
```

Since we want to use the DONOR_IND variable for clustering, we will convert that variable into two columns with 1s and 0s (that is, one hot code that variable).

```
donor_data <- mutate(donor_data,
                     donor = ifelse(DONOR_IND =='Y', 1, 0),
                     non_donor = ifelse(DONOR_IND =='N', 1, 0))
```

Let's select the variables we want to use for cluster analysis.

```
donor_data <- select(donor_data,
                    pred_vars,
                    AGE,
                    TotalGiving,
                    donor,
                    non_donor)
```

Now, let's build the clusters using the kmeans algorithm and select five clusters.

```r
dd_kmeans <- kmeans(x = donor_data,
                    centers = 5,
                    nstart = 10)
```

We'll look at the cluster distribution, but first let's convert the cluster numbers to factors and save it to the `donor_data` data frame.

```r
donor_data$cluster <- as.factor(dd_kmeans$cluster)

# Plot kmeans model
ggplot(donor_data, aes(x = AGE, y = TotalGiving, color = cluster)) +
  geom_jitter() +
  scale_y_log10(labels = dollar) +
  theme_bw(base_size = 12) +
  xlab("Donor Age") + ylab("Log (Total Giving)") +
  ggtitle("Donor Cluster Analysis") +
  scale_color_manual("Cluster Assignment",
                     labels = c("A", "B", "C", "D", "E"),
                     values = c("royalblue2", "orange",
                                "magenta3", "gray76", "limegreen")) +
  theme(plot.title = element_text(hjust = 0.5))
#> Warning: Transformation introduced infinite values
#> in continuous y-axis
```

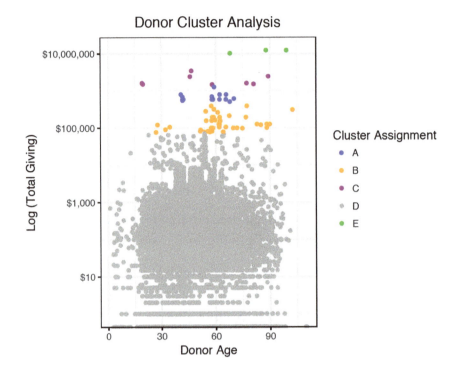

The kmeans algorithm requires that you specify *k*, which is the number of clusters used to organize the input data. In this example, the value of *k* was chosen arbitrarily, but you may also have domain expertise or business requirements informing your cluster number criteria. For smaller datasets, a rule of thumb is to define *k* as the square root of n/2 (that, sqrt(n/2)), where n equals the total number of observations in your dataset. For larger datasets, *k* can become very large and therefore difficult to manage and interpret with this cluster-selection approach. For additional details about choosing the optimal number of clusters, you can read the following article[8].

Once you've built your clustering model, it is useful to explore, compare, and describe your cluster segments using the average or median values for each of the clusters. For example, we built a cluster model with the cluster means shown in Figure 12.3 and added de-

---

[8] https://www.r-bloggers.com/finding-optimal-number-of-clusters/

scriptions. This way, you can estimate the attributes of individual members of a cluster. You can further use these attributes or labels for marketing or segmentation.

Cluster	Age	TotalGiving	ConsecutiveYears	Description
A	56	$679,385	1.6	Baby Boomers $500k+
B	63	$149,637	5.4	Baby Boomers $100k+
C	85	$11,548,090	9.0	Traditionalists $10M+
D	39	$416	1.1	Gen Y $1-999
E	55	$1,994,538	2.6	Baby Boomers $1M+

Figure 12.3: K-means donor cluster analysis

Cluster analysis, which is a type of unsupervised learning, is an effective method to explore patterns and create segments (groupings) within your data.

Using one of the machine learning recipes previously discussed as a starting point, modify the predict(model, newdata, type) function call to export probabilities instead of class predictions (that is, donor versus non-donor). Add these class probabilities into your kmeans cluster analysis, explore various segment or grouping sizes (k), and plot any useful cluster patterns (such as giving likelihood versus AGE, giving likelihood versus HAS_INVOLVEMENT_IND) with your own insight descriptions.

12.3.2 Association Rule Mining

Association rule mining (also known as **market basket analysis**) helps us find items that are frequently purchased together or, in our case, combinations of designations that are frequently donated together(that is, which designation combinations are common among our donors). This can help us uncover new prospective donors who have not given to a particular designation but have given somewhere else. For example, let's say that through our analysis we know that donors who give to athletics also give to undergraduate scholarships. What if we looked at all the donors to athletics who have not given to undergraduate scholarships yet? That population might be very likely to give to scholarships, which we identified for future marketing segmentation and appeals.

To perform market basket analysis, we need the transaction history of donors and the designations they supported. You may run the following SQL code to get this data.

```
SELECT DONOR_ID, DESIGNATION
FROM GIVING_HISTORY
```

For our recipe, we will use a synthetic data set. Let's load the `arules` and `arulesViz` libraries we need for this exercise(Hahsler et al. 2011, Hahsler 2017).

```
library(arules)
library(arulesViz)
```

Let's load the sample data set using the `read.transactions` function from the `arules` library.

```
giving_transactions <- read.transactions(
  "data/SampleGivingTransactionsAssocRules.csv",
```

UNSUPERVISED LEARNING   383

```
    format = "single",
    sep = ",",
    cols = c("donor_id", "designation"))
```

Let's see what this object formatting looks like when using the `arules` library.

```
inspect(giving_transactions[1:3])
#>     items                   transactionID
#> [1] {Arts,
#>       JARVIS Studies Center,
#>       Law,
#>       Libraries,
#>       Music,
#>       Rugby,
#>       Social Welfare,
#>       Student Life}                    1
#> [2] {Athletics,
#>       English,
#>       Innovation Fund,
#>       JARVIS Studies Center,
#>       Law,
#>       Libraries,
#>       Music,
#>       Scholarships,
#>       Student Life,
#>       Superherology,
#>       Theater}                        10
#> [3] {Athletics,
#>       JARVIS Studies Center,
#>       Law,
#>       Music,
#>       Scholarships,
```

384 MACHINE LEARNING RECIPES

```
#>        Student Life}                    100
```

Let's also add a summary of the transactions.

```
summary(giving_transactions)
#> transactions as itemMatrix in sparse format with
#>  1000 rows (elements/itemsets/transactions) and
#>  20 columns (items) and a density of 0.431
#>
#> most frequent items:
#>         Music Student Life        Law
#>           881          856        854
#>     Libraries Scholarships    (Other)
#>           760          669       4610
#>
#> element (itemset/transaction) length distribution:
#> sizes
#>   1   2   3   4   5   6   7   8   9  10  11  12
#>   7   6  13  45  52  90 114 151 135 140 108  71
#>  13  14  15  16  17
#>  39  15  11   2   1
#>
#>    Min. 1st Qu.  Median    Mean 3rd Qu.    Max.
#>    1.00    7.00    9.00    8.63   10.00   17.00
#>
#> includes extended item information - examples:
#>         labels
#> 1         Arts
#> 2 Arts Museum
#> 3    Athletics
#>
#> includes extended transaction information - examples:
#>    transactionID
```

```
#> 1                1
#> 2               10
#> 3              100
```

Let's build the association rules using the `apriori` function. Two important parameters for association rule mining are confidence and support. The confidence parameter controls the reliability of each rule. If it is set too low, we will get many rules with designations that don't show up frequently together. If it is set too high, we will get only a few rules, but with designation-combinations that are given too frequently. Similarly, support is a measure of the frequency of designations in the rules.

```
giving_rules <- apriori(giving_transactions,
                parameter = list(supp = 0.5,
                                 conf = 0.9))
#> Apriori
#>
#> Parameter specification:
#>  confidence minval smax arem   aval
#>         0.9    0.1    1 none FALSE
#>  originalSupport maxtime support minlen maxlen
#>             TRUE       5     0.5      1     10
#>  target    ext
#>   rules FALSE
#>
#> Algorithmic control:
#>  filter tree heap memopt load sort verbose
#>     0.1 TRUE TRUE  FALSE TRUE    2    TRUE
#>
#> Absolute minimum support count: 500
#>
#> set item appearances ...[0 item(s)] done [0.00s].
```

386   MACHINE LEARNING RECIPES

```
#> set transactions ...[20 item(s), 1000 transaction(s)] done [0.00s].
#> sorting and recoding items ... [8 item(s)] done [0.00s].
#> creating transaction tree ... done [0.00s].
#> checking subsets of size 1 2 3 4 done [0.00s].
#> writing ... [21 rule(s)] done [0.00s].
#> creating S4 object  ... done [0.00s].
```

Let's sort the rules by confidence (that is, the rules with highest confidence will rise to the top).

```
giving_rules <- sort(giving_rules,
              by = 'confidence',
              decreasing = TRUE)
```

Let's see a few of these rules.

```
inspect(giving_rules[1:10])
#>         lhs                 rhs           support confidence lift count
#> [1]  {Law,
#>        Rugby}        => {Music}           0.509      0.931 1.06   509
#> [2]  {Rugby,
#>        Student Life} => {Music}           0.522      0.929 1.05   522
#> [3]  {Law,
#>        Libraries,
#>        Student Life} => {Music}           0.566      0.928 1.05   566
#> [4]  {Libraries,
#>        Music,
#>        Student Life} => {Law}             0.566      0.920 1.08   566
#> [5]  {Law,
#>        Scholarships} => {Music}           0.550      0.918 1.04   550
#> [6]  {Scholarships,
#>        Student Life} => {Music}           0.537      0.918 1.04   537
#> [7]  {Law,
```

```
#>          Rugby}            => {Student Life}    0.502         0.918 1.07   502
#> [8]  {Law,
#>          Libraries}        => {Music}           0.619         0.917 1.04   619
#> [9]  {Rugby}               => {Music}           0.574         0.915 1.04   574
#> [10] {Libraries,
#>          Student Life} => {Music}               0.615         0.915 1.04   615
```

It seems like the donors who gave to Law and to Rugby also gave to Music. Similarly, the donors who gave to Rugby and Student Life also gave to Music. The lhs and rhs indicate which designations of giving go together. For example, the first rule is {Law,Rugby} => {Music}, which means donors who gave to Law and Rugby also gave to Music.

We can see rules specific to certain designations. For example, if we want to see all the rules where the rhs is Law (that is, where else the donors give to, we can use the subset function).

```
inspect(subset(giving_rules,  (rhs %in% 'Law')))
#>       lhs                  rhs     support confidence lift count
#> [1] {Libraries,
#>        Music,
#>        Student Life} => {Law}    0.566         0.920 1.08   566
#> [2] {Scholarships,
#>        Student Life} => {Law}    0.533         0.911 1.07   533
#> [3] {Libraries,
#>        Student Life} => {Law}    0.610         0.908 1.06   610
#> [4] {Music,
#>        Scholarships} => {Law}    0.550         0.908 1.06   550
#> [5] {Libraries,
#>        Music}        => {Law}    0.619         0.905 1.06   619
```

The `arulesViz` library offers multiple ways to visualize the generated rules. Let's see a few of them, but first let's store the top 10 rules for plotting.

```
top_10_giving_rules <- head(giving_rules, 10)
```

Let's plot a scatterplot between confidence and support.

```
plot(giving_rules)
```

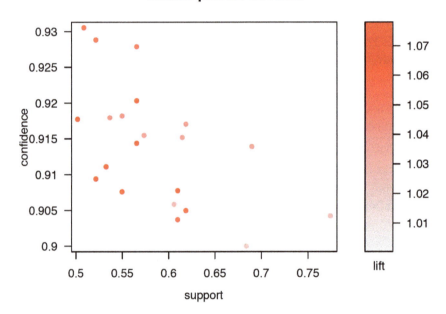

It looks like that there are many rules with high confidence and support between 0.5 and 0.6. These rules also have high lift.

Next, let's view the rules as a parallel coordinate plot.

```
plot(top_10_giving_rules,
     method = "paracoord",
```

```
              control = list(reorder = TRUE))
```

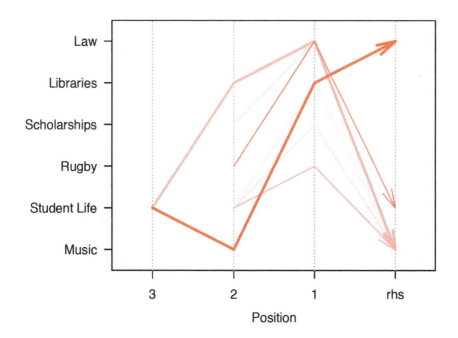

This parallel coordinate plot shows that the donors often give to Student Life, Music, Libraries, and Law designations. Also, many donors who give to other areas also give to Music.

Let's see a grouped plot. This plot shows the rules in a matrix form.

```
plot(top_10_giving_rules, method = "grouped")
```

Grouped Matrix for 10 Rules

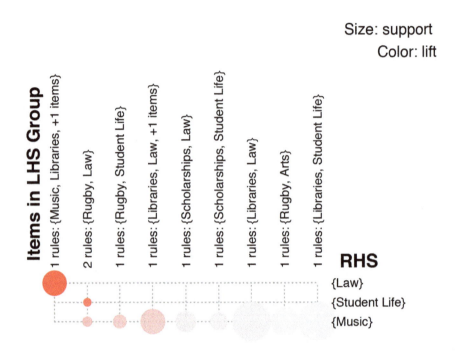

It is easy to see from this plot that many donors who gave to other areas also gave to Music and that the rule {Libraries,Music,Student Life} => {Law} has the highest support and lift.

Finally, let's see these rules in network graph format, a topic we will explore in detail in the Social Network Analysis chapter.

```
plot(top_10_giving_rules, method = "graph")
```

MODEL DIAGNOSTICS 391

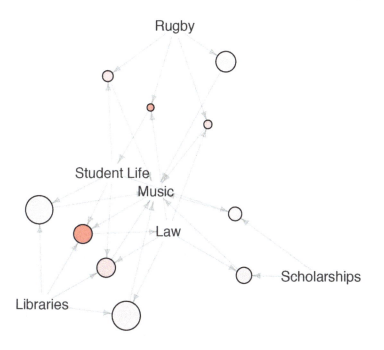

This network graph provides a different way of looking at the rules, specifically the relationships among various designations.

12.4 Model Diagnostics

As you build and refine your models, you will have to find practical ways to diagnose, tune and improve your model's performance. While detailed model diagnostics and performance tuning is beyond the scope (and purpose) of this book, it is important that you understand the fundamental concepts of bias, variance, and the bias-variance tradeoff.

392 MACHINE LEARNING RECIPES

Bias refers to errors due to incorrect model assumptions with your machine learning algorithm, such as independence of variables. Models with high bias tend to miss (underfit) important relations between the model's input and output variables. Variance refers to model errors generated due to sensitivity to small fluctuations in your training data. Models with high variance are prone to over-fitting to "noise" (random error) in your training data.

Bias and variance both contribute to your model's total error, which can be represented by the following formula:

Total Error = $Bias^2$ + Variance + Irreducible Error

Irreducible Error (also known as **inherent uncertainty**) is error usually associated with randomness or innate variability in a system. Since we cannot change irreducible error, we need to focus our attention on the bias and variance in our models. To deal with bias and variance, you can experiment with tuning your model's parameters, revisit your model specification, seek data for missing features, and/or try different machine learning algorithms.

Ultimately, to get good predictions, you will need to strike a balance between bias and variance that minimizes the overall total error of your model. To learn more about bias and variance, we recommend reading this bias-variance tradeoff[9] article as a starting point.

To learn more about using the mlr package to evaluate model performance and parameter tuning, you can check out these Evaluating Learner Performance[10], Resampling[11], and Tuning Hyperparameters[12] articles.

---

[9]https://en.wikipedia.org/wiki/Bias%E2%80%93variance_tradeoff
[10]https://mlr-org.github.io/mlr-tutorial/release/html/performance/index.html#calculate-performance-measures
[11]https://mlr-org.github.io/mlr-tutorial/release/html/resample/index.html
[12]https://mlr-org.github.io/mlr-tutorial/release/html/tune/index.html

12.5 Summary

In this chapter, we introduced and explored fundamental machine learning concepts and practical recipes using R to build fundraising solutions.

After reading this chapter, you should be able to recognize a variety of supervised and unsupervised machine learning algorithms as well as some commonly used R packages to implement solutions for both classification (categorical) and regression (numerical) tasks using your institutional data. It is important that you run these recipes on your data to cement the learning and get sensible results. Whether you are seeking to forecast numerical values or predict categorical outcomes, R, in combination with its vast array of machine learning packages, is a powerful, versatile, and evolving tool that you can use to build data analytics solutions and add value to your organization.

For a more extensive exploration of various machine learning methods and detailed coverage of model performance and evaluation techniques, you can check out the books **Machine Learning with R** by Lantz (2013) and **Practical Machine Learning Tools and Techniques** by Witten & Frank (2005).

If you're enjoying this book, consider sharing it with your network by running `source("http://arn.la/shareds4fr")` in your R console.

— Ashutosh and Rodger

394 MACHINE LEARNING RECIPES

13

PREDICTING GIFT SIZE

Among various predictive problems, predicting the next customer spend or donor gift amount is a difficult one. Although we can use—and we do—transaction history, predicting a precise amount with high confidence for every customer or donor is impossible. Even techniques as established as calculating customer lifetime value (CLV) are inaccurate. As Malthouse & Blattberg (2010) concluded, of the top 20% of customers, approximately 55% will be misclassified as not big spenders (that is, false negatives). That's a big and important population to miss. Using external and internal data can improve the results, as seen in the study of predicting the wallet size of IBM's customers by Perlich et al. (2007).

A simple, naive model can take the average of all previous transactions and predict that as the next transaction amount, which likely will be close to the actual gift amount. But this model will fail at predicting larger gift sizes, which are typically less than 1% of all transactions. The insurance industry faces the exact same challenge. For example, the majority of car drivers will not get into an accident and an even smaller minority will have high claim amounts (Yang et al. 2017), yet the auto insurance industry must offer reasonable

396   PREDICTING GIFT SIZE

premium rates to remain competitive. The auto insurance industry has had some luck predicting claim size using Tweedie distribution (Tweedie 1984, Jørgensen & Paes De Souza 1994). We can guess so because they remain profitable.

Let's try all of these approaches.

13.1   Simple Forecasting

Before our analysis gets too complicated, let's use the simplest approach we can (that is, predicting the next gift size by calculating the average of previous transactions). Let's use the sample donor data file.

```
library(readr)
library(dplyr)

donor_data <- read_csv("data/DonorSampleDataCleaned.csv")
```

We will use the previous giving columns to calculate the average. We need to clean up the dollar signs from those columns.

```
donor_data <- donor_data %>%
  mutate_at(.vars = vars(starts_with("PrevFY"), "CurrFYGiving"),
            .funs = funs(as.numeric(gsub(x = .,
                                         pattern = "[\\$,]",
                                         replacement = ""))))
```

Now, let's simply calculate the average of the previous giving columns.

```
donor_data$CurrFYGiving_pred_sa <-  select(
```

```
  donor_data,
  starts_with("PrevFY")) %>%
  rowMeans(na.rm = TRUE)
```

How does this prediction stack against the actual giving? Let's plot and see.

```
library(ggplot2)
library(scales)

ggplot(donor_data, aes(x = CurrFYGiving,
                       y = CurrFYGiving_pred_sa)) +
  geom_point() +
  scale_x_sqrt(labels = dollar) +
  scale_y_sqrt(labels = dollar) +
  theme_bw() +
  geom_smooth()
```

You can see in Figure 13.1 that our simple average model either overestimated (when there was no giving) or underestimated (when there was some giving). There are a few predictions that look somewhat accurate—we can say so because we can see some points on an imagined line that goes at 45°. If all the predictions were accurate, all the points would fall on that line. One overall but imperfect measure of accuracy is the Root Mean Square Error (RMSE). We calculate this value by taking the average of the squared difference between the predictions and the actuals. For this calculation, the formula looks like this:

$$RMSE = \sqrt{\frac{\sum_{i=1}^{n}(\mathrm{CurrFYGiving\_pred\_sa} - \mathrm{CurrFYGiving})^2}{n}}$$

In R code, the calculation is like the following:

398   PREDICTING GIFT SIZE

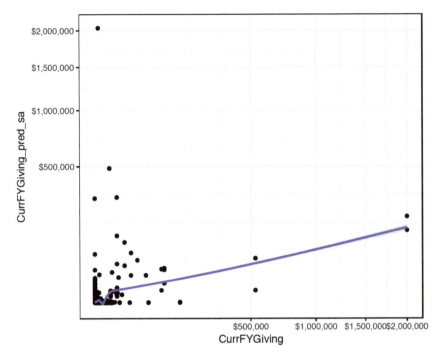

Figure 13.1: Actual versus prediction of current FY giving using simple average

```
rmse_sa <- summarize(
  donor_data,
  rmse = sqrt(mean((CurrFYGiving_pred_sa - CurrFYGiving)^2)))
rmse_sa$rmse
#> [1] 18555
```

Although such an overall statistic hides the gross mispredictions, it allows us to compare various models with each other. The RMSE for this model is 18,555.

13.2 Quantile Regression

Perlich et al. (2007) used quantile regression to predict the wallet share of IBM's customers. Since linear regression tries to minimize the mean of the prediction error, it is not helpful when only a few transactions have big values. Therefore, if we can minimize a high quantile error (such as the 90th percentile) we may get good results. Quantile regression extends linear regression by allowing us to minimize the median error or any other quantiles (Koenker 2005). We will use the quantreg package (Koenker 2017).

Before we use this technique, we need to decide the quantile at which the model will estimate (or predict) the giving. Let's find out the various quantiles.

```
quantile(donor_data$CurrFYGiving)
#>    0%   25%   50%   75%  100%
#> 0e+00 0e+00 0e+00 0e+00 2e+06
```

Even the 75th percentile is zero. So, we need to determine the quantiles between 90 and 100 then.

```
quantile(donor_data$CurrFYGiving,
         probs = seq(from = 0.9, to = 1, by = 0.01))
#>   90%   91%   92%   93%    94%    95%
#>     0     0     0     0      0      1
#>   96%   97%   98%   99%   100%
#>    25    70   110   244 2000000
```

Let's use the 98th percentile as the quantile to predict giving.

```
library(quantreg)
quant_reg1 <- rq(CurrFYGiving ~ PrevFYGiving + PrevFY1Giving +
                    PrevFY2Giving + PrevFY3Giving +
```

400   PREDICTING GIFT SIZE

```
                  PrevFY4Giving,
              data = donor_data, tau = 0.98)
summary(quant_reg1)
#> Warning in summary.rq(quant_reg1): 155 non-
#> positive fis
#>
#> Call: rq(formula = CurrFYGiving ~ PrevFYGiving + PrevFY1Giving + PrevFY2
#>     PrevFY3Giving + PrevFY4Giving, tau = 0.98, data = donor_data)
#>
#> tau: [1] 0.98
#>
#> Coefficients:
#>               Value      Std. Error t value
#> (Intercept)   100.00000  128.80697   0.77636
#> PrevFYGiving    0.26531    3.39666   0.07811
#> PrevFY1Giving  -0.00441    0.69318  -0.00636
#> PrevFY2Giving   9.34365    8.48873   1.10071
#> PrevFY3Giving   0.02039    0.36324   0.05614
#> PrevFY4Giving   0.01360    0.09012   0.15094
#>               Pr(>|t|)
#> (Intercept)    0.43754
#> PrevFYGiving   0.93774
#> PrevFY1Giving  0.99493
#> PrevFY2Giving  0.27103
#> PrevFY3Giving  0.95523
#> PrevFY4Giving  0.88002
```

Next, let's store the predictions.

```
donor_data$CurrFYGiving_pred_qr <-  predict(quant_reg1)
```

How does this prediction stack against the actual giving? Let's plot
and see.

```r
ggplot(donor_data, aes(x = CurrFYGiving,
                       y = CurrFYGiving_pred_qr)) +
  geom_point() +
  scale_x_sqrt(labels = dollar) +
  scale_y_sqrt(labels = dollar) +
  theme_bw() +
  geom_smooth()
#> Warning in self$trans$transform(x): NaNs produced
#> Warning: Transformation introduced infinite values
#> in continuous y-axis
#> Warning in self$trans$transform(x): NaNs produced
#> Warning: Transformation introduced infinite values
#> in continuous y-axis
#> Warning: Removed 1 rows containing non-finite values
#> (stat_smooth).
#> Warning: Removed 1 rows containing missing values
#> (geom_point).
```

We can see from Figure 13.2 that quantile regression is overestimating giving. This is understandable because a model that minimizes error at the 98th percentile will over-estimate. And although the regression line seen in the plot shows that this might be a good fit, the RMSE for this model was 30,253.

We can try to improve the results by adding other variables to the model.

```r
quant_reg2 <- rq(CurrFYGiving ~ PrevFYGiving + PrevFY1Giving +
                   PrevFY2Giving + PrevFY3Giving +
                   PrevFY4Giving +
                   AGE + GENDER +
                   EMAIL_PRESENT_IND,
                 data = donor_data, tau = 0.98)
```

402 PREDICTING GIFT SIZE

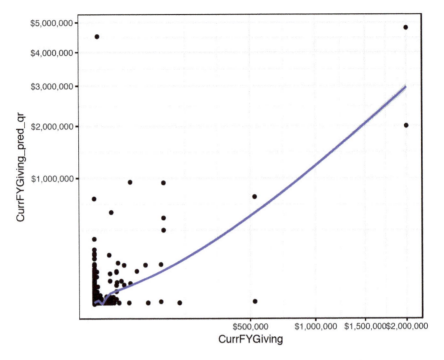

Figure 13.2: Actual versus prediction of current FY giving using quantile regression

We run into a problem, however, because of missing values. The predictions would simply omit all the missing values, or we can obtain a missing value as a prediction; both of these results are unhelpful. We can impute these missing values by taking averages or modes of the other existing values in that column, but I'll leave that exercise for you.

 Impute the missing values and fit the quantile regression model by adding these columns: AGE, GENDER, and EMAIL_PRESENT_IND.

13.3 Gradient Tree

Yang et al. (2017) described the gradient tree boosted models using Tweedie distribution for setting the auto insurance premiums. We will use the TDboost package to create this model (Yang et al. 2016). This is a complicated model with many factors at play. Explaining all the details that are happening inside the model is out of the scope of this book.

Let's go over the minimum parameters we need to use to build this model.

- Number of folds (cv.folds): We tell the model to divide the data in n folds for training and testing. If we had 10 folds, the model would create 10 different data sets by using $9/10^{th}$ portion for training and $1/10^{th}$ for testing. This is a standard approach for training models known as cross-validation and is used to avoid overfitting.
- Number of trees (n.trees): The total number of trees to grow. This parameter controls the boosting which is a method of using results from multiple models and combining them to create a superior model.

Let's build the model.

```r
library(TDboost)


td1 <- TDboost(CurrFYGiving ~ PrevFYGiving +
                PrevFY1Giving + PrevFY2Giving +
                PrevFY3Giving + PrevFY4Giving,
            data = donor_data, cv.folds = 3, n.trees = 100)
#> CV: 1
#> Iter   TrainDeviance   ValidDeviance   StepSize   Improve
#>      1        51.3634         66.5068     0.0010    0.1045
#>      2        51.3418         66.4888     0.0010    0.0001
```

```
#>     3       51.2551        66.3733      0.0010      0.0272
#>     4       51.1646        66.2574      0.0010      0.0579
#>     5       51.0787        66.1447      0.0010      0.0488
#>     6       50.9961        66.0383      0.0010      0.0401
#>     7       50.9112        65.9293      0.0010      0.0169
#>     8       50.8290        65.8209      0.0010      0.0525
#>     9       50.7475        65.7161      0.0010      0.0467
#>    10       50.7282        65.7034      0.0010      0.0095
#>   100       45.5861        59.3736      0.0010      0.0138
#>
#> CV: 2
#> Iter   TrainDeviance  ValidDeviance  StepSize   Improve
#>     1       55.1576        58.2102      0.0010      0.0470
#>     2       55.1262        58.2050      0.0010      0.0064
#>     3       55.0961        58.1995      0.0010      0.0055
#>     4       55.0106        58.0867      0.0010      0.0412
#>     5       54.9309        57.9800      0.0010      0.0396
#>     6       54.8539        57.8696      0.0010      0.0163
#>     7       54.7850        57.7780      0.0010      0.0909
#>     8       54.7665        57.7765      0.0010     -0.0038
#>     9       54.6933        57.6781      0.0010      0.0175
#>    10       54.6125        57.5697      0.0010      0.0210
#>   100       49.9403        52.1301      0.0010      0.0135
#>
#> CV: 3
#> Iter   TrainDeviance  ValidDeviance  StepSize   Improve
#>     1       61.5220        46.1652      0.0010      0.0175
#>     2       61.4101        46.1041      0.0010      0.0215
#>     3       61.3945        46.0609      0.0010     -0.0146
#>     4       61.2936        46.0091      0.0010      0.0159
#>     5       61.1935        45.9602      0.0010      0.0151
#>     6       61.1018        45.9120      0.0010      0.0903
#>     7       61.0108        45.8646      0.0010      0.0919
```

```
#>    8         60.9069          45.8031       0.0010      0.0978
#>    9         60.8033          45.7421       0.0010      0.0971
#>   10         60.7356          45.6988       0.0010      0.1073
#>  100         54.5947          41.8167       0.0010      0.0153
#>
#> Iter  TrainDeviance  ValidDeviance   StepSize    Improve
#>    1         56.1713            nan       0.0010      0.0748
#>    2         56.0834            nan       0.0010      0.0891
#>    3         55.9879            nan       0.0010      0.0355
#>    4         55.9078            nan       0.0010      0.0719
#>    5         55.8175            nan       0.0010      0.0358
#>    6         55.7961            nan       0.0010      0.0117
#>    7         55.7144            nan       0.0010      0.0851
#>    8         55.6280            nan       0.0010      0.0923
#>    9         55.5509            nan       0.0010      0.0849
#>   10         55.4682            nan       0.0010      0.0716
#>  100         49.5031            nan       0.0010      0.0595
summary(td1, n.trees = 100)
#>             var rel.inf
#> 1 PrevFY2Giving   61.63
#> 2  PrevFYGiving   37.00
#> 3 PrevFY4Giving    1.37
#> 4 PrevFY1Giving    0.00
#> 5 PrevFY3Giving    0.00
```

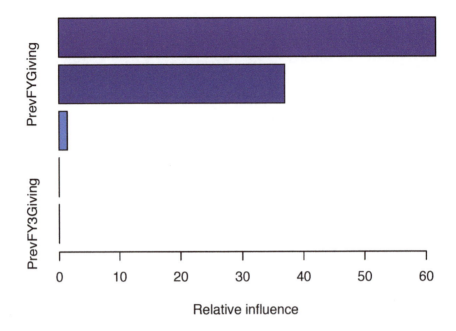

Let's save the predictions.

```
donor_data$CurrFYGiving_pred_tdb <- predict.TDboost(
  object = td1,
  newdata = donor_data,
  n.trees = 100)
```

Are these predictions any better than the previous approaches? Let's see by plotting.

```
ggplot(donor_data, aes(x = CurrFYGiving,
                       y = CurrFYGiving_pred_tdb)) +
  geom_point() +
  scale_x_sqrt(labels = dollar) +
  scale_y_sqrt(labels = dollar) +
  theme_bw() +
  geom_smooth()
```

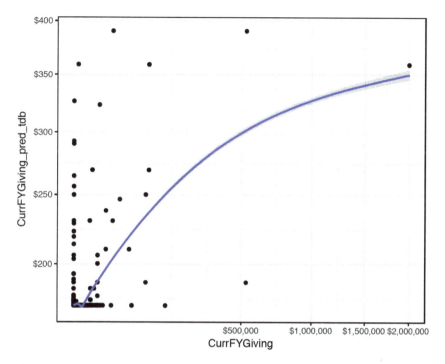

Figure 13.3: Actual versus prediction of current FY giving using TD-Boost

You can see in Figure 13.3 that TDBoost severely underestimated the gift size, but there are many parameters that we didn't change. Parameter tuning is an important task, which can yield better results. The RMSE without tuning was 15,849.

 Type ?TDboost into your R console window. Experiment with() various parameters and see whether you can obtain better results.

408 PREDICTING GIFT SIZE

13.4 Neural Networks

As we saw in the previous chapter, NNs are an extension of generalized regression models. They work by creating a layer of nodes to minimize the error between the actual values and predictions. R comes with the nnet package.

Before you use the model, let's go over the minimum number of parameters you need to provide.

- size: How many nodes should there be in the hidden layer?
- linout: Is it a regression problem?
- maxit: How many times should the minimization (and adjustment of the parameters) occur?

Let's build the model.

```r
library(nnet)

nn <- nnet(CurrFYGiving ~ PrevFYGiving +
                 PrevFY1Giving + PrevFY2Giving +
                 PrevFY3Giving + PrevFY4Giving,
        data = donor_data,
        size = 8,
        linout = TRUE,
        maxit = 500)
#> # weights:  57
#> initial  value 8670906034547.761719
#> iter  10 value 8669526260223.595703
#> final  value 8669521216347.065430
#> converged
```

Now, let's store those predictions.

```
donor_data$CurrFYGiving_pred_nn <- predict(nn)
```

Let's plot the predictions against the actuals. As you can see from Figure 13.4, this neural network did not do a good job at predicting the giving. The RMSE of this model was 15,850.

```
ggplot(donor_data, aes(x = CurrFYGiving,
                       y = CurrFYGiving_pred_nn)) +
  geom_point() +
  scale_x_sqrt(labels = dollar) +
  scale_y_sqrt(labels = dollar) +
  theme_bw() +
  geom_smooth()
```

13.5   Method Evaluation

Building one model at a time is OK, but to evaluate models against each other, we need to find a better way of building and evaluating multiple models. Fortunately, there is a way. Bischl et al. (2016) built the mlr package to do exactly this.

Let's take this step by step.

First, we need to make a list of "learners" or techniques we're interested in applying. You can view all the available learners on mlr's website[1].

If you select the techniques that come with R's installation; you don't need to install additional libraries. For example, the following code won't return any errors.

---

[1]http://mlr-org.github.io/mlr-tutorial/devel/html/integrated_learners/index.html

410 PREDICTING GIFT SIZE

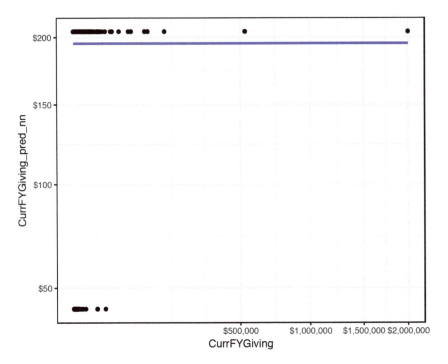

Figure 13.4: Actual versus prediction of current FY giving using neural networks

```
library(mlr)
#> Warning: replacing previous import
#> 'BBmisc::isFALSE' by 'backports::isFALSE' when
#> loading 'mlr'

reg_learners <- list(makeLearner("regr.glm"),
                     makeLearner("regr.lm"))
```

But if I want to add a random forest that's part of the ranger package, I will get an error. I will need to install the ranger package before I add a learner. If you get an error, make sure that you have installed that package.

```r
#Don't run
reg_learners <- list(makeLearner("regr.glm"),
                     makeLearner("regr.lm"),
                     makeLearner("regr.ranger"))
```

Let's select a few different learners.

```r
library(mlr)
reg_learners <- list(makeLearner("regr.glm"),
                     makeLearner("regr.lm"),
                     makeLearner("regr.randomForest"),
                     makeLearner("regr.xgboost"),
                     makeLearner("regr.earth"))
```

Next, how do you want to evaluate the models? Typically, we divide the data into training and test data sets, or we create cross-validation folds as seen earlier.

Let's use a test (also known as "holdout") set.

```r
resample_plan <- makeResampleDesc("Holdout")
#you can also do a n-fold cross-validation
#resample_plan <- makeResampleDesc("CV", iters = 10)
```

Next, mlr asks us to create a "task" that tells mlr how to build these models. We will use the same variables we have been using so far.

```r
curr_fy_reg_task <- makeRegrTask(
  id = 'donor_data',
  data = select(donor_data,
                starts_with("PrevFY"),
                "CurrFYGiving"),
  target = "CurrFYGiving")
```

412 PREDICTING GIFT SIZE

```
#> Warning in makeTask(type = type, data = data,
#> weights = weights, blocking = blocking, : Provided
#> data is not a pure data.frame but from class
#> tbl_df, hence it will be converted.
```

Finally, we build the models using the `benchmark` function.

```
benchmark_results <- benchmark(learners = reg_learners,
                               tasks = curr_fy_reg_task,
                               resamplings = resample_plan)
```

We can see the results using the `getBMRPerformances` function.

```
getBMRPerformances(benchmark_results)
#> $donor_data
#> $donor_data$regr.glm
#>   iter       mse
#> 1    1 1.01e+09
#>
#> $donor_data$regr.lm
#>   iter       mse
#> 1    1 1.01e+09
#>
#> $donor_data$regr.randomForest
#>   iter       mse
#> 1    1 52507430
#>
#> $donor_data$regr.xgboost
#>   iter       mse
#> 1    1 39058708
#>
#> $donor_data$regr.earth
#>   iter       mse
```

```
#> 1    1 5.02e+08
```

We can convert this result into a data frame and we can get the aggregate accuracy measure, which is the mean squared error (MSE) in this case, by using `as.df = TRUE`.

```
benchmark_results_df <- getBMRAggrPerformances(benchmark_results,
                                               as.df = TRUE)
benchmark_results_df$rmse <- sqrt(benchmark_results_df$mse.test.mean)
```

Since we have a data frame to work with now, it is easy to plot the results, as seen in Figure 13.5.

```
library(ggplot2)
library(scales)
ggplot(benchmark_results_df,
       aes(x = reorder(learner.id, -rmse),
           y = rmse)) +
  geom_point(shape = 21, size = 3) +
  scale_y_continuous(labels = comma) +
  coord_flip() +
  theme_bw(base_size = 14) +
  xlab("Learner") + ylab("RMSE")
```

The `mlr` package also offers some plotting functionality. Figure 13.6 shows a "violin" plot, which I don't understand fully nor use. Since the example we ran above didn't have variance in the error, I created these plots using some other criteria. But you can create such a plot by running the following command.

```
library(ggplot2)
plotBMRBoxplots(benchmark_results,
                measure = mse,
```

414 PREDICTING GIFT SIZE

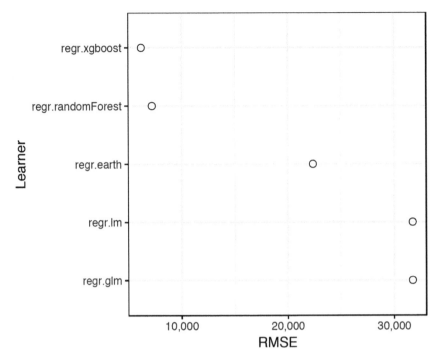

Figure 13.5: RMSE of many models

```
                style = "violin") +
aes(color = learner.id)
```

If you don't provide the `style = "violin"` option, you get a box plot, as shown in Figure 13.7.

METHOD EVALUATION 415

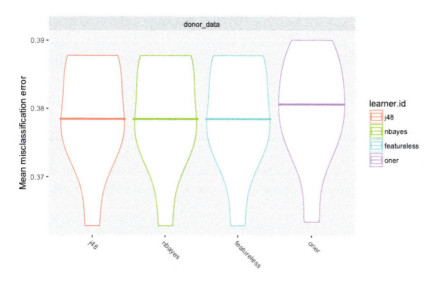

Figure 13.6: Violin plot to compare models using the 'mlr' package

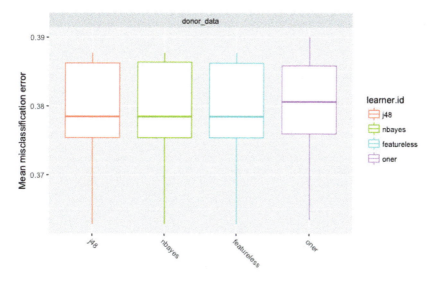

Figure 13.7: Box plot to compare models using the 'mlr' package

416 PREDICTING GIFT SIZE

 The Buy Till You Die (BTYD) package offers customer lifetime value (CLV) calculations as well as other predictions. Use the RFM sample data file and experiment with the BTYD package[2].

If you're enjoying this book, consider sharing it with your network by running source("http://arn.la/shareds4fr") in your R console.

— Ashutosh and Rodger

14

TEXT MINING

As you dive deeper into fundraising analytics, you may find you do not have the luxury of datasets that have already been organized, cleaned, and neatly prepared for you. Embracing this reality, you will first need to acquire data relevant to your purpose (*why*) and business questions *before* you begin your data analysis.

In addition to loading data from spreadsheets and databases (see Loading Data), the web offers a wealth of publicly available data for acquisition, preparation, exploration, analysis, and translation into actionable insights and recommendations using any of the data analytics methods previously covered.

R, with the installation of a couple additional packages, can connect directly to the web and harness the power of public data to further qualify, contextualize, and enhance your capacity to build data-driven solutions. In addition, the creative use of public data sources may inspire you to investigate new questions you might not have previously considered during your original analysis and research.

Let's explore some text mining recipes using R packages that highlight innovative ways to rethink, redesign, and elevate traditional deliverables and information collection processes, including prospect reports, benchmark reports, and contact reports.

14.1 Bio Generation

Forbes is a household name synonymous with success, prominence, and wealth for both individuals and businesses.

As Bresler (2016) stated in their `forbesListR` package, "Forbes is the preeminent maintainer of covering a wide range of business related topics including sports, entertainment, individual wealth, and locations. The lists are chock-full of phenomenal data that can be analyzed, visualized, and merged with other data". Specifically, the `forbesListR` package provides "an easy way to access the data contained in lists maintained by the fine folks at Forbes."

You can use the following recipe to extract wealthy individual entities from the Forbes 400 list (2017) and dynamically generate a prospect bio, including net worth, rank, geography, and so on. First, let's load the libraries.

 The following recipes are for demonstration purposes only. While we want to show how you can extract data from the web, we don't endorse any behavior that goes against the terms of services or diminishes the intellectual property of any websites. Read and follow the terms of services and copyright guidelines of each website.

```
devtools::install_github("abresler/forbesListR")
library(forbesListR)
library(dplyr)
library(stringr)
```

Then, using the `get_year_forbes_list_data` function, get all of the Forbes 400 data.

```
forbes400_data <- get_year_forbes_list_data(
  list = "Forbes 400", year = 2017)
```

Next, let's add a row number as an ID, and let's take only five of the 400 to make sure everything works.

```
forbes400_data <- mutate(forbes400_data, uniqueid = 1:n())
forbes400_data_ss <- head(forbes400_data, 5)
```

Let's use the `rvest` library functions to download the Forbes bios.

```
get_bio <- function(url) {
  read_html(url) %>%
    html_nodes(css = "#contentwrapper >
                div.content >
                div.featured >
                div.featured-text >
                ul") %>%
    html_text(trim = TRUE) %>%
    gsub("[\n\t]", "", .)
}

forbes400_data_ss <- rowwise(forbes400_data_ss) %>%
  mutate(bio = get_bio(url.bio.forbes))
```

Then, let's download the photos of people in the Forbes list.

```
if (!(dir.exists("imgs"))) dir.create("imgs")

forbes400_data_ss %>%
```

420   TEXT MINING

```r
do(d = download.file(url = .$url.image,
                     destfile = paste0("imgs/",
                                       .$uniqueid,
                                       ".jpg")))
```

Next, we will prepare LaTeXmarkup to create our final bio PDF file. LaTeX[1] is a typesetting markup language and system to create high-quality and great-looking documents.

```r
sanitizeLatexS <- function(str) {
  #http://stackoverflow.com/q/5406071/934898
  gsub('([#$%&~_\\^\\\\{}])', '\\\\\\1', str, perl = TRUE);
}


#create a bio page for every person
forbes400_data_ss %>%
  arrange(rank) %>%
  transmute(
    mrkup = paste0(
      "\\section{", sanitizeLatexS(name),
      "}\n",
      "\\begin{wrapfigure}[9]{l}[0pt]{0.35\\linewidth}\n",
      "\\centering\n",
      "\\vspace{-13pt}\n",
      "\\includegraphics[scale=0.6]{imgs/", uniqueid, "}\\\\\n",
      "\\end{wrapfigure}\n",
      "\\textbf{Forbes Rank:} ", rank, "\\\\\n",
      "\\textbf{Net Worth:} \\$", net_worth.millions, "M\\\\\n",
      "\\textbf{Residence:} ", state, "\\\\\n",
      "\\textbf{Forbes Bio:}", "\\\\\n",
      sanitizeLatexS(str_sub(bio, end = 1000)),
      "\\ldots\n",
```

---

[1]https://www.latex-project.org/about/

```r
    "\\textbf{Source:} \\url{", url.bio.forbes, "}\\\\\n")) %>%
  do(prnt = writeLines(text = .$mrkup,
                        con = "./forbesbios.tex"))


file_conn <- file('forbesbios.tex', 'r+')
file_contents <- readLines(file_conn)
writeLines(
  c(paste(
    "\\documentclass[11pt]{article}",
    "\\usepackage{graphicx}",
    "\\usepackage{wrapfig}",
    "\\usepackage[urlbordercolor={1 1 1},urlcolor=red,colorlinks]{hyperref}",
    "\\setcounter{secnumdepth}{0}",
    "\\begin{document}", sep = "\n"),
    file_contents,
    "\\end{document}"),
  con = file_conn)
close(file_conn)
```

Finally, we compile the LATEXcode to create a PDF.

```r
tools::texi2pdf("forbesbios.tex")
```

Once you run the complete code, the final PDF will look like Figure
14.1.

14.2 Endowment Benchmarking

In higher-education fundraising, endowment figures are often used
as a proxy or baseline measurement of institutional resource levels,
with the assumption that larger endowment figures translate into
increased support for educational programs, research activities, and

422 TEXT MINING

Figure 14.1: Forbes bio example

so on. You may already be familiar with or responsible for institutional benchmarking survey requests. While the purpose of benchmark reporting varies, these surveys usually involve a comparative analysis of peer institutional metrics for various purposes, including campaign-planning activities.

Suppose you receive a time-sensitive inquiry to conduct a benchmarking analysis of endowment levels of peer educational institutions across the U.S. Rather than searching for this information one by one, you would presumably prefer to find a more efficient solution to reduce the time and effort required to complete this project.

In the following recipe, we will use R to connect to the web and retrieve endowment information for various higher-education institutions.

Let's install and load the XML and httr packages.

```
# Install XML and httr packages
install.packages("XML",
                 repos = "http://cran.us.r-project.org")
install.packages("httr",
```

ENDOWMENT BENCHMARKING   423

```r
           repos = "http://cran.us.r-project.org")
```

Now, let's load the XML and httr packages to connect R to the web.

```r
# Load XML package
library(XML)

# Load httr package
library(httr)
```

Next, let's read publicly available information directly from Wikipedia:

```r
# Extract HTML data from a webpage
url <- "https://tinyurl.com/zsbw279"
webpage <- GET(url, user_agent("httr"))
```

Next, let's extract and store this information into a dataframe:

```r
endowments <- readHTMLTable(text_content(webpage), as.data.frame = TRUE)
```

Finally, let's display endowment information from 2007 to 2016 for the first 10 colleges.

```r
# Display First 10 Colleges Endowment Figures 2007-2016
endows <- endowments[[1]]
head(endows, n = 10)
```

We need to perform further clean-up to remove the dollar signs and other extra characters.

```r
remove_unnecessary_chars <- function(x){
```

```
  ret <- gsub(x = x, pattern = "\\[\\d+\\]", replacement = "" )
  ret <- gsub(x = ret, pattern = "[\r\n]", replacement = "")
  gsub(x = ret, pattern = "\\$", replacement = "")
}
endows <- mutate_all(endows,
                     .funs = funs(remove_unnecessary_chars)) %>%
  mutate_at(.vars = -1,
            .funs = as.numeric) %>%
  gather(key = "year", value = "value", -1) %>%
  mutate(year = as.numeric(str_trim(str_replace(string =   .$year,
                                     pattern = "\\(billions USD\\)",
                                     replacement = "")))) %>%
  mutate(value = value * 10^9)
```

In this recipe, we used R to pull publicly available endowment information from Wikipedia, which allows you to spend more time focusing on how to most effectively summarize and present your insights rather than having to look up this information manually.

 Modify the existing recipe to retrieve your institution's endowment figures as well as of its peer institutions. If you don't work in higher education, modify the code to pull down your alma mater's endowment information or a university you admire.

Let's continue to explore how we can use R to extract web-based text information to generate actionable insights and recommendations.

14.3 Geo-Coded Prospect Identification

Suppose you have a list of over 30,000 constituents to prioritize for prospect research and lead generation for frontline fundraisers.

Let's also imagine you have outdated and sparsely populated wealth rating information in your current database. While your first proposed solution might be to conduct a bulk wealth screening, let's also assume there is limited capacity and resources, which motivates a different approach.

To manage an inquiry of this scale or beyond, you will need a practical, efficient, and repeatable method to identify the best prospects. To put this inquiry into perspective, 30,000 constituents at a rate of 30 minutes of research per constituent translates to 900,000 minutes, which is 15,000 hours or approximately 7.8 years of work… and, hence, the motivation to find a practical solution.

Assuming you've already explored the various exploratory data analysis (EDA) and machine learning (ML) methods previously covered, another solution is to acquire public data that can be used as a proxy for wealth capacity. One potential proxy for wealth capacity is the median real estate value associated with a constituent's residential ZIP code, which is driven by census data.

While using median price ZIP code data as a proxy for wealth capacity estimates is notably sensitive to the accuracy and integrity of the constituent address information in your database, it provides a helpful way to prioritize and segment prospects. This approach assumes that prospects with higher wealth capacity tend to live on average in more expensive geographic areas relative to other prospects. This is certainly not *always* the case, but it is a useful starting point and filter for prospect research and development.

A quick search for "wealthiest zips 2017" returns a Forbes article[2] "Full List: America's Most Expensive ZIP Codes 2017," which we can use to identify affluent constituent geographies. If you are looking for a simple web-based text mining solution to acquire this data,

---

[2] http://bit.ly/2klUzwd

426 TEXT MINING

you may prefer to use the rvest package developed by Hadley Wickham. The rvest package was designed for simple web scraping and, unlike the httr and XML packages, does not require a deep understanding of the structure of web-based data objects such as XML and JSON.

The following recipe shows how to use the rvest package to extract Forbes 2017 wealthy ZIP codes and blend geo-coded wealth information acquired via the web with our example donor file.

We will also use regular expressions (also known as **regex**) to parse the text. Regexes are very powerful and help match complex patterns in strings. Read this site for more information: http://www.regular-expressions.info/ .

```
# Install Rvest
install.packages('rvest',
                  repos = "http://cran.us.r-project.org")
```

Let's load all the libraries first.

```
# Load rvest, stringr, tidyr, readr, dplyr
library(rvest)
library(stringr)
library(tidyr)
library(readr)
library(dplyr)
```

Then, let's read the HTML code of the web page with all the wealthy ZIP codes.

```
# Web page for extraction
wealth_zips <- read_html("https://tinyurl.com/yd9gzrrp")
```

Then, using the rvest library, we'll extract the list with all the details.

GEO-CODED PROSPECT IDENTIFICATION 427

```
wealth_zips_df <- wealth_zips %>%
  html_nodes("ol") %>%
  html_nodes("li") %>%
  html_nodes("ol") %>%
  html_nodes("li") %>%
  html_text() %>%
  as_data_frame()
head(wealth_zips_df)
```

```
#> A tibble: 6 x 1
#>
#>
#> 1 "94027 ATHERTON CA Median Price: $9,686,154 \n
#> 2 33462 MANALAPAN FL Median Price: $8,368,431 Days o
#> 3 94022 LOS ALTOS HILLS CA Median Price: $7,755,000
#> 4 94301 PALO ALTO CA Median Price: $7,016,631 Days o
#> 5 94957 ROSS CA Median Price: $6,939,423 Days on Mar
#> 6 11962 SAGAPONACK NY Median Price: $6,852,692 Days
```

Using `stringr` library functions and regex, extract the ZIP code and
its median home price from the extracted string.

```
wealthy_zips_medprice <- transmute(
  wealth_zips_df,
  zip = str_sub(value, end = 5),
  MedianPrice = str_extract(value, "(?<=\\$)[0-9,]+"))

wealthy_zips_medprice <- mutate(
  wealthy_zips_medprice,
  MedianPrice = as.numeric(str_replace_all(MedianPrice, ",", "")))
```

428 TEXT MINING

To filter out donor sample data with ZIP codes that have median house prices over \$1,000,000, let's join the wealthy ZIPs with the donor sample data.

```r
donor_data <- read_csv("data/DonorSampleDataML.csv",
                        col_types = cols(ZIPCODE = col_character()))

select_vars <- c('MARITAL_STATUS', 'GENDER',
                 'ALUMNUS_IND', 'PARENT_IND',
                 'HAS_INVOLVEMENT_IND', 'DEGREE_LEVEL',
                 'PREF_ADDRESS_TYPE', 'EMAIL_PRESENT_IND',
                 'ZIPCODE')

donor_data <- select(donor_data,
                     select_vars,
                     AGE,
                     TotalGiving,
                     DONOR_IND)

# Merge with SuperZip Index
dd_superzips <- inner_join(donor_data,
                     wealthy_zips_medprice,
                     by = c("ZIPCODE" = "zip"))
```

Finally, let's filter the sample data.

```r
prospects <- filter(dd_superzips,
                    TotalGiving >= 10000 & ALUMNUS_IND == "Y" &
                    HAS_INVOLVEMENT_IND =="Y" &
                    EMAIL_PRESENT_IND =="Y" &
                    PREF_ADDRESS_TYPE =="HOME" &
                    MedianPrice > 1000000 &
                    AGE >= 40)
```

Let's inspect our sample data.

```
glimpse(prospects)
```

```
#> Observations: 14
#> Variables: 13
#> $ MARITAL_STATUS      <chr> "Unknown", "Marri...
#> $ GENDER              <chr> "Female", "Female...
#> $ ALUMNUS_IND         <chr> "Y", "Y", "Y", "Y...
#> $ PARENT_IND          <chr> "N", "N", "N", "N...
#> $ HAS_INVOLVEMENT_IND <chr> "Y", "Y", "Y", "Y...
#> $ DEGREE_LEVEL        <chr> "Undergrad", "Und...
#> $ PREF_ADDRESS_TYPE   <chr> "HOME", "HOME", "...
#> $ EMAIL_PRESENT_IND   <chr> "Y", "Y", "Y", "Y...
#> $ ZIPCODE             <chr> "90265", "90265",...
#> $ AGE                 <int> 44, 60, 54, 52, 4...
#> $ TotalGiving         <int> 12850, 12309, 302...
#> $ DONOR_IND           <chr> "Y", "Y", "Y", "Y...
#> $ MedianPrice         <dbl> 4266731, 4266731,...
```

In this recipe, we used the `rvest` package to extract Forbes 2017 wealthy ZIP codes and use them as a wealth capacity proxy and filter for our example donor file. We selected the following prospect criteria: Alumni prospects who are 40 years or older with total giving of $10,000 or more, institutional involvement flag, active email address, and preferred home address ZIP with median price above $1,000,000. The resultant output is a set of 14 prospect leads for recommended research, outreach, and qualification.

14.4 Social Media Analytics

Social media is a powerful online platform that gives voice to a variety of ideas, opinions, and feedback. Platforms such as Twitter are dynamic forums driven by a broad community of users (over 300 million users as of 2017) who can instantly tap into a global conversation. Whether you actively use Twitter or other social media, you should recognize there is a wealth of social media information that you can explore and analyze to extract relevant insights.

In the following recipe, we will explore how to use R and some text mining packages to see what people are currently saying about machine learning, artificial intelligence, and deep learning on Twitter.

> In order to extract tweets, you will need a Twitter account. If you don't have one, you can sign up here[3]. Once you have an account, you can use your Twitter login ID and password to create a Twitter application here[4]. For detailed instructions on how to configure your Twitter account so you can pull data using R, you can refer to this article[5].

First, install the twitteR, rwteet packages to extract Twitter data and the tm and wordcloud packages to perform text mining analysis.

```
# Install twitteR, rtweet, tm
install.packages('twitteR',
                 repos = "http://cran.us.r-project.org")
install.packages('rtweet',
                 repos = "http://cran.us.r-project.org")
install.packages('tm',
                 repos = "http://cran.us.r-project.org")
install.packages('wordcloud',
                 repos = "http://cran.us.r-project.org")
```

SOCIAL MEDIA ANALYTICS   431

Next, load the Twitter and text mining packages.

```
# Load twitteR, stringr and tidyr
library(twitteR)
library(rtweet)
library(tm)
library(wordcloud)
library(stringr)
library(tidyr)
```

Now, define your Twitter authentication credentials.

```
# Twitter Authentication
requestURL = "https://api.twitter.com/oauth/request_token"
accessURL = "https://api.twitter.com/oauth/access_token"
authURL = "https://api.twitter.com/oauth/authorize"
consumerKey = "INSERT_YOUR_CONSUMER_KEY_HERE"
consumerSecret = "INSERT_YOUR_CONSUMER_Secret_HERE"
accessToken = "INSERT_YOUR_access_Token_HERE"
accessSecret = "INSERT_YOUR_accessSecret_HERE"
setup_twitter_oauth(consumerKey, consumerSecret,
                    accessToken, accessSecret)
```

Next, let's search Twitter for machine learning, AI, and deep learning topics.

```
# Search Twitter
tweets <- searchTwitter("MachineLearning AND AI AND DeepLearning",
                    lang = "en", n = 1000)
```

Next, let's extract tweets.

```
# Extract Text
tweets.txt <- sapply(tweets, function(x) x$getText())
```

432   TEXT MINING

Let's convert tweets to plain text format.

```r
# Convert Tweets to Plain Test
tweets.txt <- plain_tweets(tweets.txt)
```

Next, let's clean up our tweet formatting.

```r
# Remove Retweet
tweets.txt <- gsub("^RT", "", tweets.txt)
```

```r
# Remove @UserName
tweets.txt <- gsub("@\\w+", "", tweets.txt)
```

```r
# Remove Links
tweets.txt <- gsub("http\\w+", "", tweets.txt)
```

```r
# Remove Tabs
tweets.txt <- gsub("[ |\t]{2,}", "", tweets.txt)
```

Now, let's build a text corpus object.

```r
# Create Text Corpus
tweets.corpus <- Corpus(VectorSource(tweets.txt))
```

Next, let's pre-process our tweet corpus for analysis.

```r
# Text Pre-Processing
tweets.corpus <- tm_map(tweets.corpus, content_transformer(tolower))
tweets.corpus <- tm_map(tweets.corpus, removePunctuation)
tweets.corpus <- tm_map(tweets.corpus, stripWhitespace)
tweets.corpus <- tm_map(tweets.corpus, removeWords, stopwords())
```

Let's check a sample of tweets.

SOCIAL MEDIA ANALYTICS   433

```
# Inspect Pre-Processed Text Sample
inspect(tweets.corpus[1:50])
```

Finally, let's build a wordcloud of tweets.

```
# Build Wordcloud from Text
wordcloud(tweets.corpus, random.order = FALSE,  min.freq = 20)
```

Figure 14.2: Twitter wordcloud: MachineLearning DeepLearning AI

In this recipe, we used social media and text mining packages such as twitteR, rtweet, and tm to systematically pull and analyze 1,000 tweets (documents) from Twitter to understand what people are currently saying about #MachineLearning, #DeepLearning and #AI.

Based on the wordcloud visualization we created, higher-frequency words are plotted in larger text and arranged closer to the center to highlight top themes, which, perhaps unsurprisingly, include deep learning, big data, data science, artificial intelligence, and healthcare.

Other trending topics include predator vision drones using artificial intelligence to spot poachers; top virtual reality and internet of things (IOT) business trends; financial services tutorials on how to use deep learning, machine learning, neural networks, blockchain, and other cryptocurrency technologies; real estate startups using machine learning, and so on.

 Using the current recipe as a baseline, modify the code to search Twitter for recent conversations about your institution or social media campaigns. Store these tweets into a vectorized text corpus object using the tm package and build a wordcloud that reflects a snapshot or pulse of the most popular topics and trends being discussed.

14.5 Text Classification

Naive Bayes, which we introduced in the Machine Learning Concepts chapter, is one of the most commonly used machine learning methods for text classification tasks such as spam filtering. While naive Bayes makes some unrealistic assumptions of variable independence, it is both simple and effective for many real-world classification problems.

To help introduce you to text mining methods, we created a synthetic data set of prospect contact reports, which you will use to build a text classification model (also known as a **classifier**).

In the following recipe, you will build a text classifier, predict whether a contact report represents a positive prospect interaction, and evaluate these results using the `tm` package and `naiveBayes` algorithm included with the `e1071` package.

First, let's load our file manipulation and text mining libraries.

TEXT CLASSIFICATION   435

```r
# Load readr
library(readr)

# Load dplyr
library(dplyr)

# Load tm
library(tm)

# Load wordcloud
library(wordcloud)

# Load e1071
library(e1071)

# Load caret package
library(caret)
```

Next, let's load and prepare our sample contact file.

```r
# Load Data
contact_data <- read_csv("data/DonorSampleContactReportData.csv")

# Drop 'ID', 'MEMBERSHIP_ID', etc.
pred_vars <- c('Staff Name', 'Method', 'Substantive',
               'Donor', 'Outcome')

# Convert features to factor
contact_data <- mutate_at(contact_data,
                   .vars = pred_vars,
                   .funs = as.factor)

# Select Variables
```

436   TEXT MINING

```r
contact_data <- select(contact_data,
  pred_vars,
  Summary)
```

Next, let's split our contact data into training and test datasets.

```r
# Split 70% of contact_data into training
# data and 30% into test data
cd_index <- sample(2, nrow(contact_data), replace = TRUE,
    prob = c(0.7, 0.3))
cd_trainset <- contact_data[cd_index == 1, ]
cd_testset <- contact_data[cd_index == 2, ]
```

Let's confirm our training and test dataset sizes and proportions.

```r
# Confirm size of training and test
# datasets
dim(cd_trainset)
dim(cd_testset)

# Check proportions of $Outcome in training and test
# Train dataset 70% Negative, 30% Positive
# Test dataset: 63% Negative, 37% Positive
prop.table(table(cd_trainset$Outcome))
prop.table(table(cd_testset$Outcome))
```

Now, let's convert our test and training contact reports to corpus data objects.

```r
# Convert test and training contact report to corpus
cd_trainset_corpus <- Corpus(
  VectorSource(cd_trainset$Summary))
cd_testset_corpus <- Corpus(
```

```
  VectorSource(cd_testset$Summary))
```

Next, let's pre-process the contact report text.

```
# Pre-processing contact report corpora
cd_trainset_corpus <- tm_map(
  cd_trainset_corpus, tolower)
cd_trainset_corpus <- tm_map(
  cd_trainset_corpus, removeWords,
  stopwords())
cd_trainset_corpus <- tm_map(
  cd_trainset_corpus, removePunctuation)
cd_trainset_corpus <- tm_map(
  cd_trainset_corpus, stripWhitespace)
cd_testset_corpus <- tm_map(
  cd_testset_corpus, tolower)
cd_testset_corpus <- tm_map(
  cd_testset_corpus, removeWords,
  stopwords())
cd_testset_corpus <- tm_map(
  cd_testset_corpus, removePunctuation)
cd_testset_corpus <- tm_map(
  cd_testset_corpus, stripWhitespace)
```

Let's read a sample of example contact reports.

```
# Inspect contact report corpora sample
inspect(cd_trainset_corpus[1:5])
inspect(cd_testset_corpus[1:5])
```

Now, let's build document term matrices (DTM) for analysis.

438 TEXT MINING

```r
# Build Document Term Matrices (DTM)
cd_trainset_dtm <- DocumentTermMatrix(
  cd_trainset_corpus)
cd_testset_dtm <- DocumentTermMatrix(
  cd_testset_corpus)
```

Let's inspect a couple contact report DTM samples.

```r
# Inspect Contact Report DTM sample
inspect(cd_trainset_dtm[1:5,])
inspect(cd_testset_dtm[1:5,])
```

Next, let's explore associations between terms and plot term distribution.

```r
# Explore Associations Between Terms
findAssocs(cd_trainset_dtm, "meeting", 0.2)


# Plot Zipf distribution of trainset DTM
Zipf_plot(cd_trainset_dtm)
```

Now, let's create word clouds for positive and negative contact outcomes.

```r
# Create Word clouds for Positive and Negative Contact Outcomes
positive_interaction <- subset(
  cd_trainset, Outcome=="Positive")
negative_interaction <- subset(
  cd_trainset, Outcome=="Negative")

wordcloud(positive_interaction$Summary,
  random.order = FALSE,
  min.freq = 2, scale = c(3,1))
```

```r
wordcloud(negative_interaction$Summary,
  random.order = FALSE,
  min.freq = 2, scale = c(3,1))
```

Let's store a dictionary of frequent terms.

```r
# Store Dictionary of Frequent Terms
cd_dict <- findFreqTerms(cd_trainset_dtm, 2)
```

Let's use frequent terms to limit our training and test datasets.

```r
# Limit Training and Test to Frequent Terms
cd_train <- DocumentTermMatrix(cd_trainset_corpus,
  list(Dictionary = cd_dict))
cd_test <- DocumentTermMatrix(cd_testset_corpus,
  list(Dictionary = cd_dict))
```

Let's convert term counts and column counts for DTMs.

```r
# Convert Counts to Factors
convert_counts <- function(x) {
  x <- ifelse(x > 0, 1, 0)
  x <- factor(x, levels = c(0,1), labels = c("No", "Yes"))
  x
}
```

```r
# Convert Column Counts for DTMs
cd_train <- apply(cd_train, MARGIN = 2, convert_counts)
cd_test <- apply(cd_test, MARGIN = 2, convert_counts)
```

Now, let's build our naive Bayes classification model.

440 TEXT MINING

```r
# Build Naive Bayes classification Model
cd_naivebayes <- naiveBayes(cd_train,
                            cd_trainset$Outcome,
                            laplace = 0.5)


# Examine Naive Bayes model
# cd_naivebayes
```

Finally, let's use our model to make classification predictions.

```r
# Make Naive Bayes predictions
cd_prediction <- predict(cd_naivebayes, cd_test)
```

Let's explore the accuracy of the model.

```r
# Create NB crosstab
naivebayes.crosstab <- table(cd_prediction, cd_testset$Outcome)

# Confusion Matrix
confusionMatrix(naivebayes.crosstab, positive="Positive")
```

In this recipe, we built a classification model using the naive Bayes algorithm to classify contact reports as positive or negative interactions based on training (input) text data. The naive Bayes method estimates the likelihood of new observation (test) data belonging to various labeled classes (groups). The text classifier we built using example contact report data classified approximately 88% of the contact reports correctly as a positive or negative interaction based on training labels.

In the following recipe, we will explore how to analyze sentiment within text documents that don't have existing labels in our training (input) data.

14.6 Sentiment Analysis

R offers multiple packages for performing sentiment analysis (also known as **opinion mining** or **emotion AI**), which is the process of using machine learning, natural language processing, and text mining techniques to identify, extract, quantify, and study subjective information such as opinions and attitudes.

The purpose of sentiment analysis is to computationally determine user attitudes or emotional reactions to an occurrence, interaction, or event using collected data, surveys, and so on. Sentiment analysis application contexts include customer reviews, survey response analysis, social media analytics, healthcare customer experience research, and so on.

One popular package is RSentiment, which you can download with the following command.

```
# Install sentiment package
devtools::install_github("okugami79/sentiment140")
```

In the following recipe, we will build on the previous example and conduct sentiment analysis using the example contact report file.

Let's load file manipulation and text mining libraries.

```
# Load readr
library(readr)
```

```
# Load dplyr
library(dplyr)
```

```
# Load ggplot
library(ggplot2)
```

442   TEXT MINING

```r
# Load sentiment package
library(sentiment)
```

Next, let's load and prepare our sample contact report data.

```r
# Load Data
contact_data <- read_csv("data/DonorSampleContactReportData.csv")

pred_vars <- c('Staff Name',
               'Method',
               'Substantive',
               'Donor',
               'Outcome')

# Convert features to factor
contact_data <- mutate_at(contact_data,
                          .vars = pred_vars,
                          .funs = as.factor)

# Select Variables
contact_data <- select(contact_data,
                       pred_vars,
                       Summary)
```

Let's conduct sentiment analysis on the contact reports.

```r
# Sentiment Analysis
contact_data <- mutate(contact_data,
  polarity = sentiment(Summary)$polarity)
```

Next, let's summarize the sentiment score results.

SENTIMENT ANALYSIS   443

```r
# Summarize Sentiment Analysis
table(contact_data$polarity)
#>
#> negative   neutral positive
#>        9       180        7
```

Now, let's convert sentiment scores to "score" variable with numeric values between -1 to 1.

```r
# Create Sentiment Analysis Score
contact_data <- mutate(contact_data,
  score = ifelse(
  polarity == "positive", 1,
  ifelse(polarity == "negative", -1,
  0)))

result <- aggregate(score ~ Donor, data = contact_data, sum)
```

Let's select positive or negative reports.

```r
# Select positive or negative reports
result.pon <- filter(result, score != 0)
```

Finally, let's plot the sentiment results.

```r
# Sentiment Plot
p <- ggplot(result.pon,
            aes(x = score,
                y = Donor,
                colour = score)) +
  geom_point() +
  scale_color_continuous("Sentiment Score",
                         low = "red2",
```

444 TEXT MINING

```
                              high = "green3")


p + xlab("Contact Sentiment") + ylab("Donor")
```

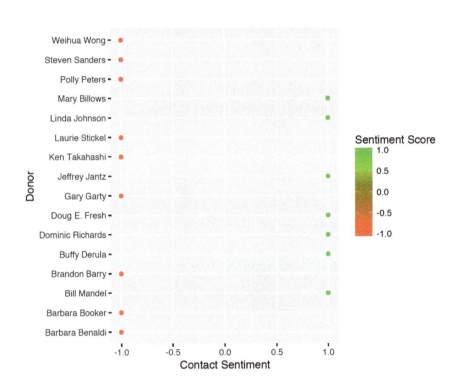

In this recipe, we used the sentiment140 package originally designed for Twitter sentiment text analysis to conduct out-of-the-box, "headache-free" sentiment scoring on our example contact report file. Unlike the previous recipe, where we built a text classifier from scratch using the naive Bayes algorithm, the sentiment140 package uses a context-free grammar (CFG) language model that is pre-tuned for English and Spanish tweets (140 characters) and requires no natural language processing (NLP) training.

For additional information about CFG models, you can check out this article[6]. To read more about `Sentiment140`, check out this link[7] and paper[8].

14.7 Summary

In this chapter, we explore how to use web and text mining packages to connect directly to the web and extract public data to build data-driven solutions. In addition, we explored how to blend public data sources with an example donor file to enhance our analysis. Specifically, we showed how to redesign information collection processes and elevate some traditional deliverables, including prospect reports, benchmark reports, and contact reports.

In the next chapter, we will explore how to analyze and explore relationship data using social network analysis and advanced visualization techniques.

If you're enjoying this book, consider sharing it with your network by running `source("http://arn.la/shareds4fr")` in your R console.

— Ashutosh and Rodger

---

[6]https://en.wikipedia.org/wiki/Context-free_grammar
[7]http://help.sentiment140.com/
[8]http://cs.stanford.edu/people/alecmgo/papers/ TwitterDistantSupervision09.pdf

446 TEXT MINING

15

SOCIAL NETWORK ANALYSIS

Social network analysis (SNA) is the study of networks formed because of connections among objects. These objects could be people and the connections could be relationships among those people. But SNA isn't limited to people. Researchers have used these types of analyses to test the reliability of electric grids (Chassin & Posse 2005), to find structure between gene expression profiles (Langfelder & Horvath 2008), to detect spam emails (Golbeck & Hendler 2004), and to find efficient hubs for air transportation (Guimera et al. 2005). Even Google's origin[1] involves a study of citation networks which later became the basis of PageRank (Page et al. 1999).

As you can see from these examples, SNA allows us to study the influential objects as well as their connections in networks. Through numbers and graphs, something that seems unfathomable can be understood and, more importantly, used in a practical application. Michael Kimmelman wrote an article in The New York Times[2] on

---

[1]https://www.wired.com/2005/08/battelle/
[2]http://nyti.ms/2jnAGnv

448 SOCIAL NETWORK ANALYSIS

Mark Lombardi's network maps on financial networks. He said, "I happened to be in the Drawing Center when the Lombardi show was being installed and several consultants to the Department of Homeland Security came in to take a look. They said they found the work revelatory, not because the financial and political connections he mapped were new to them, but because Lombardi showed them an elegant way to array disparate information and make sense of things, which they thought might be useful to their security efforts."

"[...] several consultants to the Department of Homeland Security came in to take a look. They said they found the work revelatory, [...] because Lombardi showed them an elegant way to array disparate information and make sense of things, which they thought might be useful to their security efforts."

— Michael Kimmelman

You often hear that fundraising is all about relationships. Good fundraisers know or uncover the relationships among donors or potential prospects and then use these relationships to further the non-profit's cause. A few vendors such as RelSci[3] and Prospect Visual[4] have made it easy to uncover these various relationships among our volunteers, donors, and prospective donors. This chapter will provide you with recipes to create such networks using your own data, but first let's go through a few key concepts that are useful in this field.

---

[3]https://www.relsci.com/
[4]http://www.prospectvisual.com/

15.1 Key Concepts

This is a quick introduction to SNA for our purposes; you should read Scott (2017) and Newman (2010) for more in-depth knowledge.

Node: The object of analysis is a node. It is also called as a vertex, actor, or an individual. Let's say that John is a potential donor. He will be a node in our analysis then.

Edge: An edge is the connection between two nodes. It is also called a line, relationship, or link. Let's say that Jane, our volunteer, is a friend of John. This friendship now forms an edge between John and Jane.

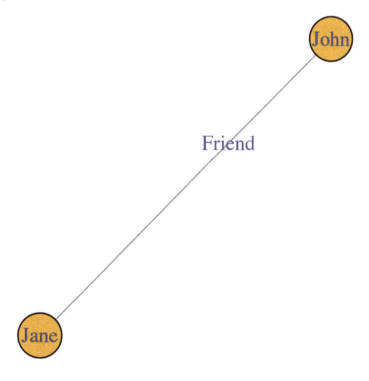

450 SOCIAL NETWORK ANALYSIS

We also know that Jesse sits on a board with John, but Jesse doesn't know Jane. Therefore, we won't see any connection between Jesse and Jane.

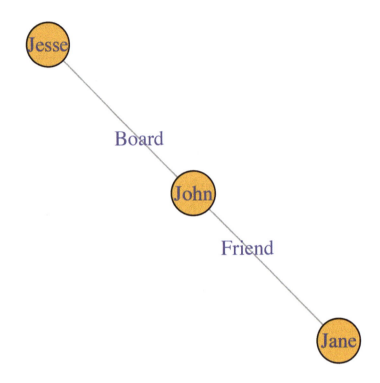

Degree: Degree is a measure of connectedness of a node (that is, the number of edges a node has). As you can guess, this is a very helpful measure because we can determine the nodes with the highest connections. Nodes with high degree are great connectors. In our made-up example, John has two degrees and both Jesse and Jane only one.

Betweenness centrality: Betweenness centrality measures the number of edges for which a node is between other nodes. This measure is helpful to find out the gatekeepers in a network. Let's say that Jack is a friend of Jane, and Jack is also a friend of Jesse.

KEY CONCEPTS 451

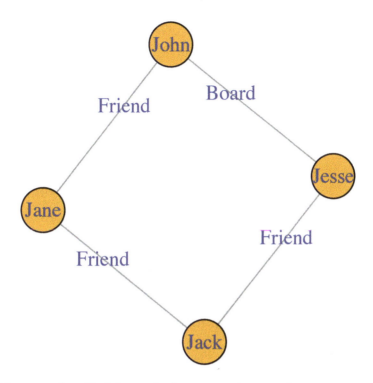

In this example, all of the nodes have two degrees, because everyone knows two people. Also, all of the nodes have a betweenness of 0.5, because every node has two connections and there are four nodes, namely, 2/4. The math to calculate this measure gets complicated quickly with many nodes and edges. For more information, you can read these lecture slides[5] by Donglei Du at the University of New Brunswick.

Communities: Communities are groups of the most interconnected nodes. A simple example of a community would be if you and I knew each other: my group of friends would form one community and your group of friends would form another.

Layouts: Layout algorithms help us see the networks and their characteristics. This is an active research field and researchers have pro-

---
[5]http://www2.unb.ca/~ddu/6634/Lecture_notes/Lecture_4_centrality_measure.pdf

vided many types of algorithms (Jacomy et al. 2014). Some common ones are random layout, circular layout, and Fruchterman Reingold layout. Figure 15.1 shows a sample network with three different layouts.

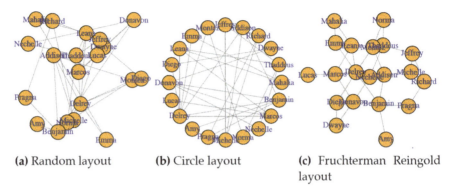

(a) Random layout (b) Circle layout (c) Fruchterman Reingold layout

Figure 15.1: Different layouts for networks

15.2 Data Structure

Relationships between two nodes is the easiest format to use for SNA in R using the `igraph` library. You could provide the data in two different ways.

- Edges or relationships only
- Edges and vertices separately

If you provide edges-only data and provide the vertex names along with it, `igraph` will figure everything out for us. This data will produce a table as shown in Table 15.1.

With this approach, you can't easily change the vertex properties, such as colors, shapes, and others. But if you were to provide edges and vertices separately, you could also provide vertex properties along with it, as shown in Table 15.2; you can see the graph this data

DATA STRUCTURE   453

Table 15.1: Edges-only data

From	To
Mahalia	Emma
Thaddeus	Leana
Mahalia	Leana
Dwayne	Diego
Thaddeus	Jeffrey
Richard	Jeffrey

Table 15.2: Edge and vertex data

From	To	Name	Label	Color	Shape
1	3	1	Jacob	burlywood1	circle
1	5	3	Danny	burlywood1	circle
1	6	9	Samantha	burlywood1	circle
3	10	4	Breyanna	orange	square
9	10	5	Nathan	orange	square
4	11	6	Amira	orange	square
		10	Briana	tomato	rectangle
		11	Marioly	tomato	rectangle

created in Figure 15.2. Providing vertex data separately also helps when you have large data sets.

You can write simple SQL statements to extract such data from your databases.

To get the edges you can write the following.

```sql
SELECT RELATED_ID, RELATED_TO_ID, RELATIONSHIP_TYPE as LABEL
FROM RELATIONSHIPS
```

To get the vertex properties you can write the following.

454 SOCIAL NETWORK ANALYSIS

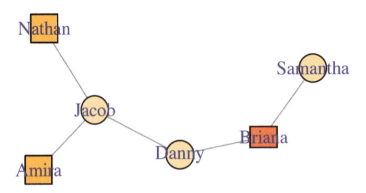

Figure 15.2: Customized vertex options

```
SELECT C.ID, C.NAME, C.CONSTITUENT_TYPE
FROM CONSTITUENT C
WHERE EXISTS
  (SELECT 0
  FROM RELATIONSHIPS R
  WHERE R.RELATED_ID = C.ID OR R.RELATED_TO_ID = C.ID)
```

You can then use the vertex properties to assign shapes or colors.

CREATING YOUR FIRST NETWORK **455**

15.3 Creating Your First Network

Enough talk. Let's create a simple network using the sample data.
It is a simple, randomly generated network data set with 20 nodes.
Let's read the data.

```r
library(readr)

sample_network_d <- read_csv("data/sample_network.csv")
head(sample_network_d)
#> # A tibble: 6 x 2
#>        from       to
#>       <chr>    <chr>
#> 1  Mahalia     Emma
#> 2 Thaddeus    Leana
#> 3  Mahalia    Leana
#> 4   Dwayne    Diego
#> 5 Thaddeus  Jeffrey
#> 6  Richard  Jeffrey
```

Let's use the `igraph` library to create a network using this data.

```r
library(igraph)

sample_network_g <- graph_from_data_frame(d = sample_network_d,
                                          directed = FALSE)
```

To plot this graph, simply use the `plot` function.

```r
plot(sample_network_g)
```

456 SOCIAL NETWORK ANALYSIS

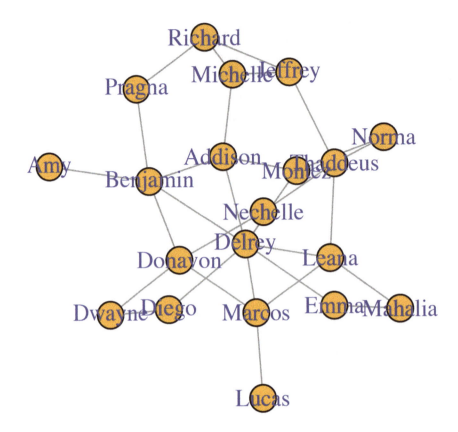

You will see that the size of the vertices is small. You can adjust that by using the vertex.size parameter.

```
plot(sample_network_g, vertex.size = 25)
```

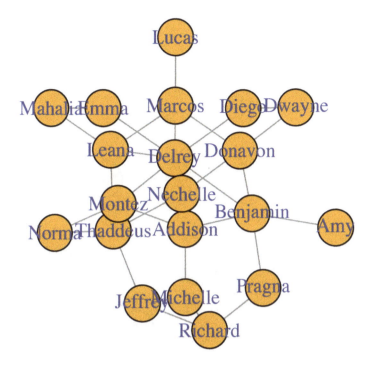

You can also play with different layouts to improve readability. Check all the different layouts by writing ?layout_ in your R console.

```
#Check out all layouts: https://stackoverflow.com/a/15365407

plot(sample_network_g, vertex.size = 25, layout = layout_with_fr)
```

458   SOCIAL NETWORK ANALYSIS

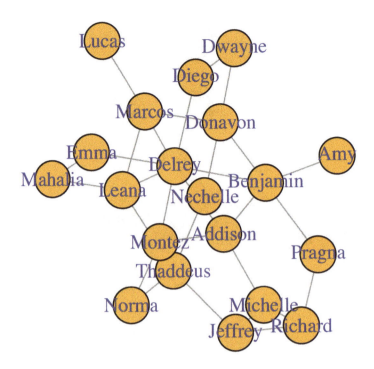

Since our sample data only had edges, we can create a separate data frame with vertex properties.

```r
#Check out all shapes: https://stackoverflow.com/a/7429938

sample_vertices <- data.frame(
  name = unique(c(sample_network_d$from, sample_network_d$to)),
  label = unique(c(sample_network_d$from, sample_network_d$to)),
  color = sample(x = c("orange", "tomato", "burlywood1", "grey"),
                 size = 20, replace = TRUE),
  shape = sample(x = c("circle", "square", "rectangle", "none"),
                 size = 20, replace = TRUE))
head(sample_vertices)
#>       name    label  color   shape
#> 1  Mahalia  Mahalia   grey  circle
#> 2 Thaddeus Thaddeus orange    none
```

```
#> 3    Dwayne    Dwayne    grey circle
#> 4    Richard   Richard orange circle
#> 5    Addison   Addison  tomato   none
#> 6    Jeffrey   Jeffrey  tomato   none
```

Use this vertex data to create the graph.

```
sample_network_g <- graph_from_data_frame(d = sample_network_d,
                                          directed = FALSE,
                                          vertices = sample_vertices)
plot(sample_network_g, vertex.size = 25, layout = layout_with_fr)
```

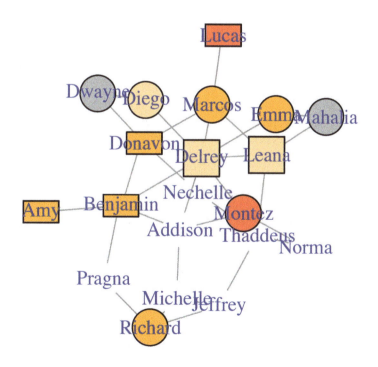

460 SOCIAL NETWORK ANALYSIS

15.4   Creating a Game of Thrones™ Network

Beveridge & Shan (2016) created a dataset using the book *A Storm of Swords*. You can find the dataset and many other fascinating applications and insights on their research page[6].

Let's read this dataset.

```
library(dplyr)
library(readr)

got_edges <- read_csv(
  file = "http://bit.ly/2Fc4Rr0",
  col_names = c("from", "to", "weight"),
  skip = 1)
glimpse(got_edges)
#> Observations: 352
#> Variables: 3
#> $ from   <chr> "Aemon", "Aemon", "Aerys", "Ae...
#> $ to     <chr> "Grenn", "Samwell", "Jaime", "...
#> $ weight <int> 5, 31, 18, 6, 5, 8, 5, 5, 11, ...
got_nodes <- data.frame(
  label = unique(c(got_edges$from, got_edges$to)),
  stringsAsFactors = FALSE)
glimpse(got_nodes)
#> Observations: 107
#> Variables: 1
#> $ label <chr> "Aemon", "Aerys", "Alliser", "A...
```

Let's build the network.

---

[6]https://www.macalester.edu/~abeverid/thrones.html

CREATING A GAME OF THRONES™ NETWORK   461

```
got_network_igraph <- graph_from_data_frame(d = got_edges,
                                            directed = FALSE,
                                            vertices = got_nodes)
plot(got_network_igraph)
```

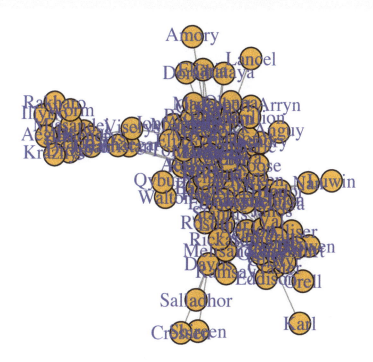

You can't really see many of the names and groups. Let's try different layouts.

```
plot(got_network_igraph, layout = layout_with_fr)
```

```
plot(got_network_igraph, layout = layout_in_circle)
```

```
plot(got_network_igraph, layout = layout_with_kk)
```

462 SOCIAL NETWORK ANALYSIS

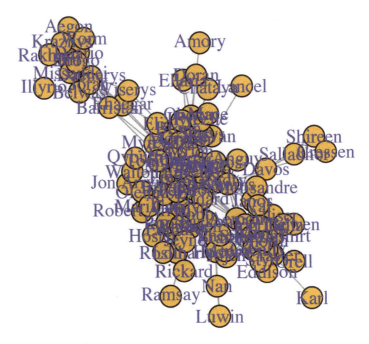

Figure 15.3: Fruchterman-Reingold layout

```
plot(got_network_igraph, layout = layout_with_lgl)


plot(got_network_igraph, layout = layout_with_mds)


plot(got_network_igraph, layout = layout_nicely)


plot(got_network_igraph, layout = layout_as_star)


plot(got_network_igraph, layout = layout_on_sphere)
```

CREATING A GAME OF THRONES™ NETWORK 463

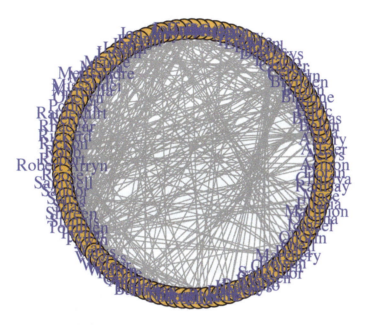

Figure 15.4: Circle layout

464 SOCIAL NETWORK ANALYSIS

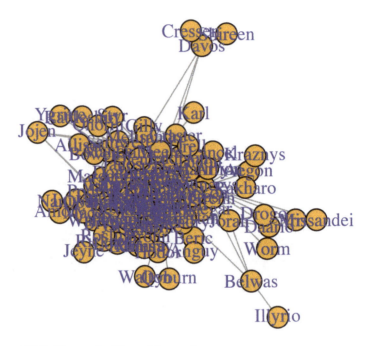

Figure 15.5: Kamada-Kawai layout

CREATING A GAME OF THRONES™ NETWORK   465

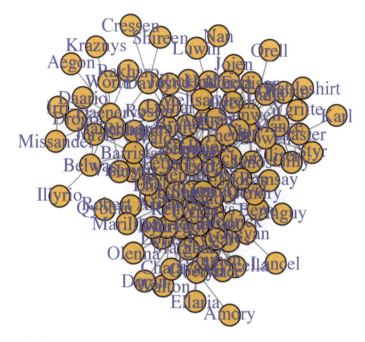

Figure 15.6: Large graph layout

466 SOCIAL NETWORK ANALYSIS

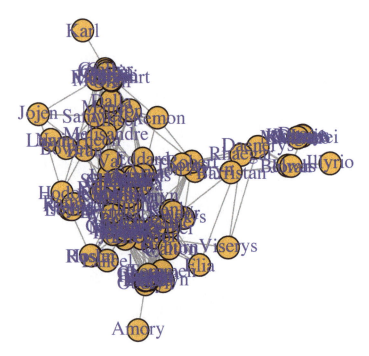

Figure 15.7: Multi-dimensional scaling layout

CREATING A GAME OF THRONES™ NETWORK 467

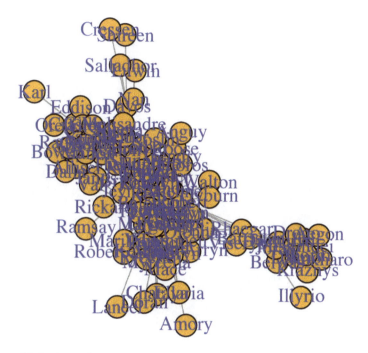

Figure 15.8: Auto layout

468 SOCIAL NETWORK ANALYSIS

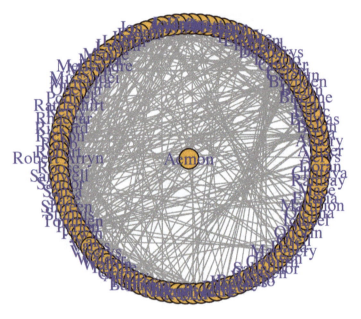

Figure 15.9: Star-shaped layout

CREATING A GAME OF THRONES™ NETWORK   469

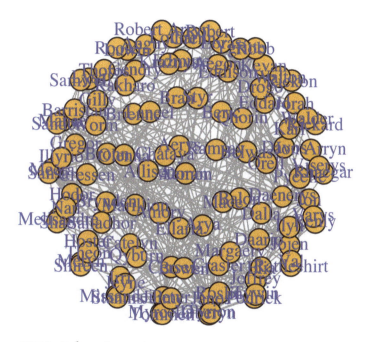

Figure 15.10: Sphere layout

470 SOCIAL NETWORK ANALYSIS

None of the layouts seem to improve the readability. We can improve the graph by deleting some of the nodes and their edges. To do so, we will need to calculate different measures.

Let's find the communities for each of the nodes using the `cluster_fast_greedy` function.

```r
membs_fc <- cluster_fast_greedy(got_network_igraph)
```

Then let's assign colors based on these communities.

```r
library(RColorBrewer)
membs_cols <- brewer.pal(n = max(membership(membs_fc)),
                         name = 'PiYG')
got_nodes$color <- membs_cols[membership(membs_fc)]
```

Let's plot the graph again with these colors.

```r
got_network_igraph <- graph_from_data_frame(d = got_edges,
                                            directed = FALSE,
                                            vertices = got_nodes)
plot(got_network_igraph, layout = layout_with_fr)
```

CREATING A GAME OF THRONES™ NETWORK

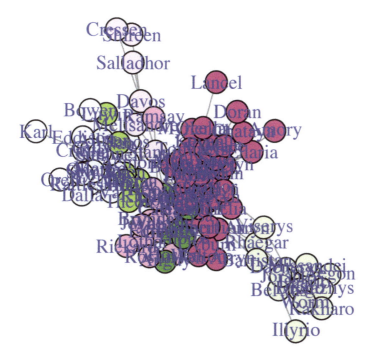

Now, although you can't see the names clearly at this resolution, you can see the different communities by their colors. We can easily find the most connected and most "in-between" characters.

Let's find the most connected characters.

```
got_degrees <- degree(got_network_igraph)
got_nodes$degrees <- got_degrees
head(sort(got_degrees, decreasing = TRUE))
#> Tyrion    Jon  Sansa   Robb  Jaime  Tywin
#>     36     26     26     25     24     22
```

Let's remove all nodes (and their edges) with the number of degrees less than 10. We will also make the node labels smaller and add curves to the edges.

```
got_network_igraph <- graph_from_data_frame(d = got_edges,
                                             directed = FALSE,
                                             vertices = got_nodes)
got_network_igraph <- delete_vertices(
  graph = got_network_igraph,
  v = which(degree(got_network_igraph)<10))
plot(got_network_igraph,
     vertex.label.cex = 0.9,
     edge.curved = TRUE)
```

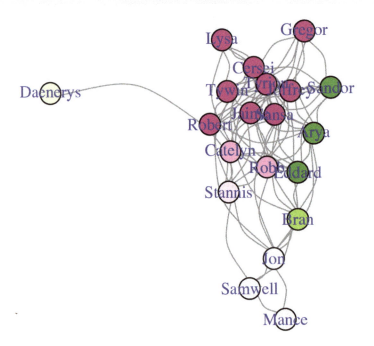

Let's find the most "in-between" characters.

```
got_network_igraph <- graph_from_data_frame(d = got_edges,
                                             directed = FALSE,
                                             vertices = got_nodes)
got_betdegrees <- betweenness(got_network_igraph)
```

```
head(sort(got_betdegrees, decreasing = TRUE))
#>  Robert  Tyrion     Jon Stannis   Sansa Catelyn
#>    1166    1164     922     697     684     598
```

Let's plot the graph with vertices which have betweenness values over 99.

```
plot(delete_vertices(graph = got_network_igraph,
                     v = betweenness(got_network_igraph) < 100))
```

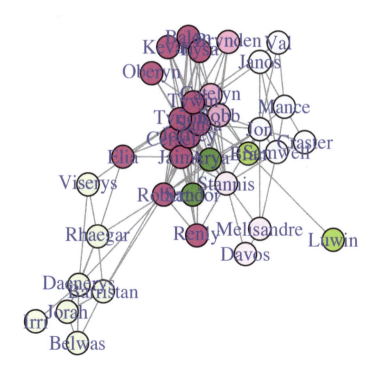

474 SOCIAL NETWORK ANALYSIS

15.5   Adding Interactivity

You can uncover many facts using numbers and graphs, but you can find the real power of SNA through interactive visualizations. The `visNetwork` library makes it very easy to create interactive networks.

Let's use the same Game of Thrones™ dataset and create an interactive network. First, let's prepare the data again, since `visNetwork` expects data in a slightly different format.

```r
library(visNetwork)
library(dplyr)
got_edges <- read_csv(
  file = "http://bit.ly/2Fc4RrO")
got_nodes <- data.frame(label = unique(c(got_edges$Source,
                                         got_edges$Target)),
                        stringsAsFactors = FALSE) %>%
  mutate(id = row_number())
got_edges <- mutate(
  got_edges,
  from = inner_join(got_edges,
                    got_nodes,
                    by = c("Source" = "label"))$id,
  to = inner_join(got_edges,
                  got_nodes,
                  by = c("Target" = "label"))$id)

got_nodes$value <- degree(
  graph_from_data_frame(d = got_edges,
                        directed = FALSE,
                        vertices = got_nodes))
membs_fc <- cluster_fast_greedy(got_network_igraph)
membs_cols <- brewer.pal(n = max(membership(membs_fc)),
                         name = 'RdYlBu')
```

```
got_nodes$color <- membs_cols[membership(membs_fc)]
```

Once the data is ready, `visNetwork` commands can be chained similar to `dplyr`, thus making it very easy to make changes as well as increasing readability. Let's see this code line by line.

- `visNetwork`: Creates a network for the specified size using the nodes and edges data frames.
- `visEdges`: Adds black edges and arrowheads from where the edge originates.
- `visNodes`: Adds circle-shaped nodes with some relative scaling of the circle sizes.
- `visInteraction`: Adds interaction to the network and enables navigation buttons.
- `visOptions`: Highlights the neighbors of a selected node.
- `visLayout`: Provides a seed to keep the final layout similar at every run.

```
got_network <- visNetwork(got_nodes,
                          got_edges,
                          height = "800px",
                          width = "100%") %>%
  visEdges(arrows = "from", color = "black") %>%
  visNodes(shape = "circle",
           value = 50,
           scaling = list(min = 40, max = 70) ) %>%
  visInteraction(navigationButtons = TRUE) %>%
  visOptions(highlightNearest = TRUE) %>%
  visLayout(randomSeed = 123)


visSave(file = "got_network.html", graph = got_network)
visExport(graph = got_network)
```

476 SOCIAL NETWORK ANALYSIS

This interactive graph, when opened in a browser, will look similar to Figure 15.11.

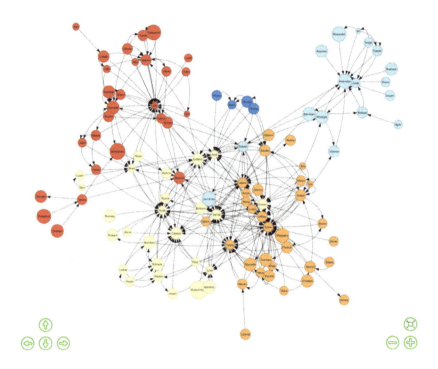

Figure 15.11: Game of Thrones™ interactive network

If you're enjoying this book, consider sharing it with your network by running `source("http://arn.la/shareds4fr")` in your R console.

— Ashutosh and Rodger

16

FINDING PROSPECTS

Prospect identification is one of the most common uses of descriptive and predictive analytics in fundraising, especially for direct mail appeals.

Whether you are acquiring new donors or reactivating former donors, identifying prospects and creating prioritized segments for direct response marketing efforts makes financial sense. For example, as we saw in Figure 1.2, if we can improve the response rate of a direct mail appeal and simultaneously reduce the number of target recipients, we can expect to generate, on average, more revenue while also reducing overall mailing costs (Bult et al. 1997).

There are many ways to experiment with prospect segmentation to increase efficiency and revenue for direct mail appeals. The following are two common methods.

- Select a target list of prospects based on giving likelihood
- Upgrade the ask amount in an appeal based on predicted gift size

First, let's establish a general framework for defining prospect segments. Next, we will explore a couple use cases which describe how

478 FINDING PROSPECTS

to use predictive analytics to create prospect segments and increase results.

16.1 Prospect Segments

Prospect segmentation involves organizing prospects into segments (groups) based on a variety of prospect attributes. One common approach is to organize prospects into a prospect quadrant defined by any two prospect characteristics such as gift capacity versus giving likelihood.

In the Data Visualization chapter, we provided a recipe to create an example text plot that displays prospects with wealth ratings of $1,000,000–$2,499,999, along with their major giving likelihood. Now, imagine a quadrant plot that displays prospects for all wealth ratings (low to high) relative to their giving likelihood. Similarly, imagine a quadrant plot that displays prospect event attendance frequency relative to their predicted gift size.

The following prospect quadrant provides a general framework for organizing prospects according to various attributes to create different segments.

Intuitively, the prospects with the highest gift capacity and giving likelihood values will typically represent the top prospects for your organization. Similarly, the prospects with highest event attendance and RFM score will often represent your top prospects. By organizing your prospects into different segments, you can identify prospect recommendations and prioritize different actions for each group.

For example, if you have prospects with high giving likelihood and low financial capacity, then you may decide to directly solicit this group, but adjust the solicitation amounts based on their gift capacity. Likewise, if you have prospects with high capacity

PROSPECT SEGMENTS 479

Figure 16.1: Prospect quadrant

and low giving inclination, you may opt to pursue peer-based solicitation rather than a direct mail approach. For low potential prospects with low gift capacity and low affinity scores, you may opt to send them a web-based survey to gauge interest or invite them to an upcoming event to learn more about your organization or cause. For the top prospects with high giving likelihood and high financial capacity, you may opt to send a highly personalized introduction appeal to a subset of this group and exclude the other portion of this group—perhaps based on prospect management or demographic attributes—in favor of individual outreach from a gift officer.

Ultimately, all of these examples reflect the importance of tailoring your solicitation and outreach approaches by using important prospect signals (descriptive indicators, predictive scores, etc.) available in your donor data. Regardless of your approach, it

480 FINDING PROSPECTS

is critical that you track, monitor and analyze your results to continuously improve your donor outreach efforts.

16.2 RFM

RFM remains a popular choice for prospect segmentation and direct response marketing efforts due to its familiarity and ease of use. In the RFM Modeling chapter, we explore multiple use cases for RFM scores and ranking, including finding donors, upgrade donors, lapsed donors, etc. If you are newer to fundraising, we recommend you explore RFM scores and identify new ways you can creatively apply this simple method to your own fundraising problems.

16.3 Giving Velocity

Giving velocity is an index that measures the rate of change in donor giving over a specific length of time. Similar to RFM, the premise is to analyze giving histories for comparative insight at the individual donor level. Giving velocity is useful for identifying donors whose change (trend) in giving has significantly increased within recent years. High degrees of positive variation in recent giving may be indicative of a significant change in wealth capacity (for example, due to a recent liquidity event). To learn more about giving velocity, check out this article[1].

The concept of giving velocity, as well as other RFM modeling variations, has been a popular topic of discussion on the Prospect-DMM forum. Prospect-DMM is a free, online discussion group you can join to connect with other development professionals who are interested in data mining and modeling (often with a focus on ma-

---

[1]http://bit.ly/2nFqmZU

jor gifts). You can access and sign up for the Prospect-DMM email group via this site[2].

16.4 Social Network Analysis

As discussed in the Social Network Analysis chapter, the degree centrality, or number of connections a prospect has relative to other prospects, can be a useful measure of social connectedness, importance, and influence.

For prospecting purposes, degree centrality can be a useful tool for finding new prospects. Degree, as well as other network centrality measures, can also help identify influencers who may be able to help connect with other important prospects who are difficult to access or reach.

> Using your own data, create prospect segments using estimated gift capacity and degree centrality. Summarize, visualize, and describe your findings. Can you identify any actionable insights, recommendations, or prospect leads?

16.5 Gift Capacity and Inclination

Gift capacity and inclination are two fundamental attributes included in most CRM databases, prospect reports, and products today, which includes wealth screening services and propensity modeling tools. Gift capacity and inclination attributes are useful and prevalent because they help identify whether a prospect has the means (capacity) and inclination (likelihood) to support your organization or cause.

---
[2]https://mailman.mit.edu/mailman/listinfo/prospect-dmm

482 FINDING PROSPECTS

Based on these two factors, we can revise our general prospect quadrant and propose some example recommendations based on each segment.

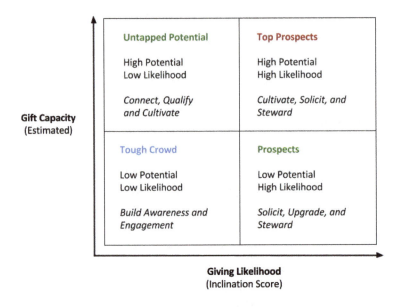

Figure 16.2: Gift capacity versus giving likelihood

Gift capacity and inclination are indeed useful attributes for prioritizing your prospects, but they are only part of the picture. Let's explore some additional attributes you can use to better understand your prospects in the context of your institution.

16.6 Engagement Scores

Affinity, connection and engagement scores remain a popular topic within the fundraising community. Why? Because giving capacity and inclination scores alone do not necessarily translate to a gift if the prospect lacks awareness, emotional engagement or a meaningful connection to your institution.

Today's donors are savvy and, with more than 1.5 million nonprofit organizations registered in the U.S. according to the National Center for Charitable Statistics (NCCS)[3], institutions have to compete for donor's time, attention, and commitment.

Given this reality, many development organizations have shifted, or have begun shifting, towards a more holistic prospecting approach that integrates traditional indicators, such as giving capacity and inclination (giving likelihood or propensity), with relationship-focused measures, qualities and appraisals such as degree of activity, engagement, and affinity. Similar to the previous attributes, we can update our general prospect quadrant to organize prospects by financial capacity and depth of engagement (perhaps using proxy measures such as volunteer involvement, event attendance frequency, etc.).

Now that we have explored some basic prospect segmentation concepts, let's explore a couple use cases of how you can use prospect segments to define solicitation groups as well as upgrade pathways.

16.7 Annual Giving

Annual giving plays an important role in any organization's fundraising efforts to broaden its donor base and strengthen its level of regular financial support.

In the short term, annual giving programs tend to focus on increasing revenue through various donor-centric engagement and annual solicitation activities. In the long term, annual giving programs often seek to build a sustainable pipeline of new donors (acquisition),

---

[3]http://nccs.urban.org/data-statistics/quick-facts-about-nonprofits

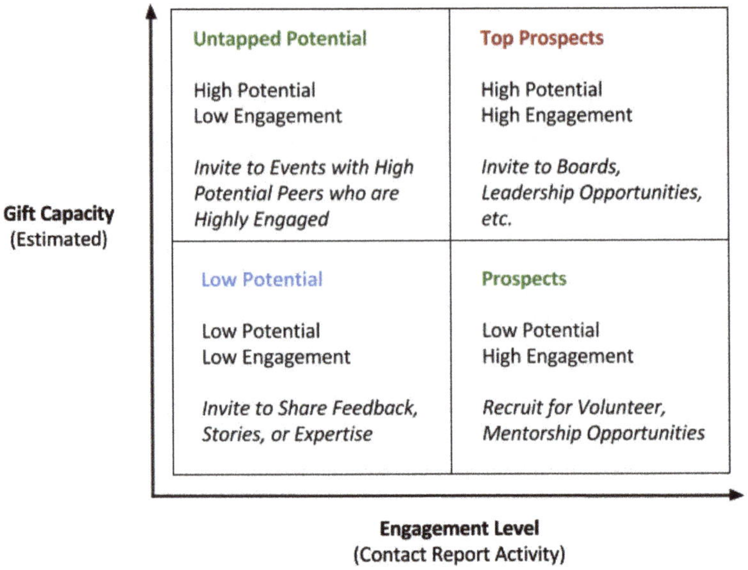

484 FINDING PROSPECTS

Figure 16.3: Gift capacity versus engagement

who repeatedly or consistently give (retention), and over time increase their level of support (upgrade) to major gifts through multi-year pledges or planned giving options such as bequests.

 The definition of major gift size varies by institution and depends on multiple factors such as existing levels of philanthropic support, current number of donors, and major gift capacity.

Annual giving programs can use multiple methods and channels to promote institutional awareness, show impact, and solicit support, including:

- Direct mail
- telefund
- E-solicitations

- Online giving
- Mobile and text-based giving
- Giving days
- Crowdfunding
- Face-to-face solicitations
- Volunteer or peer-based solicitations

For additional information on annual giving campaign fundamentals, check out this CASE resource[4].

For this annual giving example, we will assume you've already worked through the regression examples in the Machine Learning Recipes and Predicting Gift Size chapters.

Let's explore how to segment and upgrade the ask amounts in annual giving appeals based on predicted gift size. For this example, we will define annual gift size as gifts below $25,000.

The following is some example pseudocode to load your own data.

```
# Load readr
library(readr)

# Load dplyr
library(dplyr)

# Load Data
donor_data <- read_csv("data/YourDataFile.csv")

# Select variables
donor_data <- select(
 donor_data,
 pred_vars,
 TotalGiving)
```

---

[4]http://bit.ly/2FHKwtE

486 FINDING PROSPECTS

```
# Convert features to factor
donor_data <- mutate_at(donor_data,
   .vars = pred_vars,
   .funs = as.factor)
```

Now that your data is loaded and prepared, let's suppose you decide to build a multiple linear regression model to predict gift size.

```
# Fit multiple linear regression model
giving_mlg_model <- lm(TotalGiving ~ .,
  data = donor_data)
```

Next, let's store the numerical predictions.

```
donor_data$TotalGiving_pred_mlg <- predict(giving_mlg_model)
```

Based on our example definition of annual gift size, let's build a list of annual giving-level donors.

```
annual_giving_list <- filter(donor_data,
  CurrFYGiving_pred_mlg < 25000)
```

Assuming we have limited resources for a direct response marketing project, let's create targeted annual giving solicitation segments using predicted gift sizes as segment criteria:

- E-solicitation segment for predicted gift size of $1-$49
- Postcard solicitation for predicted gift size of $50-$99
- Direct mail solicitation for predicted gift size of $100 to $499
- Color brochure solicitation for predicted gift size of $500 and above

ANNUAL GIVING   **487**

Table 16.1: Annual giving mailing segments example

Group	Size	Cost	Gifts received	Gift total	Net revenue
E-solicitation	4000	$0	185	$1,825	$1,825
Postcard	1000	$500	58	$1,814	$1,314
Direct mail	500	$500	27	$2,750	$2,250
Leadership brochure	100	$500	3	$2,500	$2,000

```r
# Create e-solicitation segment
annual_giving_esol <- filter(annual_giving_list,
  CurrFYGiving_pred_mlg > 1 & CurrFYGiving_pred_mlg < 50)


# Create postcard segment
annual_giving_postcard <- filter(annual_giving_list,
  CurrFYGiving_pred_mlg > 50 & CurrFYGiving_pred_mlg < 100)


# Create direct mail segment
annual_giving_dmail <- filter(annual_giving_list,
  CurrFYGiving_pred_mlg >= 100 & CurrFYGiving_pred_mlg < 500)


# Create color brochure segment
annual_giving_cbrochure <- filter(annual_giving_list,
  CurrFYGiving_pred_mlg >= 500)
```

As long as you create segments with prospects IDs for your different annual giving solicitations, you can later monitor and measure the response rate and total giving for each segment. A simple way to compare the results is to use a table, as shown in Table 16.1.

In this example, we used predicted gift size to create annual giving segments and make annual giving upgrade solicitation recommendations. Using past giving data, we learned how to build a mockup regression model and use gift size predictions to select annual giving collateral. Specifically, we chose lower-cost solicitation methods for smaller gift size predictions and reserved more expensive print materials for larger gift sizes.

Build a classification model that predicts annual giving likelihood using your own data. Also build a regression model that predicts annual gift size. Using both giving likelihood and predicted gift size, can you identify your top predicted annual giving donor segments?

16.8 Planned Giving

Calculating the return or ROI (return on investment) on planned giving appeals or mailing requests for more information is a difficult problem. Why? Simple reasons: 1) making a planned gift is a complex "stop and think" decision, which usually requires legal and financial consultation and spousal discussion if married; and 2) there's a long delay between a person receiving an appeal and an organization receiving a gift. Nevertheless, we still can come up with a list of prospects that will likely have a higher response rate on average. Let's see how.

As you prepare your planned giving appeal, you will no doubt face the question "should I create separate lists or mailings for different planned giving options?" While this is a reasonable question, you may find that you have small sample sizes for each type of planned gift (for example, bequests, life income gifts, gift annuities, and charitable remainder trusts), which can make it difficult to make accurate planned giving predictions.

When building your own planned giving models, you may find that your classification models are less likely to overfit if you try to predict a "planned gift donor" outcome instead of a "charitable remainder trust" donor.

We recommend that you first focus your efforts on an overall higher response rate for a "request for more information" type of planned giving mailing. You will get highly qualified leads this way.

With the rise of computational advertising, there's also the option of buying Facebook ads to target people who are highly likely to make a planned gift through online giving vehicles. Regardless of the option you choose, you should include a test and a control group for targeting purposes.

As you review and finalize your planned giving appeal, your planned gift officers may tell you that planned gift donors are typically older and have no children. This makes an excellent selection criterion to test response.

 We encourage you to conduct descriptive and exploratory analysis on your own planned giving data to identify giving likelihood and age values that are practical and make sense for your target audience, especially since your predictive scores and demographics will vary relative to your institutional donor base and record of giving activity.

For the rest of this use case, we will assume that you already read the Machine Learning Recipes chapter and built your own planned giving model to generate giving likelihood scores for each constituent in your test dataset.

The following is some example pseudocode to load the planned giving scores you built.

490 FINDING PROSPECTS

```
library(reader)
library(dplyr)

donor_data <- read_csv("data/YourDataFile.csv")
```

Although based on probability, any person with a score of about 50 is a good planned giving prospect; for a higher response rate, we will select prospects with a score of 80 and above. Of course, we need to exclude current planned giving donors.

```
planned_giving_list <- filter(donor_data,
                              pg_score > 80 &
                               pg_donor_ind == 'N')
```

Let's suppose we have the budget to send a brochure to about 6,000 people. We can select 5,000 using the predictive scores and 1,000 using common knowledge. This doesn't meet the statistical need of comparable sample sizes, but let's stick to this example. If you have resources and buy-in from your planned giving office, feel free to draw different sample sizes.

```
planned_giving_list_test <- top_n(planned_giving_list,
                                  n = 5000,
                                  wt = pg_score) %>%
  mutate(group = 'test')
```

Let's select the control group.

```
planned_giving_list_control <- filter(donor_data,
                                      pg_score < 81 &
                                       pg_donor_ind == 'N' &
                                       age > 60) %>%
  sample_n(size = 1000) %>%
```

PLANNED GIVING   491

Table 16.2: Test results from a mailing

Group	Size	Responses	Gifts received	Gift amount
Control	1000	20	5	$100,000
Test	5000	100	20	$500,000

```
mutate(group = 'control')
```

Let's combine them.

```
planned_giving_final_list <- bind_rows(planned_giving_list_test,
                                       planned_giving_list_control)
```

As long as you have this list with the IDs of the prospects in both the groups, you can later calculate the response rate for each group. A simple way to compare the results is to use a table, as shown in Table 16.2.

In this planned giving example, we explored how to select a target list of prospects based on your own giving likelihood scores. Next, we outlined how to construct a test and control group of planned giving prospects using the example criteria of giving likelihood scores of 80 and above and age values greater than 60 years old.

Once the planned giving mail solicitation is delivered to your target audience, you should monitor and measure the response rates over a certain time period in consultation with your planned giving team. If your predictive model is doing its job, you should expect to see a higher response rate from the test group based on your predicted response estimates.

16.9 Summary

In this chapter, we discussed the role of prospect segmentation in donor solicitation and outreach efforts. We explored how to use descriptive and predictive methods to find prospects for a variety of use cases, including annual giving and planned giving. Building on the Machine Learning Recipes, Predicting Gift Size, and Social Network Analysis chapters, this chapter focused on applying some of these methods to finding prospects and creating segments to increase efficiency and fundraising revenue.

After reading this chapter, we hope you are inspired to further explore your fundraising problems and apply machine learning methods to your institutional data to identify actionable insights, generate recommendations, and create experiments with measurable outcomes.

In the next chapter, we will explore some important new trends, technology, and applications designed to tap into organizational data to uncover useful patterns that translate to decision support, recommendations and, ultimately, organizational knowledge.

17

NEW TRENDS

Applications of Artificial Intelligence (AI) and machine learning in the for-profit world are our signals to what's about to happen in the non-profit world. We've already seen many examples of AI and machine learning techniques. The most exciting one is natural language generation, which is exactly what it sounds like. Using text mining and natural language processing, a computer can create language, text, and narratives that read like a human wrote them. An organization that can combine all these applications to create small chunks of tasks distributed through a single, easy-to-consume platform will differentiate itself from all the other non-profits.

Let's see some of these new ideas in detail.

17.1 USC's Action Center

Using the idea of one action at a time, we built an app at USC within our Salesforce mobile instance called *Action Center*, as seen in Figure 17.1. A fundraiser with active assignments sees some of these action items on his Salesforce mobile app.

494   NEW TRENDS

1. Donor News
2. Prospect Recommendations
3. Gift Alerts
4. Proposal Cleanup

Donor News

We have built a crawling engine that looks for assigned prospects who may be mentioned in the news. We then perform some entity matching to ensure that the entity mentioned is the one we were looking for. Later, using all of the news items, we select and display news on the most important and relevant entities.

Prospect Recommendations

If a fundraiser's portfolio is active with constant visit and qualification activity, we show them an unassigned prospect who they might be interested in qualifying. These recommendations are based on the characteristics of the fundraiser's existing assigned prospects. We try to recommend a prospect that is most similar to the majority of the existing prospects. We measure similarity using the prospects' addresses, degree departments, giving likelihood, and other factors. With the simple click of a button, a fundraiser can request an assignment or see more details on the prospect without leaving the interface.

Gift Alerts

If a donor from a fundraiser's portfolio makes a recent gift, we show this to the fundraiser for an easy touch point with the click of a button. Often, if a donor has multiple giving areas, the fundraiser managing the relationship may be unaware of other gifts.

USC'S ACTION CENTER   495

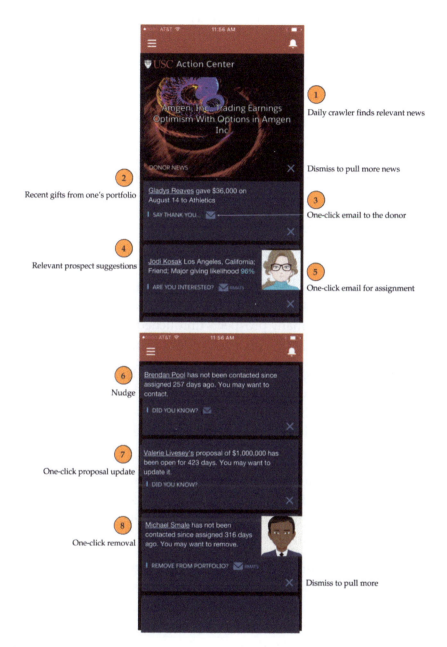

Figure 17.1: USC's action center

Proposal and Portfolio Cleanup

If a prospect has not been contacted over a certain period, we suggest that the prospect be removed. Similarly, if a proposal has been open over a year, we suggest that the fundraiser update the proposal. Again, with one click a fundraiser can complete both tasks.

17.2 Opportunity or Proposal Generation

Portfolios are obsolete.

Efforts to "optimize" a portfolio are useless.

For many years we have seen stats that fundraisers are able to contact only 50 to 60 percent of their portfolios within a year. Not only does this leave many prospects untouched, the portfolio model doesn't create a sense of urgency. It hides the urgency.

If we were to truly optimize a fundraiser's portfolio, like an investment portfolio, we would fill the portfolio with the prospects with the highest returns in the shortest duration possible. This can't happen because we still need to keep qualifying new leads. There goes the optimization.

Simple math will tell us that there's no optimization. Some sort of balance, maybe. Even the balance requires constant information searching and system updating. This is not scalable or doable with a large number of gift officers.

We can say that our return is directly proportional to the time invested in each activity. Let's define the time spent as T_{stage}, a percentage of the total available time. To calculate the total return, we simply multiply the number of prospects P_{stage} in each stage by the time spent on each of the stages.

Total Return $= P_Q \times T_Q + P_C \times T_C + P_S \times T_S + P_{ST} \times T_{ST}$

OPPORTUNITY OR PROPOSAL GENERATION

To optimize or maximize the total return, we need to change either the number of prospects or the time spent in each stage. But the maximum return, mathematically, is only possible by spending 100% of the time with prospects in the solicitation stage (that is, ask for gifts all the time).

The optimization concept is appealing, but it increases the time burden on the relationship management staff as well as on the gift officers. And the tasks with a higher burden are likely to remain incomplete. Busy people, like gift officers, appreciate the tasks that help them get closer to their goals rather than entering and updating stuff in a system.

Here's how AI can help us. Rather than assigning an abstract number of prospects, the combination of AI and human intelligence will create very targeted opportunities that the fundraisers can act on. These opportunities will come populated with the tentative ask date and ask amount, the likelihood that this ask will succeed, the potential areas that the prospect may be interested in, and the institution's resources that match up with the prospect's interest, as seen in Figure 17.2.

Figure 17.2: Auto proposal generation

The fundraiser can then add the appropriate next steps to the opportunity. If the prospect isn't responsive, the fundraiser can close the

498 NEW TRENDS

opportunity and move to the next one. If the prospect is responsive, the fundraiser can adjust the steps to move the prospect to an ask. This process will create a sense of urgency because this would be the only source of new leads. It will also help in better measurement of activities that matter and projection of future revenue rather than the obscurity hidden behind portfolios.

Portfolios are passive. Opportunities are active.

Of course, a fundraiser can add an active opportunity by himself or herself, but unlike an assignment request, an opportunity requires thinking proportionate to its seriousness.

In any case, tiny tasks with a clear outcome and action item will result in better use of one's time—optimization in its truest sense.

If we get rid of passive portfolios, we need to find ways to feed new leads. Rather than just pushing new names, we should push opportunities complete with details such as ask amount, ask date, and a brief strategy.

How do we do so? Let's see.

Ask amount: This is the easiest to predict with high confidence. Why? We can simply look at previous giving and predict the next gift size as we saw in the Predicting Gift Size chapter. We can also use wealth capacity to make better estimates.

Ask date: This isn't too difficult to predict but the confidence levels would be wide on this prediction. We can use a combination of time series forecasting and RFM to predict a time frame when the donor is likely to make a gift.

Brief strategy: This is hardest of all. We will need to know many relationships and interests of the prospective donor. We will also need to know our organization's offerings and key people.

17.3 Bio Generation

We spend many hours creating a biographical profile of a prospect or donor. This profile includes addresses, relationships, wealth, giving to our organization and others, board memberships, and a summary of all these facts.

Many organizations in a single click create such a profile after entering all the facts needed into their customer relationship management (CRM).

I have two thoughts on this process.

- Rather than us finding all these facts, can a platform be created to get this information directly from the prospect?
- If we're collecting these facts from various sources, can we create a tool that collects, cleans, and presents the information in plain English?

You may ask, "Why would a prospect give all this information to us?" A prospect would give this information if she gets something of value in return. Think Facebook. What if we can offer a glimpse of our most important work, an insider's look, based on the interest match? This customized look can include videos of the researchers showing their work, case studies, impact of this work, direct messaging, and so on. If the perceived value of the offering is high, we should see adoption. Scaling this should not be a problem once we have all of our assets created. This whole thing can run on automation, except where a personal response is necessary.

You may also say, "Auto-curated information can never match thoughtful human synthesis." And you're right. At least for the near future.

500 NEW TRENDS

We've already seen investment into this area of natural language generation. Companies like Google[1], AP[2], and even the LA times[3] have found ways to create narratives using facts and natural language generation. Do these narratives shake your brain with joy or surprise? No. That's not the goal. Yet. But this approach helps us finish template-based tasks faster.

17.4 Web Giving

I'm sure you have visited sites that show you instant chat pop-ups. These pop-ups are connected to customer service folks on their mobiles. No matter where they are or what time it is, a representative can type in her phone and answer your questions. It is simple to apply this technique to giving pages as well. A prospective donor lands on the page. We show a pop-up. The prospective donor asks a few questions. We direct them to the proper place or giving options and, of course, we capture their information and comments in the process.

17.5 Trackers + Ads

Did you search for tickets to your trip to Hawaii and now you see advertisements for flights and hotels everywhere? How does that happen? There are multiple ways in which happens, but all involve some sort of Internet cookies that captures your search and/or browsing history. This information is then traded on ad networks or given directly to the advertisers. Facebook makes it

---

[1]https://www.recode.net/2017/7/7/15937436/google-news-media-robots-automate-writing-local-news-stories

[2]https://automatedinsights.com/case-studies/associated-press

[3]http://www.bbc.com/news/technology-26614051

easy for advertisers. Any website can track your visit history using a Facebook pixel[4]. Then the website owners can pay Facebook to show ads to Facebook users with specific pixels. This is called retargetting[5].

Can't we track and advertise similarly? Of course, we can, and we should. At least for testing. This is a low-cost option, compared to a telephone program, to see whether we can acquire donors.

Another similar and simple approach is to show Google ads to people who search for "charitable contribution" but only limit the ad display to visitors in your geographic region. Finding the right keywords is a good challenge. Because when I researched, I couldn't find many searches with "charitable contribution." We need to get in the head of our potential donors. What are they thinking when they are ready to file taxes? We also need to pay attention to the timing of the ads. You'd be surprised when people search for donations. It's around April, when taxes are due. An ad like this would work well, don't you think?

17.6   Event Suggestor

Let's say that we developed a mechanism to collect the interests of our donors and prospects. These interests could be broad, like science, or narrow, like CAR-T cell therapy, but we do our best to capture specific interests. We also capture facts on our assets such as researchers, facilities, research products, and others. For higher-education institutions, this database will be rich.

Now the easy part. By creating a mashup of our constituents' interests as well as geographic location and our assets, we can suggest

---

[4]https://www.facebook.com/business/help/952192354843755
[5]https://www.facebook.com/business/learn/facebook-ads-reach-existing-customers

highly tailored events. An event suggestion could look like Figure 17.3.

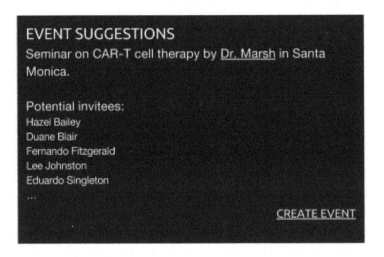

Figure 17.3: Event suggestor

Once we have a list of confirmed attendees, using all the data (relationships, location, interests, giving capacity, and board memberships), we can come up with various seating combinations that we think could spur engaging conversations and build future relationships, as seen Figure 17.4.

17.7 Donor Platforms

Websites like Donors Choose[6] and kiva[7] are popular with donors because they can see the impact of their giving immediately. The Charity Navigator[8] is similarly popular because prospective donors can

---

[6]https://www.donorschoose.org/
[7]https://www.kiva.org/
[8]https://www.charitynavigator.org/

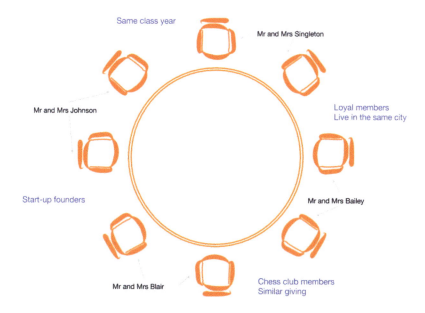

Figure 17.4: Event seating suggestor

search and find the "best" charities that they can support. But what if we build a platform that, using the social data of a prospective donor, can recommend non-profits for making gifts: an AI-driven mashup of Donors Choose and the Charity Navigator? This approach can yield a list of non-profits that are highly relevant to the donor.

17.8 Crawling + MTurks

In the Text Mining chapter, we saw a few examples of scraping data off the web. Similarly, we can set up web crawlers to store information from websites of interest. We can process this raw data using natural language processing to something useful. We can then use services like Amazon's Mechanical Turk (AMT)[9] to create small tasks that humans (called Turks or MTurks) can fulfill rapidly and cheaply.

Companies and people have used AMT to categorize paper receipts[10], transcribe audio, and even write poems [11]. A good use case for the non-profits is the styling of postal addresses. For example, if "ST" needs to be spelled out as "Street" and "AVE" as "Avenue", we can provide such instructions to the Turks and within a few days we can get thousands of stylized addresses. An example of combining crawling + MTurks would be setting up a crawler to list obituaries, using NLP to find potential matches in our database, and using the MTurks to validate the matches.

Figure 17.5: Crawling + MTurks

17.9 Auto-Generated Emails

Similar to proposal or event creation, we can auto-generate emails, ready to be sent by the fundraisers. It seems that even with all the available information, likelihood scores, and suggested actions,

---

[9] https://www.mturk.com/

[10] The supposedly "smart" platform to scan receipts used MTurks: http://bit.ly/2DLpr1s

[11] The Outline: http://bit.ly/2kRxIJ9

fundraisers don't contact (or record in the CRM) their prospects and donors. We can simplify and reduce the number of steps for the fundraisers by creating auto-generated emails. Gravyty[12], a start-up based in Boston, does exactly this [13]. Gravyty's tool "First Draft" uses machine learning on the available donor/prospect data to create emails that fundraisers can edit and send in a few clicks. When keeping in touch with prospects or donors becomes a challenge, a solution such as "First Draft" eases the burden from the fundraisers' already loaded shoulders. When we learn our fundraisers' preferences and have interest-based data on our donors and prospects, this type of solution has the power to create very targeted and personal touch points.

17.10 Interactive Data Analysis

As you saw in the introductory chapters, users are more likely to use your analysis if they understand it. Interactive data analysis offers one such vehicle to let the users be part of the analysis. Tableau, a data visualization software and a darling of many analysts, for its own marketing and sales team uses Tableau dashboard (Fink & Tibke 2012). Not only can the users see all the ingredients that make up the lead score, but they can also customize the analysis to answer specific questions. Using the "Visual Scoring" dashboard, Tableau reports a 22% increase in its conversion rate, which is the ratio of buyers from all leads.

Tableau is not the only software that lets you create dynamic and interactive dashboards. Shiny by RStudio[14] is a great open-source alternative. Rich Majerus[15] and Samantha Wren[16] are two leading

---

[12]https://www.gravyty.com

[13]Huffington Post: http://bit.ly/2BJzqXD

[14]https://shiny.rstudio.com/

[15]http://richmajerus.com/tech/2017/07/26/DRIVE-presentation.html

[16]https://www.linkedin.com/in/samkwren

506 NEW TRENDS

experts in the non-profit / fundraising field who have created interactive tools using Shiny and r. Figure 17.6 shows a Shiny app, using fake data, we built for USC users to adjust weights on an activity scoring formula. By adjusting the weights, users can compare fundraisers on the activity they think is important. For example, a manager may not value visits as much as qualification. He or she can decrease the weight on visits to zero and increase the weight prospects qualified to a higher number. Now, the fundraiser names on the chart will shift to show new scores (that is, the names farthest to the right will have more qualification activity).

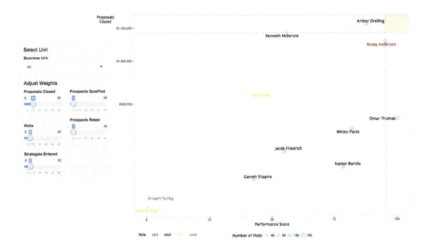

Figure 17.6: A Shiny app for fundraiser performance scoring (using fake data)

 We didn't cover Shiny app development in this book. Check out examples from the Shiny gallery (https://shiny.rstudio.com/gallery/) to get inspiration and follow the tutorials (https://shiny.rstudio.com/tutorial/) to create your own app.

If you enjoyed reading this book, can we ask you for a small favor?
It won't cost you anything, but would help us tremendously.

- Run `source("http://arn.la/shareds4fr")` in your R console to share the book with your network
- Leave a review on Amazon

With our sincere thanks,
Ashutosh and Rodger

Bibliography

Abadi, M., Agarwal, A., Barham, P., Brevdo, E., Chen, Z., Citro, C., Corrado, G. S., Davis, A., Dean, J., Devin, M. et al. (2016), 'Tensorflow: Large-scale machine learning on heterogeneous distributed systems', *arXiv preprint arXiv:1603.04467* .

Amatriain, X. & Basilico, J. (2011), 'Netflix recommendations'.
URL: *http://bit.ly/2tnLnKt*

Amblee, N. & Bui, T. (2011), 'Harnessing the influence of social proof in online shopping: The effect of electronic word of mouth on sales of digital microproducts', *International Journal of Electronic Commerce* **16**(2), 91–114.

Ashton, N., Lewis, S. G., De Groote, I., Duffy, S. M., Bates, M., Bates, R., Hoare, P., Lewis, M., Parfitt, S. A., Peglar, S. et al. (2014), 'Hominin footprints from early pleistocene deposits at happisburgh, uk', *PLoS One* **9**(2), e88329.

Beveridge, A. & Shan, J. (2016), 'Network of thrones', *Math Horizons* **23**(4), 18–22.

Bischl, B., Lang, M., Kotthoff, L., Schiffner, J., Richter, J., Studerus, E., Casalicchio, G. & Jones, Z. M. (2016), 'mlr: Machine learning

in r', *Journal of Machine Learning Research* **17**(170), 1–5.
URL: *http://jmlr.org/papers/v17/15-066.html*

Bore, I.-L. (2011), 'Laughing together? tv comedy audiences and the laugh track', *The Velvet Light Trap* (68), 24–34.

Box, G. E. P. (1976), 'Science and statistics', *Journal of the American Statistical Association* **71**, 791–799.
URL: *http://www.tandfonline.com/doi/abs/10.1080/01621459.1976.10480949*

Breiman, L., Cutler, A., Liaw, A. & Wiener, M. (2015), *randomForest: Breiman and Cutler's Random Forests for Classification and Regression*. R package version 4.6-12.
URL: *https://CRAN.R-project.org/package=randomForest*

Bresler, A. (2016), *forbesListR: Access Forbes list data*. R package version 0.1.0.

Brynjolfsson, E., Hitt, L. & Kim, H. (2011), 'Strength in numbers: How does data-driven decision-making affect firm performance?'.

Bult, J. R., Van der Scheer, H. & Wansbeek, T. (1997), 'Interaction between target and mailing characteristics in direct marketing, with an application to health care fund raising', *International Journal of Research in Marketing* **14**(4), 301–308.

Burnham, K. P.; Anderson, D. R. (2002), *Model Selection and Multimodel Inference: A Practical Information-Theoretic Approach*, Springer-Verlag.

Chassin, D. P. & Posse, C. (2005), 'Evaluating north american electric grid reliability using the barabási–albert network model', *Physica A: Statistical Mechanics and its Applications* **355**(2), 667–677.

Chen, T., He, T., Benesty, M., Khotilovich, V. & Tang, Y. (2017), *xgboost: Extreme Gradient Boosting*. R package version 0.6-4.
URL: *https://CRAN.R-project.org/package=xgboost*

BIBLIOGRAPHY 511

Cheng, H.-T., Hong, L., Ispir, M., Mewald, C., Haque, Z., Polosukhin, I., Roumpos, G., Sculley, D., Smith, J., Soergel, D., Tang, Y., Tucker, P., Wicke, M., Xia, C. & Xie, J. (2017), Tensorflow estimators: Managing simplicity vs. flexibility in high-level machine learning frameworks, *in* 'Proceedings of the 23rd ACM SIGKDD International Conference on Knowledge Discovery and Data Mining', ACM, New York, NY, USA, pp. 1763–1771.
URL: *http://doi.acm.org/10.1145/3097983.3098171*

Chua, H. F., Yates, J. F. & Shah, P. (2006), 'Risk avoidance: Graphs versus numbers', *Memory & cognition* **34**(2), 399–410.

Cialdini, R. B. (1987), *Influence*, Vol. 3, A. Michel Port Harcourt.

Cleveland, W. S. & Cleveland, W. S. (1985), *The elements of graphing data*, Wadsworth Advanced Books and Software Monterey, CA.

Cohen, W. W. (1995), 'Fast effective rule induction', *Proceedings of the 12th International Conference on Machine Learning* pp. 115–123.
URL: *http://citeseer.ist.psu.edu/cohen95fast.html*

Colvin, G. (2009), *Talent Is Overrated*, Findaway World.

Croxton, F. E. & Stryker, R. E. (1927), 'Bar charts versus circle diagrams', *Journal of the American Statistical Association* **22**(160), 473–482.

DeGraff, J. (2011), *Innovation You: Four Steps to Becoming New and Improved*, Ballantine Books.

Few, S. (2006), *Information Dashboard Design: The Effective Visual Communication of Data*, O'Reilly Media.

Few, S. (2008), 'Dual-scaled axes in graphs'.
URL: *http://bit.ly/2e5oZle*

Fink, E. & Tibke, W. (2012), 'Visual scoring – the 360° view'.
URL: *https://www.tableau.com/whitepapers/visual-scoring-360*

512 BIBLIOGRAPHY

from Jed Wing, M. K. C., Weston, S., Williams, A., Keefer, C., Engelhardt, A., Cooper, T., Mayer, Z., Kenkel, B., the R Core Team, Benesty, M., Lescarbeau, R., Ziem, A., Scrucca, L., Tang, Y., Candan, C. & Hunt., T. (2017), *caret: Classification and Regression Training*. R package version 6.0-78.
URL: *https://CRAN.R-project.org/package=caret*

Golbeck, J. & Hendler, J. A. (2004), Reputation network analysis for email filtering., *in* 'CEAS'.

Golombisky, K. & Hagen, R. (2016), *White Space Is Not Your Enemy: A Beginner's Guide to Communicating Visually Through Graphic, Web & Multimedia Design*, A K Peters / CRC Press.

Guimera, R., Mossa, S., Turtschi, A. & Amaral, L. N. (2005), 'The worldwide air transportation network: Anomalous centrality, community structure, and cities' global roles', *Proceedings of the National Academy of Sciences* **102**(22), 7794–7799.

Hahsler, M. (2017), *arulesViz: Visualizing Association Rules and Frequent Itemsets*. R package version 1.3-0.
URL: *https://CRAN.R-project.org/package=arulesViz*

Hahsler, M., Chelluboina, S., Hornik, K. & Buchta, C. (2011), 'The arules r-package ecosystem: Analyzing interesting patterns from large transaction datasets', *Journal of Machine Learning Research* **12**, 1977–1981.
URL: *http://jmlr.csail.mit.edu/papers/v12/hahsler11a.html*

Heath, C. & Heath, D. (2007), *Made to Stick: Why Some Ideas Survive and Others Die*, Random House.

Holmes, T. J. (2011), 'The diffusion of wal-mart and economies of density', *Econometrica* **79**(1), 253–302.

Holte, R. C. (1993), 'Very simple classification rules perform well on most commonly used datasets', *Machine learning* **11**(1), 63–90.

BIBLIOGRAPHY **513**

Hornik, K., Buchta, C. & Zeileis, A. (2009), 'Open-source machine learning: R meets Weka', *Computational Statistics* **24**(2), 225–232.

Hothorn, T., Hornik, K., Strobl, C. & Zeileis, A. (2017), *party: A Laboratory for Recursive Partytioning*. R package version 1.2-4.
URL: *https://CRAN.R-project.org/package=party*

Jacomy, M., Venturini, T., Heymann, S. & Bastian, M. (2014), 'Forceatlas2, a continuous graph layout algorithm for handy network visualization designed for the gephi software', *PloS one* **9**(6), e98679.

Jørgensen, B. & Paes De Souza, M. C. (1994), 'Fitting tweedie's compound poisson model to insurance claims data', *Scandinavian Actuarial Journal* **1994**(1), 69–93.

Kahneman, D. (2011), *Thinking, fast and slow*, Macmillan.

Koenker, R. (2005), *Quantile regression*, number 38, Cambridge university press.

Koenker, R. (2017), *quantreg: Quantile Regression*. R package version 5.34.
URL: *https://CRAN.R-project.org/package=quantreg*

Kohavi, R. & Parekh, R. (2004), Visualizing rfm segmentation, *in* 'Proceedings of the 2004 SIAM International Conference on Data Mining', SIAM, pp. 391–399.

Kuhn, M. & Quinlan, R. (2017), *C50: C5.0 Decision Trees and Rule-Based Models*. R package version 0.1.1.
URL: *https://CRAN.R-project.org/package=C50*

Langfelder, P. & Horvath, S. (2008), 'Wgcna: an r package for weighted correlation network analysis', *BMC bioinformatics* **9**(1), 559.

Lantz, B. (2013), *Machine Learning with R*, Packt.

514   BIBLIOGRAPHY

Liaw, A., Wiener, M. et al. (2002), 'Classification and regression by randomforest', *R news* **2**(3), 18–22.

Maier, D. (1983), *The theory of relational databases*, Vol. 11, Computer science press Rockville.
URL: *http://web.cecs.pdx.edu/ maier/TheoryBook/TRD.html*

Malthouse, E. C. & Blattberg, R. C. (2010), Can we predict customer lifetime value?, *in* 'Perspectives On Promotion And Database Marketing: The Collected Works of Robert C Blattberg', World Scientific, pp. 245–259.

Mankins, M. & Sherer, L. (2014), 'Help reluctant employees put analytic tools to work', *Harvard Business Review* .
URL: *https://hbr.org/2014/10/help-reluctant-employees-put-analytic-tools-to-work*

Matejka, J. & Fitzmaurice, G. (2017), Same stats, different graphs: Generating datasets with varied appearance and identical statistics through simulated annealing, *in* 'Proceedings of the 2017 CHI Conference on Human Factors in Computing Systems', ACM, pp. 1290–1294.

McCarty, J. A. & Hastak, M. (2007), 'Segmentation approaches in data-mining: A comparison of rfm, chaid, and logistic regression', *Journal of business research* **60**(6), 656–662.

Meyer, D., Dimitriadou, E., Hornik, K., Weingessel, A. & Leisch, F. (2017), *e1071: Misc Functions of the Department of Statistics, Probability Theory Group (Formerly: E1071), TU Wien*. R package version 1.6-8.
URL: *https://CRAN.R-project.org/package=e1071*

Milborrow, S. (2017), *rpart.plot: Plot 'rpart' Models: An Enhanced Version of 'plot.rpart'*. R package version 2.1.2.
URL: *https://CRAN.R-project.org/package=rpart.plot*

Nandeshwar, A. R. (2006), Models for calculating confidence intervals for neural networks, Master's thesis, West Virginia University Libraries.

Newman, M. (2010), *Networks: An Introduction*, Oxford University Press.

O'Neil, C. (2013), *On being a data skeptic*, O'Reilly Media, Inc.

Page, L., Brin, S., Motwani, R. & Winograd, T. (1999), The pagerank citation ranking: Bringing order to the web., Technical report, Stanford InfoLab.

Perlich, C., Rosset, S., Lawrence, R. D. & Zadrozny, B. (2007), High-quantile modeling for customer wallet estimation and other applications, *in* 'Proceedings of the 13th ACM SIGKDD international conference on Knowledge discovery and data mining', ACM, pp. 977–985.

Porter, M. E. (1996), 'What is strategy', *Published November* .

Prickett, T., Gada-Jain, N. & Bernieri, F. J. (2000), The importance of first impressions in a job interview, *in* 'annual meeting of the Midwestern Psychological Association, Chicago, IL'.

Ripley, B. (2015), *class: Functions for Classification*. R package version 7.3-14.
URL: *https://CRAN.R-project.org/package=class*

Ryan, R. M. & Deci, E. L. (2000), 'Self-determination theory and the facilitation of intrinsic motivation, social development, and well-being.', *American psychologist* **55**(1), 68.

Scott, J. (2017), *Social network analysis*, Sage.

Smith, P. (2012), *Lead with a story: A guide to crafting business narratives that captivate, convince, and inspire*, AMACOM Div American Mgmt Assn.

516 BIBLIOGRAPHY

Stadtler, H. (2015), Supply chain management: An overview, *in* 'Supply chain management and advanced planning', Springer, pp. 3–28.

Steele, J. & Iliinsky, N. (2010), *Beautiful Visualization: Looking at Data through the Eyes of Experts*, O'Reilly Media.

Tang, Y., Allaire, J., RStudio, Ushey, K., Falbel, D. & Google Inc. (2017), *tfestimators: High-level Estimator Interface to TensorFlow in R*. **URL:** *https://github.com/rstudio/tfestimators*

Therneau, T., Atkinson, B. & Ripley, B. (2017), *rpart: Recursive Partitioning and Regression Trees*. R package version 4.1-11. **URL:** *https://CRAN.R-project.org/package=rpart*

Tufte, E. R. (2001), *The Visual Display of Quantitative Information*, Graphics Pr.

Tukey, J. (1977), *Exploratory Data Analysis*, Mass: Addison-Wesley Pub. Co.

Tweedie, M. (1984), An index which distinguishes between some important exponential families, *in* 'Statistics: Applications and new directions: Proc. Indian statistical institute golden Jubilee International conference', Vol. 579, p. 604.

Verhoef, P. C., Spring, P. N., Hoekstra, J. C. & Leeflang, P. S. (2003), 'The commercial use of segmentation and predictive modeling techniques for database marketing in the netherlands', *Decision Support Systems* **34**(4), 471–481.

Voehl, F. & Harrington, H. J. (2016), *Change Management: Manage the Change Or it Will Manage You*, Vol. 6, CRC Press.

Warnes, G. R., Bolker, B., Lumley, T., Johnson, R. C. & Johnson, R. C. (2015), *gmodels: Various R Programming Tools for Model Fitting*. R package version 2.16.2. **URL:** *https://CRAN.R-project.org/package=gmodels*

BIBLIOGRAPHY **517**

Wickham, H. (2009), *ggplot2: Elegant Graphics for Data Analysis*, Springer-Verlag New York.
URL: *http://ggplot2.org*

Wickham, H. (2011), 'The split-apply-combine strategy for data analysis', *Journal of Statistical Software* **40**(1), 1–29.
URL: *https://www.jstatsoft.org/article/view/v040i01/v40i01.pdf*

Wilkinson, L. (2006), *The grammar of graphics*, Springer Science & Business Media.

Witten, I. H. & Frank, E. (2005), *Data Mining: Practical Machine Learning Tools and Techniques*, 2nd edn, Morgan Kaufmann, San Francisco.

Wong, D. M. (2013), *The Wall Street Journal Guide to Information Graphics: The Dos and Don'ts of Presenting Data, Facts, and Figures*, W. W. Norton & Company.

Yang, A. X. (2004), 'How to develop new approaches to rfm segmentation', *Journal of Targeting, Measurement and Analysis for Marketing* **13**(1), 50–60.

Yang, Y., Qian, W. & Zou, H. (2016), *TDboost: A Boosted Tweedie Compound Poisson Model*. R package version 1.2.
URL: *https://CRAN.R-project.org/package=TDboost*

Yang, Y., Qian, W. & Zou, H. (2017), 'Insurance premium prediction via gradient tree-boosted tweedie compound poisson models', *Journal of Business & Economic Statistics* pp. 1–15.

Zacks, J. & Tversky, B. (1999), 'Bars and lines: A study of graphic communication', *Memory & Cognition* **27**(6), 1073–1079.

518 BIBLIOGRAPHY

Index

acceptance, 60
accessibility, 166
adaptive boosting, 340
aggregation, 125
Alice in Wonderland, 50
analytics maturity model, 3
analytics road map, 51
annual giving, 483
 acquisition, 483
 Campaigns, 485
 retention, 484
 upgrade, 484
Anscombe, 169
artificial intelligence, 302
association rule mining, 382
axis lines, 198
axis scale, 197
axis text, 198

bar chart, 171
big data, 2
black box method, 347

Box, George, 301
box-and-whisker plot, 152
boxplot, 149, 152
business intelligence, 2

Cartesian product, 126
change effectiveness equation, 58
choropleth map, 192, 261
cluster analysis, 376
CLV, 395
comma-separated value, 90
continuous improvement, 12
correlation, 157, 190
craft, 48
Cross Validation, 403
cumulative gains chart, 6
curiosity, 11

data mining, 2
data science, 2
data visualization, 166
database, 94

520   INDEX

decision trees, 320
deep learning, 355, 359

effectiveness, 60
Einstein, 55
endowment, 422
ensemble learning, 340
Excel, 93
explanatory power, 56
exploratory data analysis, 137
extreme gradient boosting, 343
extrinsic motivation, 13

factors, 98, 100
feature selection, 303, 365
Feynman, Richard, 55
foot in the door, 57
Forbes, 418

geom, 193
GitHub, 356
Gradient Tree, 403
grammar of graphics, 193

histogram, 148

IKEA, 51
indicator variables, 100
influence, 57
innovation, 53
insights manager, 17
instance-based learning, 304
interquartile range, 152

job description, 19
joins, 125

LaTeX, 420
lift, 6
literate programming, 271

machine learning, 301
    classification
        Naive Bayes, 314
        rule based, 344
major gifts, 484
maps, 192
Martin, Steve, 60
mechanical turk, 504
mindset, 11
Minecraft, 48
minimally viable product, 54
missing values, 100

network graph, 390
neural network, 347
NFL, 48

one hot encoding, 358, 378
outlier, 152

parallel coordinate plot, 388
passion, 60
pattern recognition, 302
persuasion, 57
plan, 51
planned giving, 488
probabilistic learning, 313
Python, 17

Quantile Regression, 399

R functions
    arrangeGrob, 266

as.numeric, 105
barplot, 146
cluster_fast_greedy, 470
combine, 83
coord_fixed, 237
count, 108
CrossTable, 306
dbConnect, 95
desc, 110
distinct, 122
everything, 116
glimpse, 97, 114, 139, 306
group_by, 145
ifelse, 123, 155
install.packages, 72
is.character, 99
library, 72
list, 84
mean, 142, 149
median, 149, 152
mutate, 121
names, 92
ntile, 286
pairs, 157
plot_grid, 266
quantile, 143, 149
read.csv, 90, 98
read.table, 90
read_csv, 91
read_tsv, 91
readxl, 93
rownames, 86
select, 121, 134
seq, 83
slice, 139

spread, 134, 135
str, 92
summarize, 109
summary, 141
table, 87, 306
tally, 108
top_n, 145
write_csv, 106
R packages
    arules, 382
    arulesViz, 382
    C50, 334
    caret, 308
    class, 308
    cowplot, 266
    dplyr, 97, 99, 100, 107, 118, 139, 145, 286, 306
    e1071, 316
    forbesListR, 418
    gapminder, 234
    ggmap, 253
    ggplot, 148, 149, 193
    gmodels, 306
    httr, 423
    igraph, 455
    lubridate, 103
    maps, 247
    mlr, 409
    nnet, 408
    odbc, 95
    party, 331
    quantreg, 399
    randomForest, 341
    randomNames, 228
    readr, 91, 97, 98, 107

rpart, 320
rpart.plot, 321
rvest, 419, 426
stringr, 99, 104, 284
TDboost, 403
tidyr, 107, 130
tidyverse, 93
visNetwork, 474
xgboost, 344
XML, 423
zipcode, 125, 247
R-squared value, 370
random forests, 341
regression, 362
    coefficient of determination,
      365
    linear regression, 362
    logistic regression, 371
    multiple linear regression,
      366
    r-squared, 365
regular expressions, 426
return on investment, 8, 488
RFM, 281, 480
Rice, Jerry, 48
RMSE, 397
road map, 51

scatter plot, 169, 190
simplicity, 166
skepticism, 11
slopegraph, 239
social network analysis, 447
    betweenness centrality, 450
    communities, 451

degree, 450
edge, 449
layout, 452
node, 449
social proof, 57
SQL, 16
storytelling, 17, 61
strategy, 50, 51
supervised learning, 303
    classification, 304
      K-nearest neighbor, 305
support vector machines, 352
SVM, *see* support vector machines

TensorFlow, 356
theme, 198
trend-line, 166
trends, 166
Tukey, John W., 138

unsupervised learning, 376

wealth ratings, 122
Wikipedia, 423

ZIP Codes, 101

Lightning Source UK Ltd.
Milton Keynes UK
UKHW052315210519
343085UK00003BA/26/P